THE MIDDLE EAST
IN TRANSITION

THE MIDDLE EAST IN TRANSITION

A STUDY OF JORDAN'S FOREIGN POLICY

Mohammad Ibrahim Faddah

ASIA PUBLISHING HOUSE

LONDON

ISBN   0.210.22387.1

PRINTED IN INDIA

BY K. A. RASTOGI, PRABHAT PRESS, MEERUT AND PUBLISHED
BY P. S. JAYASINGHE, ASIA PUBLISHING HOUSE, LONDON, W.C. 2

PREFACE

This study is the first attempt to describe systematically and analyse critically the foreign policies of Jordan during the period 1947–1967. It is as much a diplomatic history as a political analysis of Jordan's foreign relations. It is concerned with the aspirations of the ruling Hashemite dynasty and the policies pursued to achieve them.

This work is an application of the triangular approach. The main feature of this approach is the study of the foreign policy of a state through the analysis of the interaction between the internal and the external settings which determine the content and direction of the policy decisions taken by the state. The internal setting emphasizes the role of personality of the decision-maker, the political culture and authority relationships, and the political socialization and recruitment. The external setting involves the geopolitical environment, the nature of the situation, and the state's capabilities to take action in the form of an initiative or in response to external stimuli.

The foreign policy of Jordan will be treated in three main areas. The first is the Arab-Israeli conflict in which Jordan played a crucial role. Due to its economic and military limitations, Jordan could not sustain prolonged hostilities. Its economic progress and political stability could be secured only if peace prevailed in the region. This situation has been the most significant factor that forced the kings of Jordan to attempt the conclusion of a peace treaty with Israel. The second is the inter-Arab relations. Despite its economic limitations and political instability, Jordan's role proved to be decisive as well as pivotal.

Jordan's problem with the Arab states has been one of leadership struggle, and to a lesser degree, its connections with the West. While the Hashemites claimed Arab leadership, they failed to appreciate the gap between the objectives and the means to achieve them. The monarchy has constituted the major obstacle to cooperation and unity between the Hashemites and the progressive regimes. Third, failing to convince the Arab people of their leadership to Arab unity and Arabism, the rulers of Jordan resorted to parochial nationalism and associated themselves too closely with the Western Powers irrespective of the popular Arab opinion. Such association was based on the Anglo-Jordanian treaties, which, until 1956, influenced all governmental activities through controlling the military, economic and political actions of Jordan. It was also based on the assumption that the Western Powers would protect the independence, the monarchy, and preserve the territorial integrity of Jordan. Jordan's attempts to accede to the Baghdad Pact and to adhere to the Eisenhower Doctrine were cases in point.

In addition, the study will focus on the application of four key factors in decision-making: the personality factor; the political culture; the political recruitment; situations, that is, the external setting and the tactical capabilities.

The study is by no means exhaustive, for it is derived mainly from already accessible materials. Ideally, the study of foreign policy should be based on the primary materials of the state documents still confined to the confidential archives. This work, however, draws on the Arabic and Western sources, both primary and secondary: general books on the region; memoirs of kings and political leaders in Jordan, the United States, Israel and Britain; official releases of these governments; the Arabic and foreign periodical literature and newspapers, and the United Nations documents.

The transliteration system applied to the Arabic names used   in this work is phonetic. For the purpose of originality, the names are rendered in English as they are pronounced in classical Arabic.

Originally, the study was approved as a doctoral thesis by the University of Oklahoma. My thanks to Professor Rufus G. Hall who read the entire manuscript and offered constructive suggestions, and to my colleagues, Professors Joe Christopher and Russel Peterson, for editing it. Finally, thanks to my wife for her patience and invaluable contribution to the production of this work.

Norman, Oklahoma   MOHAMMAD IBRAHIM FADDAH
June 9, 1971

INTRODUCTION

The study of foreign policy and international relations seeks to understand the behaviour of nations and individuals acting for these states in their capacities as decision-makers. Accordingly, there are specific aspects of foreign policy to which the study of the individual attitudes has relevance. As national ideologies have a bearing on matters of war and peace, so war and peace also depend on personality attitudes.[1]

Personality characteristics can influence the way a decision-maker responds to situations. His attitude may be affected by many factors including his cultural environment, the kind of political system in which he operates, his role in the institutional framework, and his formative background. The latter may be considered as the cause for his certainty or insecurity about his future role, his dominance, values and philosophy, need for achievement and power-seeking. His education and intelligence as well as religious values and ideology also significantly influence the method by which a decision-maker approaches the foreign policy. One author stated that the person who ultimately determines the policy should possess certain leadership qualities. Among these are: one, astute sense of socio-political climate; two, deductive capacities and talent for synthesis; and three, courage. "It is the scarcity of such talent that leads to so many political miscalculations," since significant political decisions may produce a chain reaction.[2] In studying the conduct of Jordan's foreign policy, the personality factor of the rulers can be seen as the dominant influencing factor in their approach to the development of Jordan's foreign relations.

The second factor is political culture. According to Almond, political socialization is the process of induction into the political

---

[1]Herbert Kelman (ed.), "Social Psychological Approach to the Study of International Relations," *International Behavior* (New York: Holt, 1966), p. 566.

[2]Kurt London, *The Making of Foreign Policy* (New York: Lippincott, 1965), p. 206.

culture creating loyalty of the individual to that political system.[3]
It is also the process by which political cultures are maintained and
changed.[4]   Political culture, on the other hand, refers to the propensities or the psychological dimensions of the system.   It consists of
peoples' beliefs, attitudes, values, skills and the special propensities of
sub-cultures within the system.[5]   Professor Sidney Verba has defined
the concept of political culture as follows:

> The political culture of a society consists of the system of empirical
> beliefs, expressive symbols, and values which define the situations
> in which political action takes place.   It provides the subjective
> orientation to politics.[6]

The importance of studying political culture lies in the fact that it
constitutes a sub-system of the international system.   Secondly, since
political culture reflects the attitudes and orientation of the individual
member of the society towards politics, such orientation constitutes
the latent political tendencies and the propensities for political
behaviour.   These propensities are of great importance in explaining
and predicting a state's political action, in understanding the psychological aspects of the political development and political change
in that nation.[7]   In the case of Jordan, political culture appears
to have influenced the personal conduct of King Abdullah's foreign
policy.   This was facilitated by the lack of political involvement
by the Transjordan population, and in view of the fact that the
authoritarian culture of the Middle East has been largely moulded by
Islam, which literally means submission; that the ruler is the agent of
God who must be obeyed.[8]   However, this situation changed significantly with the introduction of the Palestine Arabs who were

---

[3]Gabriel Almond and James Coleman (eds.), *The Politics of the Developing
Areas* (Princeton, New Jersey: Princeton University Press, 1960), pp. 27, 30.
   [4]Gabriel Almond and G. B. Powell, Jr., *Comparative Politics: A Developmental Approach* (Boston: Little, Brown and Company, 1966), p. 64.
   [5]*Ibid.*, p. 23.
   [6]Sidney Verba, "Comparative Political Culture," in Lucian Pye and Sidney
Verba (eds.), *Political Culture and Political Development* (Princeton, New Jersey:
Princeton University Press, 1966), p. 513.
   [7]Almond and Powell, *op. cit.*, p. 51.
   [8]Donald Eugene Smith, *Religion and Political Development* (Boston: Little,
Brown and Company, 1970), p. 187.

politically more involved, and whose loyalty to the Jordanian regime was less reliable.

The third factor is political recruitment. Each political system is constantly involved in recruiting to fill the roles of the political system. It is defined as the process of selection and induction of members of the society into specialized roles of the system by training them in appropriate skills and providing them with "political cognitive maps" and values for the operation of that system.[9] Recruitment may be accomplished by the universalistic method whereby a role is filled by election, examination, ability or performance. On the other hand, filling a role through friends, family ties and direct appointment is illustrative of the particularistic criteria. "Below the highest level, the problem of political recruitment in patriarchal societies reduces itself largely to one of obtaining the ruler's favour."[10]

During King Abdullah's reign, recruitment was mainly achieved through the particularistic method. The wealthy landlords constituted the elite who remained loyal to the Palace since their interests coincided with those of the ruler. Furthermore, the King appointed key decision-makers, the Palace Group, from the conservative loyal minority. However, unification with Arab Palestine significantly altered this situation, as the West Bankers were elected to the Parliament and held cabinet positions. However, since unification, only one Palestinian became Prime Minister. The apparent reason was that only a conservative Transjordanian could be loyal to the Palace. In any case, the inclusion of the Palestinians in the bureaucracy has diminished the use of the particularistic pattern of recruitment, while the presence of the West Bankers in the army, especially in the officer corps, has also diluted the army's loyalty to the Palace. However, the Bedouin element continued to be the most reliable guardian of the throne. The psychological reason for the Bedouins' unswerving loyalty can be found in the difference in outlook between them and the Palestinians whom the Bedouins consider to be a threat to their favoured position in the army.[11]

The study of political recruitment is important because it reveals the relationship between recruitment and personality, since the deci-

[9]Almond and Coleman, *op. cit.*, p. 31.

[10]*Ibid.*, p. 438.

[11]Robert LeVine, "Socialization, Social Structure, and International Images," *International Behavior*, ed. Herbert Kelman (New York: Holt, 1966), p. 56.

sion-makers and those aspiring for power assume their political roles through this process. Thus, by examining recruitment patterns of any nation, one can discover the attitudes, moods, morale, resoluteness, and the capacity for policy-making of the political elites of that system. Furthermore, by observing the actions of these policy-makers in both, the internal and external fields, one can predict the viability and the projected objectives of that system.

Foreign policy is defined as the courses of action and the decisions relating to them that a state undertakes in its relations with other states in order to attain its national objectives and advance national interests. It is also a reaction to external stimuli and situations requiring response.[12] A state acts when the following components can be ascertained: actors, goals, means and situations. Since the decision-makers act on behalf of the state, the key to explaining why a state reacts in a particular pattern lies in the way its decision-makers define the situation. Comprehension and appreciation of the situation require the consideration of three distinct factors: one, the political environment in which the state operates; two, the specific reactions of other states to its policies; and three, the state's capabilities to undertake action in the light of the first two factors.[13]

These three factors may be termed as the setting.[14] Comprising the internal and external aspects of the political environment, it involves the set of categories of potentially relevant factors and conditions which may affect the choices and actions of the state. Internal setting may include the skills of the population, the productivity of the industrial and the agricultural sectors, which can limit the achievement of the state's objectives. External setting, however, refers to such factors beyond the control of the state, such as actions of decision-makers in other states. The external setting is a viable factor because it depends upon what foreign decision-makers decide as important at various times. As to external response, an action by a state may be resisted nominally or extensively. In case of the latter, a state must be ready to devote a substantial portion of its

---

[12]Charles Lerche, Jr., and Abdul A. Said, *Concepts of International Politics* (Englewood Cliffs, New Jersey: Prentice Hall, 1963), pp. 30-31.

[13]*Ibid.*, p. 32; and Charles Lerche, *Foreign Policy of the American People* (Englewood Cliffs, New Jersey: Prentice Hall, 1967), p.14.

[14]Richard Snyder, H. W. Bruck, and Burton Sapin, *Foreign Policy Decision Making* (New York: The Free Press of Glencoe, 1963), p. 67.

capability to counter such resistance.

Another limitation on the states' actions is the cost-risk calculations. Due to unforeseen contingencies, these tend to delimit sharply
the scope of choice by the decision-maker.[15] A further limitation is
the consensus aspect. Execution of policy is affected by the nature
of public opinion concerning steps taken or proposed. Since any
foreign policy decision requires sacrifices on the part of the population, lack of public support reduces the credibility of the move.
Therefore, its effectiveness in influencing other nations is diminished.[16]

In the case of Jordan, achievement of its long-range political
objectives appears to have been limited to a large extent. This is
due to the fact that Jordan's internal and external settings constituted
insurmountable obstacles to achieving such goals. The discrepancy
between the objectives and the capabilities rendered the country's
foreign policy less effective, thereby curtailing the achievement
of political aspirations to bare minimum.

---

[15]Lerche and Said, *op. cit.*, pp. 37-38.
[16]Kelman, *op. cit.*, p. 571.

CONTENTS

	Page
Preface	*v-vi*
Introduction	*vii-xi*

PART ONE
Jordan-Zionist Relations

CHAPTER ONE   **JORDAN AND THE PALESTINE QUESTION**

HISTORICAL BACKGROUND—ABDULLAH DEFENDS ARAB PALESTINE — TRANS-JORDAN AND BRITAIN ON PALESTINE — THE ARAB LEAGUE AND PALESTINE — CONCLUSION   3-18

CHAPTER TWO   **JORDAN AND THE 1948 PALESTINE WAR**

BACKGROUND — JORDAN AND THE PARTITION PLAN — JORDAN'S EFFORT TO AVOID WAR — JORDAN AND THE 1948 WAR — THE TRUCE — CONCLUSION   19–30

CHAPTER THREE   **JORDAN AND THE QUESTION OF JERUSALEM**

ISRAEL AND JERUSALEM — THE RESPONSE OF THE UNITED NATIONS — THE POSITION OF THE UNITED STATES — CONCLUSION   31–43

CHAPTER FOUR   **THE RHODES ARMISTICE AGREEMENT**

CONCLUSION   44-51

CHAPTER FIVE **JORDAN AND THE 1967 WAR**

IMMEDIATE FACTORS CONTRIBUTING TO THE 1967 CONFLICT — THE QUESTION OF FREE NAVIGATION — ISRAEL'S SEARCH FOR NEW MARKETS — THE PALESTINE RESISTANCE MOVEMENT — JORDAN AND THE FEDAYEEN IN POST-1967 PERIOD — THE JORDAN RIVER DISPUTE AND THE SUMMIT CONFERENCES — DANGERS OF THE PROJECT TO THE ARABS — THE UNITED ARAB COMMAND — THE HUSAYN-NASSER PACT OF 30 MAY 1967 — JORDAN'S ROLE IN THE 1967 WAR — THE RESPONSIBILITY OF THE ZIONISTS FOR THE WAR — THE AFTERMATH OF THE WAR — CONCLUSION 52–100

CHAPTER SIX **ISRAEL'S PEACE TERMS**

THE ZIONIST-ARAB POLICY — CONCLUSION 101–116

CHAPTER SEVEN **PEACE EFFORTS BY JORDAN**

THE KHARTOUM CONFERENCE — THE POSITION OF JERUSALEM — WITHDRAWAL AND INTERNATIONAL LAW — ISRAEL DEFIES THE UNITED NATIONS — JORDAN'S PEACE PROPOSALS — CONCLUSION 117–139

PART TWO
Jordan and Inter-Arab Relations

CHAPTER EIGHT **JORDAN-SYRIA RELATIONS**

THE GREAT SYRIA PLAN — THE FERTILE CRESCENT SCHEME — ABDULLAH RENEWS HIS CAMPAIGN — ABDULLAH DEFIES THE

LEAGUE STATES — REACTION IN SYRIA
AND LEBANON — THE GREAT SYRIA
PLAN AND THE SYRIAN COUP D'ETAT —
CONCLUSION   143–160

CHAPTER NINE   JORDAN-IRAQI RELATIONS

INTRODUCTION — EARLY ALLIANCES —
PRELUDE TO UNION — FOREIGN POLICY
UNDER TALAL — KING HUSAYN'S REIGN
— MOTIVES FOR THE JORDAN — IRAQI
UNION — THE JORDAN-IRAQ FEDERATION
— DISSOLUTION OF THE UNION —
CONCLUSION   161–185

CHAPTER TEN   JORDAN AND THE ARAB
                LEAGUE

FORMATION OF THE LEAGUE: BACK-
GROUND — THE PACT OF THE ARAB
LEAGUE — THE GREAT CHALLENGE —
ABDULLAH ANNEXES ARAB PALESTINE —
THE ALL-PALESTINE GOVERNMENT —
CONFERENCES AND UNITY — THE JOINT
DEFENCE AND ECONOMIC COOPERATION
AGREEMENT — CONCLUSION   186–199

CHAPTER ELEVEN JORDAN'S ARAB POLICY

THE ARAB SOLIDARITY PACT — THE
JORDAN-SYRIA ALLIANCE — THE RISE OF
PRO-NASSER NATIONALISTS: THE NABULSI
GOVERNMENT — CONCLUSION   200–220

PART THREE
Jordan: Great Powers Relations

CHAPTER TWELVE JORDAN-BRITISH RELATIONS

INTRODUCTION — THE BAGHDAD PACT

— IRAQ'S POSITION — THE ARAB
RESPONSE — THE DILEMMA OF JORDAN
— COUNT JORDAN OUT — THE ROLE OF
THE UNITED STATES IN THE BAGHDAD
PACT — THE DISMISSAL OF GLUBB AND
ARABIZATION OF THE JORDAN ARMY —
THE ROLE OF THE ARMY IN JORDAN
— REASONS FOR THE DISMISSAL — THE
BRITISH RESPONSE — CONCLUSION   223–267

CHAPTER THIRTEEN   JORDAN-UNITED STATES
RELATIONS

BACKGROUND—THE EISENHOWER DOCT-
RINE — JORDAN AND THE EISENHOWER
DOCTRINE — THE UNITED STATES
RESPONDS — EVALUATION OF THE
EISENHOWER DOCTRINE — CONCLUSION   268–299

CHAPTER FOURTEEN   CONCLUSION   300–308

Bibliography   309–325

Index   327

PART ONE

Jordan — Zionist Relations

CHAPTER ONE

JORDAN AND THE PALESTINE QUESTION

HISTORICAL BACKGROUND

The Sykes-Picot and Anglo-French Agreements of 16 May 1916, and 15 September 1919, placed Transjordan within the British sphere of influence which included Palestine and Iraq. The San Remo Agreement of 25 April 1920, detached Jordan from Syria and included it under the Palestine Mandate.[1] Transjordan was politically and strategically important for Britain and served as a land link between British oil interests in Iraq and the Red Sea. Strategically, however, the region was crucial for the protection of the Suez Canal and the land route to the Persian Gulf. It was contemplated also to be used for the resettling of the Palestine Arabs, once a Jewish National Home in Palestine became an accomplished fact.[2]

The area of Transjordan has never been in the past a separate independent entity. Under the Ottomans, it was the southern province of Syria. However, since ancient times, it has been an inseparable part of Palestine. The Zionists have not forgotten this. They always have considered it in their expansionist plans, not as an Arab land, but purely as a Palestine territory. Today, the Herut Party, the strongest in Israel, includes Transjordan on their map

---

[1] On November 22, 1918, General Allenby issued the following declaration regarding the administration of the occupied enemy territories: 1. The southern region (Palestine) will be under direct British administration. 2. The eastern region (Inner Syria and Transjordan) will be under the administration of Amir Faysal. 3. The western region (Lebanon and the entire Syrian coastline) will be under direct French administration.

During Faysal's administration in Damascus, Transjordan was under Syrian administration. Munib Al-Madi and Suleiman Musa, *Tariekh Al-Urdun Fi Al-Qarn Al-Ishrin* (Amman: n. p., 1959), p. 83.

[2] Alec S. Kirkbride, *A Crackle of Thorns: Experience in the Middle East* (London: Murray, 1956), p. 19.

of Greater Israel and does not recognize its separation from Palestine. The majority of the Zionists blame Churchill for harming them and serving the Arabs in 1921, when he separated Palestine from East Jordan.[3]

The year 1921 ushered in a new system of administration in East Jordan by Amir Abdullah's take-over of the area under direct British Mandate. His administration succeeded in ending anarchy and tribal warfare. At the Jerusalem Conference, Churchill formally proposed that Abdullah, as agent of Britain, should form a government in the area, east of the Jordan, with British financial and military aid, and that he should help in the restoration of law and order and should check nomadic intrusions into Syria.[4] In return, Abdullah promised not to attack the French in Syria and to renounce all claims to Iraq where his brother Faysal had been installed as king.[5]

Amir Abdullah arrived in Transjordan with the intention of occupying Syria and restoring Hashemite rule in Damascus. Accordingly, he addressed a note to the "sons of the Syrian Homeland" urging them to join him as Vice-King of Syria in restoring Faysal's throne.[6] While pledging friendship to Britain, he was also anxious to gauge British reaction to his plan. However, the British Government was committed to the recognition of the French

[3]Ahmad Baha'uddin, *Iktirah Dawlat Filistin* (Beirut: Al-Sharikah Al-Hadithah Lil-Tiba'ah, 1968), p. 89.

The British delegate to the Permanent Mandate Commission declared that "Transjordan is not a part of Palestine, but it is a part of the area administered by the British Government as mandatory under the authority of the Palestine Mandate." The League of Nations, 11th Session, 1927, p. 111. See *Al -Difa'*, October 16, 1959.

[4]F.G. Peak, the British Military Agent in Transjordan communicated with his government that Abdullah should not be allowed to use Transjordan as a base of operations against the French. F.G. Peak, "Transjordan," *Journal of the Royal Central Asian Society,* Vol. XI (1924), p. 300; also his book, *A History of Jordan and its Tribes* (Miami: University of Miami, 1958), pp. 105, 383.

[5]Although without a throne, Amir Faysal held that the Iraqi throne was to be Abdullah's. Only when Abdullah renounced it, did Faysal accept the kingship of Iraq. Ben-Jamin Shwadran, *Jordan: A State of Tension* (New York: Council for Middle Eastern Affairs Press, 1959), p. 132.

[6]Musa, *op. cit.*, p. 133. The British Government was opposed to Abdullah's plan and asked Faysal and Husayn I to use their influence to stop him. Rohan Butler and E.L. Woodward (eds.), *Documents on British Foreign Policy, 1919-1939* (London: His Majesty's Stationery Office, 1952), p. 412.

sphere of influence in Syria, while maintaining a vague obligation to the Hashemites. Due to British objection and for financial reasons, Abdullah accepted the British offer to head an administration in Transjordan, as a face-saving device for giving up his highly ambitious plans.[7]

The offer provided a basis for his future schemes. While the British offer satisfied his ambitions temporarily, Abdullah hoped that with the support of a great power like Britain, he could legitimately achieve his goals. Thus, while Transjordan was accepted by Abdullah as a nucleus for his future kingdom, the creation of Transjordan was intended by Britain to place Abdullah in an "unwanted territory."[8] Nonetheless, Abdullah was promised independence at a later date.[9]

The establishment of "Transjordan" under Hashemite administration severed this particular area from the jurisdiction of the proposed Jewish National Home in Palestine and formally demarcated the Western frontier of Transjordan. These two measures gave Abdullah effective protection against Zionist colonization.[10] At

---

[7]Abdullah accepted the British offer without arguing. This led the British Resident to observe, "...Whether his (Abdullah's) bellicose intention toward Syria had ever existed was a moot point." Kirkbride, *op. cit.*, p. 27. See Abdullah Bin Husayn, *Al-Amali Al-Siyasiyya* (Amman: n. p., 1939).

[8]John Bagot Glubb, *The Story of the Arab Legion* (London: Hodder and Stoughton, 1948), p. 58; also Kirkbride, *op. cit.*, p. 19.

[9]The Abdullah-British agreement included a provision that Great Britain should use its good offices with France to secure the restoration of the Arab government in Syria, "with Amir Abdullah as its head." Baha'uddin Tuqan, *A Short History of Jordan* (London: Luzac, 1945), pp. 42-45; also Phillip Ireland, *Iraq: A Study in Political Development* (New York: The Macmillan Company, 1938), p. 310.

Abdullah claimed that Churchill promised him Syria as a price for surrendering the throne of Iraq to Faysal. "In six months he (Churchill) would be able to congratulate us on the return of Syria to our hands." Phillip Graves (ed.), *Memoirs of King Abdullah of Transjordan* (London: Jonathan Cape, 1950), p. 45.

However, according to Jarvis and Abu Al-Sha'ar, Britain never committed itself for such a project. In fact, the British government was doing its utmost to obstruct the realization of this plan so that it would not antagonize the French, and perhaps, not to create obstacles which might obstruct the realization of establishing a Jewish National Home. C. S. Jarvis, *Arab Command* (London: Hutchinson, 1943), p. 80; and Ameen Abu Al-Sha'ar, *Muthakkarat Al-Malik Abdullah Bin Al-Husayn* (Sao Paolo: n. p., 1953), pp. 179-82.

[10]No Jews lived within the boundaries of Transjordan. Jewish National

the same time, Britain appeased Abdullah in partial fulfilment of its promises to his father for joining the side of the Allies in 1915.[11]

ABDULLAH DEFENDS ARAB PALESTINE

During the first decade of his rule, Abdullah kept himself scrupulously aloof from involvement in the Palestine problem. His greatest ambition was to create a geographic Syria under his leadership, to include Syria, Lebanon, Palestine, and Transjordan. This plan was his major obsession until his death in 1951. Since Syria and Lebanon were under French mandate, he envisioned a partial fulfilment of this dream by uniting only Palestine with Transjordan, this time with the help of Britain which was in control of Palestine. But in Palestine, there were two forces—Arab nationalism and Zionism—and both were in opposition to such a plan.[12] Nevertheless, in 1934, he laid claim, first, to the religious and then to the political leadership of the Arabs in Palestine. In his letter to the British High Commissioner dated 25 July 1934, he said:

> As the ruler of an Arab country neighbouring Palestine, and as a Moslem descendant of the Prophet, who is near to its Holy Places, especially the Aqsa Mosque, and as a leader who bears a large responsibility for the Great Arab Revolt, and as overseer of the conditions at which my people, the Arabs of Palestine, have arrived...I saw it imperative to write to your Excellency about the Arabs in Palestine for the time had come....I communicate to you the fears of my people in Palestine as frankly as possible.... My loyalty to my Arab people and my British friends equally.[13]

By so doing, Abdullah made Transjordan the base and the nucleus for an expanding kingdom.

Home was made "inapplicable to Transjordan." Great Britain Parliament, *Papers by Command* (London: H.M. Stationery Office, December 1922), p. 1785.

[11]Royal Institute of International Affairs, *Documents on International Affairs* (London: Oxford University Press, 1928), pp. 213–19.

[12]Palestine Arabs were divided: one group led by the Huseinis who opposed Abdullah, Zionism, and the British; the other, led by the Nashashibi family, were pro-Abdullah and more conciliatory.

[13]Abu Al-Sha'ar, *op. cit.*, 4th ed., pp. 258-61.

Abdullah adopted the Palestine case.[14] Persistently, he expressed his frank opinion to the High Commissioner regarding the Balfour Declaration and Jewish immigration.[15] On 18 October 1933, he wrote to the High Commissioner in Transjordan:

The Arabs in Palestine believe that the Jews aimed at exploiting the catastrophe of their expulsion from Germany in order to expedite fulfilment of their known desire to Judaize Palestine. They have revealed their intentions in a manner that exhausted Arab patience....If the Arabs, Muslems and Christians began to feel the danger of extinction and decline due to those intruders, I do not blame them, especially when they realize that a great nation like Germany despite its organization and civilization had feared for its existence from those Jews who persisted to feel like strangers despite their connection with the indigenous people there for long periods of time. What can we say of the Arabs in Palestine who have been surprised by the Jewish immigration ?...How can they protect themselves from this great catastrophe when other nations are releasing to them Jews with European education in science and industry, and with mechanical and military knowledge such as the German Jews.... Compelled by impartial co-operation and in fulfilment of my duty to the common interest, I must be frank....Nationalism is a moving force for this turbulence. This is the same spirit that drives the Palestine Arabs to demonstrations and rebellion. Added to that is their fear of extinction whose manifestations have been shown in a disturbing manner throughout the country while threatening the neighbouring Arab countries....[16]

---

[14]Musa, *op. cit.*, p. 453.

[15]"His Majesty's Government views with favour the establishment in Palestine of a national home for the Jewish race and will use its best endeavours to facilitate the achievement of this object, it being clearly understood that nothing shall be done which may prejudice the civil and religious rights of existing non-Jewish communities in Palestine, or the rights and political status enjoyed in any other country by such Jews who are fully contented with their existing nationality." Leonard Stein, *The Balfour Declaration* (New York: Simon and Schuster, 1961), p. 521.

[16]Abu Al-Sha'ar, *op. cit.*, pp. 255-57. Jewish immigration increased from 4,755 in 1931 to 30,327 in 1933 and reached a peak of 61,854 in 1935. The Jewish Agency for Palestine, *Statistical Handbook of Jewish Palestine, 1947*, p. 103.

The Balfour Declaration was a betrayal of all promises made to the Arabs and that betrayal was to condition subsequent events. Arab hostility was not slow to show itself in Palestine and in the most violent fashion, a clear indication of the Arabs' hostility to the Zionist project of making Palestine Jewish. The British became aware of the enormous difficulties that Jewish immigration and colonization would cause. But the British had gone too far in their support for Zionist ambitions to retreat, especially since the Zionist lobby was extremely powerful. But to the British Government, the Balfour Declaration was intended to facilitate the creation of a "National Home" and not a "Jewish State." In a statement on British policy in Palestine, Churchill stressed that the Jewish National Home did not mean "the imposition of a Jewish nationality upon the inhabitants of Palestine."[17]   Accordingly, there was no intention to bring about the "disappearance or the subordination of Arabic population, language, or culture in Palestine."[18]

Transjordan and Britain on Palestine

As the disturbances in Palestine grew more menacing, the High Commissioner met Abdullah in Amman and requested his mediation in the Palestine issue. While Abdullah agreed to undertake the task, he, in return, asked the British government to intercede with France for the unification of Transjordan and Syria under his leadership. The alternative to the unity with Syria was his demand to join Palestine to Transjordan. A treaty similar to that between Iraq and Britain would be entered into by the unified state.[19]

Under criticism and pressure from the Arab nationalists, Abdullah decided to maintain a policy of non-intervention, declaring that the conflict in Palestine was the concern of the Arabs in Palestine only.

As the pace of strife in Palestine was accelerated, the leading tribal chiefs in Jordan met on 26 June 1936, and decided to enter Palestine to aid the Arabs, and warned Abdullah that:

[17]J.C. Hurewitz, *Diplomacy in the Near and Middle East* (New York: Van Nostrand, 1956), p. 15.

[18]Great Britain, *Parliamentary Papers* (*Correspondence of the Colonial Office with the Palestine Arab Delegation and the Zionist Organization*), Cmd. 1700, 1922.

[19]*Oriente Moderno*, April, 1936, pp. 180-81.

...We must cross the Jordan to win Palestine....We will warn
the Amir that the Arabs of Palestine must be given freedom and
be liberated from Jewish dominance within ten days or we will
go to free them....Freedom for Transjordan is useless without
freedom in Palestine.[20]

While Abdullah was able to convince the chiefs to delay their action
hoping that the British government would do justice to the Palestine Arabs, he expressed his fears as he declared:

...I do not know how much longer I will be able to hold them.
Thousands of Transjordan...Bedouins edge near the Palestine
borders....I have held them for two months....But if the problem is not quickly settled, I fear grave troubles in Palestine....
We cannot interfere....But the Arabs will hold tight to their
rights until Great Britain realizes the justice of the Arab claims.[21]

Abdullah's influence over the Transjordan volunteers had prevented them from entering Palestine, and the British government expressed its gratefulness.[22]

As the Arab heads of state, Abdullah, Ibn Saud, and Ghazi, King
of Iraq, assured the Palestine Arabs of their support, they urged
them to avoid violence. The British government, in an effort to
allay Arab fears, declared that Jewish immigration would not be
unlimited.

...There can be no question of the total stoppage of Jewish immigration into Palestine. The guiding principle as regards the admission of immigrants is the policy of absorptive capacity. His
Majesty's government contemplates no departure from that
policy.[23]

Britain was then confronted with two fronts: the Arabs who resolved to prevent the creation of a Jewish commonwealth, and the
Jews who were determined to establish their national home through

[20]*New York Times,* June 27, 1936.
[21]*Ibid.,* June 14, 1936.
[22]Great Britain, *Parliamentary Debates* (5th series), (Commons), Vol.
CCDXIII, Col. 1320.
[23]*The Palestine Report,* 1936, p. 21.

immigration and land purchases. The British, not really knowing
what they were trying to do, found themselves fighting the Jews on
one side and the Arabs on the other.[24] Burdened by the Balfour
Declaration, Britain was committed to the Jewish cause and political cooperation between the Arabs and the Jews. The ultimate
result would have inflicted serious injuries upon the Arab community
for the "crux of the problem was the bearing of Jewish national progress upon the Arab national prospect."[25]

On 10 January 1937, Abdullah sent a memorandum to the Royal
Commission which was sent to investigate the Palestine situation,
explaining the Arab rights and aspirations, and the falsified Jewish
claims. He said:

The Jews argue that the Balfour Declaration gave them a national
home in Palestine. This could have been possible, logically and
legally, if Palestine were desert without people. But Palestine
was inhabited by its original people when this declaration was
issued. What right has a nation to dispose of another's homeland
and award it to others while its people are still living?

Balfour did not have a limit to his declaration, but left it open
as if he wanted it to continue forever, until no Arab is left in
Palestine, or as the Jews say, until they accomplish the eviction
of the Arabs from their homeland and the establishment of a
Jewish kingdom on its ruins....[26]

[24]Husayn, *Uneasy Lies the Head* (New York: Geis, 1962), p. 119.

[25]Arnold Toynbee, "The British Mandate for Palestine," *Survey of International Affairs,* 1930, p. 227.

[26]Musa, *op. cit.,* p. 457.

The Balfour Declaration was included in the Versaille Treaty of 1919, the
provisions of which were approved by Faysal, Abdullah's brother, on condition
that the Arabs obtain their independence as demanded by Faysal in his memorandum to the British Foreign Office dated the 4th of January 1919. George
Antonius, *The Arab Awakening,* 3rd ed. (New York: Capricorn Books, 1965),
p. 439.

The Versaille Treaty was not ratified nor acknowledged by King Husayn I
(father of Faysal and Abdullah), in view of the great injustices done to the Arabs
by the Allies, particularly their refusal to create the promised Arab kingdom.
Had this promise been fulfilled, Zionism would not have entrenched itself within
an Arab Kingdom, and the Middle East would have been a peaceful region today. Stewart Erskine, *King Faisal of Iraq* (London: Hutchinson, 1933), p. 99.

In an interview with Turkish Prime Minister Ismat Inonu, he was asked if

Although Abdullah appeared to reject the Balfour Declaration,. he nevertheless accepted it. Abdullah had trust in Britain that ultimately, it would redeem her promises to the Arab nation. That was the core of abdullah's political belief. But, at the same time, he understood that Britain also had to redeem the promise she had given to the Jewish people in the Balfour Declaration. Accordingly, he warned the Arabs not to ask Britain to break her promises to the Jews—for he might have feared that one broken promise would justify another.[27]

When the British Royal Commission arrived in Palestine in the summer of 1937 to investigate solutions to the problem, such as partitioning, Abdullah sent them a memorandum showing the danger of such division and decided to assume the role of a mediator. He submitted a twelve-point proposal, the key-point of which was uniting Transjordan with Palestine under an Arab monarchy with adequate safeguards for the Jewish minority.[28]

---

the Arab criticism of Turkey's support of Israel was justified. He replied:

> We were not those who allied with the Jews in the previous war. We were not those who agreed to the Balfour Declaration....It was the Arabs that did this, the Arabs themselves....They are, namely, El-Said,. and the like....Faysal....because those were the allies of England, allies with the Jews, allies with the enemies. They sacrificed us for their personal ambitions.

Nasir Eddin Al-Nashashibi, *Matha Jara Fi Al-Sharq Al-Awsat* (Beirut: Al-Maktab Al-Tigari, 1961), pp. 103-4; also see Appendix 4 in Frank Gervasi,. *The Case for Israel* (New York: The Viking Press, 1967), p. 191.

[27]*The London Times*, April 6, 1921.

[28]The proposal included the following recommendations:
1. A united Arab Kingdom of Palestine and Transjordan to be established under an Arab monarchy that is able to execute its responsibility and to implement its obligations.
2. The Kingdom will award special regime to the Jews in the Jewish areas which will be designated by a committee of Britishers, Arabs, and Jews.
3. The Jews will enjoy complete privileges similar to those enjoyed by privileged administrations.
4. The Jews will be represented in the Arab state parliament according to their number; they will be represented in the ministry.
5. Jewish immigration—at a reasonable scale—will be restricted to the areas of special administration.
6. The Jews will not have the right to purchase land or receive immigrants. outside the Jewish area.

Abdullah believed that by uniting Palestine with Transjordan as a first step in the Syrian unification plan, he could put an end to the problems which had plagued Palestine. By creating a larger Arab government with an army to defend it and with an efficient administration to run it, he believed that peace could reign, once illegal immigration was checked. With these proposals, Abdullah challenged the Commission to propose a more efficient solution than this.[29]

Having investigated the conditions in Palestine, the Royal Commission under the chairmanship of Lord Peel came to the conclusion that partitioning was the best solution. It reported:

...manifestly, the problem cannot be solved by giving either the Arabs or the Jews all they want.... While neither race can justly rule all Palestine, we see no reason why, if it were practicable, each race should not rule part of it.... Partition seems to offer, at least, a chance of ultimate peace.[30]

The Peel report recommended the termination of the mandate and the partitioning of Palestine into two independent states : a Jewish state, and an Arab state consisting of Transjordan united with the Arab part of Palestine.[31]

---

7. These provisions are for 10 years only, 8 for experiment, the remaining two to give a final decision; then independence will be announced and mandate terminated.

8. If the Arabs detect the good intentions of the Jews, Jewish immigration to the Arab parts will be allowed at Arab discretion.

9. The British mandate will continue during the ten years symbolically, merely for observation and control in the united state.

10. No objection will be made to the stay of the British army for these ten years.

11. At the end of the eighth year and the beginning of the ninth, the government of the united state and its parliament must make a final decision and implement the choice.... Musa, op. cit., p. 459.

[29]Husayn, op. cit., p. 120.

[30]Great Britain, Parliamentary Papers (Palestine Royal Commission Report, Peel), Cmd. 5479, 1937, p. 375.

[31]Ibid., p. 381.

A third sector was to include the holy cities of Jerusalem and Bethlehem with the immediate surrounding areas and a narrow corridor to the sea. This sector was to remain under British mandate

This idea pleased Abdullah. The scheme, however, did not materialize. After the British government changed its mind regarding the Partition Plan, it invited the Arab governments of Transjordan, Iraq, Egypt, Yemen, and Saudi Arabia to the London Conference to discuss the Palestine problem.[32] After the convening of the conference, late in January 1939, the British government issued the famous White Paper which recommended the creation of an independent Palestine state after ten years.[33]

Pre-World War II British policy methods had antagonized most of the Arab world. Britain now tried to improve its reputation by actually taking the initiative for a Pan-Arab policy which would remove the grievances which had been hampering Anglo-Arab relations. One observer commented: "It is possible that the future history of the British Empire may in the end depend on its Arab policy now than any other single factor."[34]

Britain's major considerations for such a shift in policy were several. First, Britain would strengthen the Anglo-Arab alliance if she gave support to Arab nationalistic aspirations. Second, unification of the Arab states under British influence—considered a tactical measure to drive the French from the Levant—could realize Britain's policy of creating a Hashemite-dominated state, thereby fulfilling its long-awaited promises. Third, Britain may have wanted to convey to the United States and the Zionists the fact that she no longer would allow herself to be the Jewish catspaw in Palestine. Britain hoped that an Arab political body would be more effective in dealing with the Palestine problem than the Palestine Arabs themselves, and that a pan-Arab front would be more effective in

---

[32]On 9 November 1938, Britain issued a statement recognizing the ties that bound Arab Palestine to the other Arab countries. Toynbee, *op. cit.*, 1938, p. 443.

[33]Musa, *op. cit.*, p. 462.

The Conference which ended on 17 March 1939, showed that the major obstacle to any compromise lay in the judicial basis of the problem. The Arabs demanded the abrogation of the Balfour Declaration and replacement of the mandate by a treaty similar to that concluded with Iraq in 1930. In order to secure Arab acceptance of a compromise, the McDonald White Paper was issued on May 17. It was considered a positive step in the interest of the Arabs since it stated that the Arabs in Palestine should not be made subjects of a Jewish state against their will. Great Britain *Parliamentary Papers*, Cmd. 6019, 1939.

[34]J.G. Frere, "Arab Chessboard," *Spectator*, June 7, 1946, p. 577.

counterbalancing the Zionist ambitions than was the case at the
London Conference.[35]

Amir Abdullah's initiative and communications to the British
Government regarding the future of Palestine brought him severe
criticism from Arab political leaders who suspected his personal
ambitions in Palestine. In a letter to Abdul-Hameed Said, head
of the Young Men's Muslim Association in Egypt, Abdullah
defended his position.

> ...I was fortunate to have established a government in
> Transjordan and excluded it from the provisions of the Balfour
> Declarations....The Declaration was implemented quietly. The
> number of Jews has increased and their influence augmented....
> In 1921, their number did not exceed one hundred thousand;
> today, it increased to four hundred fifty thousand. Now they
> own the most fertile land, as they have established themselves
> everywhere....Zionism is based on three pillars: the Balfour
> Declaration; the European nations which decided to rid them-
> selves of the Jews, and which recommended Palestine for their
> National Home; and the Arab extremists who do not accept any
> solution—except on their terms. In the meantime, Palestine is
> breathing its last breath. I was informed that the Jews have
> requested the extension of the Mandate so that they would be able
> to purchase more land and bring in new immigrants....Palestine,
> in its catastrophe, is unlike any other country.... Palestine
> suffers the danger of dominance by one nation over another.
> The remedy for Palestine lies in the hastening to halt this danger
> and limiting the invasion....I find it my religious duty and nation-
> alistic obligation to prevent the disaster by uniting Palestine with
> Transjordan, thereby increasing the Arab population by one
> half million—to maintain majority. In addition, the Palestine
> Arabs will be in control of the administration of the state, the
> Parliament, and the army which will defend it...controls its
> shores, and closing its doors to secret immigration....[36]

The outbreak of World War II also dimmed Abdullah's plans in
Palestine. But with the proposed French plan to make Syria a

---

[35] J. S. Raleigh "Ten Years of the Arab League," *Middle Eastern Affairs*, Vol. VI (March, 1955), p. 68.

[36] Musa, *op. cit.*, p. 460.

monarchy, the Great Syria Plan was revived, especially when certain Syrian elements were reported to be supporting Abdullah for the Syrian throne.[37]

As World War II broke out, Abdullah commenced his call for the unification of geographic Syria, the aim of which was to combine the Arab forces to check the Zionist invasion. "Syrian unity must precede any other Arab unification. It is imperative to have Palestine in this unity...."[38]

The report of the Anglo-American Investigating Commission of 13 March 1946 was disappointing to Arab aspirations. Abdullah communicated to the British government that:

> The report placed the case in the worst situation ever. The report, which permitted one hundred thousand immigrants to enter Palestine, also indicates a policy of turning Palestine into a Jewish country....If there is value or weight to the Muslim East from Burma to Tangiers, it is then, the duty of Attlee and Bevin to correct the situation.[39]

In his reply to Abdullah, King George VI said that his government awaits the opinions of the Arab governments before finalizing the decisions taken by the Commission. Similarly, President Truman, in his reply to Abdullah's cable said that there would not be any basic changes in the Palestine situation without consulting Arab and Jewish leaders, and that the United States would not take any decision regarding the Commission's report without consulting the government of Jordan.[40] However, despite these assurances, both the western powers proceeded with their pro-Zionist policies.[41]

Jordan's negotiations for independence were received with indig-

---

[37]G.E. Kirk, *The Middle East in the War, 1939–1946* (London: Oxford University Press, 1952), p. 84.

[38]Musa, *op. cit.*, p. 462.

On March 3, 1944, Abdullah cabled F.D. Roosevelt drawing his attention to the pro-Jewish attitude of Congress whose stand "brings pain which is felt by every Easterner. Further, the deliberations of Congress contradict the principles of national freedom and eliminating tyranny which the United States is fighting for." *Ibid.*

[39]*Ibid.*, p. 463.

[40]*Ibid.*

[41]*Ibid.*

nation by Zionist circles. Although the Jewish Agency had reconciled itself to the separation of Transjordan from Palestine, many radical Zionists still insisted that Jordan was included within the provisions of the Jewish National Home. Realizing the Zionist danger, Abdullah called upon all the Arabs to cooperate more closely and to be ready to defend the Arab homeland with their lives if necessary.[42] In his coronation speech on 25 May 1946, Abdullah affirmed his defence of Arab Palestine: "We promise God a holy war in defense of Palestine to keep it an Arab country."[43]

THE ARAB LEAGUE AND PALESTINE

At the Bludan Conference, 8-12 June 1946, the Arab countries, including Jordan, decided on direct Arab intervention in support of the rights of Arab Palestine. The Zionist reply to the Bludan decision was the dynamiting of ten bridges connecting Palestine with its Arab neighbours and the attacking of police and customs posts inside Jordan.[44]

After the end of the War, the British government was still indecisive regarding its policies in Palestine. While the Arabs persisted in their intransigence, the Zionists acted positively and vigorously. While the Palestine Arabs were backed by the Arab League, the Zionists too had found a new and powerful support in America.[45] This widened the scope of the problem and caused it to become an international rather than a localized dispute.

In an effort to bridge the gap between the Jews and the Arabs, the British government held conferences in London with the representatives of the Arab governments. In the first conference, which lasted from 10 September to 2 October 1946, Britain proposed the Morrison Plan which was rejected by the Arabs. The second conference took place on 28 January 1947, when Britain proposed a new plan, the Bevin Plan, which was also rejected by the Arabs.[46]

---

[42]*New York Times,* January 28, 1946.

[43]Musa, *op. cit.,* p. 464.

[44]*Ibid.*

[45]Aqil Hyder Hasan Abidi, *Jordan: A Political Study: 1948-1957* (New York : Asia Publishing House, 1965), p. 24.

[46]The Morrison Plan was based mainly on the recommendations of the Anglo-American Committee of Inquiry. The Plan envisaged converting the

Commenting on Britain's handling of the Palestine question, an Arab politician wrote :

Britain came to realize that, in her handling of Palestine, she had launched an irresistible force of Jewish aspirations against the immovable obstacle of Arab nationalism, and that no practical solution lay in her hands. Like a signalman who had mistakenly set two trains rushing at each other on the same set of lines, she could only bury her face in her hands and refer the matter to Providence.[47]

At this time, the British government declared that she would take the case to the United Nations.

CONCLUSION

The establishment of the Transjordan Amirate came as a face-saving solution to both, Amir Abdullah and Great Britain. Having forfeited the throne of Iraq, Amir Abdullah's purported destination was Syria, to restore King Faysal's throne from the French. The British felt that it was time to come to an understanding with him, for they suspected that, if Abdullah should attack Syria, the French would crush him and occupy the territory east of the Jordan. This the British had to prevent. With British persuasion, Abdullah abandoned his plan and remained in Transjordan. His decision was dictated by economic, military and political considerations. He realized that a campaign against the French would require vast funds which he did not possess, nor have access to. The force which he

---

Mandate into a trusteeship and dividing Palestine into Jewish and Arab provinces. The Plan would ultimately lead to either a unitary state or to partition.

According to the Bevin Plan, Palestine would be divided into sectors with considerable self-government. oth nationalities would be represented in the High Commissioner's Advisory Council. The Mandate would be terminated in five years, and Jewish immigration would be allowed at the rate of four thousand per month for a period of two years. After that trial period, a new arrangement would be made; Palestinians would progressively be taken in the central government, and at the end of four years, a constituent assembly would be convoked to establish an independent state. *Ibid.*

[47]Emil Bustani, *March Arabesque* (London: Ebenzer and Sons Ltd., Trinity Press, 1961), p. 70.

could assemble was no match for the French army in the Levant. A third factor was that since Britain would have prevented him from advancing through its Transjordan territory, the Amir knew that he could not cope with this situation either. Fourth, though the British considered Transjordan to be of little value, they hoped to pacify Abdullah by installing him as its Amir. This would have benefited Britain in two ways: first, the British domain would be increased by precluding French occupation of the territory, and second, Britain would impress upon the Arabs and the world their sincerity with regard to her promises and international obligations, namely, to create an independent Arab kingdom.

By consenting to administer Transjordan, Abdullah may have achieved a tactical victory. He considered the territory as a nucleus for an expanded kingdom, since he never abandoned his ambitious plans to unite the Syrian provinces.

The external setting, namely, opposition of Syria, Lebanon, Egypt, Saudi Arabia, France and, to some extent, Britain precluded for all practical purposes the realization of this plan. However, Abdullah's loyalty to Britain was rewarded when the Arab sector of Palestine came under his administration in 1948, thereby partially fulfilling his personal as well as the national dream.

CHAPTER TWO

JORDAN AND THE 1948 PALESTINE WAR

BACKGROUND

The United Nations' Partition Plan for Palestine was approved by the General Assembly on 29 November 1947, by thirty-three to thirteen, with ten abstentions. This was followed by a British declaration to terminate the Mandate on the 15th of August 1948, which was revised on May 15.

The Arab governments, including Jordan's, met at Alai in Lebanon on 7 October 1947 and decided to "support Palestine Arabs in order to enable them to defend themselves and their existence."[1] The Arab League convened a conference in Cairo on 8 December 1947, in which they declared that partitioning was illegal and promised their support in the form of weapons and funds to the *Jaysh Al-Inqath* (Army of Liberation) under the command of the Iraqi General, Ismail Safwat. Furthermore, despite the advice of the military experts, the League decided that, in the event of partition, the Arab armies would enter Palestine to restore it to its inhabitants who possessed the inviolable right to self-determination.[2]

Of all the Arab states, Transjordan alone had a long-standing interest in Palestine, since it was considered a part of the Great Syria Plan. Thus, when King Farouk announced in the League Political Committee that the Arab armies would enter Palestine to liberate it and hand it over to its people, Abdullah in order to assuage the fears of the Arabs declared to the Arab News Agency on 14 April 1948:

...this is not a time of greed for any Arab government....

[1]Musa, *op. cit.*, p. 466.

[2]Had a plebiscite been conducted, the partition would have been defeated, since two-thirds of the populations were Arabs. Further, some local Jews led by Magnes and Poper objected to the Partition Plan. From a speech by King Husayn at the Press Club, Washington, D.C., 7 November 1967.

After liberating this land, [Palestine]...its people will have the last word [to determine their destiny] without compulsion. No doubt, Jordan and Palestine are one. Any assistance from any Arab state given Palestine, I shall consider an assistance to Jordan.[3]

However, despite his claim to quiet Arab public opinion, Abdullah's approach to the partition resolution preceded the determination of the League to intervene militarily in Palestine. Jordan's discussions with Britain through Prime Ministers Tawfiq Abul-Huda and Ernest Bevin at the time of the revision of the Anglo-Jordan Treaty in February 1948, indicated that Jordan planned to administer the parts of Palestine adjacent to Transjordan after the British evacuation. Since the Palestine Arabs, unlike the Jews, did not possess organized administrative machinery, the greatest majority of the Palestinians urged Abdullah to send his army to protect them after the British withdrawal.[4] It was reported that Bevin had agreed to the plan and that both Syria and Egypt would, in the same manner, administer the adjacent parts of Arab Palestine according to the Partition Plan. However, Bevin warned Huda that jordan should not go beyond the partition lines to occupy any area of the Jewish part.[5]

The discussions between Jordan and Britain were based on the fact that partition was forthcoming, and thus, all parties had to accept it without any choice. Furthermore, Jordan's acceptance of the proposed partition should be considered in the light of the inability of the Arab governments to take effective action in Palestine, as was evident later on.[6]

[3]*Arab News Agency*, 14 April 1948.

[4]Musa, *op. cit.*, p. 469.

[5]John Bagot Glubb, *A Soldier With the Arabs* (New York : Harper & Brothers Publishers, 1957), p. 63; also Nashashibi, *op. cit.*, p. 77. In his memoirs, Glubb said it was decided that the Legion, in case it entered Palestine, was not to fight but was only to occupy the Arab part according to the Partition Plan of 1947.

I personally was against the idea of the Legion's entry in Palestine. I told Abdullah and Huda of this, but Huda told me, 'I assure you, Glubb, we will not fight. I know that the League wants. It does not want war at all. Nashashibi, *op. cit.*, p. 146.

[6]Ironically, the idea of partition which Jordan had welcomed in 1947 is today the official demand which the Arab states desire to attain.

JORDAN AND THE PARTITION PLAN

King Abdullah's interest in the Partition Plan was determined by three considerations: his ambition for territorial expansion; the indecisiveness and evasiveness of the British Government regarding a Palestine settlement; and finally, inter-Arab rivalries toward Abdullah's political aspirations.[7]

The Government of Jordan had suggested to the Arab League that its army alone be given the task of containing the Zionists, provided that the Arab states finance the increase in troops and the purchase of arms. Jordan's argument in this connection was based on the fact that it was not a United Nations member. But the Arab states refused this suggestion for several reasons: first, Jordan's political and military life was tied exclusively with that of Britain. The Jordan army was commanded and officered by British personnel. Thus, the danger of leakage of operational plans was present. Second, cognizant of Abdullah's ambitions, they feared, once he was in full control of Arab Palestine, he would annex it to Jordan. Third, they suspected that he, under pressure from Britain, might reach a settlement with the Zionists. Fourth, his control would perpetuate British presence in the Arab world. However, in their meeting of 25 April 1948, the Foreign Ministers finally decided that the Arab armies would enter Palestine.[8] Accordingly, the Jordan army was given a subsidy of one and a half million pounds for the proposed combined military operation.[9]

Having been well informed about the Zionist strength, the Jordan Government counselled the Arab states to arrive at a peaceful solution. Jordan did not wish to devote its scarce resources to a military effort.[10] From the day partition was voted in the United Nations,

---

[7]Jon and David Kimche, *Both Sides of the Hill: Britain and the Palestine War* (London: Secker and Warburg, 1960), pp. 55-60.

[8]The decision was based on two main reasons: one, to prevent loss of Arab land to the Zionists; and two, to prevent the "Zionist terrorists" from expelling Arab farmers and townsmen from their properties. King Husayn's Speech at the Press Club, Washington, 7 November 1967.

[9]Musa, *op. cit.*, p. 470.

[10]On 15 May 1948, the combined Arab force was 21,500. In the final phase of the war, the Arab force numbered 40,000, facing 60,000 Israelis. Musa, *op. cit.*, p. 472; Max Rodinson, *Israel and the Arabs* (New York: Pantheon Books, 1968), p. 39.

Abdullah accepted it, though not openly.[11]   He had hoped that his earlier proposals to the Royal Commission would materialize this time.

JORDAN'S EFFORTS TO AVOID WAR

King Abdullah wished to make his intentions clear to the Zionists, while maintaining his position *vis-a-vis* the Arab leaders.   Against odds, he steered tactfully.   He would explore every means to secure peace.[12] While he was eager for a peaceful settlement, he sensed that the Zionists were uncompromising.   On 21 April, he told the Arab News Agency:

The present conflict aims at displacing a nation by another....
I still had remnants of hope to find peace and cooperation before the incidents at Deir Yassin, etc. I told the Arab League delegation last fall: if the Jews want peace, we also want peace; but if we are compelled to defend Palestine, that we shall do. The matter of peace is in the hands of the Jews, if they can get rid of their haughtiness and accept a compromise with the Arabs....   As to Jerusalem, it is the responsibility of the United Nations to advise the Zionists not to come close to it because that would mean fighting and Jerusalem is Jerusalem. . . .   The national and religious feelings compel us to preserve its holiness regardless of cost. My desire for compromise compels me to mention this.   Further, the Arabs are compassionate if the Jews try for an understanding.[13]

Realizing the futility of Arab cooperation and that the conflict would be a collision between two movements a colonizing Zionism and a xenophobic Arab nationalism each seeking to destroy the other— Abdullah decided to pave the way for peace to avert bloodshed in the

[11]Abidi., *op. cit.*, p. 25.

[12]In February, 1948, at Lake Success, King Abdullah made a bold international venture. It was reported that Jordan's representative at the United Nations, Omar Al-Dajani, had offered a scheme in Abdullah's name whereby a partition plan be effectuated in return for American recognition of Transjordan. Shwadran, *op. cit.*, p. 249.

[13]Abdullah At-Tall, *Karithat Filistin: Muthakkarat* Abdullah At-Tall (Cairo, n.p., 1959), pp. 62-63.

Holy Land.[14] Accordingly, on 5 May 1948, he directed a message to the people of Palestine:

> We are trying for peace settlement which would give the Jews the right of citizenship in Palestine.... If they inclined to peace, then peace is our goal. We will give them local government in the areas in which they constitute a majority within the Arab State.[15]

On the following day, he warned the Jews saying: "the journey is long and the Arabs are numerous. You have espoused tyranny and no victory accrues to tyrants."[16] His message portrayed him as a peace-maker and the Zionists as warmongers.

JORDAN AND THE 1948 WAR

When the Jordan army originally planned to enter Palestine at the termination of the Mandate, "no war with the Jews had been visualized."[17] Its mission was to occupy the Arab part according to the

---

[14]Uri Avnery, *Israel Without Zionism: A Plea For Peace in the Middle East* (New York: MacMillan, 1968), p. 193.

[15]Musa, *op. cit.*, p. 472. T.E. Lawrence testified to Abdullah's peaceful inclinations. He found him "too balanced, too cool, too humorous to be an armed prophet." *Seven Pillars of Wisdom* (Garden City, N. Y.: Doubleday, 1951), p. 68.

[16]Musa, *op. cit.*, p. 472. In reference to the atrocities committed by the Zionists such as the Deir Yassin massacre, Abdullah told *Al-Ahram* on 17 April 1948:

I received a telegram from the Jewish Agency in which they expressed indignation at the crime committed by the terrorists. The Agency said that the new state would respect international law and principles in the fighting. I interpret this as tantamount to a declaration of war on Transjordan and the Arab states. I do not recognize the existence of a Jewish state, and give no weight to this telegram.

At-Tall, *op. cit.*, p. 62; also Terrence Pritties, Israel: *Miracle in the Desert*, Revised Edition (Baltimore: Penguin Books, 1968), p. 177.

[17]Glubb, *op. cit.*, pp. 82, 96.

Prime Minister Abul-Huda was reported to have declared: "We never initiated battles....There has never been any inclination to war at all...." At-Tall, *op. cit.*, p. 531. Furthermore, while the Egyptian Parliament appropriated forty five million pounds for the war, Abul-Huda expressed his indignation at dragging Jordan into the conflict. He said, "... Those who insist on making

United Nations Partition Plan, and to restore order which had broken, following the withdrawal of the British.[18]

According to General Glubb, the British commander of the Jordan army, the military action undertaken by the jordanian army was designed to prevent the well-organized Israeli forces from overrunning the entire country, and from inflicting more massacres on the peaceful Arab population and driving them into exile.[19] Thus the issue became a matter "not of securing something for the Jews but of trying to salvage something for the Arabs."[20] General Glubb realized that if the Israeli forces had moved forward on May 15 and the Arab Legion had not crossed into Palestine, the Jews, in a very short time, would have conquered all Palestine up to Jordan.[21]

High on the list of priorities of King Abdullah was to prevent the fall of Jerusalem in the hands of the enemy. "The absence of an Arab military force in Jerusalem when the Mandate ended offered the Jews the irresistible temptation to seize the whole defenseless city and incorporate it into the new Israel."[22] Furthermore, the main road, connecting Jerusalem with Tel-Aviv, also had to be brought under Jordan's control, particularly, the strategically crucial Latrun heights to prevent the introduction of new Israeli forces into Jerusalem.[23] In other parts of eastern and central Palestine, the Jordan army merely held its positions along the partition line, since there had been no plan to occupy any part of the Israeli sector.

---

war had better pay for it." Immediately, the Arab League paid to Jordan twenty-five thousand pounds. Glubb, *Soldier With the Arabs*, pp. 82-85.

[18]Shwadran, *op. cit.*, p. 258.

[19]See the "situation" which made imperative the intervention of the Jordanian army as illustrated by Glubb. Glubb, *Soldier With the Arabs*, p. 97.

[20]John Marlowe, *The Seat of Pilate* (London: The Cresset Press, 1959), p. 249.

[21]Glubb, *op. cit.*, p. 107.

[22]*Ibid.*

[23]*Ibid.*, p. 110.

The Jordan army was subjected to greater military pressure than expected, due to the larger Israeli forces and their resolve to occupy the entire city. Abdullah's desperate efforts to save the City seemed to have weakened the Israeli determination. One observer remarked: "...The Israelis apparently decided that they could not afford the heavy casualties which their attacks on Jerusalem were causing to their army and diverted their offensive to other parts of the front. Kirkbride, *op. cit.*, p. 163.

THE TRUCE

The military objectives of the Jordan army were concerned with containing the advance of the Israeli forces and with isolating Jerusalem from the coastal plain where the majority of the Jewish population was concentrated. Due to Jordan's victories inside Jerusalem and around it, the situation of the besieged Jews in Jerusalem worsened due to the lack of water and supplies.[24] Failing to save the city militarily, the Israeli government with the help of its supporters throughout the world, pressed the United Nations for a truce. On 23 May the security Council issued an order for a cease-fire which the Israelis accepted immediately because the city would fall to the Arabs if fighting continued. However, Jordan refused the truce declaring that it would not stop the fighting unless the Israelis changed their plan of establishing a Zionist state.[25]

The Security Council continued its discussions of the Palestine issue. On 29 May it approved a British resolution for stopping any military aid to either side. To complicate matters for Jordan—which at the time had the upper hand in the City—the British Government informed Jordan on May 30 that it had decided to withdraw all British officers in the Legion. This would have had significant repercussions because these officers were in full command and in charge of the operations on which Jordan's military and political positions depended.[26] Furthermore, the British Government threatened to stop sending arms and ammunition, and end its subsidy unless Jordan complied with the four-week truce ordered by the Security Council.[27] The British action was ostensibly influenced by their respect for the International Organization, world public opinion and in response to the American pressure.[28]

[24]Musa, *op. cit.*, p. 498. A telegram from Tel Aviv to the Mayor of besieged Jewish Jerusalem said: "Patience. Help will come, but it will be political." See At-Tall, *op. cit.*, pp. 198-200.

[25]Musa, *op. cit.*, p. 498.

[26]Glubb, *op. cit.*, pp. 133-34.

[27]Musa, *op. cit.*, p. 502; also U.N. Security Council official Record, Document S/801, 1948.

[28]The United States exerted great pressure on Britain to stop her military and monetary aid to Jordan. Senator Brewster found support in the Senate for his suggestion that American financial aid to Britain, under the European Recovery Program, should be reconsidered "to determine to what extent the United States is assisting those, who, both, at Lake Success and in the Middle East, are

While King Abdullah felt the absolute necessity to comply, the other Arab states refused the truce. However, when Jordan threatened to accept the truce and withdraw from the League unilaterally—which would have meant also the withdrawal of Iraq—they acquiesced.[29] Thus, in order to save the Arabs' so-called unity, the political committee of the League decided on accepting the truce. This decision proved to be a major disaster to the Arabs because it ended the siege of Jewish Jerusalem thereby allowing tens of thousands of Jews to leave the city and join the Zionist fighting forces on other fronts. Most importantly, however, it enabled the Zionists to procure sorely needed armaments. This, undoubtedly, was a tactical victory for the Zionists and the beginning of the decline of the Arab military position, as Gabbay observed:

The Israelis could do only very little to stop the Arab military advance during the first days of the battle. This was due to the scarcity of modern arms, such as heavy weapons, tanks, anti-aircraft guns. Only one or two weeks had elapsed after the truce than weapons and ammunitions as well as airplanes began to fly to Israel to be readied within hours. .... Israel was also flooded with volunteers from all over the world....And when fighting

---

apparently so milatintly opposing the United States.

On May 22, Warren Austin, the American Ambassador to the U.N., accused Jordan of 'contumacy' and urged the Security Council to 'keep Abdullah where he belongs.'

In response to these pressures, Britain through its representative at the U.N., Sir Alexander Cadogan, announced that immediate steps were being taken to ensure that those officers seconded to the Arab Legion from the British army should not serve in Palestine; that the obligation to pay the next instalment of the subsidy to Jordan, which fell due on July 12, would be reviewed in the light of the United Nations decision; and that the British Government would suspend its deliveries of arms to Egypt, Iraq and Transjordan in completion of existing contracts, if the Security Council should decide on a general embargo effectively preventing the supply of arms to Arabs and Jews alike. *U.S. Congressional Record,* 94 (1948), pp. 6279-81; also U.N. SCOR, 301st Meeting, No. 72, 3rd Year, pp. 42, 44; also Glubb, *op. cit.,* p. 133.

[29]Mahmoud Hafez, *Istiragiat Al-Gharb Fi Al Watan Al-Arabi* (Cairo: Al-Mutba'ah Al-Fanniyyiah Al-Hadithah, 1967), p. 153.

Jordan's dire need was explained by Glubb, as he told Abdullah in 1948: "We have very little ammunition, and the depots are empty. I cannot fight for more than FIVE hours. The army is tired and we must accept the truce. Nashashibi, *op. cit.,* p. 151.

was renewed on July 9, 1948, the Israeli army was not the unarmed or untrained army.[30]

In order to maximize his advantages, Prime Minister Ben Gurion, broke the truce and the cease-fire on various occasions.[31] Significantly, *fait accompli* was the code name for such violations.[32]

In an interview regarding the Arab-Israeli conflict, and the truce arrangement which Israel had pressed for to be able escape the Arab military pressures, Ben Gurion said:

The fate of Israel would be determined in Palestine either in battle or in peace negotiations between the Arabs and Israel and not in the United Nations conference rooms.... Even if the truce would have been carefully observed by the Arab countries, we would not have accepted it for an indefinite period....and Israel would force the Arab armies out of Palestine if the United Nations failed to accomplish this itself.[33]

By this time, Israel had become convinced that Egypt was its principal enemy, not only due to its strength but also because it took a harder policy towards Israel, as compared to Jordan. In October, the clamour for resumption of hostilities in order to deal one more blow against Egypt and seize the Negeb had increased.[34] A plan to attack the Egyptian front was contemplated for the following reasons: first, the confidence that the Egyptian forces would be defeated, and second, Ben Gurion's interest in conquering the Old city of Jerusalem which was high on his priority list. If his army gained control of the Negeb, it could readily attack Jerusalem from the rear.[35] This plan was made

---

[30]Rony E. Gabbay, *A political Study of the Arab-Jewish Conflict: The Arab Refugee Problem* (Paris: Libraire Minard, 1959), p. 154.

[31]Vick Vance and Pierre Lauer, *Hussein of Jordan: My "War" With Israel* (New York: William Morrow, 1969), p. 109.

[32]Rodinson, *op. cit.*, p. 39.
Only an Anglo-American ultimatum prevented Ben Gurion from pressing into Sinai beyond the Egyptian frontier, *Ibid.*

[33]*New York Times,* July 30, 1948; Kimche, *op. cit.*, p. 272; also Gabbay, *op. cit.*, p. 155.

[34]*New York Times,* October 15-16, 1948.

[35]Fred J. Khouri, *The Arab-Israeli Dilemma* (Syracuse : Syracuse University Press, 1968), p. 86.

by the military minded Ben Gurion despite the warnings of his foreign Minister Moshe Sharette who declared that such aggression could seriously harm Israel's international standing. Thus, military preparations for the invasion of the Negeb were underway.[36] On 14 october 1948, Israel surprised the world by breaking the truce and attacking the Egyptians in the Negeb area.[37]

This decision to attack was due to several factors: the Soviet Union had indicated that she would not seriously consider applying sanctions against Israel; the American presidential elections were at a climax, thus, the least reaction to an attack would be voiced; but mainly, distrust, disunity, and lack of cooperation between the Arab armies enabled Ben Gurion to concentrate a large striking force against Egypt in the Negeb without having to worry about an attack from the rear. As a result, the Egyptians lost a large part of the territory which was under their control, while the Zionists made substantial gains. On October 17, they announced that Israel "stands by its claim to the whole Negab." Only strong opposition from his cabinet prevented Ben Gurion from marching and occupying the Old City of Jerusalem and the area eastward to the Jordan River.[38]

The Security Council ordered a cease-fire to take place on October 19, but Israel, certain of victory, ignored it and continued attacking until October 22.[39] When the Security Council Resolution of 4 November 1948, was passed, ordering both sides to go back to the lines prior to the attack, Israel refused again, and the U.N. did nothing about it.[40] According to O'Ballance, an Israeli victory over the Egyptian army was made possible, since the Israeli Government was assured of non-interference of the Hashemite armies.[41] This created bitter reaction by the Egyptians who felt abandoned by their Arab allies and considered entering into separate negotiations with Israel to extricate themselves from their dangerous military position.[42] Egypt did so in January 1949, influenced by three factors: The

---

[36]Kimche, op. cit., p. 274.

[37]Shwadran, op. cit., p. 267.

[38]New York Times, 17 October 1948.

[39]U.N., S. C. O. R., Document S/1058, 26 October 1948; At-Tall, op. cit., p. 409.

[40]377th meeting of the Security Council, 4 November 1948.

[41]Edgar O'Ballance, The Arab-Israeli War, 1948 (New York : Praeger, 1957), p. 198; At-Tall, op. cit., p. 543.

[42]Khouri, op. cit., p. 94; and O'Ballance, op. cit., p. 198.

critical military situation which would have resulted in loss of more territory and men; secondly, the fact that fighting alone would not yield victory, since Egypt had been abandoned by its Arab allies; and thirdly, the American and British pressure made it imperative to sign the Armistice Agreement with the Zionists. It was followed by other agreements with Jordan, Syria, and Lebanon. Only Iraq refused to sign, since it had no boundaries with Israel.

CONCLUSION

Jordan's intervention in Palestine in 1948, was not calculated to wage a war, but to implement the United Nations Partition Resolution by occupying and administering the Arab sector. In view of its lack in military capability to wage an offensive, Jordan's position was a defensive one. The army of Jordan depended for its supplies on the goodwill of Britain; its commanders were British officers, who in effect were implementing Britain's Palestine policy. This diplomatic venture determined to a large degree Jordan's military operations, as well as Abdullah's political aspirations in Palestine.

In any case, avoiding a protracted military conflict was, without doubt, in Jordan's interest for tactical, political and economic reasons. First, Abdullah did not see the logic of devoting Jordan's scarce resources to a military effort which would not benefit him more than negotiations would. Secondly, his information about the enemy's military and political strength dictated that negotiations, rather than fighting, would be more advantageous, since hostilities might result in loss of Arab land. Thirdly, hostilities would not secure more land for Jordan, since world public opinion would not allow depriving the Zionists from the minimum area designated by the Partition Plan. Lastly, King Abdullah realized that Jordan's political interests had to be preserved. To him, a peaceful solution was most desired. Accordingly, he insisted on a Jordanian solution rather than an Arab one.

Although Abdullah was determined to avoid military conflict, he, nonetheless, under popular pressure, joined the Arab League states in their so-called Palestine campaign. His decision to participate—at least on the surface—was occasioned by external forces, some beyond his control. As a founding member of the League, the King could not afford to be the Maverick of the Arabs. His refusal would inevitably make him a traitor to Arab nationalism. As well, Abdullah might have wished to impress upon his critics that he enjoyed independence in foreign and military policies as any other Arab ruler. Since the avowed objective of the Arab expeditionary force was to protect Arab Palestine, and since he intended to do so in any case, his participation did not alter his plans. Moreover King Abdullah's personal rivalries, especially with King Farouk, made him eager to take part as commander-in-chief of the Arab forces, in an attempt to prevent Egypt from sharing Arab Palestine with him. This appears to have precipitated the ever-present Jordan-Egyptian cold war, considered by many students of Arab affairs to be a major cause for Arab disunity.

CHAPTER THREE

JORDAN AND THE QUESTION OF JERUSALEM

According to the Partition Plan, Jerusalem was to be international-ized.[1] But on the 14th of May, the Zionist forces commenced the occu-pation of key strategic buildings in the city, including those directly overlooking the old section, like the Notre Dame building.[2] The Arab defenders were merely volunteers with no organization. They feared that the organized Zionist forces could overwhelm them and occupy the Old City.

Abdullah's plan in Palestine was governed by certain objectives, mainly the annexation of Arab Palestine and reaching a final peace settlement with the Zionists.

As to Jerusalem, it was exempted from the Legion's military operations because:

(i)   The Arab League had agreed to exempt Jerusalem from the military plans of the Arab armies;

(ii) due to the existence of a truce in Jerusalem supervised by foreign counsels of the U.S., France, and Belgium; and

(iii) on account of the political situation of Jerusalem and the possibility of internationalizing it.[3]

---

[1]The General Assembly Resolution, 181 (II), 12 November 1947, provided that Jerusalem would be a *corpus separatum* under a special international regime and administered by the United Nations. Article 4 designated the boundaries of the territory of the city: "The territory of the city shall include the municipality of Jerusalem as delimited on 29 November 1947, together with the surrounding villages and towns, the most eastern of which is Abu Dis; the most southern, Bethlehem: the most western, Ein Karim (including also the built-up area of Motsa); and the most northern, Shu'fat." U.N. Special Committee on Palestine, *Report to the General Assembly,* Vol. I, Doc. A/364, 1947, p. 27.

[2]David Ben Gurion, *Rebirth and Destiny and of Israel* (New York : Philoso-phical Library, 1954), p. 530. Replying to a question, Bevin said, "They [Jews] first started it. . . . I certainly say that they [Arabs] did not start the battle, the attack was made on the Holy places of the Arabs." Great Britain, *Parlia-mentary Debates,* 451, Col. 2145.

[3]At-Tall, *op. cit.,* p. 78; also Musa, *op. cit.,* p. 484; Glubb, *op. cit.,* p. 98.

Ahmad Hilmi, leader of Arab Jerusalem, cabled the government of Jordan saying, "Unless you rescue us immediately, Jerusalem will fall finally into the hands of the Jews."[4]   Accordingly, Abdullah met with his Prime Minister Tawfiq Abul-Huda, regarding the situation in Jerusalem, but Abul-Huda emphasized that military intervention would be considered a violation of the agreement with Bevin.[5]   Consequently, it would lead to international complications, in view of the U.N. resolution to internationalize the city.[6]   Aggravated by the Zionist violations, being highly emotional about the religious importance of the city and the need to defend the civilian Arabs and concerned about the city's future, Abdullah decided to intervene. He ordered a cabinet meeting immediately to form a regency council, since he decided to take command of the operational forces personally regardless of the consequences.[7]

At this juncture, Abdullah communicated with Glubb:

> The importance of Jerusalem to the Arabs, Muslims and Christians is known.   Any catastrophe that might befall its people by the Jews—such as being murdered or evicted—is a matter of grave importance for which we are responsible.   The situation is not desperate yet.   I order you to preserve what is in hand: the Old City and the Jericho road.... I ask the implementation of this order with dispatch.[8]

On May 19, the Jordan army intervened and the Old City was secured for Abdullah.

For a detailed account on the battle of Jerusalem; see pp. 105- 118 in *Ibid.*

[4]Hazza'a Al-Majali, *Muthakkarati* (n.p., 1960), p. 67.

[5]Shwadran, *op. cit.,* p. 246.

[6]Majali, *op. cit.,* p. 68.

[7]*Ibid.*

[8]Musa, *op. cit.,* p. 489; Glubb, *op. cit.,* p. 118.

According to At-Tall, Glubb did not agree to sending troops to defend Jerusalem.   But Abdullah issued an order for the movement of the 6th Regiment overruling Glubb. The task of this regiment was to defend the walls of the Old City and to occupy the Jewish quarter in the Old City which the Zionist force decided to defend.   Musa, *op. cit.*

Further, King Abdullah, on 18 May 1948, sent an ultimatum to the Belgian Consul, who at the time served as chief of Truce Commission: "I shall bombard the Jewish section of New Jerusalem to the ground if the Jews refuse to surrender."   At-Tall, *op. cit.,* p. 455.

The control of the Arab part of Palestine including the Old City by Jordan brought Abdullah a step closer to the realization of his Great Syria Plan. The armistice gave Israel and Jordan a *de facto* division of the city, and non-internationalization was crystallized.[9] When the General Assembly voted for internationalization on 9 December 1949, the Arab states, except Jordan, voted for it.[10] However, when count Folke Bernadotte, the U.N. mediator, suggested that all of Jerusalem become part of Abdullah's domain, they agreed because it was more preferable to have Jerusalem under Arab control rather than under international or Zionist control.[11] By previously voting for internationalization, they intended to prevent both Zionists and Jordan from controlling the city. Disappointed at this policy, Abdullah emphasized his interest in the city as he commented:

... the demand for the internationalization of Jerusalem was one of the most unbalanced [Arab] national aims. It was one that disregarded the Arab rights and interests by handing the Holy Places over to international control and wrenching Jerusalem from the possession of the Arabs. It was my duty to stand resolutely and firmly in defense of the Arab character of the Holy City and resist internationalization in all its aspects.[12]

Abdullah realized that internationalization could never become a reality as long as each side opposed it and occupied a part of the city. The Zionists did not favour territorial internationalization, since they wanted to expand their domain and make the city their capital.[13] To them, if the city was internationalized, 680,000 Arab refugees would have to be returned to the international sector.

[9]Frank Sakran, *Whose Jerusalem* ? (Washington: American Council on the Middle East, 1968), p. 1.

[10]U.N., *G. A. O. R.,* 75th meeting, 4th year, p. 607.

[11]After the failure of the Crusades and 400 years of Turkish rule, the Christians agreed to Muslim sovereignty over the Holy City. Thus, the idea of Muslim rule under Jordan remained familiar and not wholly repugnant. There was no Christian protest against the Bernadotte proposal that Jerusalem be under Jordanian rule. On the other hand, Jewish rule seemed contrary to the natural order, especially when some Arabs are Christians, and Israel has no connection with Christianity. Further, there might have been fear that Israel might extend its authority to the Old City. Walter Eytan, *The First Ten Years: A Diplomatic History of Israel* (New York: Simon and Schuster, 1956) pp. 77-78.

[12]Sha'ar, *op. cit.,* p. 339.

[13]Eytan, *op. cit.,* p. 72.

To Abdullah, Jerusalem constituted the heart of annexed Palestine. Recognizing the strategic, political, religious, and economic importance of the Old City, Jordan informed the General Assembly that "no form of internationalization... would serve any purpose as the Holy Places under Jordan's protection ... were safe and secure without the necessity for a special regime."[14] Jordan, however, gave the assurance to guarantee full freedom of worship and ready access to Holy Places.[15]

From the Arab side other influences dictated Abdullah's decision. First, there was his response to the decisions taken by the Jericho Conference of 1 December 1948, which reflected his territorial ambitions. On 1 December 1948, after the Zionist aggression culminated in the occupation of a large sector of Arab territory, the Palestine Arabs in the Jordanian sector held a conference in Jericho and adopted the following resolutions:

(i)   ...Resumption of fighting to liberate Palestine;
(ii) the call for Jordan-Palestine unity...;
(iii) the call for a comprehensive national unity in which uniting Palestine to Transjordan must take place first; and
(iv) to proclaim Abdullah, king of all Palestine.[16]

Abdullah's attempts to annex Arab Palestine were opposed by the Mufti, president of the All-Palestine Gaza Government. In a telegram to the president of the United Nations Trusteeship Council dated 4 March 1950, he stated: "Transjordan does not represent the views of the Muslim and Christian inhabitants of Jerusalem area.

The Zionists accepted internationalization as the price for obtaining an independent state under the Partition Plan. Government of Israel, *Jerusalem and the U.N.* (Washington: Office of Information, July 1953), p. 1.

[14]Khouri, *op. cit.,* p. 107.

[15]Abdullah did not close the door to a possible change in his position. In an interview, he stated that he would consider withdrawal from the Old City if Israel gave up the Arab area allotted to the Arab state by the Partition Plan. *The London Times,* 21 November 1949.

While Jews were not given access to their Holy Places in the Old City or in the Jordanian sector due to security measures, "There is no recorded instance of any Christian being refused access to any of the Holy Places of this faith in Jordan." Eytan, *op. cit.,* p. 72.

[16]Musa, *op. cit.,* p. 536; *New York Times,* 14 December 1948; Edmund Wright, "Abdullah's Jordan: 1947-51," *Middle East Journal,* V (Autumn, 1951), p. 456.

Their views can only be ascertained by free plebiscite covering both residents and refugees.[17]

Second, opposition to the All-Palestine Government of Gaza, which was created by the Arab League under Egypt's sponsorship. The Gaza government was viewed by Abdullah as an attempt to block Jordan's annexation and as a reaffirmation of opposition to the Zionist state as well as to partition.[18] In order to silence the Gaza government and to assuage Arab fears with regard to Abdullah's ambitions, the Jordanian parliament approved on 24 April 1950 the bringing of both the banks of the Jordan river under Jordan's control in defiance of the League's resolution to the contrary.[19]

To authenticate his control over the Old City, and in opposition to internationalization, Abdullah appointed a custodian for the Holy Places with the rank of a cabinet member on 2 January 1950. He also appointed a Mufti replacing Haj Ameen Al-Husayni, his main opponent.[20] On 27 July 1953, the cabinet proposed transferring certain government ministries to the Old City and holding parliamentary sessions there. This proposal was not implemented in view of the dangerously exposed position of the City.[21] However, on 21 August 1959, Arab Jerusalem was designated as the second capital.[22]

[17]United Nations, *Trusteeship Council Official Records*, Annex Vol. 1, 4th Year, 6th Session, T/487, 4 March 1950, p. 116.

[18]Ben Gurion, *op. cit.*, p. 530.

[19]The League's reaction to the annexation was negative. The political committee decided on 16 May 1950, that annexation violated the Organization's resolution of April 12, which prohibited annexing any part of Palestine unilaterally by any Arab state. Egypt, Saudi Arabia, and Lebanon voted for the expulsion of Jordan from the League. However, the negative vote of Iraq and Yemen, together with Iraq's mediation, resulted in a compromise. Accordingly, Jordan declared that annexation was without prejudice to the final settlement of the Palestine question.

The unity was recognized by Britain, subject to the reservation that, "pending final determination of the status of the Jerusalem area, they are unable to recognize Jordan's sovereignty over any part of it." *Whiteman's Digest of International Law*, Vol. II, pp. 1163-68. Quoted in Elihau Lauterpacht, *Jerusalem and the Holy Places* (London: n.p. October, 1968), p. 47.

[20]Raghib Al-Nashashibi and Shiekh Husam Eddin Jarallah respectively.

[21]*Daily Star* (Beirut), 5 January 1954.

[22]*New York Times*, 21 August 1959.

The United States declared that it would recognize such a step. United States Department of State, *Digest of International law*, Vol. I (Washington D. C., 1963), p. 594.

ISRAEL AND JERUSALEM

Although the Armistice Agreement of 1949 recognized the *de facto* occupation of Jerusalem by Israel and Jordan, without reference to internationalization, the United Nations Trusteeship Council proceeded to make plans to administer the City, and called upon both parties to cooperate in establishing international administration. However, in defiance of the International Organization, Ben Gurion countered by ordering the transfer of his government ministries to Jerusalem.[23] Characterizing the international proposal as "wicked council,"[24] he declared that "the Jews will sacrifice themselves for Jerusalem no less than the English for London."[25] Determined to perpetuate their control over the City, the speakers at the dedication of the new parliament building made it known to the world that Israel intended Jerusalem to remain their capital forever.[26]

In view of these violations, the president of the Trusteeship Council, in a letter to the Israeli Foreign Minister, inquired about the legality of transferring the ministries to Jerusalem, and counselled Israel "to abstain from any action liable to hinder the implementation of the General Assembly Resolution of 9 December 1949."[27] Challenging the authority of the Trusteeship Council, the Israeli representative to the United Nations replied:

...only a minority of the Council [five out of twelve] associated themselves with the resolution. In the view of the government of Israel, the powers of the Trusteeship Council as fully defined in the Charter of the United Nations do not include a capacity to call for the revocation of administrative acts by the governments of Member States in Territories for whose administration and security they are responsible. In this connexion, the Government of Israel has noted the doubts expressed in the debates of the Trusteeship Council on 20 December 1949, 'whether the Council was

[23]The United States disapproved of the move and maintained its embassy in Tel-Aviv. United States Department of State, *American Foreign Policy, 1950-55* (1957).

[24]Sakran, *op. cit.*, p. 1.

[25]Khouri, *op. cit.*, p. 107.

[26]*Ibid.*, p. 112.

[27]Trusteeship Council Official Records, Document T/431, Annex, Vol. I, 4th Year, 6th Session, 5 January, 1950.

entitled to make a direct appeal to the Government of Israel'
or, in particular, 'whether the Council has authority under the
General Assembly resolution to pass a condemnatory resolution
addressed to any particular government.'

My Government believes that it had full and complete authority
for deciding upon the measures announced in the Kenesset on
17 December 1949. These measures mark the continuation
of a process begun long ago as part of an effort to restore
Jerusalem to its traditional place in the life of the country.... [28]

In a speech to the parliament on 13 December 1949, Ben Gurion
rejected internationalization and stressed Israel's determination to
restore Jerusalem as its capital. He said:

As you know, the General Assembly...has...by a large majority
decided to place Jerusalem under international regime as a
separate entity. This decision is utterly incapable of implementation—if only for the determined unalterable opposition of
the inhabitants of Jerusalem themselves. It is to be hoped that
the General Assembly will, in the course of time, correct this
mistake which its majority has made and will make no attempt
whatsoever to impose a regime on the Holy City against the will
of its people .... But for the State of Israel, there has always been
and always will be one capital—Jerusalem, the eternal. So it
was three thousand years ago—and so it will be, we believe,
until the end of time.[29]

Ben Gurion's rejoinder to the Trusteeship Council's demand confirmed the belief that Israel intended to annex all of Jerusalem as
soon as an opportunity presented itself. This opportunity came
in June 1967, when the Israeli forces occupied the Old City. Shortly
after the cease-fire, Israel's Parliament enacted a statute annexing
it. In justifying this action, Deputy Prime Minister, Yigal Allon,
in a news dispatch on 5 July 1967, said: "The world must reconcile
itself to the fact that the city has, at last, returned to the nation
that founded it and turned it into a Holy City."[30] Two days after

[28]*Ibid.*
[29]*Ibid.*, ; also Eytan, *op. cit.*, p. 74.
[30]Sakran, *op. cit.*, p. 2.

the City fell under Israeli military control, approval was given by the Israeli municipal council of Jerusalem to include the Old City in the Greater Jerusalem Master Plan.[31]

THE RESPONSE OF THE UNITED NATIONS

The General Assembly convened on 17 June 1967, at the request of the Soviet Union and, after extensive debate, approved Resolution 2253 on 4 July.[32] Ten days later, Resolution 2254 (ES–V) was also approved. These two resolutions reflected a widespread sentiment within the World Organization that territorial aggrandizement cannot be the product of conquest by force. Secretary-General, U Thant, stated it as follows:

> It is indispensable to an international community of states—if it is not to follow the law of the jungle—that the territorial integrity of every state be respected and the occupation of one state cannot be condoned.[33]

The Resolution was adopted by a vote of ninety-nine to nothing with twenty abstentions including the United States. Its delegate stated that peace in the Middle east would not be achieved by a resolution dealing with one aspect of the question and emphasized that the United States does not "recognize or accept" the measures taken by Israel which he regarded as "interim and provisional."[34]

The Resolutions invalidating Israel's annexation of East Jerusalem evolved from earlier proposals that Israel withdraw from all occupied areas. The Yugoslav draft resolution of June 28, was supported by seventeen states in addition to the Arab countries. Although it

---

[31]*Jerusalem Post*, 8 June 1967.

[32]In the main, the Resolution stated that the General Assembly "Calls upon Israel to rescind all measures already taken and to desist forthwith from taking any action which would alter the status of Jerusalem." UNGA, *Official Records, 5th Emergency Special Session, Supplement 1*, p. 4.

[33]U N. General Assembly, *Official Records, Introduction to the Annual Report of the Secretary-General on the Work of the Organization*, June 16, 1967, Document A/7201, p. 5.

[34]*New York Times*, 15 July 1967, p. 5.

received a majority, it failed to obtain the required two-thirds vote. These states made up a significant part of the Third World.[35]

On 30 June another draft resolution sponsored by twenty other members of the Third World—virtually, all of the Latin American states—called upon Israel to "withdraw all its forces from all territories occupied by it as a result of the recent conflict."[36] This proposal, too, failed for lack of two-thirds majority.

Thus, opposition to Israeli occupation became evident by the developing nations, for either religious reasons or for the anti-colonial character of the occupation. Furthermore, other nations, as noted above, supported this stand.

Discarding conciliation by the Vatican, Britain and the United States, and in defiance of the world organization, Israel decided to present the world with a *fait accompli*. Foreign Minister Eban's speech at the General Assembly declared that Israel had no intention to comply with the resolutions just adopted, and announced that Jerusalem's future would no longer be considered a negotiable issue.[37] Israel's decision was influenced by emotionalism of its own people and by the political, strategic, economic as well as by religious considerations.[38]

The United States refused to recognize the validity of the Israeli action and took the position that these measures could not be considered as "prejudicing the final and permanent status of Jerusalem."[39] To that end, on 7 November 1967, the United States submitted a draft resolution in which it declared its policy of "just and lasting peace in the Middle East," and the "withdrawal of armed

[35]The Yugoslav resolution was co-sponsored by Indonesia, Cambodia, Malaysia, India, Pakistan, Ceylon, Afghanistan, Cyprus, Somalia, Tanzania, Zambia, Congo (Brazzaville), Burundi, Mali, Guinea and Senegal.

[36]Formally presented by Trinidad and Tobago, it was co-sponsored by Argentina, Barbados, Bolivia, Brazil, Chile, Colombia, Costa Rica, the Dominican Republic, Ecuador, El Salvador, Guatemala, Guyana, Honduras, Jamaica, Mexico, Nicaragua, Panama, Paraguay, and Venezuela.

[37]Lauterpacht, *op. cit.*, p. 48.

Israel did not vote for the resolution on the grounds that the issue of Jerusalem was "outside the legal competence of the General Assembly." *New York Times*, 5 July 1967.

[38]*New York Times*, 18 June 1967; Khouri, *op. cit.*, p. 113.

[39]United Nations, Document AP/V, p. 154, 14 July 1967.

forces from occupied territories."[40]   The draft resolution, it was assumed, would apply to East Jerusalem.[41]

A fourth resolution was submitted by India and co-sponsored by Mali and Nigeria. It was cast in a stronger language than the United States draft resolution. However, neither resolution was adopted. Instead, on 22 November the British draft resolution was unanimously adopted.[42]

While Israel insisted on keeping the City under its control, it promised to give free access to the Holy Places.[43] However, it emphasized that it would not give up the Old part regardless of the Assembly's resolution.[44] Just as King Abdullah had stressed to the United Nations that an international regime would be impractical;

---

[40]Although the United States had hitherto held to a policy of "territorial integrity of all states in the Middle East, omitting 'all' from the phrase "all territories, reflected the partiality of the United States Government towards Israel on the issue of retaining some Arab land, such as Jerusalem, the Golan Heights and, perhaps, other sectors. Significantly, the United States' representative to the United Nations at the time was Arthur Goldberg, an American Jewish leader.

[41]United Nations Security Council, *Official Record, Supplement for July-August-September,* 1967, Document S/8229.

[42]The resolution read as follows:

"The Security Council ... emphasizing the inadmissibility of the acquisition of territory by war. . .

i   Withdrawal of Israeli armed forces from territories occupied in the recent conflict;

ii   Termination of all claims or states of belligerency and respect for and acknowledgement of the sovereignty, territorial integrity and political independence of every state in the area and their right to live in peace within secure boundaries, free from threats or acts of force;

2   Affirm further the necessity :

(a) for guaranteeing freedom of navigation on through international waterways in the area;

(b) for achieving a just settlement of the refugee problem;

(c) for guaranteeing the territorial inviolability and political independence of every state in the area...;

(d) requests the Secretary-General to designate a special representative to proceed to the Middle East to establish and maintain contacts with the states concerned in order to promote agreement and assist efforts to achieve peaceful and accepted settlement in accordance with the provisions and principles of the resolution...." United Nations Security Council, Document S/8247.

[43]Ibid., Document S/8052.

[44]*New York Times,* 12 July 1967.

that peace and safety of the Holy Places be assured under Jordan's protection, so Israel did the same in 1967.[45]

On 2 May 1968, Israel decided to hold an Independence Day military parade in violation of the agreement that the City should permanently be demilitarized.[46] Israel explained its action on the basis of three points; one, that Jerusalem had become a united city; two, the Armistice Agreement was no longer operative, for it had been destroyed by the June war; and three, the Israelis "are free to move, and to parade as they see fit."[47] Thus, the parade was planned and held in the face of warnings by the Security Council to desist from taking any action which might result in changing the status of the city.[48]

Jordan's accusation that Israel was contemplating the final liquidation of the Arab character of Jerusalem was supported by the Arab population of the city. In a memorandum sent to the Israeli authorities, they deplored Israel's action, insisting that the Old City still belonged to Jordan.[49]

THE POSITION OF THE UNITED STATES

Israel has persistently disregarded United Nations resolutions and emphasized that the decisive factor, as far as she was concerned,

[45]Khouri, op. cit., p. 115. Israel's representative at the U.N., in defence of his government's action, said:

. . . Since June 7, the entire city of Jerusalem has experienced peace and unity. The Holy Places of all faiths have been opened to those who held them sacred....The term 'annexation' used by the supporters of the resolution is out of place. The measures adopted referred to the integration of Jerusalem in the administrative and municipal spheres, and furnishing a legal basis for the protection of the Holy Places in Jerusalem.

United Nations Security Council, Document S/8052, pp. 74-75.

[46]Avnery, op. cit., p. 20.

[47]Yosef Tekoah, Barbed Wire Shall Not Return to Jerusalem (New York: Israel Information Service, n.d.), p. 42.

[48]United Nations, Document S/8549, 18 April 1968; New York Times, 28 April 1968. The Israeli authorities refused to cooperate with the U.N. Mixed Armistice machinery by preventing them from investigating the military parade. U.N., S.C.O.R., Document S/7893.

[49]U.N., S.C.O.R., Document S/8109, 3 August 1967; New York Times, 22 July 1967.

was the attitude of the United States.[50]   The American policy position regarding the annexation of Old Jerusalem could have been
derived from the United States' concern with the territorial integrity
of Jordan. This explains Washington's refusal to recognize
the validity of the Israeli annexation move. "It should be
equally clear that boundaries cannot and should not reflect the
weight of conquest."[51]   And "a just and lasting peace will require
...withdrawal of Israel's armed forces from territories occupied in the
Arab-Israeli war of 1967."[52] However, two weeks after President
Johnson's moral stand in his speech on 19 June 1967, the United
States refused to support the General Assembly resolution which
called on Israel to refrain from annexing East Jerusalem. This
resolution censured Israel on the grounds that her move to change
the status of Jerusalem was invalid.

Two years later, however, it was reported that, "on one major and
crucial issue, the Administration appears to accept Israel's
position: Jerusalem should remain a unified city."[53]   This apparent
deviation in the U.S. policy may have been possible by "trading"
of Old Jerusalem by Jordan for the right of access to the Mediterranean, through Israeli territory.[54]   While Britain and France were
urging Israel to postpone action on annexation until a peace
settlement was reached, the United States, while declaring non-
acceptance of the move, refused to apply effective pressure on Israel
"without obtaining something from the Arabs in return."[55]   With this
backing, unification of Jerusalem became an accomplished fact and
outside the framework of any negotiated settlement.

The United Nations has, demonstrably, been unable to dissuade
Israel from annexing Arab Jerusalem.   Some observers ascribe this
failure to the absence of wholehearted support by the Johnson
administration, whose declarations proved incompatible with its
voting at the United Nations, as lacking sincerity and consistency.[56]

[50]U.N., *S.C.O.R.*, Document S/8650, 21 June 1968.

[51]President Johnson's address to the B'nai B'rith, 10 September 1968.

[52]Secretary of State Rodgers before the Senate Foreign Relations Committee,
27 March 1969.

[53]*Near East Report*, 14 May 1969.

[54]*Manchester Guardian*, 9 April 1969.

[55]*New York Times*, 13 July 1967.

[56]Richard Pfaff, *Jerusalem: Keystone of an   Arab-Israeli Settlement*,

CONCLUSION

The United Nations Resolutions had recommended that the City of Jerusalem be placed under international administration, but the World community and the Organization never seriously tried to enforce its will.

The occupation of the new part of the City by Israel, and the subsequent transfer of Israeli government's ministries in defiance of the United Nations, complicated the task. However, Jordan's position was not dissimilar. King Abdullah's decision not to surrender the Old City to international administration was based on political, military and personal considerations. From the political view-point, controlling the Old City endowed Jordan with international importance as guardian of the Holy Places. Furthermore, by occupying half of the City which the Zionists called their capital, Jordan was placed in a stronger bargaining position in the event of territorial adjustments. By administering part of the City, considered the centre of Palestine—spiritually, economically and politically—Jordan's presence was tantamount to legalizing Arab rights against the claims of the Jews. Placing the Holy Places under Jordan's control, provided Abdullah with a sense of achievement, which he hoped would encourage the revival of the Great Syria Plan. Economically, the Old City became the source of a significant part of foreign exchange, sorely needed by Jordan. Militarily, the Jordan army had suffered large casualties in the defence of the Old City. Thus, preserving it became a symbol of the King's determination.

Most importantly, however, Abdullah was under no pressure from the Middle Eastern Christian community to internationalize the City. While they viewed Jewish control as repugnant, since Israel had no connection with Christianity, the idea of a Muslim rule under Jordan was acceptable in the light of recent history. For centuries since the Crusades, the City and the Holy Places had been under Muslim administration.

(Washington: American Enterprise Institute, 1969), p. 44; also *Financial Times,* 21 November 1967.

CHAPTER FOUR

THE RHODES ARMISTICE AGREEMENT

After Egypt decided to begin armistice talks on 12 January 1949, under the direction of Ralph Bunche, the United Nations Mediator, Jordan also consented to enter such talks on 8 February 1949. Jordan's military position was drastically weakened due to the withdrawal of the Iraqi army. Iraq had decided not to start the talks herself but authorized Jordan to negotiate on her behalf.[1] However, King Abdullah's eagerness to arrive at a final peace dictated his entry in the Rhodes Armistice negotiations.

However, while Jordan assumed that her consent to start peace talks would also end military operations on both sides, the Israelis, anxious to acquire more Arab territory in the East Negeb and to obtain an outlet to the Red Sea at the Gulf of Aqaba, sought to delay peace talks as long as possible. Only after her military objectives were achieved, did Israel sign a cease-fire with Jordan on 11 March 1949.[2]

As the Egyptian front became quiet, Israeli forces were deployed along the Jordan-Iraqi front. Fearing that Israel might use its military power to invade and occupy parts of Transjordan, the King's interest was intensified in the direction of peace. In the meantime, Abdullah invoked his treaty with Britain. The British answer was that they would defend all area under Abdullah's control —including the newly won West Bank. This reply caused a wave of protest in Israel and in the countries that supported it. Thus, under international pressure, Britain declared that it would defend the original areas east of the river only.[3] Although a British force

---

[1]Musa, *op. cit.*, p. 531.

[2]Khouri, *op. cit.*, p. 96.

[3]Musa *op. cit.*, p. 530. In explaining Jordan's dilemma, Prime Minister Abul-Huda said : "The arrival of the British forces at Aqaba was at our request in order to prevent the Jews from reaching the shore, thereby cutting us off from Egypt.... But the British did not interfere. When we inquired from Sir Alec Kirkbride—Britain's ambassador to Amman—about the reasons...he said that the British force came to defend Aqaba only. ...The British Government

arrived in Aqaba and took battle positions, their duty was merely to prevent the Israeli forces from crossing into Transjordan.

During the armistice talks, the Jordan delegation proposed that the cease-fire take effect on the Iraqi lines. The Israeli delegation refused and informed Bunche that they did not approve of replacing the Iraqi army by the Legion, and they would "consider this act as a violation... and reserved for themselves in that situation complete freedom of action."[4] They threatened to "obtain what they want by war, if not by peace,"[5] and demanded that the truce line be moved several kilometres to Israel's advantage. Accordingly, if their demands were met, they would: "...sign a permanent truce with Jordan; that this demand be the last request for they consider it vital to them in view of the military necessities."[6]

Confronted with a serious situation, Abdullah requested for aid from his ally, Britain. Bevin's reply was discouraging. He advised the King to seek the mediation of President Truman. On 29 March, 1949, Truman answered advising submission to the Jewish demands, but promised to intervene to stop further Israeli expansion in the Jordanian sector of Palestine.[7]

Thus, when the British and the Americans were unwilling to intervene, Abdullah, who was already alienated from the other Arab states, accepted the Jewish demands.[8] The decision to cede a number

---

apologizes for its failure to fulfil its obligations for two reasons: one, because the United States advised her not to clash with the Jews; and two, because the majority of the British Commonwealth nations did not agree to a confrontation with the Jews." See At-Tall, op. cit., p. 521.

[4]Ibid., p. 530.

[5]Ibid.

[6]Ibid. When the Israeli demand reached Jordan, the Prime Minister inquired from Glubb, the Legion's commander: "One, if we refuse these demands and fighting was renewed, can we repel them on all fronts ? Two, if we cannot repel them and the Legion faced them alone, is there a possibility of their occupying more territory than they demand now ?"

The army chief replied that "the Legion cannot hold its positions on all front lines; and it is possible that if fighting is renewed, the Zionists would occupy a larger area than what they demand now." Musa, op. cit., p. 531; also Majali, op. cit., p. 92. See n. 13, p. 96.

[7]Glubb, op. cit., p. 210; also Musa, op. cit., p. 531; At-Tall, op. cit., p. 527.

[8]Glubb, op. cit., p. 234. The cession of the central belt deprived many villages of their farm land and were left without adequate means of support. Ibid.; Kirk, op. cit., p. 297.

of strategic mountain positions and good farm land along the truce line was an alternative to renewal of hostilities and as an attempt to pacify the enemy, in the quest of future peace: "If they inclined to peace you should also do so and leave it to God."[9]

The Rhodes Agreement was considered a first step to eliminate the threat of war and to facilitate the transition from hostilities to permanent peace in Palestine. Its most immediate objectives were related to military matters, such as the reduction of forces and exchange of prisoners.

According to Colonel Abdullah At-Tall the King's confidante, Prime Minister Abul-Huda, in order to placate the Israeli Government stated:

> If we recall the past, we see how Jordan was dragged into the war, the immediate causes of which were the Old City of Jerusalem, and the attempts of your forces to occupy it. This resulted in actual battles between the Jordan army and your troops. Aside from that, we never initiated battles.
>
> ...Our original policy, which we followed, was that the Arab army [Jordan] was to stop its advance at the partition line which we never crossed. ... There has never been any inclination to war at all .... You can appreciate our difficult position in implementing this policy and being swept in the current of Arab policy merely as camouflage. Today, we are not tied with Arab policy, nor do we accept outside advice. From all our hearts we desire to reach peace and a settlement with you. If your intentions are as good as ours, our problem will be solved as dictated by our mutual interests and good neighbour policy between our two countries.
>
> The present problem is the permanent truce, according to which you demand altering the boundaries. That will bring us untold difficulties. His Majesty's Government suggests the implementation of the partition plan which gives you a state and

---

For an excellent description of the plight of the border villages, see Ann Dearden, *Jordan* (London: Robert Hale, 1958), p. 132.

This "deal" intensified bitterness among the Arab nationalists who accused Abdullah of betraying the Arab cause in return for personal gains. As a result, the monarchy became upset with serious unrest among the refugees and the whole Palestinian polulation on the West Bank.

[9]From the Koran; Abu Sha'ar, 4th edition, *op. cit.*, p.242.

which gives us the other part. Why don't we proceed accordingly so that our problems would not multiply especially the refugee problem

...Submitting to your demands places the Government and the King in a precarious position and impedes progress toward a final settlement with you.[10]

Insisting on the absolute demand that the northern triangle be ceded to Israel, and encouraged by the apparent weak bargaining position of the Government of Jordan, Eytan, on behalf of the Israeli government replied:

...The basis of strong friendship between Israel and Jordan is a settlement of the northern triangle which will be satisfactory to Israel and insures her security....The Government of Tel-Aviv would like to calm public opinion regarding the situation in the triangle over which the people want to go to war.

Israeli demands in the triangle are not negotiable. No part of it can be given up since the military experts had recommended that these demands are the absolute minimum to insure the security of the new Jewish state in that region. Their recommendations are considered by the Government to be more important than Palestine problem—compensations and the like—because the security of Israel is the most important demand we present. When this demand is fulfilled, an agreement would be reached tonight.[11]

The Israeli-Jordan Armistice agreement was concluded following extensive diplomatic activities carried out by Israel, Jordan, Great Britain, the U.S., and the U.N. In an attempt to reach a peace settlement, Abdullah decided to sign the agreement. Accordingly,

The results achieved at Shuneh were incorporated in the armistice agreement signed there on April 3, 1949. The demarcation line was not drawn strictly in accordance with the position of the armies but further east. It involved the cession to Israel of considerable territory. The governing factor being in the main topographical.

---

[10]Abdullah At-Tall, *op. cit.,* p. 531.
[11]*Ibid.,* pp. 517, 532.

The Jordanians were anxious to keep as many villages as possible
on their side of the line, but they cared less about village lands. As
a result, a good many farmers were cut off from their land and some
from their wells.   Here again, however, this was regarded as a
temporary expedient pending peace and the establishment of a
definite frontier.   It is not likely that either Israel or Jordan would
have agreed to this particular demarcation line except as a provisional measure.[12]

The delegation, which included Glubb, was personally picked by
Abdullah and were expected to merely sign rather than negotiate
since negotiations were being carried on secretly in Jordan.   The
Jordan delegation was entirely composed of men from the East Bank
who were not aware of the land values, the water resources, or the
conditions of the villages in Palestine.[13]
Walter Eytan of the Israeli Foreign Office observed:

The quality of the Jordan delegates, however, was not equal to the
mission on which they had been dispatched .   The Egyptian delegation had been skilful, tenacious, and well-briefed.   That of
Lebanon was fully adequate to its task which proved the easiest of
all.   The delegates of Syria were fiercely argumentative regarding
diplomacy as a form of aggression and were well able to stand up
for the rights of their country.
    Jordan's delegation, however, was not of this mettle. When they
arrived at Rhodes, they were seen to be an unimpressive set. They
looked helpless and lost, apparently not sure of their instructions;
it had seemed possible indeed that no clear instructions had been

[12]Eytan, *op. cit.*, p. 41.
[13]Majali, *op. cit.*, p. 90; also Eytan, *op. cit.*, pp. 40, 41.
    A delegation from Palestine pleaded to Abdullah the necessity of including
Palestinians in the delegation.   While the King agreed, the Prime Minister Huda
refused because "these negotiations were of military character which could not
affect the final settlement if a peaceful settlement is possible." Majali, *op. cit.*, p.
92; and Glubb, *op. cit.*, p. 241.
    The critics of Huda accused him of voluntarily signing the agreement with-
out outside pressure, for he could have resigned to avoid this painful catastrophe,
since he used to resign for trivial reasons.   The Zionists had refused to sign any
agreement unless it was signed by Huda personally. It seems that the ghost
of the agreement continued to haunt him until he committed suicide in 1954.
Majali, *op. cit.*, pp. 91 -93.

given them. King Abdullah, their master, soon indicated that he did not trust them to negotiate on his behalf, and that he proposed to take matters in hand himself. It was agreed that the talks at Rhodes should continue as a facade, but that the real negotiations should be conducted in secret with the King at his winter palace at Shuneh. Only the King's closest confidantes were to know; the rest of the world was to go on watching the show at Rhodes. This had, perhaps, been the King's intention from the outset and determined the choice of delegates.[14]

To King Abdullah, whatever land in Palestine he could bring under his control was an improvement. Thus, his accommodation to the Israelis aimed at ending hostilities and establishing peaceful relations with his neighbour, Israel. He condsidered the armistice as the beginning of his quest for an enlarged kingdom and a fulfilment of his ambitions. Walter Eytan of the Israeli Foreign office commented:

Abdullah alone of the Arab rulers was sincere in regarding the armistice as a major step toward peace. After the agreement was signed, he sought more permanent arrangements with Israel. To that end, negotiations with him and his closest advisers were carried on intensively, especially between November 1949 and March 1950. A draft treaty was prepared and initialled, but Abdullah, under the rising pressure of Arab extremism which scared his ministers, was unable to carry it through.... It came to be suspected that the King was planning to make peace with Israel. This, in the eyes of Arab nationalists, was treason.... His death served as a warning to others, and nowhere in the Arab camp has there been talk of peace with Israel since.[15]

[14]Eytan, *op.cit.*, p. 40. The delegation was forbidden to agree to anything without reference to Amman, "Thus, in reality, every phrase has been approved or even dictated by Taufiq Pasha (Abul-Huda)." Glubb, *op. cit.,* p. 241.

[15]Eytan, *op. cit.*, p. 43.

As to direct negotiations, no Arab state or personality has ever been willing to undertake them without the intervention of the United Nations. An example is the present Jarring mission.

When the Rhodes delegation returned by air to Amman, they were told to go quietly and separately to their homes. It was feared that if they entered the town together, riots might start. Glubb, *op. cit.,* p. 243.

The war of 1948 which ended in the armistice of 1949, insured the existence of the Zionist state, and enabled it to extend its boundaries well beyond those allotted by the Partition Plan.[16] Furthermore, by resorting to war to achieve its objectives, a significant growth of the influence of the military mentality in the internal and external affairs of Israel was manifested. Thus, the political and military goals went hand in hand.

The agreement defined the armistice "demarcation line" which, although was not a political or territorial boundary, nevertheless, has been the frontier.[17]

To Jordan, the Rhodes agreement signified military as well as political defeat due to the following reasons: one, the agreement was made under duress, since Jordan had no alternative. It was the least of the two evils—war or signing the Agreement—since Jordan was incapable of defending its territories. Two, the agreement did not represent the opinion or the desires of the population, especially the Palestinians. Three, the outcome of the Armistice was catastrophic to the Arabs, even to King Abdullah personally, since his aim was to secure more land for the Arabs. Thus, since the agreement yielded maximum benefits to the enemy, Jordan could not expect any advantages from its revision, especially since Israel defaulted in giving Jordan the port of Asqalan[18]

Reacting to the oppressive character of the agreement, the Jordanian Parliament demanded that Prime Minister Abul-Huda revoke it, but their demand was refused. In any case, the agreement continued to be the sole legal instrument of relationship between Jordan and Israel. Ralphe Bunche likened the agreement to the "unequal treaties" imposed by the Western powers on China in view of its oppressive results and commented, "the Jewish delegation

---

[16]Israel with the help of the Western powers parcelled the Palestine problem: the refugees, freezing funds, division of the Jordan waters, shipping through the Suez Canal, the U.N. Conciliation Commission, and the internationalization of the city of Jerusalem. This policy aimed at keeping the Arabs attention diverted to deal with secondary issues rather than the central one, freeing Palestine. Fadhil Al-Jamali, *Thikrayat Wa Ibar: Karithat Filistine* (Beirut: Dar Al-Kitab Al-Jadid, 1965), p. 49.

[17]Eytan, *op. cit.*, p. 29. Full text in Muhammad Khalil, *The Arab States and the Arab League: Documentary Record*, Vol. II, (Beirut Khayyat, 1962), p. 599.

[18]At-Tall, *op. cit.*, pp. 453, 489.

asked for the shirt, but the Arab delegations were very generous and handed both the shirt and the trousers."[19]

CONCLUSION

The deteriorating military position of the Egyptian army led to the signing of an Armistice Agreement. Since Egypt, the largest Arab state had signed it, the others, except Iraq, followed suit.

Jordan's political and military situations had reached a point which demanded that peace replace hostilities. On the military front, the Jordan army was left facing a determined enemy force fifteen times larger, and resolved to hold to every inch of territory it occupied. In this light, General Glubb warned that the army, with its depleted supplies could not possibly challenge a superior enemy force, and that any attempt to attack would inevitably result in loss of more Arab land. Furthermore, resumption of hostilities, it was feared, would encourage the enemy to occupy the Old City, even the entire West Bank. To Abdullah, such a nightmare was tantamount to losing his dream of enlarging his domain.

Aside from the military aspect, the King was also faced with external pressures. His appeals to the U.N., the United States and to his ally-by-treaty, Britain, went unheeded. This signalled Jordan's inability to protect its interests and made imperative the signing of the Armistice Agreement which was characterized as the "unequal treaties."

No doubt, King Abdullah's self-confidence had become shaken, as he expected a final peace treaty on equal terms. But the resultant weak bargaining position of Jordan and Abdullah's desire to end present hostilities and avoid future wars dictated his decision to sign the peace agreement. The Zionists' oppressive demands reflected their expansionist policy. Colonel At-Tall wrote that after the agreement was initialled, the Zionists presented a surprise gift from Ben Gurion to King Abdullah. It was a copy of the Old Testament with a map of ancient Israel which included Palestine, Transjordan, Syria, Iraq, and parts of Hijaz.[20]

[19]Majali, *op. cit.*, p. 91.
[20]At-Tall, *op. cit.*, p. 517.

CHAPTER FIVE

JORDAN AND THE 1967 WAR

IMMEDIATE FACTORS CONTRIBUTING TO THE 1967 CONFLICT

All factors that had induced Israel to go to war in 1956 were present in 1967. The conflict revolved round the blockade of the Suez Canal, the Straits of Tiran, the search for new markets by Israel, the increase in frequency and daring of the Arab commandos across the cease-fire line, the policy of the Zionists to dispose of the Palestine people and their national liberation resistance, the Jordan River question, the United Arab Command and Jordan's signing of the military pact with Egypt and Syria on 30 May 1967.

THE QUESTION OF FREE NAVIGATION

Egypt justified its mobilization and the closing of the Straits as purely defensive measures, claiming that it had the legal right to prevent Israel from using the Gulf because: (*i*) the Arab states were still in a state of war with Israel; (*ii*) Israel's occupation of the Port of Elat on the western shore of the Gulf was illegal, since it was done after the signing of the Rhodes Agreement with Egypt and in complete violation of Security Council resolutions; (*iii*) the tripartite aggression of 1956 did not change the legal status of Egypt's rights, since Israel's privileges to use the Gulf were guaranteed only by her Western supporters, particularly the United States, Britain, and France; (*iv*) Egypt was not denying any country innocent passage nor actually blockading the Straits, since normal shipping was not being interfered with (the U.A.R. had the right to prohibit Israeli ships and strategic material from passing through her territorial waters because in the state of war such passage could not be considered innocent; and (*v*) the Arab states consider the Gulf as primarily an internal, not an international, body of water, since its only entrance is one mile wide surrounded by Arab land.[1]

[1]Khouri, *op. cit.*, p. 251.

Israel's insistence on keeping the Straits open, even at the risk of war, was dictated by the belief that diplomacy will produce nothing practical. The best Israel could hope for was less than free and open passage through the Straits. Moreover, while opening the Straits through diplomatic efforts might provide a solution to the immediate problem, it would be temporary and unsatisfactory. To Israel, diplomacy or reliance on United Nations' intervention would not satisfy its aspirations of absolute control of the Straits; thus, Israeli leaders expressed that they had no confidence in the U.N. peace-keeping force as a means of insuring the right of navigation in the Straits.[2] To that end, "Israel must chart her own course."[3] Foreign Minister Abba Eban expressed this policy in the Security Council when he threatened that, "Nothing less than complete non-interference with free and innocent passage is acceptable."[4]

Seemingly, sure of Israel's capability to back its threat to force the opening of the Gulf, Eban, in a press conference on 30 May 1967, stated that the Egyptian action caused a change in the security balance in the region. He threatened that unless Egypt immediately rectified these changes, Israel would take retaliatory measures.[5]

To Israel, security was placed above every other consideration. She had insisted that the major Powers implement the 1957 commitment to create "a regime of international security and law."[6] This included open navigation in the Gulf of Aqaba. Israeli Prime Minister Levi Eshkol had acted upon that assumption, but President Johnson responded by indicating that the United States was not in a position to uphold international law and warned Israel against taking unilateral action. Since the Big Powers did not respond to Israel's expectations, the Zionist leaders began to believe that international order had been abandoned by the Great Powers, to the detriment of Israel. It decided to chart its own course and take unilateral action:

[2]*New York Times*, 15 December 1968.

[3]*Ibid.*, 11 November 1968, p. 2.

[4]*Ibid.*, 4 June 1967.

[5]Charles Yost, "The Arab Israeli War: How it Began," *Foreign Affairs* (January, 1968), pp. 304-20.

[6]Terrence Prittie, *Eshkol: The Man and the Nation* (New York: Pitman Publishing Corporation, 1969), p. 319.

The international order had been challenged and abdicated. The Israeli soldiers took over.... They believed that they had to get very fast results before any great power could act. The instinct that there is a great power system built up over the years faded away gradually.[7]

To Israel, the closing of the Straits constituted a threat to its vital interests since ninety-nine per cent of its oil imports were handled by the Port of Elat. However, the closure did not pose a threat to its survival since no Israeli ships crossed the Straits for over two and a half years before the conflict.[8] According to King Husayn:

The latest attack is not an isolated example but a part of a deliberate Israeli expansionist policy, although they have somehow made it appear that they are a tiny unarmed country surrounded by Arab willies.[9]

The strategic problem of Israel was not a military or an economic one, but political and psychological. Mohammad Haykal of *Al-Ahram* explained:

The closure of the Gulf of Aqaba to Israeli navigation and the ban on import of strategic goods, even when carried by non-Israeli ships, means first and last that the Arab nation represented by the UAR has succeeded for the first time *vis-a-vis* Israel in changing by force a *fait accompli* imposed on it by force. This is the essence of the problem, regardless of the implications surrounding it and future contingencies....
...To Israel this is the most dangerous aspect of the current situation.... Therefore, it is not a matter of the Gulf of Aqaba, but something bigger. It is the whole philosophy of Israeli security. It is the philosophy on which Israeli existence has pivoted since its birth and on which it will pivot in the future.

---

[7]*London Times*, 2 January 1969.

[8]Husayn's speech at the General Assembly Emergency Session, 26 June 1967 (Amman: Ministry of Information), p. 3.

The port of Elat handled 90 per cent of Israel's oil imports, though only 5.9 per cent of the rest of its trade. See Malcolm Kerr, *The Middle East Conflict* (New York : Foreign Policy Association, 1969), p. 28.

[9]Husayan's G.A. speech, 26 June 1967, p. 6.

Hence I say that Israel must resort to arms.[10]

Egypt's action was primarily based on Soviet Intelligence. By closing the Gulf and the Straits, "the Soviets wanted an Egyptian show of strength, but only one that would be "limited exercise in brinkmanship, not war."[11]

Miles Copeland of the Central Intelligence Agency insisted that Nasser's move was merely a show of strength aimed at enhancing his prestige, while the Israeli action was calculated to win a decisive battle. He wrote:

Except that I would add that Nasser did not exactly stumble, and that Israel was not exactly unprepared, Nasser planned his operation in detail right up to the moment Vice President Zakaria Mohieddin, in Nasser's name, was to back down magnanimously (over the Straits of Tiran issue) in response to appeals from the United Nations; the Israelis had no wish to let Nasser get away with such a prestige-building gesture. Despite their promise to President Johnson that they would hold off until Zakaria got to New York, the Israelis struck on the very morning Zakaria was supposed to depart. After all, they had been rehearsing their assault for years, and never again would they get such favourable circumstances in which to launch it.[12]

Since its conception, Israel has been a garrison state. Its army's ideology of expansion and security has been tied closely to its foreign policy. Thus, the army played a major role of implementing and determining to a large extent the course of Israel's foreign relations.[13] It was the military rather than the politicians that made the strike unavoidable.

There had grown up a myth of Israeli invincibility which weighed heavily behind the Israeli policy of armed reprisals. Thus, in June 1967, a retreat from attacking the United Arab Republic first, Jordan and Syria second, would have given the impression that Israel did not dare to tangle with the Arab armies. The mere possibility that

---

[10]Kerr, *op. cit.*, p. 26.

[11]Miles Copeland, *The Game of Nations* (New York; Simon and Schuster, 1969), p. 276.

[12]*Ibid.*

[13]Amos Perlmutter, "The Israeli Army in Politics," *World Politics*, Vol. 20, No. 4 (July 1968). p. 625.

Nasser personally would benefit from such retreat, strengthening his position of Arab leadership upset the Zionists who wished to minimize, even to eliminate his power. By maintaining military superiority over the combined Arab force, Israel could successfully preserve the safety of its frontier. Since offence is the best defence, offence was employed to establish peace through strength. This theory became the policy of the Israeli army.[14] Therefore, it became imperative that Israel must strike first. By so doing, Israel had achieved an unchallengeable military superiority over the entire region.

ISRAEL'S SEARCH FOR NEW MARKETS

As to the internal economic conditions in Israel, the German reparation payment expired in 1965. Thus, a substitute source of funds had to be found. The rising unemployment and frequent recessions in Israel's economy had reached an alarming level in 1967.[15] In order to halt the economic decline, the state embarked on a policy in the direction of armed conflict that would attain certain economic objectives, as increased commercial transactions in the immediate vicinity of Israel, it was argued, could alleviate some of the pressing economic problems.[16]

[14]*Ibid.*, p. 626.

[15]Ibrahim Abu-Lughod, "Israel's Arab Policy," *The Arab World*, XIV, Special Issue, Nos. 10–11, p. 35.

The Zionist economists knew that Agriculture and services—the nation's principle source of employment—had been expanded to the maximum limits. Virtually, all arable lands were being tilled and cultivated. Furthermore, by 1964, there were surplus housing units as immigration had been reversed.

The war solved the unemployment problem overnight, but demobilization recreated it. However, by occupying large territories, new markets were created, new enterprises established, and new jobs for administering the populated occupied areas were found. *New York Times*, 13 August 1967, IV, p. 5. See also "Israel's Economy Slows Down," *New Outlook*, June 1966, pp. 9–18; and "Anatomy of a Crisis," *New Outlook*, March 1966, pp. 21-25.

[16]The United Jewish Appeal, the Israeli bonds, and the Israel Emergency Fund have been the major source of funds.

On May 15 and 25, 1967, following Eshkol's threatening declarations, top American Jewish leaders journeyed to Israel and were taken on a tour of the front. There, it was decided that war is the "only solution" and the launching of the Israel Emergency Fund drive to finance the war was to start on 22 May, *Jerusalem Post*, 3 July 1967, quoted in Lughod, *op. cit*, p. 39.

One major result of the 1956 aggression was the opening of markets for Israeli trade in certain Asian and African countries. However, the volume of trade was low and its proportion of Israeli export market remained negligible and continued to decline, despite improvement in relations between Israel and these states.[17]

At this point, it became evident to Israel that there was no substitute for normalization of trade with the immediate Arab neighbours. To that end, a policy was directed towards a long-range objective of reaching a form of settlement with the Arabs, by either voluntary peace or by force.[18] The Zionist leadership differed on the method of attaining this goal. Dayan and the militarists were of the opinion that there was only one way to solve the problem conclusively, and that "was by defeating the Arabs so decisively in battle that they be forced to accept a dictated settlement at the conference table."[19] The logic behind this premise was that "force was, after all, what Arabs understood best."[20]

The alternative proposal was adopted by Eban, who, while agreeing to the same principle, pursued a subtle strategy which required a great deal of skill in execution. He viewed the Middle East as a region of fragmented sovereignties which eventually would accept the Zionist state as a partner for mutual benefits.[21] Further, he foresaw the dominant role of Israel in the region. However, in order to realize this dominance, a peace settlement on Israeli terms was the only feasible solution. Accordingly, in his view:

[17]Odeyo Ayagu "Africa's Dilemma in the Arab-Israeli Conflict," *Pan-African Journal*, Vol. 1, No. 219 (1968), p. 114.

[18]An Israeli English daily commented on this issue: "The only way to reach a settlement is for the Zionists to recognize the rights of the Palestinian people—according to the Partition Plan and repatriation of the refugees and compensating them. Israel's relations with the Arab states will continue to be abnormal until Israel finds a way to accommodate positively the rights of the Palestinian people." *Jerusalem Post*, 18 October 1966.

All studies indicate that while Israel is eager to reach a settlement, it insists on the *status quo* which is abhorrent to the Palestinians and the Arabs as a whole. The alternative to the Zionists is to force such settlement by force of arms, a policy which, in fact, has precipitated three major confrontations.

[19]Lughod, *op. cit.*, p. 37. Dayan said after the 1967 war, "If one thinks military defeat brought the Arabs closer to peace, he is very much mistaken." Avnery, *op. cit.*, p. 206.

[20]Lughod, *op. cit.* p. 37.

[21]See Chapter VIII, n. 1,

The challenge to Israel's foreign policy lay in its ability to organize pressure on the Arabs to normalize their relationship with Israel and at the same time make it crystal clear that under no circumstances would the Arabs ever be in a position to bring about a solution other than one envisaged by Israel.[22]

Realizing that direct negotiations with the Arabs were not yet possible, Eban envisaged international pressure to compel the Arabs to accept Israel's terms for peace. To him, therefore, the road to a Middle-East settlement must pass through Washington and Moscow and to a lesser extent through London and Paris. His plan was to persuade these Powers that peace in the Middle East was of direct concern to them, and that they could initiate such steps as pressurizing the progressive regimes and influencing the conservative ones. On the other hand, they could impose sanctions by withholding arms shipments to their Arab allies, thus depriving them of the capacity to counter Israel's power.[23] Consequently, the Arabs would sue for peace.

The Great Powers were inclined to ignore the Middle East issue if the situation was calm. On the other hand, they became alarmed when border incidents intensified, lest the confrontation between the Powers might develop. The retaliatory raids by the Zionists, while intended for offensive military purposes, had great propaganda value. The raids signified that a helpless alien state was being perpetually harassed by those who wanted its destruction. Thus, while the raids were primarily for offensive reasons, they conveyed the impression that they were initiated in self-defence, to repel the attacks by the neighbouring hostile states. By this strategy, world opinion was alerted to the fact that tension existed in the region, and, in

[22]Lughod, *op. cit.*

[23]This policy means that, while the Zionists will have adequate military power, the Arab states will have a much smaller quantity. This leads the observer to the conclusion that a settlement for Israel in order to be enforced must place Israel in a position to dictate her own terms. The only position from which to bargain is that of the conqueror. This doctrine now dictates the policy which the Zionists had maintained since the 1967 war, namely, to force the Arab states to sign a peace treaty on Israel's terms. Perlmutter, *op. cit.*, p. 627.

For example, Israel protested against the sale of Mirage Jets by France to Libya on 9 January 1970, as she had protested against all arms sales to the Arabs from any source including the U.S.S.R.

pursuit of peace, it would pressurize the Arabs to reach a peaceful settlement of the issue.[24]

Thus, by escalating the military situation along the Syrian-Israeli armistice line in April 1967, the Zionists succeeded in re-alerting the Powers to the explosiveness of the region, as the surprise attack on 5 June 1967 brought these Powers and the U.N. into international crisis.

The Palestine Resistance Movement

The Zionist policy towards the Palestine Arabs in particular and the Arab states in general was guided by two factors: ideology and practical needs. As to the latter, the Zionists, in pursuit of acquiring the maximum amount of territory, took advantage of Arab disunity and lack of military cooperation as manifested in the Rhodes Agreement and violated the cease-fire agreements whenever it was to their advantage.[25] As to the ideological factor, Israel's most immediate objective was to stake a claim to mandate Palestine by liquidating the cultural and natural affinity of the Arab inhabitants and ultimately to excise them from the territory.[26]

For that reason, Zionist policy towards the Palestine issue fluctuated according to expediency. At first, they considered the palestine issue merely a local one, concerning the Palestine Arab community and the Zionists alone.[27] However, since the Palestine Arabs had no organization, the Arab states had to adopt their problem. For that reason, the Zionists began to recognize the Arab states as party to the conflict.

Despite the fact that the Palestine Arab community became conquered people and a Zionist state was established in their land, they

[24]*Ibid.*, p. 626.

[25]Rodinson, *op. cit.*, p. 39.

[26]Christopher Sykes, *Crossroad to Israel* (London: Collins, 1965), p. 65.

[27]As the impasse persists, Israel is trying to persuade the Arabs in the occupied territory to have local autonomy thereby severing all connections with Jordan. But this policy has not succeeded mainly due to the fact that the West Bankers prefer to be under an Arab government and because the Jordan Government had declared that : "Every Jordanian on the West Bank of the Jordan is still and will continue to be a Jordan citizen. The Government declares that any collaboration with the enemy...will be considered treason...." *New York Times*, 22 June 1967.

have not capitulated nor weakened their resolve to liberate their homeland. This is manifested in their recognition by the Arab states and especially by the formation of the Palestine Liberation Organization (P.L.O.) under Arab League sponsorship. This development is of grave political importance since two opposing nationalisms compete for the same territory. "There can be no real resolution to the conflict, short of political elimination of one or the other protagonist."[28]

To Israel, this was an imminent and clear danger. It realized that the long dormant Plaestine Arabs, whom it called hitherto "conquered people" or simply "Arab refugees," were emerging as an independent force and that a Palestine national liberation movement was in the making.

This movement represented a resistance to occupation of their homeland. To the Zionists, this resistance violated the basic principle upon which the concept of Israeli defence and border security was based. The commando movement was directed from the neighbouring states. This turn of events caused discomfort with the Zionists who had always taken the position that the Palestine Arabs were merely conquered people and they were the occupying-power. As the resistance movement intensified in frequency and daring and became a fact which the Zionists were reluctant to live with, it gave the Zionists a pretext for retaliatory action against the neighbouring states from whose territories this resistance was initiated.[29] The policy of reprisals was in accordance with the basic strategic principle which the Zionists had espoused, namely, of waging war outside Israel's boundaries.

In both the 1956 and 1967 wars, the Palestine resistance movement gave rise to major conflicts. In fact, from 1953 on, violence along the armistice line was occasioned by infiltrators' activities initiated by border villagers not organized by the central government at Amman.[30] Nevertheless, these activities brought about reprisals carried

[28]Moshe Dayan, "A Soldier Reflects on Peace Hopes," *Jerusalem Post* (December 30, 1968). On this point, see also Hashim Sharabi, *Palestine and Israel* (New York, Pegasus, 1968), p. 128.

[29]Lughod, *op. cit.*, p. 35.

As commandos were showing increasing proficiency, Eshkol stated on 17 May 1967, that Israel had "no... other choice but to adopt counter measures against the foci of sabotage and the abettors." *New York Times*, 6 March 1967.

[30]Eytan, *op. cit.*, p. 105.

out by regular Israeli army units. A United Nations observer verifies this condition:

> But when the Arabs do something wrong, it is usually stealing a sheep or picking a fruit in Israel. When the Israelis act, it is usually to take over more land or set up military positions, or clobber the Arabs somewhere.[31]

In pursuing this policy, Israel followed a precedent.[32]

[31]Samuel Merlin, *The Search for Peace in the Middle East* (New York: Thomas Yoseloff, 1968), p. 226.

[32]The United States Government sent troops into Mexico on 15 March 1915, after the failure of all its other efforts to contain the marauders who harried the frontier zones. The American forces were not withdrawn until early the following year. On 20 June 1916, the Secretary of State, Robert Lansing, addressed a note to the Mexican Government:

> It would be tedious to recount instance after instance, outrage after outrage, atrocity after atrocity to illustrate the true nature and extent of the widespread conditions of lawlessness and violence which have prevailed . During the past nine months in particular, the frontier of the United States along the lower Rio Grande has been thrown into a constant state of apprehension and turmoil because of frequent and sudden incursions into American territory and depredations and murders on American soil by Mexican bandits. . . . Representations were made to General Carranza, and he was emphatically requested to stop these reprehensible acts. . . . In the face of these depredations. . . the perpetrators of which General Carranza was unable or possibly considered it inadvisable to apprehend and punish, the United States had no recourse other than to employ force to disperse the bands of Mexican outlaws who were with increasing boldness systematically raiding across the international boundary. . . . This Government has waited month after month for the consummation of its hope and expectation. . . . Obviously, if there is no means of reaching bands roving on Mexican territory and making sudden dashes at night into American territory, it is impossible to prevent such invasions unless the frontier is protected by a cordon of troops. No government could be expected to maintain a force of this strength along the boundary. . . for the purpose of resisting this onslaught of a few bands of lawless men, especially when the neighbouring states make no effort to prevent these attacks. The most effective method of preventing raids of this nature, as past experience has fully demonstrated, is to visit punishment or destruction on the raiders. . . . The first duty of any government (is) the protection of life and property. This is the paramount obligation for which governments are instituted, and governments failing or neglecting to perform it are not worthy of the name.

Quoted in Eytan, *op. cit.*, pp. 106-7.

Thus, the Israeli-Arab policy had the objective of destroying the Palestine resistance in embryo, as in the cases of Kibya, Essamu and Karamah. By breaking this resistance they hoped to maintain peace and stability along the armistice line and to serve notice to the neighbouring states that, should they tolerate commando actions from their territories, they will automatically invite reprisals.[33] To achieve this objective, border incidents were increased and intensified in order to force the Arabs, especially Jordan which had the longest border of four hundred and fifty miles with Israel, to sign a peace treaty legitimizing Zionist conquest. This attitude of Israelis was a calculated policy to serve its political purposes. Maintaining a high but tolerable level of tension served to consolidate its hold over external supporters for political and financial ends. Internally, it solidified and strengthened the nation's unity. Explaining Israel's psychology in this respect, Professor Max Rodinson, a French Jew wrote:

Zionist Israel throve on a bellicose atmosphere and threat of danger. The world could not allow her to be destroyed. Jews, the world over, would rally to the aid of those who in time of peril they could not help regarding as their brothers. Zion's salvation lay in permanent danger.[34]

Jordan, under King Abdullah, was receptive to such pressures, but it came to a halt when Husayn became the ruler. Thus, a new policy of systematic coercion was embarked on, the assumption of which was that the language of force was the best the Arabs could understand. Its principal aim was to compel Jordan to sue for peace with the assumption that if Jordan, the country most involved in the conflict, agreed to a peace treaty, the other Arab states would follow. But this policy produced the opposite reaction in Jordan, for instead of suing for peace, Jordan embarked on a counter policy of reprisal to the raids by organizing the National Guard, arming the Jordan population, especially the border villages.[35]

For a decade after the Suez crisis, despite some border incidents, the threat of armed conflict was at a minimum. The lull was inter-

[33]Hashim Sharabi, "Prelude to War: The Crisis of May-June 1967," *The Arab World*, Vol. XIV, No. 10-11 (n.d.), p. 23.

[34]Rodinson, *op., cit.* p. 70.

[35]Lughod, *op. cit.*, p. 33.

preted as signifying a potential for peace.[36] However, with the large-scale military attack on the Jordanian village of Essamu in December 1966, a sudden confrontation seemed imminent. Though this was attributed to increasing activity of the Palestinian resistance, but, in fact; it was a calculated move to test the cohesiveness and the capability of the newly formed Arab Command, particularly, since the activity had not appreciably disturbed the lull. The commando activities meant to the Palestinians the right to their land and homes. To the Zionists, by contrast, this was not an issue, for, in the logic of the latter's strategy, the question of Arab rights to their ancestral homeland in which they lived for fourteen centuries, like the question of Jerusalem, now belonged to the non-negotiable category.[37] Micheal Ionides, an old observer of Middle Eastern politics, commented:

> They [Palestine Arabs] were attacked both ways. It was morally wicked of them to fight to prevent the Zionists enjoying what was theirs; they were weak and incompetent to fight and failed. As aggressors, they had no right to win; for their military incompetence they deserved to lose. They should have been loyal to the United Nations decision to partition, for the rule of law must be honored; they must accept the consequences of defeat, for victory goes to those who are strong. The Jews were there of right; anyway they had beaten the Arabs in war. It is right for the Jews to fight to acquire; wrong for the Arabs to fight to hold.[38]

To Jordan, in particular, it appeared that the commando activities precipitated Israeli reprisals which Jordan wished to avoid. Cognizant of their weak military posture, the states of the Arab

---

[36]The president of the Carnegie Endowment for International Peace, Joseph Johnson, was dispatched to the Middle East by the Palestine Conciliation Commission for another attempt at conciliation in the early '60s (New *Outlook*, Vol. VII, No. 6, Tel Aviv, 1964, pp. 16-24). Also the French philosopher, Jean-Paul Sartre, visited the Middle East in an attempt to bring about a dialogue between the Arabs and the Zionists (*New Outlook*, Vol. IX, No. 4; cited by Lughod, *op. cit.*, p. 34).

[37]Sharabi, *op. cit.*, p. 29; *Manchester Guardian*, 8 May 1969.

[38]Micheal Ionides, *Divide and Lose: The Arab Revolt, 1955-58* (London: Goeffrey Bles, 1960), p. 79.

Command made it a point not to furnish Israel with the slightest
pretext for starting a premature war. Accordingly, at the Arab
Summit Conferences, it was agreed that:

> all commando actions against Israel had to be submitted to re-
> view by the United Arab Command before they were carried out,
> since it alone had the authority to judge if the proposed operation
> was a 'coordinated action' as defined by the Arab states.[39]

In Jordan, however, Husayn refused to permit the commandos
to roam freely in his territory, to have headquarters in Jordan, or
even to use the radio station. Furthermore, he forbade the P.L.O.
to tax the refugees or recruit them into the liberation army.[40]

JORDAN AND THE FEDAYEEN IN POST-1967 PERIOD

The Palestine commandos (Fedayeen) became a formidable force
guarding Jordan's frontier and cooperating with the army alongside
of which they fought the so-called six-day war in 1967. This changed
the image of the Fedayeen who no longer were men in hiding
operating from secret bases. Now they were viewed as great fighters and patriots. Even Husayn acknowledged their prestige when
he remarked, "If this continues, we might all reach the stage where
we are all Fedayeen."[41]

The new role of the commandos made it clear that the June War
had not ended on the 6th day because Israel had not won a victory,
especially not against the commando anyway. Nor had Husayn
won the battle to halt their operations inside his country because
they became: "...a law unto themselves, obeying commanders in
Syria and Egypt....Above all, they forced Jordan to maintain the

---

[39]Vance and Lauer, *op. cit.*, p. 27.

[40]On January 27, 1967, Husayn withdrew his recognition of the P.L.O.
Furthermore, Jordan declared that it would boycott all organizations connected
with the Arab Summit in which Ahmad Al-Shuqayri, head of the P.L.O., would
take part. *Al-Ahram* reported that Jordan attack on Shukayri was a pretext to
boycott the summit and disable the U.A.C. At the same time, Husayn requested
700,000 pounds of the League's budget for River Jordan projects. *Al-Ahram*,
28 January 1967.

[41]*New York Times*, 7 April 1968, IV, p. 131, and 8 December 1968, IV, p. 14.

illusion of continuing a war with Israel when the King wanted to continue the search for peace."[42]

In order to minimize the Israeli retaliation after the War, Husayn declared that he would not tolerate the commando operations in his country and sought to hold back all-out commando escalation. He was confronted with a critical situation. While commando activities were keeping the enemy off balance, they were inviting reprisal raids which adversely affected Jordan's economy, especially by damaging the irrigation canals, dams and other projects.

Replying to criticism and challenging other Arab governments, he continued: "If anyone thinks he is a better Arab national than I am, let him show it in his own country and not use Jordan as a base."[43]

Husayn's stand on the Palestine issue since 30 May 1967, and his cooperation with the commandos during the war transformed his position into a positive light. Even Nasser declared that as long as Husayn's policy aimed at ridding Palestine of Zionism, no Arab would stand against him.[44]

In Jordan, the support given the commandos by the presence of the Iraqi army placed their activities largely beyond the control of Husayn. In any case, after the 1967 War, it became imperative for Husayn to give full support to the commandos who enjoyed the support of the majority of his subjects. In the Press Club speech he defended the legality of the commando activities:

I am asked "Why don't you stop the Fedayeen, the commandos, in their raids against Israel?" I reply, 'I would not stop them.' It's their land that the Israelis are occupying and they see no way out for them except to struggle to achieve their rights. If they can't succeed in regaining the occupied land, then their aim is to exercise their right of active resistance to the forces of occupation. To practical people this may seem quixotic but to people with anger in their hearts and a conviction that they are in the right, the practicability of their acts is of no consequence.

[42]*New York Times*, 7 April 1968, IV, p. 131.

The conflict between the Palestine commandos and Husayn precipitated the Jordan Civil War in September 1970.

[43]*New York Times, op. cit.,* p. 132; and Vance and Lauer, *op. cit.,* p. 27.
[44]*New York Times, op. cit.,* p. 134.

Nor the sacrifice. And I am not willing to be responsible for the security of the forces of occupation.

...There is no difference in my aim in seeking a peaceful settlement and their aim in a settlement by conflict. What we both want is a restoration of our rights. I would never accept a peace that did not fully restore these rights. When we have regained them there will cease to be a reason for commando action. It is the intolerable situation that produces the commandos; not the commandos who provoke the situation.[45]

The Fedayeen leaders have repeatedly insisted that they do not want to take over political administration in Jordan. Such a move, they argued, would only play into the hands of Israeli military "hawks" who want total polarization brought about by the departure of Husayn, the ending of British–American influence in Jordan, and the growing of Soviet influence instead.

The Fedayeen and Nasser testify to the value of having an ally on good terms with the West. Furthermore, the moderation of Husayn made Nasser look relatively tough. Yet there are more important reasons for cooperating with Husayn. One, until the Fedayeen agree on a unified leadership of their own, they would like to see cooperation and direction from Husayn. Two, the commandos consider Jordan the best place from which to regain their usurped land. Consequently, they would not like to see Jordan swallowed by any of its Arab neighbours, for such contingency would invite Israeli intervention which could result in the occupation of parts if not all of Jordan. Lastly, by establishing a "Commando Government" to replace Husayn's regime would mean the end of Jordan as a state which would cost the Arabs a seat in the United Nations.[46]

---

[45]King Husayn's Speech at the Press Club, Washington D. C. 19 April, 1969; also *Al-Risalah Al-Malakiyyiah* (Amman: Ministry of Information, n. d.), p. 27.

Adopting the same attitude regarding the Fedayeen, Syrian Premier Zayn said in a Damascus Press Conference on 10 October, 1966: We are not guardians of Isreal's safety. "We are not resigned to holding back the revolution of the Palestine people...." Theodore Draper, *Israel and World Politics* (New York: Viking Press, 1968), p. 37.

[46]*The Economist*, 14 December 1968, p. 25.

Major-General Ezer Weisman warned that if a "Commando Government" takes over in Jordan, the Israeli army would intervene, *Christian Science Monitor* 21 February 1970.

THE JORDAN RIVER DISPUTE AND THE SUMMIT CONFERENCES

By 1960, the Arabs showed mounting anxiety over the progress being made by Israel to divert the Jordan waters to the Negeb. In response, the Arabs threatened to divert the "Arab River" from its sources in Syria and Lebanon. Jordan was the first to call for joint Arab action declaring that the water problem was a part of the Palestine question which concerned all the Arabs. Jordan was especially concerned because the Israeli projects would deprive her of badly needed water for irrigation, since the Israeli project was designed to divert these waters before entering the Jordan territory.

The loudest provocation was made by Dayan in 1959, when he threatened that "unless the Arabs cooperate in finding a solution to the Jordan waters, we will take it by force...."[47]

The first call for a summit was made by President Nasser on 23 December 1963. The conference was convened in Cairo from January 13 to 17, at which the heads of states decided to create a special commission to supervise the diversion of the Jordan waters, and entrusted the Unified Arab Command with the task of preventing an enemy aggression aiming at obstructing the plan. It was also agreed that a budget of fifteen million pounds be spent in arming Jordan, Syria and Lebanon.[48]

The Arab summit caused an immediate response in Israel which viewed the Arab plan as an act of physical aggression. As work began, Israel bombarded the sites of the operation.[49] Furthermore, Prime Minister Levi Eshkol in a speech in the Parliament on 16 January made his government's policy clear. He warned that the Arab plan would be regarded as an "encroachment on our soil; hence military confrontation would be inevitable."[50]

Recently, Dayan stated that Husayn's "Western friends" were the deterrent to a large-scale military action in Jordan, *Ibid.*

[47] *Filistin*, 20 October 1959.

[48] Mohammad Faraj, *Al-Ummah Al-Arabiyyiah Ala-Al-Tareeq Ila Wahdat Al-Hadaf* (Cairo: Dar Al-Fikr Al-Arabi, 1964), p. 474; also Khalil, *op. cit.*, Vol. II, p. 172.

The only project of any significance was the Mukhiba Dam in Jordan. The other projects were abandoned for lack of military security. Malcolm Kerr, *The Arab Cold War* (New York: Oxford University Press, 1967), p. 153.

[49] Merlin, *op. cit.*, p. 23.

[50] *Ibid.;* also Israel Ministry of Foreign Affairs, *The Arab Plan to Divert the Headwaters of the River Jordan* (April 1965), No. 14, p. 7.

Appealing to world public opinion, Israeli Foreign Minister Sharette declared to an Amsterdam conference: "The summit meeting should be considered a defiance to all the world and should not be looked upon casually as long as it represents defiance to the world which created the state of Israel."[51]

In the meantime, Golda Meir in an interview with *Le Monde* threatened, "...We know our power and capability to confront every attempt to do us harm."[52]

The Arab argument was based on the fact that the diversion of the waters by Israel will present a problem of salinity.[53] "In due course," the *Jerusalem Post* stated, "The Jordan will be reduced to a little more than a seasonal trickle and the Negeb shall live."[54] While the Negeb prospers, thousands of Jordanian farmers would lose their only means of livelihood.[55] Furthermore, the Arab states reject Israel's claim which is based on territorial sovereignty, and insist that the creation of the Zionist state was an illegal act by the United Nations.[56]

[51]Faraj, *op. cit.*, p. 481.

[52]Quoted in *Ibid.*, p. 483. Under Secretary of State, Alexis Johnson in a speech to the Citizens Committee of American Foreign Policy in the Near East declared that the United States was determined "to avoid taking sides in the regional disputes...but this does not mean that we will stand idly by if aggression is committed." He also warned that, "In the coming months many of our policies will be put to test." "The Arabs took Johnson's statement as a warning to them not to attack Israel militarily or by diverting the Jordan waters before they reach Israel." *New York Times*, February 3, 1964.

Senator Keating further threatened: "The United States must declare that it will not allow the Arabs to obstruct Israel's diversion of the river waters, and it should explain its opposition in this matter, and that the Sixth Fleet should stand now and in the future ready to stop any Arab adventure or military activity against Israel." Quoted in Faraj, *op. cit.*, p. 486.

Senator Harrison Williams also added, "We must explain to the World continually that we will support Israel, and oppose anyone who opposes it with all our resources." Quoted in *Ibid.*, p. 487.

[53]*Daily Star*, November 3, 1965.

[54]*Jerusalem Post*, 15 August 1962.

[55]The Jordan Ministry of Agriculture claimed that almost 50 per cent of the country's vegetable produce would be lost. Such produce was sold in Kuwait and Saudi Arabia, yielding a substantial income.

[56]Omar Z. Ghobashy, *The Development of the Jordan River* (New York: Arab Information of Centre, 1961) p. 43.

DANGERS OF THE PROJECT TO THE ARABS

The water-carrier project was designed to irrigate the Negeb desert.
In his introduction to the Israel Year Book of 1956, Ben Gurion
elaborated on the importance of the Negeb. He wrote:

> The Negeb is the weakest point of Israel and a source of danger
> to its future. In the Negeb are the greater Jewish aspirations....
> The small state of Israel cannot wait any longer leaving the Negeb
> desert in its present condition which constitutes half of the
> territory, because if this state does not exploit it, this very desert
> will plan the evident end of Israel.[57]

"The battle of the Negeb is the battle of Israel's survival."[58] To
the Zionists, the Negeb has economic, military and strategic importance. Economically, this water scheme has been referred to as
"the backbone of the national water project."   Irrigating the area
would enable Israel to increase its population by 500,000 by 1970,
and by 1,500,000 by 1980.[59]   Haim Weisman, Israel's first President,
estimated that five million Jewish immigrants would enter Israel.[60]
Ben Gurion was even more optimistic as he urged all Jews to emi-
grate. "This is not a state of 600,000 or so Jews who live in it...
but a state destined for the whole people and its doors are open wide
to every Jew."[61]   In a speech before the Parliament, he declared,
"By tempo of immigration and the speed with which it is absorbed
...will Israel's security be determined."[62]

As to strategic importance, Israel's population are concentrated in
a small coastal area on the Mediterranean. The emptiness
of the Negeb is a source of danger to Israel, as it is a factor
to help the Arab forces attack from the south. Realizing this, the
Israeli militarists and Ben Gurion agree that "the development of the
Negeb and living in it is an absolute necessity to the security of

---

[57]*Israel Government Year Book,* 1956.

[58]Ali M. Ali., *Nahrul Urdun Wal Mu'amarah Al Sahyouniyyiah* (Cairo:
National Publishing House, n. d.), p. 14.

[59]*Economist* , 14 December 1963.

[60]*Jewish Observer,* 28 February 1964.

[61]*Israel Government Year Book*, October 1952; also Alfred Lilienthal,
Other side of the Coin (New York: Devin-Adair, 1965), p. 261.

[62]*Israel Government Year Book*, October 1951.

Israel...."[63]   Thus, while Israeli planners dream of "dispersing settlements throughout the length of the state for political and security reasons,"[64] they also plan to transform the desert into a productive centre. Furthermore, the Negeb borders on the Red Sea, an essential outlet to Africa and Asia. The existence of Elat on the Sea represents a wedge separating Egypt from Jordan, thus, in fact, dividing the Arab world into East and West. Earlier, as a condition for peace, Nasser had demanded that the Negeb be returned to Arab control, according to the Bernadotte Plan. Israel rejected this demand because the Negeb, if in the hands of the Arabs, would constitute a danger to Israel. Denying it to the Arabs prevents military encirclement extending from Morocco to Kuwait. Thus, it was not an accident that in 1948, in violation of the Truce agreement, the Israeli forces penetrated the sector and occupied Elat, a strategic point of Arab territory.[65]

In order to reap maximum results from the Negeb, that desert must be irrigated and colonized. Ben Gurion has been a major proponent of the agricultural settlements.[66]
He wrote:

The aim of agriculture is not only food production. There are also problems of statesmanship, sociology, colonization and defense involved....There is great need for distributing the population over the whole country; conquest and development of the desert and changing the professional structure of the settlers.[67]

Settling and colonizing the Negeb requires hundreds of thousands of immigrants. Such large numbers would be needed not only to increase agricultural production but also to augment the present population and help in the defence of the state. Ben Gurion elaborates:

Israel can have no security without immigrants. The population of Egypt alone numbers 23 millions. ...Aliyah (the return of the Jews to the Land of Israel) is not only the redemption of Jews

    [63]Ali, op. cit., p. 13.
    [64]Israel Government Year Book, October 1958, p. 61.
    [65]Shwadran, op. cit., pp. 275-78.
        [66]Though Prime Minister, he lives in the Negeb. The idea is to be the example for "youth go south.'
    [67]Israeli Government Year Book, 1951, p. 37 and 1959 p. 182.

from physical and spiritual extinction in the diaspora and the supreme historic mission of the state of Israel; it is paramount for our security.

Security means settlement and peopling of the empty areas north and south; the dispersal of the population and the establishment of industries throughout the country; the development of agriculture in all suitable areas; the building of an expanded economy that will provide our people with a livelihood and liberate them from dependence on material aid from without. These things are imperative for our survival. Upper Gallilee and the expanses of the south and the Negeb are the country's weak points, and no military force can assure us their continued possession until we settle them as speedily and as closely as possible.[68]

Here lies the crux of the Arab opposition to diverting the Jordan waters to the Negeb. To the Arabs, it would be self-defeating, for otherwise they would give the enemy a prosperous life economically and strengthen his position militarily.

Verifying the critical character of the situation, the *London Daily Telegraph* concluded that the plans to divert the Jordan headwaters together with Arab arms build-up were "leading step by step to an inevitable collision involving missiles and possibly nuclear weapons."[69]

Diversion of the Jordan waters by Israel which she considered her share under the Johnston Plan, had not yielded the anticipated results for purely technical reasons.[70] In order to obtain the full benefits from these waters, Israel needed the control of the headwaters which were located in Syria. Only through military occupation, in the absence of a peace treaty, could the Zionists' water plan materialize.

To that end, Israel used the Palestine commando activities as a pretext to reach these headwaters. Israel was doing its best to create the same situation that preceded the 1956 tripartite aggression,

[68]*Ibid.*, 1959, p. 22. See *Security and the Middle East* (a report submitted to the President of the United States, April 1954), pp. 142–47, for the economic value of the Negeb.

[69]Quoted in Merlin, *op. cit.*, p. 24.

[70]There was an unwritten agreement between Jordan and Israel to' take 40 and 60% respectively. *Jerusalem post*, 14 April 1965; also *New York Times* 17 April 1965, p. 2.

particularly, by giving world-wide publicity to the Palestinian resistance, which, cleverly exploited, won for the Zionists world-wide sympathy.[71]

THE UNITED ARAB COMMAND

The United Arab Command was established at the Cairo Summit Conference in 1964. Its aim was to consolidate the Arab armed forces in the face of expansionist Zionism. However, its immediate objective was to prevent Israel from diverting the Jordan River waters. Accordingly, the forces of Jordan, Syria, and the United Arab Republic were placed under the command of the Egyptian commander, General Abdul Hakim Amer.

According to the Command's plan, each state became responsible for repulsing Israeli attacks on its own territory, unless such attacks involved the occupation of Arab land. "The Joint Defense Agreement does not mean the immediate intervention of the Egyptian army.... The raids must remain the responsibility of the various fronts, even if there were one single army."[72]

This principle was applied during the Israeli raid on the Jordanian village of Essamu on 13 November 1966, and the Israeli-Syrian aerial battle on 6 April 1967.

Though a dramatic expression of Arab military unity, the United Arab Command could not have represented any immediate danger to Israel, for it would have required many months to make the command an effective instrument against her.[73]

[71]Vance and Lauer, *op. cit.*, p. 11.

[72]*Al-Ahram*, 18 November 1967.

[73]Although Husayn expected a future Arab-Israeli confrontation, he had hoped that it would not occur before the Arabs were ready for it. In an interview with the *Der Spiegel* he reflected that "the Israeli aggression took us a year or a year and a half too early." Quoted in Draper, *op. cit.*, p. 96.

Husayn charged that since the Essamu attack, Israel had been trying to build up the Arab-Israeli differences into an East-West struggle with deliberate intention of embroiling the Big Powers. P. J. Vatikiotis, *Politics and the Military in Jordan: A Study of the Arab Legion, 1921-1957* (New York: Praeger, 1967), p. 155.

In this policy, Husayn saw a crisis which most probably would culminate in "an Israeli plot to bring about a war before the Arabs were ready.... I hope we are not moving towards a trap set for us into which we might fall." *New York Times*, 29 May 1967, p. 3.

Jordan had an important role in any Arab plan for an offensive against Israel. It had a 450 miles long border with Israel and the easiest access to the latter's vital centres. Only from the West Bank could an Arab invasion be successfully mounted and a thrust to cut Israel at her narrow waist could take place. However, Arab nationalists argued that Jordan could not be relied upon because it benefited most from the Palestine conflict with minimum military operations; that it was basically opposed to the revival of Palestine nationalism as well as to any change in the territorial *status quo* which had existed since the Rhodes Agreement of 1949. Furthermore, Jordan's very existence was dependent upon Western financial, military, and diplomatic support, it was amenable to Western pressures. This dependence limited her participation in any serious Arab action against the Zionist state. Viewing Jordan as a weak link in the Arab front, some Arab nationalists concluded that this situation could be resolved by a change in the Jordan regime. But, succinctly, this meant liquidation of the Jordan reactionary regime should precede the liberation of Palestine; "the road to Tel Aviv leads through Amman."[74]

The Jordan official stand on this question was that Jordan was the inheritor of the sorrows and aspirations of Arab Palestine, as it was the main bulwark against the Zionists. Accordingly, in the view of the Jordanian Government, Jordan had the prime responsibility to be the frontline for the defence of the rights of Arab Palestine, and that any Arab invasion of Israel should be spearheaded by the Jordanians.[75]

As late as March 1966, Nasser had taken the position that an attack

---

In September 1965, at the Casa Blanca Conference, General Amer, head of the U. A. C. told the Arab heads of state, "It would take at least four years of intensive preparations before the Arab armies would be in a position to challenge Israel." Aubrey Hodes, *Dialogue with Ishmael* (New York: Funk & Wagnals, 1968), p. 22.

In an interview with *Le Monde*, on 16 September 1966, Amer declared: "Our problem at present is less to destroy Israel than to contain her in her frontier and dissuade her from aggression on the Arab world."

[74]Y. Harkabi, "Fedayeen Action and Arab Strategy," *Adelphi Papers*, No. 53 (London: The Institute of Strategic Studies, December 1968), p. 19.

[75]Ministry of Information , *Al-Urdun Wal Quadiyyiah Al-Filistiniyyiah Wal-Alaqat Al-Arabiyyiah* (Amman: n. d.), p. 29. See also *Al-Husayn Ibn Talal* (n p., 1957), p. 60.

on Israel from the south was militarily not possible. An attack must come from the east, from the territories of Syria and Jordan. In an interview with the Lebanese newspaper *Al-Hawadith* on 26 March 1966, Nasser declared:

> We could annihilate Israel in twelve days were the Arab states to form a united front. Any attack on Israel from the south is not possible from a military viewpoint. Israel can be attacked only from the territory of Jordan and Syria. But conditions in Jordan and Syria have to be in order so that we in Egypt can be sure we would not be stabbed in the back as in 1948.[76]

Nasser held the position that only unifying and organizing the Arab armies into one unit could prevent Zionist aggression and that a united Arab command could not be effective unless the forces of one Arab state could operate freely and fight in the territory of any other Arab country.

The Israel attack on the border village of Essamu, which ostensibly was aimed at the commando bases in that town, was out of proportion to the objective. Husayn's failure to retaliate resulted in demonstrations and riots throughout Jordan, and the government was urged to arm border villages. For several weeks, the monarchy was seriously threatened, and Husayn's position was weakened within Jordan and within the Arab world.[77] The raid made it more difficult for Husayn to continue his moderate policy towards the Zionists.[78]

In response to the Essamu incident, the Arab League Defence Council met in early December 1966, and unanimously agreed that Iraq and Saudi Arabia should advance troops to Jordan to help strengthen its defences. However, this was prevented for two reasons: one, Husayn feared that the presence of these military contingents might be used to intervene in Jordan's internal affairs, and they might serve as a pretext for an Israeli attack. Two, the Israeli government warned that it would not tolerate the stationing of troops in Jordan from other Arab countries as it did in 1956.

These influences climaxed in Husayn's declaration that his agreement to accept outside military assistance was dependent upon two

---

[76] *Al-Hawadith* (Beirut), 26 March 1966.

[77] *New York Times*, 20 November 1966, pp. 24-49.

[78] Khouri, *op. cit.*, p. 235. Husayn disclosed that the incidents were fabricated o create a case for retaliation. *New York Times*, 28 May 1967.

conditions: one, Jordan must be faced with an immediate military threat from Israel; two, Egypt must request the withdrawal of the United Nations Emergency Force and replace them with the Egyptian troops fighting in Yemen.[79]

Thus, inter-Arab conflicts, particularly, the Husayn-Nasser rivalry, prevented the realization of the Nasser plan: the creation of an integrated Arab army which could operate from any Arab territory for the express objective of halting Israeli aggression, and eliminating Zionist expansionist policy. Jordan's strategic importance in such a plan was paramount in view of the fact that its cease-fire line with Israel extended over a 450-mile long border and the greatest length of it almost cuts through densely populated areas of Israel. Another fact was that the salient at Latrun and Qalqilia were but fifteen miles from the sea, which placed Tel Aviv within shelling range. In addition, any Arab pincer attack from Jordan could result in cutting the Zionist state into two parts disrupting its lines of communication, which could result in a decisive victory for the Arabs.[80] A third fact was that unlike the situation in Sinai, no expanse of desert or long line of communications separated either Syria or Jordan from Israel, a tactical necessity for the Arabs.

Only when Husayn became convinced that the Zionist threat to his country was imminent, did he consent to the entry of Arab forces into Jordan and requested the reactivation of the United Arab Command.

Jordan's position was that all the Arab states should be exposed to the Israeli borders, so that the pressure on Jordan be minimized.[81]

---

[79]*Ibid.* Jordan accused the U.A.R. of failing to send its air force to defend Essamu. The U. A. R.'s reply was that it had no long-range bombers for such a mission, and blamed Husayn for his refusal to permit the armies and the air-forces of the Arab Command to be stationed in Jordan.

Most Arab governments were of the opinion that Jordan had accepted the League Council decision only to play a trick, to intimidate Egypt into withdrawing its forces from Yemen. Others accused Husayn of sabotaging Arab defence plans.

[80]Glubb, *op. cit.*, p. 132.

General Glubb, commander of the Jordan Army, was of the opinion that, as long as Jordan cooperated with the Arab states, its front lines near the waist-line of Israel prevented the latter from mounting any attack upon any Arab country. *Ibid.*, p. 244.

[81]Iraq declined Jordan's offer to allow Iraqi troops to be stationed in Jordan, declaring that the offer "has come too late." Husayn had refused entry to Arab

With this in mind, Jordan and Saudi Arabia accused Egypt of having become "a pane of glass" hiding behind the U.N.E.F. shield. Jordan's Prime Minister Wasfi At-Tall accused Nasser of having entered into a "gentleman's agreement" with Ben Gurion in setting up a buffer patrolled by the U.N.E.F.[82]

> The whole question of the U.N.E.F. has been brought up by Jordan in the Arab Defence Council where Jordan has been under heavy pressure to admit foreign troops to defend the country against Israeli attacks.

> Jordan responded by insisting that other Arab states also go on a war footing for the battle with Israel and specifically Egypt was asked to get rid of the U.N.E.F. so that the Egyptian army—the biggest in the Arab World—can take part in the battle.

> The Egyptian response has been that the U.N. force was symbolic (it numbered about 3,000 men) and would have no effect whatsoever if it tried to stop Egyptian army movements.[83]

As border incidents became more intense, particularly, on the Syrian sector which resulted in an aerial battle in which seven Syrian jets were downed on 7 April, Husayn declared that the situation looked serious and feared that "Israel and Zionism might succeed in setting off an explosion."[84] Aggression on Syria could be followed by others on Jordan. Husayn's position following the Essamu affair resulted in his further alienation from the Arab states. Since the moral and political support which he enjoyed outside the Arab world had also waned, he felt isolated. At this point, he reversed his policy, deciding on joining the Arabs for good or for worse. Under these circumstances, Husayn came to the conclusion that the Arabs, in order to face the common enemy, must achieve unity at all costs: "It would be a great tragedy if we were not able to face the threat

---

troops after the Essamu incident in December 1966, as advised by the League's Council. *New York Times*, 25 May 1967; also see Vance and Lauer, *op. cit.*, p. 39.

[82]*New York Times*, 21 May 1967, IV, p. 1. ; also Copeland, *op. cit.*, p. 280.
[83]*Washington Post.*, 8 January, 1967.
[84]*New York Times*, 29 May 1967, p. 3.

as one. This is the time when we feel that our quarrels and differences are put aside."[85]

In an interview with the *New York Times,* Husayn declared that, should the war result in the defeat of the U.A.R., "Our position here is finished."[86] Jordan would inevitably be attacked because "Israel views the Arab World as one."[87]

Earlier, Husayn had refused to allow any Arab armies to enter Jordan. However, after realizing the extent of the enemy threat, he requested such forces to enter Jordan, declaring "but now things are serious, [so] that we need all the help we can get."[88] As late as May 29, just one day before his signing of the Pact in Cairo, Husayn declared: "Even at this time I am trying to establish a link with all our brethren in the Arab World to meet this threat to our future. If things do go terribly wrong, I expect help from anywhere."[89]

In Husayn's view, political unity was unattainable under the prevalent conditions, but military unity was feasible. To head off further Zionist expansion of Israel's geographical frontier, reactivation of the United Arab Command was the answer. The major goals of the U.A.C. were:

> ...Re-establishing a balance between Arab and Israeli forces in three years allotted. To mean anything, this balance had to give the Arabs a slight superiority in order to make the Israelis stop and think and to discourage them from planning any kind of military adventure.[90]

The idea of the U.A.C. caused the Israeli leadership and its press to become increasingly concerned about the planned military strength in the Arab states. Husayn was reportedly planning on doubling the strength of his army and an increase in his air force.[91] In this connection, the Israeli Chief of staff, General Rabin, declared that "If this increase really materialized, Israel would have no choice but to reappraise some of its basic policies toward Jordan."[92]

[85]*Ibid.*
[86]*Ibid.*
[87]*Ibid.*; also Vance and Lauer, *op. cit.,* p. 35.
[88]*Ibid.*
[89]*Ibid.*
[90]Vance and Lauer, *op. cit.,* p. 17.
[91]*Ibid.*, p. 18.
[92]Merlin, *op. cit.,* p. 24.

THE HUSAYN-NASSER PACT OF 30 MAY 1967

Although Jordan's security, unlike Syria's, was not directly threatened at the time of the closing of the Straits, she, nevertheless, could not stay out of the conflict for the following reasons: first, she was a signatory to the Arab defence pact of 1964, which had never been revoked despite the frequent disagreements among the Arab states which rendered the Pact unoperational. The adherence of Jordan to the Syria-U.A.R. Pact was almost inevitable because any Israeli military initiative of a serious nature would involve the three Arab governments jointly. Under the legal dictum of *Pacta sunt servanda*, it would have been just as inappropriate and unlikely for Jordan and Syria not to come to the assistance of the U.A.R., as it would have been for the United Kingdom and France to abandon Poland to the German invasion of 1939.

Second, Jordan constituted the "center of gravity" in the Arab world in regard to occupied Palestine. Convinced that Israel was the main and permanent threat to his kingdom, and well aware that "Tel Aviv's principal objective was to occupy the West Bank of the Jordan,"[93] Husayn came to the conclusion that it was best for Jordan to join the pact in order to strengthen its position against another, Essamu.[94]

With 450 miles of firing line, Jordan could not stand alone separated from Arab cooperation, Arab support, and Arab sympathy, no matter how long foreign assistance was extended. As long as Jordan's borders were exposed to the Zionist front, to an enemy that initiated offensive action, and which could occupy Jordan territory, Jordan felt threatened and insecure.

As long as there is Zionist ambition in the Arab part of Jerusalem, no Rhodes Agreement, not a thousand treaties like that of Rhodes, are capable of preventing the Zionists from violating the truce line

[93]Ministry of Information , *Al-Urdun Wal, Qadiyyiah Al-Filistiniyyiah Wal-Alaqat Al-Arabiyyiah* (Amman: n. d.), p. 35.

[94]Winston Burdett, *Encounter in the Middle East* (New York: Atheneum, 1969), p. 291.

To this end he invited Saudi Arabia and Iraq to send reinforcements. While Saudi Arabia sent troops, "The Iraqis gave us a flat 'No!'" Vance and Lauer, *op. cit.*, p. 39.

and occupying the Arab part where the Solomon Temple and the Wailing Wall are located.[95]

The Israelis were well aware that the Arab Legion alone could not prevent their forces from occupying the West Bank, not only because of the smallness of the Jordanian army but also due to the extent of its weapons, especially the virtual absence of an air force.[96]

Third, in case of an Egyptian-Israeli confrontation, Jordan would not be excluded despite the assurances of the Western powers and Israel that it would be saved in case of an Arab defeat. From experience, it appeared Jordan would be involved, as the 1956 and 1966 incidents showed. In both cases, Jordan became the target because the Fedayeen operated from its territory.[97] The conclusion was obvious: the differences among the Arabs were significant only to the Arab camp. "To Israel, we were all alike. We were all Arabs."[98]

Fourth, since the Palestine issue was central, and Jordan's commitment was uncontestable, the "Jordanians take the Palestine question very seriously," because it affects Jordan more than the Egyptians, the Syrians, the Iraqis, or any other Arab nation. Thus, it became clear that without Jordan's cooperation, the possibility of an Israeli

[95]Nashashibi, *op. cit.*, p. 355.

[96]In 1948, Prime Minister Abul-Huda commenting on this condition said:

It is not a sign of greatness or power in a nation to have the army deprived of war planes to protect its skies and defend it against aggression.... Jordan had previously forwarded these requests to Britain, but received only promises. Abdullah sent a delegation to London to buy war planes and the delegation returned after it had bought three passenger planes.... I had seen Israeli planes invade Jordan's skies and pass over Amman almost touching the roof of the Palace. Every day, Israeli planes pass over Jordan in comfort and security as long as Israel knows the extent of the Jordan air force.

Nashashibi, *op. cit.*, p. 177.
At the time Jordan joined the pact on 30 May 1967, its air force consisted of twenty-two Hawker Hunters with sixteen pilots. Jordan was to receive thirty-six Star-fighter, F-104s, from the United States within the following fifteen months. Vance and Lauer, *op. cit.*, p. 35.

[97]The Syrian Chief of Staff, General Sweidani, in support of the Fedayeen activities said: "These activities are legal and it is not our duty to stop them, but to encourage them. We are constantly ready to act inside Jordan and inside Israel in order to defend our people and their honour. We will mobilize volunteers and will give them arms." United Nations Security Council, *Provisional Verbatum Record*, 14 October 1966, p. 13.

[98]Vance and Lauer, *op. cit.*, p. 35.

defeat would be absolutely impossible.[99]

Fifth, internally, the country needed stability. The majority of the population were Palestinians, who, although were offered citizenship and shared in the economy, were not assimilated. For two decades, they viewed the Jordan rulers with suspicion, even as traitors to their cause. They regarded Husayn as strongly pro-Western, and thus, somehow pro-Israeli. This made him anti-Nasser, their Saladin. Their suspicions were verified every time Husayn attacked Nasser and embarked on a propaganda wave against the Arab progressive regimes, considered by the Palestinians as their only hope of recovering their usurped land. In addition, Husayn, on several occasions, broke diplomatic relations with Egypt and Syria.

Economically, Jordan has been non-viable. Its economic capabilities were small and limited; half of the country is a desert and a high percentage of the population consists of unproductive refugees, who for two decades have lived under the auspices of the United Nations. The most productive economic activity in Jordan was tourism which brought in thirty-five million dollars, while, budget deficits were covered by British, then Arab, then American, then again by Arab subsidies.[100]

Because outside assistance could not last forever, and since internal factors could not guarantee the continuation of Jordan as an independent political entity, it became imperative that Husayn march in the procession of Arab nationalism, if he wished to save his position. Thus, the political currents in Jordan, such as the disturbances following the Essamu affair, popular emotions, political pressure, and even certain manoeuvres by the United States, all made it imperative for rapprochement with Nasser. Having been constantly branded by the progressive regimes as the stooge of imperialism, Husayn could not resist the pressures from Cairo, Syria, Iraq, the refugees, the Palestine Liberation Organization and the Nationalists. His move, it appears, "was a political, not a military calculation."[101] This

---

[99]*Ibid.*, p. 127.

[100]Nashashibi, *op. cit.*, p. 355.

[101]Burdett, *op. cit.*, p. 291.

From 1965 onwards the P.L.O. became established and assumed the role of an independent force. "It became a state within the Arab states." In Jordan, government restrictions on their activities, politically and militarily, were harshly imposed. This was a part of Husayn's policy to completely eliminate their raids into Israel in return for which Israel would not take

agreement enhanced Nasser's position as leader of the Arab world and strengthened his hand militarily. Another advantage was to put an end to the enmity between Nasser's socialist regime and Husayn's conservative monarchy. A third advantage was the strengthening of Husayn's position *vis-a-vis* his population who had been accusing him of "being soft on Israel." Husayn's move may have been intended to keep Nasser and Cairo-controlled P.L.O. from fomenting opposition to his rule. Thus, the agreement aimed at lessening the likelihood that the Nasserites and the P.L.O. in Jordan would try to overthrow his regime.[102]

Sixth, the U.A.C. had actually worked, as the U.A.R. came to Syria's aid and Israel had, in fact, been deterred. Impressed by Nasser's confidence in his command to the extent that he could hold his own against the aggressor, Husayn decided that he "could not be absent from a spectacular Arab victory."[103] For personal as well as tactical reasons, he decided to cooperate, for the alternative would be militarily dangerous and politically suicidal. The rising fever of nationalism presented Husayn with no other course. If the Arabs won the war and he stayed out, he would be isolated. If they lost, it would be his fault, and he would be viewed as a traitor. Thus, the signing of the pact "was simply the less of two evils."[104]

Seventh, he apparently realized that Israel was surprised by the show of Arab might and decisiveness when it was not receiving encourage-

---

punitive actions against Jordan.

As the P.L.O. threat to Husayn's regime was intensified, especially through dividing the population of the East and the West Banks, Jordan responded by declaring the P.L.O. as subversive, and illegal political party. Husayn ordered its offices to be closed, for to him the aim of the Organization was "to replace Jordan's monarchy with some other political authority." Vance and Lauer, *op. cit.*, p. 22; also James Chace, (ed.), *Conflict in the Middle East*, Vol. 40, No. 6 (New York: H. W. Wilson, 1969), p. 98.

In reply to Husayn's action, Ahmad Shukayri, head of the P.L.O. declared, "The kingdom of Jordan must become the Palestine Republic," and "the first that must be done is to station an army of the P.L.O. in Jordan." Vance and Lauer, *op. cit.*, p. 29.

[102]*New York Times*, 31 May 1967, p. 16; Vatikiotis, *op. cit.*, p. 162.

[103]Burdett, *op. cit.*, p. 291. "The proof of this is that Nasser never called on us. It was we who called on him." Vance and Lauer, *op. cit.*, p. 49; Vatikiotis, *op. cit.*, p. 163.

[04]*New York Times*, April 7, 1968, p. 130.

ment from Washington which counselled reason and negotiations rather than fighting.[105]

Eighth, Husayn's policy, ever since he came to power, had been to avoid the mistakes of Abdullah who unilaterally disconnected himself from the rest of the Arab public opinion. To Husayn, therefore, Jordan's destiny was imperatively connected with that of the entire Arab nation.[106] To that end, cooperation became a must, especially when dealing with the Zionist threat. Being a man of honour with ancestral pride, it was better to go down as a loyal Arab in victory or defeat.[107]

In view of the deteriorating military situation which resulted from Israel's large-scale raid on Essamu, and the Syrian-Israeli air battle on 7 April, Husayn anticipated possible confrontation with the opposing superior force, which he alone could not possibly repel.[108] To him, it became absolutely essential that the United Arab Command be revitalized.[109] Thus, a pact similar to that between Syria and the U.A.R. was signed by Husayn and Nasser on May 30.

While the U.A.R. was to be the mainstay of the United Command in view of its greater strength, the position of Jordan was to be secondary. "We Jordanians tried to pull our weight as a diversion, thus minimizing the damage when war came. This was the plan, because unlike Israel, the Arabs were without a unified plan.[110] "All we had in Jordan was a plan for defence."[111]

---

[105]Burdett, *op. cit.*, p. 290.

[106]*Al-Urdun Wal Qadiyyiah Al-Filistiniyyiah Wal-Alaqat Al-Arabiyyiah*, p. 3.

[107]Burdett. *op. cit.*, p. 291.

To an interviewer, Husayn said: "How could I face my people and the Arab Legion if I ever forgot the oath I made to them: Jordan acknowledges the brotherhood that links together all the people of the great Arab nation. Jordan is but a part of the Arab nation and the Arab Legion is but one of its armies." *New York Times*, 7 April 1968, p. 130

The Pact was in accordance with the Arabic proverb, "My brother and I will fight my cousin, but my brother, my cousin, and I, will fight the outsider."

[108]Six Syrian MiGs were brought down in one hour. Vance and Lauer, *op. cit.*, p. 11.

[109]*Ibid.*, p. 45.

Due to disagreements after the Summit in 1964, relations among the Arab States deteriorated and the Pact was put out of commission.

[110]*Ibid.*, p. 48.

[111]*Ibid.*, p. 56.

Jordan, since Abdullah's reign, had experienced frightful indecision in political direction. It had been under the stress of internal difficulties: economic and political, and under constant external threat from a relentless enemy whose unlimited objectives included the occupation of Jordan's territories. Unable to stand alone and having been in cross-currents of inter-Arab conflicts, Jordan changed allies as circumstance dictated: once with Iraq, once with the Saudis, once with the Arab nationalists, once signing the Defence Pact, trying to sign the Baghdad Pact, dismissing Glubb, retaining British officers in the army, then once attacking Israel and once Nasser, once to the right and once to the left. What is the secret? The secret is that Jordan did not know where it was and what it wanted. "I mean, the Jordan rulers."[112] It was evident that "the events that dictated the policies of London and Washington, found their echoes falling in Amman."[113]

Perhaps, desiring to liberate himself from the subordinate and extremely dangerous circumstances in which he found himself and his country engulfed—dictation from certain Western Powers under whose shadow he was sustained, the clear and immediate threat of expansionist Zionism, and the Arab Cold War—Husayn decided to plunge into the international arena as an equal partner. This culminated in his calling on Nasser in Cairo and signing the Defence Pact on 30 May.

Husayn signed the pact after Israel's mobilization. By joining the Pact, he agreed to open the borders of Jordan to Iraqi, Syrian, and Egyptian forces and to allow the P.L.O. to operate freely in his territory. The Pact placed his army under the operational command of an Egyptian General. The sudden revival of the U.A.C. meant one thing to the Zionists: the Arabs had decided to attack. The Husayn-Nasser agreement settled the internal debate between "hawks" and "doves" in Israel.[114]

JORDAN'S ROLE IN THE 1967 WAR

On June 5, an all-out Israeli air and land attack was conducted against Egypt. After the start of the fighting, Eshkol sent an ultimatum

[112] Nashashibi, *op. cit.*, p. 356.
[113] *Ibid.*, p. 357.
[114] Hodes, *op. cit.* p. 90.

to Husayn through General Bull, chief of the U.N. Truce Supervisory Organization, in which he summarily told Husayn that operations had started against the U.A.R. and added that, if Jordan did not intervene, it would suffer no consequences. The message read:

> We shall not initiate any action whatsoever against Jordan. However, should Jordan open hostilities, we shall react with all our might, and he [King Husayn] will have to bear the full responsibility for all the consequences.[115]

Infuriated at such an ultimatum, Husayn remarked, "Did the Israelis think that Jordan was a nation of desert mice ?"[116] Husayn replied to General Bull, "They started the battle. Well, they are receiving our reply by air."[117]

The Zionists claim that Jordan could have stayed out of hostilities, especially after an ultimatum was delivered to him. To Husayn, this was inconceivable since it was imperative that Jordan should come to the aid of her ally, the U.A.R.

Israel's surprise at Jordan's involvement can be attributed to either inattention or to duplicity, particularly, since Israel considered as inevitable two or three fronts, should war come.[118] This policy was

---

[115]Draper, op. cit., p. 115.

[116]New York Times, April 7, 1968, p. 131.

Brigadier General Aluf Uzzi Narkis, commander of the front facing Jordan stated in a press conference in Tel Aviv on 13 June 1967, that the Zionists had hoped that "King Husayn would limit his participation in this war to symbolic air and artillary attacks, which could have been pictured as fulfilling his obligations to Nasser under the terms of the May 30 U.A.R.-Jordan military alliance." Quoted in Richard Pfaff, Jerusalem: Keystone of an Arab-Israeli Settlement (American Enterprise Institute for Public Research, Washington, 1969), p. 34.

However, it became apparent that a unique opportunity to occupy Jerusalem and the West Bank availed itself, following the annihilation of the Egyptian airforce. Thus, Husayn's "limited participation" in the war became the pretext for conquering the West Bank.

[117]Vance and Lauer, op. cit., p. 65.

On June 7, when Husayn requested a negotiated cease-fire, Dayan answered: "We have been offering the King an opportunity to cut his losses ever since Monday morning (the 5th). Now we have 500 dead and wounded in Jerusalem, so tell him that, from now on, I'll talk to him only with the gunsights of our tanks!" Ibid.

[118]Two Zionist pilots taken prisoner by Jordan told that they had been training for a year and a half on models that were exact replicas of the objectives they each would have to attack. Ibid., p. 106.

declared on June 2 when Allon, at a rally in Tel Aviv, said: "There isn't the slightest doubt about the outcome of his war and each of its stages, and we are not forgetting the Jordan-Syrian fronts either."[119]

The Zionist ultimatum to Husayn could be interpreted as a mano-euvre to keep the Jordan forces from attacking and possibly thrusting towards the sea, thereby cutting Israel into two and disrupting its communications. To counter this, a substantial part of the Israeli army had to be deployed against the Jordan forces, thereby delaying, if not preventing, a full attack against Egypt.

To Husayn, it must have seemed that, sooner or later, a full thrust to occupy the West Bank, possibly even the East Bank, would be made. Since Husayn's decision did not give comfort to the Zionists' plans, Eban in the Security Council announced:

Jordan's responsibility...is established beyond doubt. This responsibility cannot fail to have its consequences in the peace settlement....Jordan had become the source and origin of Jerusalem's first ordeal. The inhabitants of the city can never forget this fact or fail to draw its conclusions.[120]

Another interpretation of Husayn's decision to share in the hostilities might have been based on the remote possibility of eliminating the Egyptian air force. Even if Husayn stayed out, his position would be highly precarious, and inevitably, he would have had to comply with the Zionists demands, such as ceding the West Bank, including the Old City of Jerusalem, perhaps, the irrigated land on the eastern bank of the River Jordan too. Under such circumstances, he would be in danger internally and subjugated externally. Thus, a decision to enter the war, whatever the consequences, seemed morally appropriate.

Embittered about the defeat in the so-called six-day war, Husayn said:

---

[119]*Harretz*, June 4, 1967, quoted in Howard Kock, "June 1967: The Question of Aggression," *The Arab World*, June 1969, p. 10.

[120]Abba Eban, "Never have Freedom and International Morality Been so Righteously Protected," text of the address by Israel's Foreign Minister in the General Assembly of the U.N. 19 June 1967 (Washington: Embassy of Israel), p. 16.

I did'nt fight under real war conditions.   I never declared war on Israel and I never made war with Israel.   Naturally, I responded to each of Israel's acts of aggression in 1956, 1967, and still more recently in 1968.

A state of war has existed in the Middle East since 1948. During this period we have had an armistice, not peace.   Nor have the conditions of this armistice been easy; more often than not, they have been ruptured by the Israelis.[121]

Husayn, however puts the blame on Arab politics, as being responsible for the debacle. In particular, he blamed Syria for the delay in sending its air force which, combined with the Iraqi and Jordanian air forces, were supposed to bomb Israeli air bases in the hope of neutralizing as much as possible the enemy's air power.[122]   The King justified his military action as a "response" to a planned Israeli aggression against an ally, the U.A.R.; that Jordan did not initiate hostilities, since "a formal declaration of war in the sense of the Third Hague Convention of 1907, would naturally have meant the recognition of Israel."[123]

THE RESPONSIBILITY OF THE ZIONISTS FOR THE WAR

Prior to the conflict, Husayn-Nasser disagreements, together with

---

[121]Vance and Laeur, *op. cit.*, p. 109.

[122]*Ibid.*, p. 61.

While Israel started out with excellent intelligence, supply and communication services, and a well-planned offensive strategy and a unified command, their air-force superiority was the decisive factor in winning the war.   On the other hand, the Arabs had not had the time to unify their forces, or plan an offensive strategy. The New York Military analyst, Hanson Baldwin, testified:

> Since the vaunted superiority in numbers of the Arab armies was never brought to bear on the fighting front, Israel, probably, had an over-all numerical superiority in troops, actually involved and a clear-cut superiority in fire power and mobility in the actual battles.... Many of the 2,000 tanks and self-propelled guns used by the principal Arab armies do not appear to have been engaged at all....

New York Times, 8 June 1967.

[123]Shabati Rosenne, "Directions for the Middle East Settlement—Some Underlying Legal Problems," *Law and Contemporary Problems*, Duke University School of Law, Vol. XXXIII, No. 1 (Winter, 1968), p. 50.

Arab disunity, enhanced Israel's security.[124] But Israel's armed attacks on border villages and the subsequent threatening statements by high Zionist officials regarding the Arab proposals for diverting the River Jordan altered the picture. The Arabs, in order to discourage an Israeli attack, entered into a military alliance.[125]

According to the U.N. observers, the raid on Essamu resulted in eighteen soldiers and civilians killed, and fifty-four wounded. Many buildings were demolished. The fact that moderate Jordan was the target of retaliation seemed ill-judged to most of the world.[126]

By a vote of 14-0-1, the Security Council censured Israel for the large-scale military action in violation of the armistice agreement, and warned against repetition of such acts.[127] Similarly, the severe retaliation in the air over Syria and Jordan was disproportionate in size and effects, and increased the pressure on Nasser to intervene if his ally, Syria, was attacked. An American diplomat commented:

It is difficult to see how an Israeli leader could have failed to foresee that such repeated massive reprisals must eventually place the leader of the Arab coalition (Nasser) in a position where he would have to respond.[128]

To Nasser, the most prestigious leader of progressive Arab nationalism, the overthrow of the Ba'ath government in Syria by an Israeli attack would seriously upset the balance of power of the Middle East in favour of Zionism and its allies, the conservative regimes of colonialism.[129]

By closing the straits and concentrating some of his troops in Sinai, Nasser was discharging his obligation to his ally, Syria. The Russians informed Nasser that the Israelis had timed the swift strike at Syria for the end of May "in order to crush it and then carry the fighting over into the territory of the U.A.R."[130] The *New York Times*

[124]As late as 22 January 1967, Husayn withdrew his ambassador to Cairo when Nasser assailed him for preventing the Arab armies from entering Jordan. Draper, *op. cit.*, p. 44.

[125]Khouri, *op. cit.*, p. 281.

[126]Yost, *op. cit.*, p. 305.

[127]*Ibid.*, New Zealand abstained.

[128]*Ibid.*, p. 319.

[129]Sharabi, *op. cit.*, p. 23.

[130]*Ibid.*

reported on 12 May that Israeli leadership had decided that the use
of force against Syria "May be the only way to curtail increasing
terrorism." The *Jerusalem Post* in an article entitled "It May Be
Time to Act Against Syria" reported that the Minister of Trans-
port, Moshe Carmel, one of the leaders of the Ahdut Haavoda Party,
suggested that "the time may have come to act vigorously against
Syria whatever her relations with the Soviet Union."[131]

By signing the pact with Husayn, Nasser hoped that the Israeli
threat to attack Syria had abated sufficiently to allow him to
de-escalate Egyptian military pressure.[132] According to Eric Rouleau,
Cairo correspondent for *Le Monde*: "All that the U.A.R. now
required to withdraw its troops from the frontier was public declaration by Israel renouncing its intention to attack Syria."[133]

To the Zionists, the signing of the pact by Husayn completed the
encirclement of Israel by hostile states. While Nasser's action
was defensive in nature to remove the threat of invasion of his ally,
Syria, to the Zionists it meant that if war started, the conflict would
be waged all along their extensive frontier.[134]

Arab-Israeli relations were based on the following assumptions:
one, due to Arab encirclement, and to a large measure, the presence
of Jordanian forces in close vicinity of populated centres, particularly
in the central sector and Jerusalem, the entire country became a

---

An announcement by *Tass* on May 23 stated:

The Foreign Affairs and Security Committee of the Knesset have accorded
the Cabinet on 9 May, special powers to carry out war operations against
Syria. Israeli forces concentrating on the Syrian border have been put in a
state of alert for war. General mobilization has also been proclaimed in the
country....

Cited in a speech in the General Assembly in June 1967 by Abba Eban.
[131]*Jerusalem Post*, 23 March 1967.
[132]Sharabi, *op. cit.*, p. 24.
In reply to a question by British M.P., Christopher Mayhew, on 2 June 1967,
"And if they don't attack, will you let them alone ?" Nasser said, "Yes we will
leave them alone. We have no intention of attacking Israel." Similar assurances
were repeatedly given to the U.S. by the highest Egyptian authorities (Yost,
op. cit., p. 317). Haikal of *Al-Ahram* said, "Even if Egypt left Israel alone, Israel
would not leave Egypt alone. Israel can only feel secure with Egypt impotent,
wounded under its feet, bleeding and near to death. ' Prittie, *op. cit.*, p. 312.
[133]Sharabi, *op. cit.*, p. 26.
[134]Avnery, *op. cit.*, p. 30.

frontier. Two, the state, therefore, lived under the shadow of destruction. Three, the existence of the Resistance Organizations which waged guerilla warfare created unrest. Four, to liquidate these dangerous conditions, the alternative policy of Israel was to turn the armistice agreement into a final peace. However, since peace was unattainable under normal conditions, a policy of imposing peace through military superiority was, therefore, adopted. A pre-emptive strike, it was calculated, would eventually bring the adversary to the peace table.

As to the Jordanians, although under the command of a U.A.C. general, they could not mount an offensive. They had a negligible air force and their troops had been defensively deployed since 1948— a policy which General Glubb had implemented. However, it was the introduction of Iraqi, Syrian and Egyptian forces into Jordan's territory that the Israeli leaders had always worried about, not just the arrival of the Egyptian General.[135]

"If Husayn thought by May 30 that he could not afford to stay out of Nasser's war, Israel's reaction was not too different."[136] Strategically, Israel has always been fearful of encirclement. A British study in 1965 revealed that,

> whereas Israel fighting on narrow fronts might be able to hold both Egyptians and Syrians at once, even against superior odds, she would be extremely vulnerable to a simultaneous broad-fronted attack from Jordan which would quickly cut her communications between north and south.[137]

The theory of encirclement adopted by Ben Gurion led to organized raids between 1953 and 1956, under the direction of Dayan's "units 101" and culminated in the Sinai invasion in October 1956.[138] "It is this doctrine that moved the army to war on 5 June 1967, when Dayan became defence minister."[139]

[135]Kerr, *The Middle East Conflict*, p. 30.

[136]Draper, *op. cit.*, p. 97.

[137]David Wood, "The Middle East and the Arab World: The Military Context," *Adelphi Papers* No. 20 (London: The Institute of Strategic Studies, July 1965), p. 5.

[138]Special units 101, for retaliatory raids such as the one on Kibya, in which 40 houses were destroyed and 50 civilians were killed. See Avnery, *op. cit.*, p. 108.

[139]Perlmutter, *op. cit.*, p. 626.

Striving to avoid war, Nasser requested reactivating the Egyptian-Israeli Armistice Commission, which the Zionists boycotted since 1956, and he proposed open discussion with the World Powers concerning the Palestine problem. He came to consider the totality of the question rather than the individual aspects, such as straits, commandoes or even the attack on Syria.[140] "Nasser's intention was not to restore the *status quo ante bellum*, obtained before the Israeli attack of 1956, but that of 1948."[141] He had already told the United States that he "was prepared to let all ships, even those carrying oil, pass through the Straits of Elat, as long as none of them carried the Israeli flag."[142]

The Armistice Commission, like the U.N., was an institution held in great contempt by the Zionists.[143] The Sinai invasion of 1956 caused the Armistice machinery to break down. Thus, the United Nations Emergency Force was created to replace the Armistice machinery.

The stationing of the U.N.E.F. on the Egyptian side of the border was a bilateral agreement between the U.N. Secretary-General and the Egyptian government. The force, accordingly, could be withdrawn at the request of the host nation.[144] Although relative quiet reigned on the frontier, the absence of progress towards a settlement of outstanding questions continued. Realizing this, the Secretary-General cautioned:

It is an unhappy statement to have to make, but it is a reality all too apparent that, despite almost a decade of relative quiet along the long line on which the U.N.E.F. is deployed, relations between the peoples on the opposite sides of the line are such that if the United Nations buffer should be removed, serious fighting would, quite likely, soon be resumed.[145]

[140]Sharabi, *op. cit.*, p. 25.

[141]*Ibid.*; also *New York Times*, 29 May 1967, p. 1.

[142]Avnery, *op. cit.*, p. 30.

[143]Khouri, *op. cit.*, p. 236.

[144]The confusion over the legal basis for U.N.E.F. operations was increased in 1967. The views of the present Secretary-General are contained in his report on the withdrawal of the force. United Nations, *G.A.O.R.*, Fifth Emergency Special Session, Annexes Agenda, Item No. 5, pp. 4, 9; and U.N. Document A/6730, 1967 .

[145]The Secretary-General indicated that the continued presence of the U.N.

As Nasser became a target for ridicule by the heads of the Arab states who accused him of hiding behind the shield of the United Nations Emergency Force, there was no alternative to requesting the withdrawal of the force. In an effort to prevent confrontation, the Secretary-General offered to station the U.N.E.F. on the Israeli side of the truce line. His offer was rejected.[146] By removing the U.N.E.F., the Israeli strategy had been less interested in thwarting an Egyptian attack than to make sure that U.N. forces did not affect her ability to strike at her neighbours from a short distance whenever she chose. On the other hand, had the Israeli leaders really believed that Israel's survival was at stake, they could have easily precluded an Arab invasion by accepting U Thant's appeal to station the U.N.E.F. on their side of the Armistice line.[147] Israel's goal had been to destroy the Arab military manpower and military equipment before the Arabs had an opportunity to unify their forces and develop a superior capability.[148]

The Israelis were convinced that the Middle East arms race would ultimately lead to a balance in favour of the Arabs. This, in the Israeli view, required 'pre-emptive' action to place Israel in a strong military position guaranteeing Israeli existence.[149]

Conditions were favourable, indeed. Egypt deployed its forces according to a defensive plan.[150] Militarily, such deployment was erroneous, since the units were isolated from each other by difficult terrain, creating gaps through which the enemy did in fact penetrate, surprise, and surround the Egyptian forces with unbelievable efficiency.[151] The same mistake was committed by the Syrian and Jordanian military tacticians. Thus, the defensive plan devised

---

E.F. as a buffer might contribute to prolonging the efforts towards a settlement. U.N.E.F. Report of Secretary-General, 21 U.N., *G.A.O.R.* Annexes, Agenda Item 21, p. 2, U.N. Document A/6406, 1966.

[146]Khouri, *op. cit.,* p. 282.

[147]*Ibid.*

[148]*Ibid.*

[149]James F. Sams, "U.S. Policy and the Middle East Crisis," *Middle East Forum,* Vol. XLIII, No. 2 (1967), p. 53.

[150]Mohammad Haykal, "This is the Actual Crisis," *Al-Ahram,* 19 June 1970, p. 3.

[151]*Ibid.*

before the June War "was an omen for an unavoidable defeat."[152]

The news agencies reported a declaration by Israeli military leaders regarding the deployment of the Arab force: "One look at the map of deployment of the Egyptian forces in the front persuades every one of us that before him was a unique opportunity which may never occur again to administer a smashing blow to the Egyptian forces."[153]

At Washington, Eban, in a meeting with Secretary of State Rusk and Secretary of Defence McNamara, General Earl Wheeler, Chairman of the Joint Chiefs of Staff, gave his official estimate of the Defence Department. Eban related:

General Wheeler was called in to join the meeting and he gave the official evaluation. He had no information of any Egyptian intention to attack; he declared, if anything, it was the Israeli army that was pressing to begin hostilities. And he repeated that in the Pentagon's view, Israel had nothing to fear. Her army was in their estimation far superior to that of Egypt.[154]

This evaluation was shared by the C.I.A. Director, Richard Helms, i.e. an Israeli initiative in the air against the Arabs would result in a victory in three to four days.[155]

The Arab plan was defensive, and no war was contemplated or planned. In a report from Cairo by James Reston of the *New York Times*, he stated that the U.A.R. did not wish war and was "certainly not ready for war" and had been making no preparations within the country itself.[156]

In an interview with *Le Monde*, General Izhaq Rabin, Chief of the Israeli General Staff, conceded to the afore-mentioned analysis by declaring: "I don't believe that Nasser wanted war. The two divisions he sent into Sinai on May 14 would not have been enough to unleash an offensive against Israel. He knew it and we knew it."[157]

[152]*Ibid.*

[153]*Ibid.*

[154]David Kimche and Dan Bawly, *The Sand Storm: The Arab-Israeli War of 1967* (New York: Stein and Day, 1968), p. 126.

[155]*Ibid.*, p. 13; *L' Oriente*, 13 June 1967.

[156]*New York Times*, 4 and 5 June 1967.

[157]*Jerusalem Post*, 29 February 1968.

For Israel, therefore, the issue was not one of security. It became evident that her real intention was not to defuse the crisis but to choose the appropriate moment to strike, as favourable conditions prevailed.[158] Thus, a pre-emptive strike to cripple the Arab air forces was administered. It was of the Pearl Harbour variety with devastating results.[159]

On the ideological side, *Eretz Israel* (Greater Israel), which entailed territorial acquisition and the "ingathering" of the Jews from diaspora through accelerated immigration, has been for a long time the guiding principle of the official policy of the Zionist state.

From the Israeli standpoint, the anticipated rewards of military action by far exceeded those of diplomatic negotiations. Armed with highly sophisticated intelligence, with analysis of the over-all political and military situation of the Arab states, with favourable world opinion, and with a disunited and neutralized United Nations, it acted not spontaneously, but calmly.[160]

But, if the Zionist aim was to teach Egypt a lesson by annihilating its air force, why go on to seize the Jordan West Bank and the Syrian Heights? The answer can logically be found in the fact that the temptation was overwhelming to make the most of the chance of a lifetime. However limited its ambitions were, the Zionist state could only defend itself by taking the offensive action and could only safeguard its territory by expanding it.[161]

To the military-minded Zionists, this gave a pretext to strike first:

Our security is based, first of all, on our ability, by the prestige of our army, to deter any enemy from threatening our existence. And secondly, if this deterrent fails, to hit first and win quickly. Thereby avoiding any invasion of our constricted territory.[162]

[158]Sharabi, *op. cit.*, p. 26.

[159]Copeland, *op. cit.*, p. 282.

[160]Sharabi, *op. cit.*, p. 26.

Al-Ahram reported that *Newsweek* said that Israeli intelligence was in co-operation with the intelligence of the Maghrib, and that led to, or was the main reason for, the Arab defeat in 1967 because Israeli intelligence was very effective in getting the secret information of the Rabat Arab Summit. *Al-Ahram* 28 February 1967. See also Vance and Lauer, *op. cit.*, p. 106.

[161]Kerr. *op. cit.*, p. 29.

[162]Avnery, *op. cit.*, p. 23.

Having mobilized the entire population and allowing the economy to come to a halt, Israel's only alternative was to go to war.

If we back down now, every Arab will believe that our military force is a bluff. If this belief spreads, there is nothing to hold back the Arabs from starting a guerilla war along all our fronts, cutting off the Jordan waters, and doing anything else they like. So we had better fight now.[163]

By the spring of 1967, it was clear that neither the U.A.R. alone nor the United Arab Command were in a position to attack Israel or to withstand a surprise assault.[164] But, world public opinion was led to believe otherwise. The skilful Zionist propaganda, as always, had simplified the issue to an Israeli "David" versus an Arabian "Goliath."

Thus, the Zionists came to the conclusion that the time was right to effect a crippling blow to the combined Arab force. This decision, like that of 1956, was for "a preventive war" to render the United Arab Command inoperative.[165] At the same time, it aimed at effectively eliminating the Palestine Resistance Movement. On 29 May 1967, Eshkol gave an assessment of Israel's military capability and announced, "The Israeli defense forces are capable today of meeting any test with the same capacity that they demonstrated in the past."[166] This estimate was based on the declaration by Rabin on March 24 when he said that the arms balance had definitely tipped in favour of Israel and it would continue to be so in the future. Significantly, he added that there was no chance for a peace settlement with the Arabs and that, in case of war, Israel would

---

[163]*Ibid.*, p. 26.

[164]Michael Howard and Robert Hunter, "Israel and the Arabs, the Crisis of 1967," *Adelphi Papers,* No. 41 (London: The Institute of Strategic Studies, October 1967), p. 11. Also see Allen Horton, "The Arab-Israeli Conflict of June 1967," *American University's Field Staff,* Vol. XIII, No. 2, p. 4.

[165]Israel had been planning for the 1967 War, long before it took place. Israel's Chief of Staff, Rabin, was quoted as having stated, as early as 1965, that Israel would have to strike first while she was still able "to disrupt any Arab time-table for war against us." George de Carvahlo, "Desperate Arab-Israel Struggle for Scarce Water: An Ancient Hatred Builds Toward War," *Life,* 8 June 1965, p. 50.

[166]*Israel Digest,* 2 June 1967, a speech on 29 May 1967.

win.[167]

This confidence in military capability led Eshkol to his threatening statement on May 19 in which he said:

We shall hit when, where, and how we choose....Israel will continue to take action to prevent any and all attempts to perpetuate sabotage within her territory. Israel will continue to foil every scheme to divert the sources of the Jordan River, and will defend its rights to free navigation in the Red Sea.[168]

THE AFTERMATH OF THE WAR

The victory accomplished the following for the Zionists: one, it destroyed large amounts of Arab military equipment, and, in so doing, it was able to alter the balance of power, at least, for the time being.[169] Two, the Straits were opened. Three, Egypt was prevented from using the Canal as a source of revenue.[170]   This resulted in more dependence on the U.S.S.R.   Four, occupation of the West Bank added coveted, strategically and agriculturally valuable territory, and, at the same time, Israeli victory increased Arab hatred which has and will continue to be a major factor of Israel's internal as well as external security.   Five, it regained emotional, economic, and political support from world Jewry, and enabled her to strengthen ties with the United States.   Six, it enhanced Israel's self-confidence,

[167]*Ibid.,* 7 April 1967.

[168]Howard and Hunter, *op. cit.,* p. 14.

The *New York Times* seemed to indicate that Israeli threats and declarations were backed by certain Senate leaders.   On 6 June, Senators Dirkson and Javits announced "Legally, we are an ally of Israel." *New York Times* 7 June 1967, p. 18.

[169]"There were those who thought that Israel's 1967 blitzkrieg had won her 10 years of peace, but, in fact, her strategic position, never brilliant was, only marginally improved, since her power was the key to the situation." Peter Young, *The Israeli Campaign , 1967* (London: Kimber, 1967), p. 185.

There was also the belief that "Israel's victory had substantially eased its defence problems.   It had not." Prittie, *op. cit.,* p. 284.

[170]Dayan said that "Egypt does not want the Suez Canal to operate while we are sitting on the east bank.   It might turn into a permanent arrangement.... While Cairo wants to have us withdraw, any attempt to force such a withdrawal would mean war." *New York Times,* 5 November 1968, p. 9.

heightened the morale and prestige of the army, and magnified its feeling of superiority. Seven, the territory under its control was quadrupled, thus adding to her security by removing the military threat of the Arab armies from the population centres. The new borders gave Israel every strategic advantage, its military ever sought. The expansion after the 1967 War has shortened the Jordanian border, and the military threat of Jordan was minimized since the Jordan forces were pushed back to the River where they are remote from Israeli settlements. In the south, the Negeb and Sinai separate Jordan and the U.A.R. forces from population centres as does the occupation of the Golan Heights. The Zionists wanted the territory, but not the inhabitants, as Eshkol stated, "We received a beautiful dowry, but unfortunately we got the bride."[171] Eight, the result placed her in a strong bargaining position to demand a peace treaty on her own terms.

The war brought no solutions to the basic problems since not all of its objectives were obtained. Nasser, Husayn and the Syrian President Attasi continued in power and emerged more united.

During the course of the June War, Nasser's attitude toward Jordan and myself had changed completely. Perhaps, he learned the truth about us, as we did about him.

As a result of our several meetings...his point of view turned out to be quite similar to mine....We want to make common cause in the diplomatic battle we were to wage and to bring about Arab unanimity in the viable solution. We agreed on this at the time of the summit conferences in Khartoum; it holds true today.[172]

The P.L.O. activities had increased to dangerous proportions in frequency, intensity, and daring. Further, the war created another major refugee problem. By occupying the West Bank and the Holy Places, in particular, Israel weakened the position of the moderates led by Husayn. By annexing all Jerusalem and insisting that it is non-negotiable, Israel minimized the chances of peace while antagonizing non-Arab Muslim countries, such as Turkey and Iran with whom it had economic and diplomatic relations.

[171]Prittie, *op. cit.*, p. 229.
[172]Vance and Lauer, *op. cit.*, p. 116.

Furthermore, as it defied the advice of the French not to strike first, Israel lost the confidence of its former close ally which stopped shipping military equipment. The position of the French Government in this regard was stated on 2 June 1967:

France is not pledged in any way or any matter to any of the states concerned. For her own part, she considers that each of these states had the right to live. But she deems that the worse would be the opening of hostilities. Consequently, the states that would be the first—wherever it might be—to take up arms will have neither her approval nor, even less, her support.[173]

However, the most consequential negative result was the breaking of relations by the Soviet Union, which assumed a pro-Arab policy and looked with suspicion on the loyalty of its Jewish nationals.

Furthermore, by renouncing the armistice agreement, claiming that only a cease-fire situation existed, Israel, in fact, invited the resumption of hostilities. In view of her military superiority, this condition is to her advantage, as she has been conducting frequent air strikes as well as military operations inside the Arab territories, under the pretext of retaliation. This situation resulted from the fact that a cease-fire is imposed by the Security Council, while an armistice agreement is considered a legal commitment by the parties themselves to end hostilities. However, despite Israel's disregard for the International Organization, the U.N. still insists that the armistice arrangement and the U.N. machinery are legally in force.[174]

As to Jordan, the loss of the entire West Bank, which constituted the backbone of the kingdom, dislocated its economy and multiplied the number of refugees on the East Bank.[175] The West Bank

---

[173]Murville, speech before the U.N., 22 June 1967., cited in *Vital Speeches*, Vol. 33, No. 19, 15 July 1967, p. 590.

[174]Khouri, *op. cit.*, p. 287.

[175]By occupying the West Bank, and the Gaza Strip, Israel also inherited one million inhabitants, whose loyalty continues to be to Jordan. The occupation government has partially solved some economic problems in the West Bank. It authorized the export of surplus agricultural products to Jordan, its original market. In the first year after the war, $16 million worth of exports reached Jordan. To that end, the occupied areas as well as Jordan have become a useful market for Israeli exports. Prittie, *op. cit.*, p. 301.

Through this commerce, Israel has fulfilled a part of its long-range policy to secure markets for its products in the Arab states. At the General Assembly,

was the most fertile and most productive part of Jordan, while tourism constituted the largest source of foreign exchange. "Most experts agree that the East Bank cannot survive without outside economic assistance.[176]

Although Jordan lost the battle, it did not lose the war. King Husayn, instead, gained popularity among the Arabs because he dared to fight in fulfilment of a Pact in defence of Arab nationalism.[177]

CONCLUSION

The Rhodes Armistice aimed at ending hostilities and was considered as a first step towards peace. However, this optimism did not materialize as the Arab-Israeli relations assumed a unique character: a state of war existed and a no-peace no-war situation persisted.

Although Jordan did not participate in the 1956 Suez War, different circumstances, however, confronted it in 1967 which dictated its involvement in the six-day war. Immediately prior to the war, Jordan's security was threatened, a situation which required an immediate response.

Israel had posed an immediate threat to the economies of Syria, Lebanon and Jordan by its plans to divert the Jordan waters. Since the Arab states were militarily unprepared to challenge the enemy, they decided on merging their armed forces under the command of an Egyptian General.

Faced with an external situation, King Husayn embarked on the

---

Eban declared this policy as his fourth principle, which he called, "open frontier." Speech on 8 October 1968. Also, see Nabil Sha'ath, "The Newly Occupied Territories," *Fateh*, 23 March 1971, p. 15.

[176]Khouri, *op. cit.*, p. 288.

At the Khartoum Summit Conference, Jordan was given an Arab subsidy of $100 million annually. The U.S.A., accordingly, ended its subsidy which lasted since 1957.

[177]Vatikiotis, *op. cit.*, p. 164.

As a result of Husayn's decision to fight, he emerged as a hero of the Arab masses and gained admiration abroad. Even Nasser, on June 9, gave him accolade by calling him "a noble and courageous man." Considering past discord between them, this public recognition changed Husayn's status in the Arab world. George Lenczowski, "Arab Bloc Realignment," *Current History* (December 1967), p. 348.

most critical decision in the history of Jordan. On 30 May 1967, he signed an alliance which would include Egypt, Syria and Iraq. The result was the six-day war and its devastating consequences to Jordan's economic, military and political positions.

Husayn's decision not to stay out, of what appeared to be an Egyptian-Israeli confrontation, was determined by several factors. The most disturbing factor was the fact that Jordan had been persistently threatened. Husayn was aware that Israel's policy was to occupy the West Bank. Only if Jordan became a member of an Arab command, would such a threat diminish. Another factor was Husayn's personality. Since Jordan was signatory to the Arab Command, it was inappropriate for him not to come to the assistance of his allies. To avoid this negative characteristic of Abdullah, and to appear as a national hero, he had no alternative. Husayn was under no illusion that the destiny of Jordan was connected with the Arab states, and that without his cooperation, elimination of Israel would be an impossibility. Even if he would not fight, he could not place obstacles before an Arab plan to conquer Palestine or, at least, limit the Zionist danger. In any case, Husayn might have decided that he could not be absent from a spectacular Arab victory from which he would benefit greatly. A fourth factor of great significance was Jordan's need for stability. Husayn's association with the West in defiance of Arab nationalism, the Arab states, and the majority of Jordan's population rendered his regime endangered. By joining the Arab venture he could alter internal and external conditions to his personal advantage: he would pacify the turbulent public opinion and appear as a hero to all. In any case, Husayn had no alternative but to take that course of action even if given assurances by Israel and the Western powers.

The 1967 War resulted in a new phase of Jordan-Israeli relations. Faced with a highly dangerous situation, Husayn was placed in an exceedingly weak position. The war resulted in the loss of the valuable productive land which Abdullah had acquired in 1948, and a new wave of refugees entered the East Bank rendering the bad economic situation intolerable. Most important, however, was the bringing of the war to the East Bank. The economic, social and military problems forced Husayn to submit an unprecedented proposal for peace. Paramount among them was the recognition of Israel as a state within secure and recognized boundaries. This was a drastic departure from the Arab's earlier position: that Israel was "Mazoumah" —an imaginary state.

Husayn's decision was further dictated by external forces, which limited his alternative courses of action. His Western allies—the U.S. and Britain—who wished to see Nasser and the Ba'ath regime in Syria fall, also became unhappy about Husayn's participation in the war, but both governments refrained from supporting Jordan's position. Furthermore, the fact that the international community—including the U.S.S.R.—had resolved that Israel "was there to stay," made any other decision impractical.

Peace had become Jordan's most urgent objective as the economic crisis ensued. The loss of the West Bank deprived Jordan from sorely needed foreign exchange. Israeli military attacks and air strikes on the East Bank rendered the irrigated land useless, thus, compounding unemployment and causing inflation which an unviable state like Jordan could not endure for long.

Husayn's efforts to reach a "Jordanian solution" were futile in view of the objection of the Arab states and due to the stand taken by the Palestine Resistance Organization, which always rejected any peace on enemy terms.

CHAPTER SIX

ISRAEL'S PEACE TERMS

At the General Assembly on 8 October 1968, Foreign Minister Abba Eban proposed nine principles by which peace in the Middle East can be achieved.

First, the establishment of peace. The situation to follow the cease-fire must be one of just and lasting peace....Peace is not just mere absence of fighting....We propose that the peace settlement be embodied in treaty form. It should lay down the precise conditions of our coexistence including an agreed map of secure and recognized boundaries....

Second, secure and recognized boundaries....We are willing to seek agreement with each Arab state on secure and recognized boundaries within the framework of a permanent peace....

Third, security agreements....The instrument establishing peace should contain a pledge of mutual non-aggression.

Fourth, open frontier....The freedom of movement now existing in the area, especially in the Israel-Jordan sector, should be maintained and developed....We should emulate the open frontier now developing within communities of states, as in parts of Western Europe (Scandinavian type frontier). Within this concept we include free-port facilities for Jordan on Israel's Mediterranean coast and mutual access to places or religious and historic association.

Fifth navigation....The arrangement for guaranteeing navigation should be unreserved, precise, concrete, and founded on absolute equality of rights and obligations between Israel and other littoral states....

Sixth, refugees. A conference of Middle-Eastern States should be convened together with the governments contributing to refugee relief and the specialized agencies of the United Nations to chart a five-year plan for the solution of the refugee problem in the framework of a lasting peace and the integration of the refugees into productive life....Under the peace settlement, joint refugee integration and rehabilitation commissions should be established in order to approve projects for refugee integration in the Middle East with regional and international aid....

Seventh, Jerusalem....Our policy is that Christian and Muslim Holy Places should become under the responsibility of those who hold them in reverence.

Eighth, acknowledgment and recognition of sovereignty and right of national life....It should be fulfilled through specific contractual agreement to be made by the governments of each Arab state...by name.

Ninth, regional cooperation....Examination of a common approach to some of the resources and means of communication in the region in an effort to lay the foundation of a Middle-Eastern community of sovereign states.[1]

THE ZIONIST-ARAB POLICY

Israel's major objective is the signing of peace treaties with the Arab states which, under international law, would be binding and would replace the cease-fire and the armistice agreement with recognized boundaries.

To the Israeli leadership, the cease-fire line and the armistice regime "have been killed by the war."[2] According to them, this regime was inadequate for the security of their state, because the 1949 armistice clearly stated in Article 4, paragraph 3, that "the conclusion of a partial or general armistice agreement does not end the state of war." Thus, the Zionist policy seeks transition from cease-fire to a negotiated settlement designed to end all acts of hostility.

Accordingly, Eban declared that apart from the cease-fire agreement, there was no valid contractual engagements. Thus, a durable edifice of relations embodied in treaties should be erected. "The old era is ended ....In our view, the transition must be from

---

[1]Embassy of Israel, *Forward to Peace* (Washington, D.C.: n.p., October, 1968), pp. 11-13.

[2]Prime Minister Golda Meir on "Meet The Press,' 28 September 1969.

It should be emphasised that Israel's continued disregard for the U.N. Armistice machinery which she boycotted precipitated almost every dispute since 1949.

suspended war to stable peace."[3]   At the Security   Council, he
said:

> We cannot return to the shattered armistice regime or any system
> of relations other than a permanent contractually binding peace
> ....The fragile armistice lines must be superseded by agreed and
> secure national boundaries. After the cease-fire lines, a permanent
> and mutually recognized territorial boundary is our only possi-
> ble destination.[4]

At the Khartoum Conference in December 1967, the Arab
states, including Jordan, emerged more moderate than before.
They decided on a political rather than on a military solution. However, they held to the principle of no recognition, no negotiation,
and no peace, until the Zionists responded to Arab demands of complete withdrawal from all territories occupied in the 1967 War.
This demand had been rejected in view of their feeling of invincibility and the resultant military superiority.

Although the Israelis had achieved a military victory, they have
not succeeded in reaching a peaceful solution to the twenty-year
conflict, particularly, recognition from the Arab states. Recognition to the Israelis is paramount because it would end all acts of
belligerency and boycotts; it opens markets with unrestricted trade
in the neighbouring Arab states; it channels the huge military expenditure to peaceful development of their state. Thus, the most
urgent item in the Zionist policy is the need for authentic recognition by the Arabs of Israel's roots in the Middle-Eastern reality.
Eban attacks the Arab leaders for their reluctance to recognize the
depth and authenticity of Israel's roots in the life, the history, the
spiritual experience and culture of the region.[5] Integrating the
Zionist state in the area had been of vital importance, as Foreign
Minister Sharette had declared: "It is a cardinal principle of our

---

[3]*New York Times*, 4 October 1967, p. 1.

[4]Israel Information Service, *From a State of War to a State of Peace* (New
York: n.p., November, 1967), p. 10.

[5]Israel Information Service, *Not Backward to Belligerency But Forward
to Peace* (New York: n.p., June 1967), p. 12.; also *New York Times* and *London
Times*, 4 June, 1953.

While Dulles gave credence to Arab fears of "expansionist Zionism," he urged
Israel to cease considering itself an alien state. *Ibid.*

foreign policy to seek integration in the region to which we
belong."[6]

The Zionists recognize Arab resistance to the establishment of an
alien state in their midst. Eban verifies this point:

> It became evident that the neighbouring countries have deep
> abhorrence toward this new state which was established against
> their will, for it is the first time in many generations that a non-
> Arab, non-Muslim nation was able to have independence in the
> Middle-East.   The neighbouring countries have been used to
> see the Middle East as a compact Arab area.[7]

At the same time, the Israeli leadership resolved to continue the
occupation of the Arab territories which came under their control
legally or illegally.[8]   As Prime Minister Levi Eshkol declared:
"Today, the whole world bears witness that there is no power that
can uproot us from this land.[9]

In a speech before the Security Council, Eban emphasized
the permanence of the Zionist state, and seems to threaten that the
Middle East is doomed unless the "God Chosen" people save it.
He declared:

> This, then, is the first axiom.   A much more conscious and unin-
> hibited acceptance of Israel's statehood is an axiom requiring
> no demonstration.   There will never be a Middle East without
> an independent and sovereign state of Israel in its midst.[10]

Israel has not abandoned its insistence on direct face-to-face
negotiations with the Arab states. Prime Minister Meir insists
that:

> It's not enough that even the Arab countries would make a state-
> ment that we have a right to exist.   Actually, we are not in need

[6]*London Times*, 12 March 1952.

[7]Cited in Hafez, *op. cit.*, p. 161.

[8]Both Jordan and the U.A.R. complained that Israeli forces continued their
advance and occupied territory not held by them before the cease-fire had gone
into effect.   U.N. Document *S/7953*, 8 June 1967; *New York Times*, 8 June 1967.

[10]Israel Information Service, *Not Backward to Belligerency But Forward to
Peace* (New York: n.p., June 1967), p. 13.

of that kind of a statement.... We want them to sit down with us and conclude peace agreements and for them to, by the signature of the peace agreements, say, 'No more wars.'"[11]

Similarly, at the General Assembly, Eban, expressed Israel's need for security; he said that a mutual non-aggression pledge should be signed to insure the future security of the area.[12]

To the Israelis, the Arab insistence on returning to the armistice line which prevailed on June 4, is an alibi for refusal to make peace.[13] From the Zionist point of view, this is tantamount to Israel giving up her security without obtaining a genuine and irrevocable binding peace. Eban declared:

We shall do no such thing. After 21 years of siege and thousands of years of struggle to maintain and preserve our identity, we cannot put Israel's existence under the mark of interrogation which hovered over no other nation.[14]

The existence of Israel as a sovereign state is the point of departure for any solution.[15] Only a signed peace treaty can guarantee this demand.

We shall not commit the irrational course of returning to the poli-

[11]Meir on "Meet the Press," 28 September 1969. The Zionist leadership declared that recognition of Israel by the Arab states is not essential to the continuation of it. *New York Times*, 4 October 1967, p. 1.

[12]*New York Times*, 9 October 1967, p. 3.

Regarding the fragmentation of the region, the Israeli leadership differs. The first believes that instead of contending with one huge pan-Arab state surrounding it, Israel prefers much rather to deal with several smaller states, like Jordan and the Lebanon with whom the prospects of arriving at a settlement are far brighter. Merlin, *op. cit.*, p. 340.

Ben Gurion and the Leftist groups, however, believe that as long as the Middle East is divided into small states, each must show that it is more anti-Israeli than others, and, especially, than Nasser himself. If, however, the Middle East were consolidated into a unified framework, this need for outbidding would gradually disappear. A strong, unified Arab leadership enjoying the necessary prestige, would not be inhibited in negotiating with Israel. *Ibid.*, p. 340.

[13]Eban, Security Council, 13 November 1967.

[14]Eban, General Assembly, 19 September 1969.

[15]Avnery, *op. cit.*, p. 211.

tical anarchy and strategic vulnerability from which we have emerged. National suicide is not an international obligation.... We cannot reconcile ourselves with the intermediate situation of neither war nor peace. Thus, the armistice lines must be superseded by accepted frontiers. It is in our view that the new situation should rest on contractual agreement which commit and engage the responsibility of Israel and each Arab state.[16]

On 18 September 1967, Israel rejected "foreign guarantees" of her security, and reiterated her position that peace can only come about through direct negotiations with the Arab states. Eban declared:

No external declarations or guarantees...can replace the sovereign responsibilities of the governments concerned....May and June teach us a lesson about the limitations of international guarantees in the present state of world power balance. The Middle Eastern peace with its relevant provisions and agreements for enforcement must spring up from within the region. It cannot be grafted on to it from outside. The Middle East is not an international protectorate. It is a region of sovereign states which bears the main responsibility for adjusting their mutual relations.[17]

However, the main conviction, common to all Zionist leadership, is that the Arabs do not want peace, that Arab nationalism is an inherent threat to Israel, that the support of Western Powers is important for Israel's security, and that the superiority of its military is essential for its very existence. All of these elements are of a vicious circle that have contributed to the present impasse.[18]

Furthermore, the Israeli leaders insist that if concessions were to be made in reaching a final peace settlement, the Arabs should make

[16]Eban, General Assembly, 25 September 1967.

Israel's insistence on peace treaties and fixed boundaries can be ascribed to their fear of international pressure to withdraw:

"People in the U.S., Britain, and France have forgotten 1956, but we haven't. The memory haunts us. We won the Sinai campaign with guns and lost it with words." *New York Times*, 20 August 1967.

[17]Eban's, speech before the General Assembly, 25 September 1967. Also *Washington Post*, 9 September 1967.

[18]Avnery, *op. cit.*, p. 105.

them.[19] Ex-Prime Minister Ben Gurion shares this conviction, that peace was impossible because the Arabs were and would remain unwilling to make peace. He, like most Zionist leaders, insists that making peace is entirely up to the Arabs and that Israel could do nothing to initiate it. Peace means Arab recognition of the *status quo* from which Israel could not and would not budge.[20]

[19]Merlin, *op. cit.*, p. 224.

[20]In December 1952, Israel informed the U.N. of its willingness to negotiate peace treaties and gave "a blueprint" for the general economic, political and diplomatic issues. "The Israeli view was that a peace settlement should include a non-aggression clause and gave assurance that any Arab fear of expansion by Israel was unfounded...." *London Times*, 2 December 1952.

In 1948, Israel increased its territory by 30 per cent and in 1967, it quadrupled its land area. The 1956 and 1967 wars, in particular, refute such assurances, especially, when Israel refuses to abide by the U.N. withdrawal resolutions, which can mean only expansion. Thus, the Arab distrust of the Zionist aims and policies have so far precluded Arab initiative for peace settlement. Vance and Lauer, *op. cit.*, p. 120.

The frequent statements by major Zionist leaders, who, at the same time, have been the decision-makers in Israel, indicate expansionist policies. The following are examples:

On 18 July 1967, Walter Eytan declared that, "Israel has not taken anything that belongs to another person." Cited in Ministry of Education and Guidance, *Yawmul Naksah* (Amman: Al-Mutbaah Al-Wataniyah, 1969), p. 11.

As late as November 1966, hardly six months before the Israeli attack of 5 June 1967, the Israeli representative to the U.N. declared:

I should like to inform the committee quite categorically that the government of Israel covets no territory of any of its neighbours....We have all signed the Charter obliging us to respect each other's political independence and territorial integrity. My government, fully and unreservedly, accepts this obligation toward the other 120 state members of the United Nations (U.N., *Document A/SPC/PV*. 505, November 8, 1966).

Menachem Beigin, leader of the Herut Party (the largest in Israel) and a cabinet member declared in 1955:

I deeply believe in launching a preventive war against the Arab states without further hesitation. By so doing, we will achieve two targets: first, the annihilation of the Arab power; and secondly, the expansion of our territory (From a statement made in the Parliament, 12 October 1955).

Another spokesman of the Herut declared in 1956: "Peace with the Arab countries is impossible with the present boundaries of Israel which leave Israel open to attack." He advised that "Israel should take the

Israel gives the impression that unless peace prevails, the Zionist state will be destined to extinction. Though victorious in three wars, and with military and political superiority, she had refused the United Nations' resolutions as well as the mediation of the major Powers to reach what she claims indispensable. Thus, while peace is most advantageous to her, for it would free military expenditure to developmental plans and open new markets in the neighbouring Arab states, allowing Israel to become the Switzerland of the Middle East and to achieve its goal of economic, financial domination of the region, the question still stands, "Why is Israel so deficient in the art of peace?"

The answer may be found in the fact that the Zionist leadership wished to concentrate on building a superior military machine to impose its will on the people of the region, enforcing a *pax judica*.[21]

In the Zionist viewpoint, there is no alternative to direct negotiations, normalization of relations, and a peace treaty concluded by intimidation. This is their current official stand, since post-1967 War conditions yielded for them more territory, brought their forces closer to the Arab capitals, and at the same time, removed the threat from their population centres. Due to the military weakness of the Arab states, these conditions are highly advantageous

---

offensive immediately and capture strategic points along its borders including the Gaza strip and then should take over the British-backed Kingdom of Jordan" (*New York Times*, 25 January 1956).

In 1951, Prime Minister Ben Gurion also stated that the state of Israel has been resurrected in the Western part of the Land of Israel and that independence has been reached in a part of our small country....It must now be said that it has been established in only a portion of the Land of Israel. Even those who are dubious as to the restoration of the historical frontiers as fixed and crystallized from the beginning of time will hardly deny the anomaly of the boundaries of the new state. (Israeli Government Year book, 1951-52, p. 64; and 1952, pp. 63, 65.)

President Chaim, during his visit to Jerusalem on 1 December 1948 told his audience: "Do not worry because all of Jerusalem is not now within the state....The old synagogues will be rebuilt anew and the way to the Wailing Wall will be open again. With your blood and sacrifices you have renewed the covenant of old. Jerusalem is ours...." Dov Joseph, *The Faithful City: The Siege of Jerusalem, 1948* (New York: Simon and Schuster 1960, p. 322.)

[21]Sharabi, *op. cit.*, p. 27.

to Israel.

A Jewish Commentator had rightly opined in the *New York Times*, "For the first time in our history, time is working in our favour. The cease-fire situation may not be ideal for Israel but it is infinitely worse for the Arabs."[22]

The overriding concern of the Zionist policy is to maintain military superiority and adopt an aggressive policy because it is rooted in a movement of colonization. Its relationship with its adversary is based solely on force. Thus, any peace settlement for Israel had to be enforced by bargaining from a position of strength.[23] Prime Minister Meir emphasized this point:

> I maintain that a strong Israel is not only the best guarantee for peace, but is the best incentive for peace because there is no sense in making peace with a weak Israel. A weak Israel can be thrown into the sea....The less hope there is to bomb Tel Aviv, the more hope there is for peace.[24]

Since the Arab counter-demands are not acceptable to the Israeli leadership, in view of the latter's superiority of military stance, Israel planned to strengthen its deterrence, maintain military power and hence induce peace. In 1956, Israel tried to impose the *status*

[22]*New York Times*, 20 August 1967, IV, p. 5.

[23]Sharabi, *op. cit.*, p. 26.

[24]"Meet The Press," 28 September 1969.

Subsequent American Administrations share this view. Recently, President Nixon said:

> We recognize that Israel is not desirous of driving any one of the other countries into the sea. The other countries do want to drive Israel into the sea....Once the balance of power shifts where Israel is weaker than its neighbours, there will be war....We will do what is necessary to maintain Israel's strength *vis-a-vis* its neighbours, not because we want Israel to be in a position to wage war...but because that will deter its neighbours from attacking it.

White House Release, "A Conversation With the President," 1 July 1970, pp. 15-16.

It is regrettable that the U.S.A., which claims "neutrality" on this issue, failed to recognize the fact that while the Jews have not been "thrown into the sea, the so-called American "neutral" policy has significantly contributed to "throwing the Arabs in the desert." Al-Fatah [P.L.O.] (Beirut), Vol. I, No. 6, 1970.

quo by force of arms.   Following the 1967 War, the Zionist leader-ship hoped that the Arabs become weary of waiting, and, therefore, sue for peace.

Since peace settlement is still a remote possibility, Israel operates according to the policy that a state can grow and prosper without peace.   Eban declared that "peace with the Arabs is an important objective of our policy but is not a condition for the existence of the state of Israel."[25] In the meantime, Israel embarked on absorbing new immigrants, integrating the varied communities into a national entity and developing its economy.

The 1967 War placed Israel in the strongest bargaining position they ever envisioned. With a superior military machine, they hoped to dictate peace.[26]   Accordingly, on June 12, the Israeli cabinet agreed on the following general policy:

> First, a peace settlement would be sought to replace the 1949 armistice agreement....Second, negotiations would be sought directly with the Arab states rather than relying on any U.N. machinery or the good offices of Powers outside the region. Third, no territory captured...will be returned unless the Arabs re-cognize Israel's right to access from the Red Sea to Elat, her southern port and Israel's right to complete military security.[27]

In this connection, Eban declared that the war did, in fact, bring Israel closer to the achievement of its ancient empire.   Hoping for a positive Arab response, he declared that "the objective of such negotiations will be to resolve some of Israel's historic problems and to insure the nation's stability."[28]   Eban may well have envisioned the revival of "Greater Israel" open to unlimited immigration, its commerce thriving and its boundaries secure.

Regarding the proposed secure frontier, Eshkol, in early September

---

[25]Merlin, *op. cit.*, p. 244.

[26]The late Israeli Foreign Minister Sharette, in his book, *Travelling in Asia*, disputed those who believed the axiom, "you can reach peace through force." Quoted in *ibid.*, p. 245.

[27]*New York Times*, 12 June 1967, p. 1.

  Except for recognition, Husayn and Nasser have indicated that the Arabs would agree to all Zionist demands put forth before the 1967 War. See King Husayn's speech in *New York Times*, 11 April 1969.

[28]*New York Times*, 12 June 1967, p. 18.

1967, declared that: "No better natural border can be found between Israel and the U.A.R. than the Suez Canal....The River Jordan must become the natural boundary with Jordan."[29]

Similarly, as early as 11 June 1967, Dayan had declared that he had no intention of returning the Gaza Strip to the U.A.R. or the West Bank to Jordan, and urged that Israel "dig its claws into the areas it had occupied." Applying force to compel the Arabs to come to the peace table, Israel threatened that "nothing was to be returned until the Arabs make peace and recognize the state of Israel."[30]

It was also declared that "Israel has more right to the West Bank of Jordan than the Hashemite Kingdom of Jordan."[31] Inside Israel and outside it, there are organizations which oppose territorial concessions by Israel as a price for peace. Zionist statesmen, both hawks and doves, have been in agreement regarding plans for the establishment of "Greater Israel." This plan has become the official policy of that state.[32] There is ample evidence to this con-

---

[29]K. Ivanov, "Israel, Zionism and Imperialism," *International Affairs* (Moscow), No 6 (June 1968), p. 13.

The issue of long-range peace vs. the demands for short-term security has been widely discussed inside Israel. Professor Levontin of the Hebrew University Law School cautioned:

> A secure border... isn't a natural boundary like a mountain or a river.... A border is secure when those living on the other side do not have sufficient motivation to infringe on it... we have to remind ourselves that the roots of security are in the minds of men, since that is where the sources of insecurity also lie.... The term "secure borders"...ceases to be an honest one when you [Zionists] expand settlements up to the new border, so that in order to make the new line "secure" you need still another strip of some ten kilometres...."

"To Make War or to Make Peace in the Middle East." *New Outlook*, pp. 5-6, quoted in Parker T. Hart, *The Annals of American Academy of Political and Social Sciences*, Vol. 390, July 1970, p. 105.

[30]*New York Times*, 7 April 1968, IV, p. 24.

[31]*Ibid*.

A Syrian spokesman commented: "We no longer know whether Israel is trying to guarantee its rights to exist or its rights to expand." Ivanov, *op. cit.*, p. 15.

[32]*Ibid*., p. 13.

clusion.   At the end of February 1968, the Minister of the Interior
issued an order that Israeli law was to apply to the occupied territories.   Discarding international reaction, he officialy announced,
these territories were no longer enemy territories, and declared that
new settlements were to be set up in the occupied areas.[33]   Confir-
ming this policy, Labour Minister   Allon declared   earlier, that
"new villages should be established in the occupied zone to make
Israeli existence there an approved fact."[34]

As Arab resistance to peace talks persisted, Israel began to revise
its policy.   In November 1968, Eshkol said in Parliament that the
River would be Israel's security border as distinguished from the
political frontier.[35]   But added that, in any settlement, no Arab
army would be permitted to be stationed in the West Bank. This
plan agreed with Allon's which entailed that the river be the eastern boundary between Israel and Jordan.[36]   The Allon plan also
involved the return of most of the West Bank to Jordan, provided
all Jerusalem remains in Israeli hands. In addition, a nine-mile wide
strip along the river, broken by entry points, should be retained by
Israel.   This proposal, however, was rejected by both the U.A.R.
and Jordan.   The major reason for the rejection was Israel's insistence that Jerusalem must be retained by it, therefore, was not a
negotiable issue.[37]

A distinctive characteristic if Israel's strategy has been to pro-
tract conflict rather than solving it.   To the   Zionist leadership,
attitudes   of compromise by the Arabs, ever since the Geneva
Protocol in 1949, has been a source of embarrassment.   Even the

[33]Ibid., p. 14.

[34]U.N. Document S/8581, 8 May 1968.

[35]New York Times, 18 June 1968, p. 17; also The Economist, 23 November
1968, p. 29.

[36]U.N. Security Council Document 8581, 18 May 1968; also The Economist, 23 November 1968, p. 29.

The Israelis declared their intention of retaining wedges of land jutting along
the River from Beisan valley to the Dead Sea. This would provide for a security belt of fortified settlements along the mountain ridges. Israeli guns would
be placed on high precipitous cliffs controlling an expanse of twenty miles to the
east, thus, preventing Arab tanks from crossing the River or reaching the West
Bank. Essentially, therefore, since no Arab troops would cross the River,
then, the "Israeli Maginot Line" would in effect become the frontier." New
York Times, 18 June 1968, p. 41.

[37]Sabin et al., op. cit., p. 12; The Economist, 22 June 1968, p. 30.

peace mission of Tunisian President Habib Bourgiba provoked discomfort in the Israeli ruling circles.[38] Accordingly, a change in the attitude of Israeli leadership would require a radical transformation in their military-diplomatic thinking and a shift from the offensive to a conciliatory strategy. Due to Arab disunity and military weakness, and in view of the Zionist apparent resolve for expansion, Israeli decision-makers are not yet prepared for such a change. Israel needs some fifty years of friction and tension to establish strong and stable institutions capable of bringing about conditions of permanent equilibrium.[39]

The philosophy of the Israeli military establishment, as personified in Defence Minister Dayan, is one of a crusader who sees no doors open towards peace, and who believes that the very thought of peace is demoralizing. A Member of his Parliament described him saying, "He is and will always be an Arab fighter. He is the Israeli equivalent of what the Americans used to call an Indian fighter."[40] His views seem to reflect those of the majority of the Zionist leadership: that alien settlers must fight the native population. Dayan counselled:

Let us not today fling accusations at the murderers. Who are we that we should argue against their hatred. For eight years now, they sit in their refugee camps in Gaza, and before their very eyes we turn into our homesteads the land and the villages in which their forefathers have lived.... We are a generation of settlers and without the steel helmet and the cannon; we cannot plant a tree and build a house.... Let us not shrink back when we see the hatred fermenting and filling the lives of hundreds of thousands of Arabs who sit all around us. Let us not avert our eyes so that our hand shall not slip.... This is the fate of our generation to be prepared and armed, strong and tough, or otherwise, the sword will slip from our fist and our life will be snuffed out.[41]

[38]Sharabi, *op. cit.*, p. 27.
[39]*Ibid.*
[40]Avnery, *op. cit.*, p. 133.
[41]*Ibid.*

A neutral observer of the U.N. commented: "It seems to me to be symptomatic of a certain blindness to the human reaction of others that so many Israelis professed not to understand why the Arabs, who had been driven from their lands should continue to hate and try to injure those

In December 1967, Dayan proposed a solution to the Palestine question, which should guarantee the Jewish character of Israel, settle the refugees elsewhere and secure Arab recognition of the new state within demarcated boundaries.[42]   Such solution could mean the outright annexation of Arab territories and the creation of the historical "Greater Israel."   This solution is based on the premise that, "If everything was achieved until now by war, why should we be interested in peace now?   Why shouldn't we expect further gains in future wars?"[43]   Such policy reflects a colonizing, expansionist movement,[44] and such philosophy seemed to have precluded any hope for peace in the foreseeable future.

Contrariwise, as the impasse persisted, the Israeli leadership proposed prescriptions for peace.   They came to believe that a change in Arab outlook could be induced, thereby making it possible that a peaceful resolution of the conflict could be achieved.   Eban proposed:

...You must achieve two processes in the Arab mind.   First, eradicate the concept of irredentist war which will make Israel disappear from the future of the Middle East....Then you might, after a period of time, make transition to a more affirmative relationship in which they think not only of the absence of war but the presence of peace.[45]

Whatever methods and instruments Eban had in mind, such as economic incentives or economic deprivation, the use of force, exiles and "reservations" are reminiscent of the stick-carrot approach applied to subdue the American Indians and the Africans inside their own territory.   The Zionist leadership have placed the entire blame on the Arabs for not submitting to their demands of negotiation, recognition and the conclusion of peace treaties.   By causing bad economic, social and political conditions in the Arab states, Israel hoped to induce a change in Arab attitude towards peace.   At the end of 1968, Eshkol wrote that peace had:

---

who had driven them out."   E.L.M. Burns, *Between Arab and Israeli* (London: Harrap, 1962), p. 162.

[42]Avnery, *op. cit.*, p. 146.

[43]*Ibid.*

[44]*Ibid.*, p. 148.

[45]Merlin, *op. cit.*, p. 224.

...now entered the realm of practical politics in which Egypt and Jordan could no longer conceal from themselves a long-standing truth, namely, that they need peace with us, no less than we need peace with them.[46]

Although Israel had thought that a military victory would convince the Arab leaders of the need for peace, only Husayn responded affirmatively in view of the immediate economic need, for, while Egypt and Syria could live without their lost territories, Jordan could not survive without the economics of the West Bank. But Israel also knew that Husayn had declared that he was never strong enough to oppose Nasser and negotiate a separate treaty.[47] In fact, Husayn, in order to avoid King Abdullah's mistake of conducting secret and separate peace talks with Israel, declared that he would not do such a thing behind Nasser's back.[48]

CONCLUSION

Israel's offers for peace in the Middle East are addressed to the Western world, not the Arabs. Such pronouncements portray the Zionists as desirous of peace, while picturing the Arabs as war-like.

The Israeli leadership insist on changing the Armistice Agreement of 1949 with a lasting peace arrangement signed into treaties with each of the Arab states and legalizing the Zionist conquests, while preserving the *status quo*. While Israel demands recognition and secure frontiers, it insists on retaining certain parts of the Arab land which the Israeli military establishment consider as strategically essential for the security of their state.

Jerusalem is the key to any successfully peaceful solution. Despite Jordan's declarations which stressed that the return of the Old City would be basic to any negotiated settlement, Israel's answer was that the City had become the united capital, hence a "non-negotiable"

---

[46]Prittie, *Eshkol*, p. 309.

[47]Vance and Lauer, *op. cit.*, p. 119.

In this connection, Dayan had declared that "Jordan informed Israel that she did not want to negotiate a separate peace with Israel without Cairo's approval." *New York Times*, 6 November 1968, p. 41.

[48]Sabin, *et al.*, *op. cit.*, p. 13; *New York Times*, 8 December 1968. See also King Husayn's *Uneasy Lies The Head*, *op. cit.*, p. 109.

question.

Integrating Israel in the region became a cardinal principle of the Zionist foreign policy. They insist on establishing and developing economic relations with the neighbouring states based on the "Open Frontier" idea, to enable Israel to become the Switzerland of the Middle East, whose industrial product would be marketed in the vast and populous, yet underdeveloped Arab countries.

To achieve this goal, normal relations must be established: recognition extended and cooperative attitude installed. Thus, the Israeli leadership insist on face-to-face talks; that peace negotiations must be conducted directly by the parties to the conflict; that a third party such as the United Nations would only hinder progress towards a final peace.

While the Israeli leaders demand acceptance of their state and integrating it in the cultural, political and economic life of the region, they, however, persist in regarding it essentially as European in character. In the meantime, in order to preserve Israel's "racist" character, they disclaim any responsibility for the Palestine refugees. Yet, Israel indicates her readiness to participate in programmes for their rehabilitation and re-settlement elsewhere.

In pursuing a policy towards recreating the "Greater Israel," and a *Pax Judica,* the Israeli leadership place maximum emphasis on the military machine. They maintain that peace in the region could be guaranteed only if Israel is militarily stronger than her neighbours. This military mentality has precluded Arab positive response to Israel's demands which appeared to be coercive in nature rather than aiming at any just and equitable settlement. One may conclude that by making demands backed by force, Israel's leaders may very well have been influenced by their current thinking that "If everything was achieved until now by war, why should we be interested in peace now."[49]

[49]Avnery, *op. cit.,* p. 148.

CHAPTER SEVEN

PEACE EFFORTS BY JORDAN

The Rhodes Armistice Agreement of 1949 constituted the only legal instrument of relations between Jordan and Israel. King Abdullah's aim was to convert it into a permanent peace, but Israel's refusal to abide by U.N. resolutions, and Arab opposition to any negotiations from a position of weakness precluded such a possibility. Thus, in view of the strong anti-Zionist feeling, King Abdullah sought substantial concessions, which Ben Gurion and his militarists opposed while advocating provocations on the Jordanian frontier in the hope of forcing Jordan to submit and sign a separate peace treaty.[1]

King Abdullah had been engaged in secret negotiations with the Zionists until shortly before his assassination. However, the more the Zionists reached an agreement with Abdullah, the less they became interested in responding to Egypt's proposals, thus, in effect, destroyed excellent chances for peace. For, if the most important Arab state—Egypt—had reached an agreement, the smaller states, such as Jordan, would follow as it did take place at Rhodes.

Israel had hoped that the 1956 Tripartite Aggression would force Egypt and the Arabs to the peace table. But their hope was not fulfilled because the Arabs became less willing than ever before to deal with Israel. The insistence of the U.N. and the United States on Israeli withdrawal from the Sinai, and the support given to the Arabs by the Soviet Union, strengthened the Arab position, hence the refusal to negotiate.

Following the 1967 War, the Zionists rejected all efforts for mediation by the U.N. and others, and insisted on direct negotiations. Having suffered most from the war, Husayn took the initiative and urged the Arab leaders to meet at a summit conference. With permission from Nasser and other leaders, he set out to seek a compromise in the political solution to the Palestine question. It was reported that Husayn, through a third party, had expressed willingness to end the state of belligerency, to demilitarize the West Bank, to

---

[1]*New York Times*, 15 October 1950.

guarantee for Israel its borders as existed under the armistice on 4 June 1967 and to provide the Jews with safe access to their holy places inside the Jordanian sector. But the most important concession, however, was his offer not to press the implementation of the U.N. resolution calling for the repatriation of the refugees. Israel, however, rejected these offers and insisted on more concessions by Jordan and on direct negotiations.

Continuing his efforts for peace, Husayn called for an Arab summit, but to no avail, due to a split within the Arab leadership on matters of policy. Finally, when Sudanese President Ismail Al-Azhari joined Husayn and Nasser in their call for a summit conference, the other Arab leaders agreed, and the Khartoum Summit began at the end of August 1967.[2]

THE KHARTOUM CONFERENCE

At this summit, the Arab leaders agreed to have a permanent peace among themselves.[3] Husayn and Nasser emerged as the moderates advocating a political rather than a military solution to the Palestine question. Husayn was chosen to improve Arab-American relations and to help impress on the United States the need to pressurize Israel to reach a peaceful settlement. However, the leaders of Syria, Algeria and the Palestine Liberation Organization advocated initiating guerilla warfare against the Zionists to keep them off balance and to force them to give up the conquered lands. But the moderate argument prevailed. They all agreed on three important decisions: non-recognition of the state of Israel; indirect negotiations to be conducted through the U.N. or the Great Powers; withdrawal of Zionist forces from all occupied lands before negotiations; elimination of all traces of aggression; and that the Arab states would

[2]The Syrian representative boycotted the conference and departed for Damascus before the end of the meetings. The King of Lybia and the President of Tunisia, unable to attend because of ill health, sent high-ranking officials. The King of Morocco opposed to Arab top-level conferences and sent his Prime Minister. Ahmad Shukayri, leader of the P.L.O., attended, but left the meetings protesting against the decisions reached. Khouri, *op. cit.*, p. 312.

[3]An agreement was reached to end the Yemeni war. Jordan became involved, as it sided with the monarchists of Saudi Arabia and the Royalists of Yemen. Khouri, *op. cit.*, p. 313.

continue to protect the rights of the Palestine Arabs. Despite these decisions, no reference was made to any military action or to the need for destroying Israel.[4]

The Arabs have always insisted on indirect negotiations. They feared that such face-to-face talks or recognition before withdrawal would enable Israel to gain legal status prior to her withdrawal. The Arabs had learned a lesson. After the Rhodes Agreement of 1949, it was hoped that the Partition Plan and the U.N. resolution regarding the refugees would be implemented. However, once Israel had gained *de facto* status as a result of the armistice negotiations, it refused the Partition Plan and stated that there was now "a new reality."

At Khartoum, both Husayn and Nasser made clear their readiness to make substantial concessions to Israel. In exchange for their occupied lands, they offered important concessions short of actually recognizing the Zionist state and negotiating a formal peace treaty with her.[5] Husayn was eager to reach an early peace settlement along the lines suggested by the U.N. resolution which he accepted without reservation. In compliance with that resolution, he explicitly stated that Jordan was prepared to accept the demilitarization of the West Bank and to grant Israel a corridor to the Wailing Wall in the Old City. Jordan, however, was not prepared to reach any agreement with Israel without Egyptian accord.[6]

Since the War of June 1967, a major objective of Jordanian foreign policy has been the recovery of those territories occupied by Israel in the course of that war. In an effort to realize this objective, an accommodation with the Zionists had to be reached. In return, Husayn was prepared to adjust the June 4 frontiers. He proposed to "consider the possibility of adjustments of the Israeli frontier to take into account the military insecurity created by the narrow waist-line around Tel Aviv and the Salient of Latrun."[7]

The United Nations resolution of 22 November 1967 provided for the withdrawal of Israeli armed forces from the occupied territories; the termination of the state of belligerency, respect for territorial

[4]*Ibid.*

[5]*Ibid.*, p. 314.

[6]*Issues in U.S. Foreign Policy, No. 1, The Middle East* (Washington: Department of State, n.d.), p. 10.

[7]Sabin, *op. cit.* See *Washington Post*, 7 July 1967.

integrity and political independence, and the right of every state in the area to live in peace within secure and recognized boundaries.

The establishment of the cease-fire was followed by a long period of negotiations which culminated in the Security Council Resolution 242 of 22 November, adopted unanimously by all its fifteen members.[8] Israel, however, insisted that its acceptance of the Resolution was conditional upon direct negotiations with the Arab states. Husayn's comment on this insistence was that direct negotiations are not the only method for solving disputes. According to Article 33 of the Charter, mediation, conciliation, arbitration, adjudication by the U.N. Security Council and General Assembly are recommended as legitimate methods for settlements. To Husayn, therefore, Israel's refusal to implement the U.N. resolution was tantamount to rejecting its provisions of withdrawal. This refusal contradicts President Eisenhower's statement in 1956 which stated:

Should a nation, which attacks and occupies foreign territory in the face of the United Nations disapproval, be allowed to impose conditions on its own withdrawal? If we agree, then I fear we have turned back the clock of international order.[9]

THE POSITION OF JERUSALEM

Husayn believes that Jordan's destiny is tied with the issue of Palestine and its people; that Jordan is the primary home and base for all the sons of Palestine; and that Jordan constitutes the first line of defence of the Arab nation against the Zionist danger. If the Palestine problem was an Arab problem as a whole, it is for the most part a Hashemite, Jordanian problem.

We [in Jordan] believe that the Palestine issue is our most important and most dangerous problem. To us, it is a matter of life or extinction. It is the greatest challenge which we face in this region before others . . . . Therefore, whatever we had done and will do in

[8]See *supra*, Chapter IV, pp. 40-41.
[9]Quoted by Husayn in his address to the National Press Club, Washington D.C. 10 April 1969.

this country [Jordan] is for Palestine and because of Palestine.[10]

During his tour throughout the Arab countries in April 1968, Husayn appealed to the heads of the Arab states for more funds to strengthen his armed forces which were being attacked daily. At the same time, he declared that he was speaking as the King of both the banks of the River Jordan, and also as guardian of the holy places of Jerusalem.[11]

Although Husayn made it clear that, while immediate withdrawal from all occupied territories, including the Old City, was not a prerequisite for negotiations, he, however insisted that Israel must publicly declare its acceptance of the principle of withdrawal. He further emphasized that the Arabs have certain inalienable rights which cannot be abandoned under any circumstances. "I announce firmly and distinctly that we will stand by our rights and not to move one inch from our position....All occupied lands are ours; sacred Jerusalem is ours."[12]

To Jordan, therefore, any form of settlement must include the return of the Old City to her control. The issue of Jerusalem concerns Jordan more than any other matter. In addition to its spiritual importance to the Arab people, Muslims and Christians, it is vital to the Jordan economy. Without it, Jordan would not be complete. It would be "England without London, France without Paris, or Italy without Rome."[13]

The Arab states are adamant that East Jerusalem should be returned to the Arabs. At the Press Club in Washington, Husayn gave Jerusalem a special place:

Any plan of withdrawal must include our greatest city—our spiritual capital—the Holy City of Jerusalem....We cannot envision any settlement that does not include the return of the Arab part of

[10]Husayn's Ajlun speech, 14 July 1966, p. 4; also see *The Economist*, 20 February 1960, for Jordan's claim. Jordan declined a proposal by the U.A.R. for an Arab Palestine entity in the West Bank and Gaza. However, Husayn agreed to a plebiscite. *New York Herald Tribune*, 8 March 1960.

[11]*New York Times*, 21 December 1968, p. 12.

[12]*New York Times*, 21 December 1968, p. 12. Husayn denied the rumour circulated in the *London Observer* that he was willing to renounce sovereignty over the West Bank as a price for a political settlement.

[13]Husayn's speech at the Press Club, 7 November 1967.

the City of Jerusalem to us with all our Holy Places.... [14]

In his biography, Husayn further emphasized the place of Jerusalem as spiritual with universal application:

As far as Jerusalem is concerned, it is not a question of our giving up our rights. They are not our rights alone, but those of all Moslems. This is no longer a Jordanian problem, but a Moslem problem, an Arab and a Christian problem.... But we cannot give up our rights to Jerusalem for they go back more than a thousand years. Jerusalem is a religious problem.... [15]

[14]Husayn's Press Club Speech, 10 April 1969.

In March 1968, for example, King Faysal of Saudi Arabia called for holy war, "Jihad," to restore Old Jerusalem. See Faysal's statement in *New York Times*, 7 February 1968; and for King Husayn's position see *New York Times*, 17 February 1968, 21 December 1968, and 11 April 1969.

[15]Vance and Lauer, *op., cit.,* p. 121.

The Islamic conferences held in many Islamic cities, all voiced strong objection to the present status of East Jerusalem. The resolution adopted by the World Muslim League at its meeting in Mecca, Saudi Arabia, in October 1967, was indicative of this attitude:

The Muslims must realize that the problem of Jerusalem and the territory usurped in Palestine is a general Islamic problem, and a sacred problem, and that struggle (jihad) in the cause of God for the liberation of al-Masjid al-Aqsa and the occupied lands from the grasp of the aggressors is a sacred duty imposed upon all the Muslims, and not merely upon any one Muslim people.

...No solution or settlement will be acceptable if it does not involve the restoration of Jerusalem to its previous status. *Islamic Review and Arab Affairs*, January 1968, p. 11.

While the Vatican wished to see Jerusalem established as a *corpus separatum* as originally envisaged in the 1947 Partition Plan, the National Council of Churches also urged the creation of an international control over the Holy City. In its resolution of 7 July 1967, it declared:

We support the establishment of an international presence in the hitherto divided city of Jerusalem which will preserve the peace and integrity of the city, foster the welfare of its inhabitants, and protect its holy shrines with full rights of access to all. We encourage the earliest possible advancement of U.N. proposals to make such arrangements practicable.

We cannot approve Israel's unilateral annexation of the Jordanian

Israel says that it cannot retreat from the issue of Jerusalem reunification which it regards as a mere extension of municipal services and integration rather than annexation. However, the Israeli Government insists on two points: one, retention of Jerusalem; two, the necessity of negotiations prior to withdrawal. The Jordanian official stand regarding Jerusalem is that "as long as Israel insisted that East Jerusalem is not negotiable and must remain a part of Israel, there can be no negotiations."[16] Accordingly, in the Jordanian view, "The way Israel can help towards a settlement is to end all talk about East Jerusalem not being negotiable and stop the changes they are making in the city."[17]

---

portions of Jerusalem. This historic city is sacred not only to Judaism but also to Christianity and Islam; *New York Times*, 14 January 1968.

[16]Sabin *et al.*, *op. cit.*, p. 12.
The two positions on this issue are irreconcilable. Upon his visit to Old Jerusalem following the June War, General Dayan declared: "The Israeli Defense Forces liberated Jerusalem. We have reunited the torn city, the capital of Israel. We have returned to this most sacred shrine, never to part from it again," *Facts on File*, XXVII, 7 June 1967.
In an interview with Eric Rouleau of the *Le Monde* in April 1969, Ben Gurion stated his formula for peace. "In exchange for peace...I would return all the territory conquered in June 1967." When asked if this would include East Jerusalem, Ben Gurion answered, "Certainly not!" *Le Monde*, 23 April 1969, p. 4.
[17]Sabin *et al.*, *op. cit.*, p. 14; *New York Post,* 21 October 1967. Examples: within a week after occupation of the Old City, some 100 Arab homes near the Wailing Wall were razed; *New York Times*, 19 June 1967. A month later, again one hundred Arab houses were levelled in the same vicinity. *New Outlook* (Israel), September 1968, p. 39. *The Washington Post* also reported that "buses and trucks at the Damascus Gate were waiting to take displaced Arabs to Jericho and beyond," *Washington Post*, 20 June 1967. At the same time, the Israeli *Jerusalem Post* of 19 June was urging Israeli settlers to move into the Old City. *New York Times,* 18 June and 3 July 1967, carried the programme for settling Zionist families in East Jerusalem, aiming at changing the demographic character of the Old City. See Jordan's protest to the U.N. Secretary-General on this issue, *U.N. Document* A/7107 (S/8634).
Describing the condition in the Old City, *The Economist* reported that:

The U.N. mission investigating occupied territory will find that the Muslims and Christians in Jerusalem are in poorer shape than other West Bank Jordanians. They can be blamed for not wholeheartedly accepting the Israeli conquest and be seen as the principle victims of the Arab refusal to negotiate on Israel's terms, but even on those the majority who at least co-operate, Israel's legislation bears hard. All Arabs are classed as 'absent'

WITHDRAWAL AND INTERNATIONAL LAW

The Security Council Resolution (242) of 22 November 1967, emphasized "the inadmissibility of the acquisition of territory by war."
This unanimous decision is in accordance with the Stimson Doctrine of 1932.   Similarly, the Spanish expression, "La victoria no
da derechos," which means victory bestows no rights, has been the
basis for many important treaties in the Americas.

International law is clear on the issue of conquest by force and the
fruits of aggression.   The Stimson Doctrine explains the position of
the United States regarding the invasion of China by Japan in 1932.
In the Buenos Aires Declaration of 1936, and the Lima Declaration
of 1938, the United States took the position that:

> The occupation or acquisition of territory or any other modifica-
> tions or territorial or boundary arrangement obtained through
> conquest by force or by non-pacific means shall not be valid or
> have legal effect.[18]

The Charter of the O.A.S, signed at Bogota in 1948, also declared,
"no territorial acquisition or special advantage obtained either by

---

but have to pay high income-tax. Their tourist trade is gone. They are losing
more and more land through Israel's land expropriation. What is clear
is that no new Jerusalem is being built in the Holy Land.   There is simply
this sad Old Jerusalem whose treatment by Israel may well prove the crux of
whether there is peace or war. *The Economist*, 4 May 1968, pp. 30–31.

Comparing the economic conditions of the Jerusalem Arabs before and after
the June War, G. Lenczowski noted that the Arabs of East Jerusalem were enjoying a rate of economic growth even greater than those in Israel, prior to the war.
Per capita agricultural production in Jordan reached an index of 193 (1957-59=
100) just before the war, compared to only 146 for Israel.   The over-all rate of
growth for Israel between 1958 and 1966, averaged 9.3 per cent annually, while
for Jordan, it was almost 9.7 per cent.   Moreover, Israel has been the recipient
of almost $5 billion in outside financing since 1948, while capital flow into Jordan
was much more modest during this same period. George Lenczowski, (ed.),
United States Interests in the Middle East (Washington: American Enterprise
Institute, 1968), pp. 64-73.

[18]Report of the United States delegation to the Eighth International Conference of the American States, 1938, pp. 132–33, quoted in Marjorie M.
Whiteman, *Digest of International Law*, Vol. 5 (Washington: Government Printing Office, 1965), pp. 880–81.

force or by other means of coercion shall be recognized."[19]

On 16 November 1956, Under Secretary of State, Herbert Hoover, told the General Assembly that "the basic purpose of the Charter is peace with justice....Peace without justice is not enough, for, without justice, peace is illusory and temporary."[20] Similarly, King Husayn told the Assembly on 26 June 1967, that "peace to be the future relations in the Middle East."[21] He also made the Arab position clear: that a military solution or any forced solution is a "prescription for war," that it is necessary to go back to the situation that existed before June 5, and that all traces of aggression must be erased. He added: "To permit Israel to retain its gains as a bargaining weapon is to permit the aggressor to use the fruits of his aggression to gain the ends for which he went to war. This is immoral.... Should all traces of aggression not be completely erased, Jordan will survive and with us will arise the Arab nation."[22]

Stressing the illegality of conquest by force, and that military supremacy cannot create legal rights in occupied territories, Secretary General Dag Hammarskjöld, in a report concerning the Suez invasion of 1956, stated the position of the World Organization:

> The United Nations cannot condone a change of the status juris resulting from military action contrary to the provisions of the Charter. The Organization must, therefore, maintain that the status juris existing prior to such military action be re-established by a withdrawal of troops, and by the relinquishment or nullification of rights asserted in territories covered by the military action and depending upon it.[23]

[19]U.N. General Assembly Official Record, 91, 1956.

[20]U.N. *G.A.O.R.*, 91, 1956.

[21]King Husayn's speech at the General Assembly Emergency Session, 26 June 1967.

[22]King Husayn's speech at the Press Club, Washington. D.C., 7 November 1967.

[23]Report in connection with G.A. Resolution, 1123, 11, U.N. *GAOR*, Annexes, Agenda Item No. 66, at 47, U.N. Document A/3512 (1957).

The Arabs in Old Jerusalem since 1967 have been deprived of their freedom to belong to the Arab community. In 1948, Eban, then Israel's representative at the U.N., argued that internationalization of Jerusalem would deprive 110,000 Jews of their right to belong to Israel and that such action by the U.N. would be morally incorrect, politically unwise, and a violation of U.N. principles.

It is academic that living under international administration differs greatly

Before the outbreak of hostilities in June 1967, Israel and the U.S. Ambassador Goldberg insisted that peace could be achieved through the restoration of the *status quo ante* in the Gulf of Aqaba. However, when Israel emerged victorious and in control of large territories, Goldberg changed the formula and stated that reverting to the *status quo ante* would be a "prescription for renewed hostilities."[24] Such declaration by the representative of a major Power had, in fact, encouraged Israel to refuse to withdraw. Confident of its military dominance, Israel has been insisting on face-to-face talks with the individual Arab states under duress, and only on "conqueror's terms."[25]

While debating the Tripartite Aggression on Egypt in 1956, Ambassador Henry C. Lodge reiterated the U.S. position regarding acquisition by military means. At the General Assembly on 1 March 1957, he said that the U.S.

> ...called upon Israel to withdraw and called for the withholding of assistance to Israel if it did not withdraw. The U.S. views in this respect have been steadfast.... We have recognized that it is incompatible with the principles of the Charter and with the obligations of membership in the U.N. for any member to seek political gains through the use of force or to use as bargaining point, a gain achieved by means of force.[26]

Similarly, the position of the French Government was stated by its Foreign Minister Murville at the General Assembly:

> ...The French Government has taken a stand since the end of the military operations. It goes without saying...that no *fait accompli* on the spot regarding the territorial boundaries and the situation of the citizens of the states concerned should be consi-

---

from living under conqueror's laws. See Memorandum on the Question of Jerusalem submitted to the U. N. Trusteeship Council, Seventh Session, Lake Success, May 1950.

[24]U.N. Document A/PV 1527, 30 June 1967, pp. 16-17.

[25]Anthony Nutting, "The Tragedy of Palestine From the Balfour Declaration to Today,' Address delivered at the annual conference of the American Council for Judaism, 2 November 1967 (London: Arab League Office), p. 6.

[26]U.N. *GAOR*, 1956, p. 1277.

dered permanent.[27]

Accordingly, Israel should not dictate conditions for peace since its behaviour and occupation are illegal as they are governed by military considerations. This places her in violation of the international as well as the U.N. resolutions.

ISRAEL DEFIES THE UNITED NATIONS

One crucial factor contributing to the deadlock is that Israel does not regard the Security Council Resolution as an instrument ready for implementation, but considers it as "a set of principles subject to discussion and agreement and not a self-executing document."[28] Such unilateral interpretation frees Israel from the obligation of implementing it, particularly when implementation is to her disadvantage.

Israel's refusal to abide by the U.N. resolutions can be ascribed to certain attitudes which have been borne by its leadership for the last twenty years. Although it was created by a U.N. Resolution, Israel has violated the orders of the International Organization throughout its history.[29] In 1966, in an interview with Premier Eshkol, Eric Rouleau of *Le Monde*, put the question that the Arab states think Israel

[27]French Foreign Minister Maurice Couve de Murville, Speech before the United Nations General Assembly, 22 June 1967, quoted in *Vital Speeches*, Vol. 33, No. 19, 15 July 1967, p. 591.

[28]*New York Times*, 7 November 1968, p. 2.

[29]The following are examples:

1. Resolution (181)—II of 29 November 1947, regarding partition;

2. Resolution 194 (III) of 11 December 1948, which provided for the return of the refugees and compensating those who desired not to return;

3. Resolution 273 (III) of 11 May 1949, which provided for the admission of Israel to U.N. membership on the condition that it will respect and implement the afore mentioned resolutions;

4. Resolution 394 (V) of 14 December 1950, which entrusted the Palestine Conciliation Commission with the protection of the interests and properties of the refugees;

5. Resolution 237 of June 1967, regarding the return of the refugees;

6. Resolution 2253 (ES–V) of 4 July 1967, which restrained Israel from annexing Jerusalem; and

7. Resolution 242 of 22 November 1967, which provided for the withdrawal of Israeli troops from all occupied territories.

should abide by the U.N. resolutions, "Wouldn't you think that these
offer a basis for negotiations?" Eshkol's reply was: "Absolutely
not."[30]

The Zionist leadership have been dissatisfied with the U.N. for not
giving them what they always asked for. They seem to insist that
the World Organization owes them statehood, protection and
survival. Thus, they demand to be treated by the U.N. as *primus
inter pares.*" Recognizing the impotence of the U.N. and assured of
unswerving support of the major powers, Israel embarked on a policy
of *fait accompli,* which never failed. Not even the murder of the
U.N. Mediator, Count Folke Bernadotte by Zionist terrorists of the
Stern Gang on 17 September 1948,[31] was to count against her.[32]

[30]Quoted in Samuel Merlin, *The Search For Peace in The Middle East* (New
York: Thomas Yoseloff, 1968), p. 233.

[31]Glubb, *A Soldier With the Arab,* p. 448.

[32]Rodinson, *op. cit.,* p. 40.

In a security review of top Parliamentary members of Eshkol's Party, Dayan
rejected the U.N. resolution and added that the decisive factor, as far as Israel
was concerned, was the position of the United States; that the attitude of the U.S.
has more importance for Israel than the Security Council Resolution. U.N.
Document S/8650, 21 June, 1968.

In connection with the use of force policy which had been the landmark in
Israel's behaviour, a leader of the British Labour Party, T.E.M. McKitterick
observed:

> What brought Israel into existence was in the end not an agreed decision but
> the force of arms, and all the U.N. was able to do afterwards was to take note
> of the fact and try to prevent any further changes from being made by similar
> methods. The implication is a very far-reaching one—that a collective security
> organization is bound by its very nature to favour the status quo, while ini-
> tiative for change comes not from agreement but from force. T.E.M.
> McKitterick, *Fabian International Essays* (New York: Praeger, 1957), p. 121.

Before 1948, the British, the Arabs and the U.S.S.R. were trying to show that
the Partition Plan could not work. Accordingly, the U.S.A. tried to create a
U.N. Trusteeship instead. The Secretary of State, James Forrestal, who objected
to the establishment of the Zionist State failed to persuade President Truman to
commit U.S. troops to enforce the Trusteeship Plan. Warren Austin, the U.S.
Ambassador to the U.N., was about to present a joint American-British Trusteeship Plan instead. However, the U.S. decided on an alternative: to support the
creation of Israel, to recognize it, and to insure its survival as a part of the Western
world. This policy was dictated by the fear of Soviet infiltration in the region.
It should be recalled that the U.S.S.R. voted for the creation of Israel, and
recognized it only a few days after its proclamation.

According to the Israeli leadership, the crisis of 1967 resulted from the fact that for twenty years, the U. N. was unable to solve the Palestine conflict, and that in early summer of 1967, the Security Council had abdicated its function when it could not prevent the diversion of the River Jordan and the activities of the Fedayeen. In this connection, a spokesman in Tel Aviv communicated that "the Prime Minister doubts whether the United Nations could do much either for us or for the Arabs."[33] Thus, the Israelis conclude that the present condition of the U.N. clearly indicates to the small Powers that they cannot yet count on obtaining their security from the World Organization.[34] Israel's problem, therefore, for the most part, is political and psychological, given its character as an alien national entity, forcibly thrust into a hostile environment. To the Zionist, it was logical that they must chart their own course by displaying military strength.[35]

This military strength has been the vehicle for their expansionist policies, and is currently being applied to force a peace settlement. French Foreign Minister Murville does not approve of or support such policy. He said:

The Israeli Government, basing itself on such a war map and deliberately putting aside for the future and further intervention by the U.N. Organization or third Powers, declares that it intends to discuss peace terms with each of the Arab countries concerned individually, without, however, defining these terms, even though they seem to go beyond freedom of navigation through the gulf of Aqaba.[36]

The Secretary of State, Rusk, voiced the thinking of the U.S. in adopting this policy:

If we did nothing, it is likely that the Russians could and would take definite steps toward gaining a control in Palestine through the infiltration of specially trained Jewish immigrants.

See Avnery, op. cit., p. 194.

[33] Jerusalem Post, 2 April 1967.

[34] Embassy of Israel, Forward to Peace (Washington: n.p., October 1968), p. 4.

[35] Kerr, The Middle East Conflict, p. 28.

[36] Vital Speeches, op. cit., p. 590.

JORDAN'S PEACE PROPOSALS

In 1967-68, Israel had been saying that the June War had "shattered beyond repair" the armistice agreement and that a new reality had come about. The Arabs are now willing to convert the 1949 Armistice arrangement into a peace settlement. Israel, however, persistently rejected these proposals. Even the peace campaign of President Bourgiba in 1964 was ignored, but, at the same time, it succeeded in exposing Israel's real intentions and policies.[37] The Zionists' consolidation of their grip on the occupied territories makes the Arabs apprehensive of direct negotiations, much less recognition.

Israel's peace offers are not, by their very nature, directed to the Arabs at all. They are directed to the Western world.[38] The Arab position has been that there is nothing to negotiate as long as Israel assumes this attitude. Therefore, a promise from the Arabs for direct talks remains slender. John C. Campbell, a student of the Middle East politics observed:

Israel, for its part, consistently expressed its desire to sit down with the Arabs and talk peace terms. Basically, Israel's attitude was more reasonable in that it wanted peace while the Arabs did not, but from the viewpoint of the latter, what Israel wanted was recognition and legal confirmation of unjust gains won by the sword. Israel's attitudes, moreover, did nothing to disarm Arab suspicion or mitigate Arab hostility even if that had been possible. . . . Israel paid remarkably little heed to the necessity of coming to some terms with the fact of living in the heart of the Arab World. . . . The Government of Israel did nothing toward the solution of the problem of the Arab refugees.[39]

---

[37] Erskine B. Childers, "Palestine: The Broken Triangle," *Modernization of the Arab World,* J.H. Thompson and R.D. Reischauer (editors), (Princeton, N. J.; D. Van Nostrand Company, Inc., 1960), p. 154.

[38] *Ibid.*

[39] John C. Campbell, *Defense of the Middle East* (New York: Praeger, 1960), pp. 82-83. The Israeli Government rejected the return of the refugees since 1948. In a letter to Bernadotte from the Israeli Foreign Minister, the reasons given were security and economy; *Spectator,* 12 May 1961, p. 675.

For the Arabs, direct negotiations as a first step are inconceivable. They suspect that direct talks could lead to a trap due to the fact that the power equation is manifestly in Israel's favour. Any settlement thus arrived at would inevitably conform to the actual distribution of power between Israel and the Arabs. In other words, it would enable Israel to impose maximum penalties on the Arabs in terms of territories, refugees, control of waterways and recognition. It means that by coming to the conference table, the Arabs will be required to sign on the dotted line.[40] Interestingly, a member of the Israeli Parliament, Uri Avnery, understands the Arab position regarding direct talks with Israel. Assuming an Arab viewpoint, Avnery asks:

What does Israel want from us? Only recognition of its lawful existence. We, on our part, have many concrete demands: retreat from the cease-fire lines, repatriation of the refugees, and so forth. If we agree to direct peace negotiations, we are ready to accord to Israel recognition. In other words, we are giving you in advance what you want without receiving anything in return. After making such a mistake, Israel could say at the negotiating table that it does not want to concede anything. Therefore, secret negotiations by mediators must come first. We must know what Israel wants to give up in return for recognition before any Arab leader can make any open move.[41]

Conversely, Husayn declares his trust in the U.N. and the judgement of the Big Powers, and realizes the necessity of their involvement in the Middle East conflict. To him, the issue of peace in the region is too important to be left to the parties concerned, particularly, when failure to find peace could precipitate World War III.[42] The Zionists,

40 M.S. Agwani, *Mid East* (March-April 1969), p. 11.
41 Avnery, *op. cit.*, p. 184.
42 "The role of the U.S. was again problematical. She was on the winning side and superficially her policy seemed successful. But, on the deeper level, it was clear that the swiftness of Israel's victory had saved the U.S. from having to make some very difficult decisions. Had the war gone badly for Israel, the U.S. might have been forced to intervene and risk a confrontation with the Soviet Union." John G. Stoessinger, *The United Nations and the Superpowers* (2nd ed.; New York: Random House, 1970), pp. 73-4.
According to *New York Times* of 12 June 1967, "The Johnson Administration appeared content to let the Israelis capitalize on their strength" by not pressing

however, are walled up behind the cliche that only the parties to the conflict must be parties to the peace, and that no external intervention could replace the direct negotiations by the parties concerned.

In November 1967, at the Press Club, Husayn declared that he was not speaking for Jordan alone but for the entire Arab nation. He stated that a grave injustice had been suffered by Arab Palestine in 1948, and unless justice was restored, there would be no hope for peace. This is still the Arab position in its true meaning. Although the Arabs in the past were reluctant to find a solution, today they are desirous of cooperating with maximum efforts to reach a permanent peace with justice.[43]

In accordance with the Security Council Resolution, and as a basis for "just and lasting peace," Husayn offered the following proposals:

1. The end of all belligerency.
2. Respect for and acknowledgement of the sovereignty, territorial integrity and political independence of all states in the area.
3. Recognition of the right of all to live in peace within secure and recognized boundaries, free from threats or acts of war.
4. Guaranteeing for all, the freedom of navigation through the Gulf of Aqaba and the Suez Canal.
5. Guaranteeing the territorial inviolability of all states in the area through whatever measures necessary, including the establishment of demilitarized zones.
6. Accepting a just settlement of the refugee problem.[44]

Husayn's position is that Jordan was prepared for an over-all

---

for a cease-fire. "The administration's greatest pressures to have Israel halt the fighting did not develop until June 9, while Israelis were making their final bid to seize high ground in Syria."

Although Israel accepted the cease-fire on June 7, the fighting stopped on June 9. The delay of Israel's compliance with the cease-fire order caused by the U. S. attitude resulted in Israel's occupation of more land not held by it on June 7.

[43] Husayn, Press Club, 7 November 1967.

There was also a tacit understanding that an effort would be made primarily through King Husayn to improve Arab relations gradually with the U.S.A. and win American support for an Israeli withdrawal from the occupied area. Khouri, *op. cit.*, p. 313.

[44] *Ibid.*, 10 April 1969.

political settlement which included Jordan's recognition of Israel's right "to live in peace and security." Thus, Husayn indicated that the Arabs would agree virtually to all the demands put forth by Israel before 5 June 1967. He knows that an accommodation of some kind would restore the Arab-occupied areas in the West Bank to his king-dom, making it viable economically.[45] Thus, he could declare, "if we cannot achieve an Arab solution, then we must have a Jordan solu-tion."[46] To that end, the King shuffled his cabinet and brought in new members who were willing "to follow the king in seeking a poli-tical settlement in the Middle East."[47] Prime Minister A.M. Rifa'i was sent on a tour throughout the Arab states to consult the Arab rulers about "how far they will back Jordan in any settlement with Israel."[48]

This attitude represented a major change from Jordan's position, since such a statement indicated that the Arabs face a Zionist state as a fact of life.[49] The King also called upon Israel to match this new and positive approach by offering terms to consider, for, if the Zionists wish to live in peace with one hundred million Arabs and become accepted neighbours, they should initiate proposals leading to a just solution. He demanded that:

Israel must contribute to a solution to the Palestine problem as a whole so that the peace will be definitive, and now is the time to do it. A peace between Jordan and Israel or Palestine and Israel is simply useless. We have shown that we are ready to go a long way toward its realization and to accept the challenges of building a better future for this region as an indivisible whole. Now it is Israel's turn. It is up to them, the victors, to prove by actions that they really mean to live in peace with the Arabs and be

[45] *New York Times,* 11 November 1968, p. 5.

[46] *Ibid.,* p. 4.

[47] *Ibid.,* 27 December 1968, p. 2.

[48] *Ibid.,* 1 December 1968.

[49] "Middle East Stalemate," *Newsweek,* 20 November 1967, p. 73. King Husayn wrote about his visit to many foreign nations following the 1967 War:

Wherever I went, one point was made abundantly clear: in spite of the tragic turn in Palestine problem, world opinion was convinced that Israel is in this part of the world to stay (Vance and Lauer, *op. cit.,* p. 115).

accepted in this world on which they have encrusted themselves like a scab.[50]

It became apparent that the deadlock has been caused by Israel's insistence on face-to-face talks and recognition, and due to the fact that these conditions are beyond implementation at present. Since the Zionists' demands denote dictated peace and intimidation, the Arabs, including Husayn, rejected them. A European official remarked that the Zionists should have recalled that intense hatred of the Germans had prevented the Israeli Government from holding direct talks with West German officials, and added:

> How can it be expected that these Arab countries, which for twenty years have refused to negotiate with Israel—however great a shock they may have suffered and possible even because of this shock—will be any more ready to negotiate today than they were yesterday? It is probable that never has any dialogue been harder to imagine. . . .[51]

To Jordan, the alternative is indirect talks through the United Nations Mediator, Jarring. This alternative is not wholly acceptable to the Israeli leadership. Eban, whose tactics is to have the Rhodes talks repeated, agreed to hold such talks in Cyprus, but on condition that the Arabs will yield some day to direct talks. He said:

> We do not mind Jarring being there making it a United Nations conference as at Rhodes, but we eventually will all have to come to the same table. We have to see the whites of their eyes.[52]

Eban recognizes Husayn's special position in view of his great losses in terms of territory, revenue, and population. Added to that are

---

[50] Vance and Lauer, *op. cit.*, p. 119.

[51] Murville, *Vital Speeches*, p. 590.

[52] *New York Times*, 7 April 1968, p. 129. Commenting on this attitude, Husayn described the Zionist position as one which does not differ from that of a man who robbed a bank, and wanted to open an account in the same bank with the money he had robbed. The Arab position can be summerized, "return our money first, then we will discuss the matter of opening the account." Husayn's speech at the Press Club, 7 November 1967, cited in *Kalimat Al-Husayn, July 1967-July 1968* (Amman: Ministry of Information, n.d.), p. 58.

his unrelenting efforts to arrive at a satisfactory peace settlement. Accordingly, Eban declared that in the framework of face-to-face negotiations, Husayn, most especially, would get a fair shake. Enticing Husayn to negotiate, Eban added:

> We don't intend to negotiate a deal which would humiliate him in the least. He will receive new boundaries commensurate with his dignity, though I do not think he can expect to get back to June 4 lines.[53]

The Economist reported that while the U.A.R. rejected the offer officially, Husayn seemed more inclined to accept it. Hard pressed by the activities of the Palestine Resistance Movement, by Israeli retaliation and by economic dislocation, Husayn was anxious to get some form of talks going so long as Egypt gave its consent.[54] However, to confirm his stand on the issue of direct talks, Husayn consistently declared that Jordan would make no move for peace without the U.A.R. Simultaneously, he transmitted a sense of crisis and urgency about the need for an early break in the impasse.[55]

To Husayn, who suffered most damages from the war, peace is most urgent.[56] Thus, accommodation with the Israeli leaders became imperative. However, due to his sensitive political position in relation to the Arab states, particularly, the U.A.R., a peace settlement has to include the other Arab countries. "Jordan will not make a separate peace treaty with Israel without Cairo's approval."[57] Although both Jordan and the U.A.R. receive Arab subsidies, it appears that contributors trust the judgement of Cairo as to the conditions of such peace.

In clarifying his feeling about the Zionist state, and reflecting the

---

[53] *New York Times,* 7 April 1968, IV, p. 129.

[54] *The Economist,* 2 March 1968, p. 23.

[55] Sabin *et al., op. cit.,* p. 12. Jordan's Prime Minister Abdul-Mun'em Al-Rifa'i said in connection with separate peace that: "It was impossible without the United Arab Republic, although not necessarily without Syria, Iraq or other Arab countries." *Ibid.,* p. 13; also *New York Times,* 8 December 1968.

[56] The material losses of the armed forces amounted to seventy million Jordan dinars (approximately $200 million). *Al-Risalah Al-Malakiyyiah* (The Royal Message), Amman: Ministry of Information, 1968, p.22.

[57] *New York Times,* 6 November 1968, p. 41; also Vance and Lauer, *op. cit.,* p. 130.

feeling of all the Arabs too, Husayn, in November 1967, told a press conference in Paris, "We are not against the right of any nation to exist,"[58] and declared further that the Arabs do not object to the Jews living among the Arabs peacefully, but they object to the creation of a foreign political state within the Arab world. This is what Israel represents.

> The Jews could live with the Arabs as a nation, not as a military or political danger . . . . The future of the Jews does not reside in racist Zionism, but in free association as fellow countrymen.[59]

Husayn's attitude towards peace has been influenced by the attitudes of many foreign nations. World public opinion is convinced that "Israel is in this part of the world to stay." Accordingly, Husayn had to adjust his position and declare that Jordan recognizes the right of Israel to live in peace and security. However, his fear of expansionist Zionism is real, as the aftermath of the 1967 conflict clearly shows. President Charles De Gaulle told King Husayn in Paris that "if Israel has the right to live in peace and security, Jordan certainly has earned the same right."[60] In this light, Husayn sees that Israel's relations with the Arabs have two alternatives: it can defeat the Arabs, expand into their territories and compel them to accept it as a conqueror; or it can live in peace as an unwelcome neighbour. This state of affairs would change if the Jews end the military nature of their state and abandon their racist philosophy.

In conclusion, two crucial matters seem to stand out in Husayn's peace initiative: one, the return of the refugees to their homes and properties, for the "refusal to accept a solution to this issue constitutes a fatal blow for any hope for accepting other Arab proposals;"[61] two, Israel must return the occupied territories in which the Zionists conducted themselves as no occupation army had done in recent years. For, instead of occupying and establishing military and civilian controls, they expropriated the land and colonized it. Such conduct

[58] Aubrey Hodes, *Dialogue With Ishmael: Israel's Future in the Middle East* (New York: Funk & Wagnalls, 1968), p. 159.

[59] King Husayn's Press Club Speech, 7 November 1967; also *New York Times*, 16 April 1964, p. 1.

[60] *Ibid.*

[61] *Ibid.*

has never been observed throughout the last two hundred years.[62]

As the deadlock for peace continues, Husayn persisted in his challenge to the Zionist leadership to modify their position as the Arabs had done. He expressed: "We are reaching the end of the line. Either of two things can happen: we take our chances to establish peace, or we lose it forever. . . . If it is lost, this would be the fault of Israel and not of the Arabs. Israel must take the next step to show that she really wants peace."[63]

The Israeli hawks may win and go on winning, but without attaining peace, thereby demonstrating Hegel's aphorism about the impotence of victory. Dictating peace, by force of arms, would inevitably lead to absolute despair which would render any peaceful settlement impossible. Cautioning about this dangerous consequence, Jacob Talman, Professor of History at the Hebrew University said, "We Jews have shown how strong the power of despair could be."[64]

CONCLUSION

Peace efforts by Jordan had started even before the Mandate ended. Although hostilities erupted in 1948 and ended in the Rhodes Agreement, King Abdullah continued his efforts to reach a final peace with Israel, for he realized that only under peaceful conditions could Jordan prosper and his plans materialize.

Aside from border incidents, a technical peace prevailed. However, the 1967 War ended the calm. As Jordan lost all the territory acquired by Abdullah in 1948, a new reality was created, and a new political situation established.

Despite King Husayn's moderation and offers for a just and

[62] King Husayn, Press Club Speech, 7 November 1967.

[63] *New York Times,* 7 April 1968, IV, p. 24. Compare Israel's position after the 1967 War when it emerged dictating peace terms, with its position in 1958, when the U.A.R. and the Arab Union were formed. In 1958, Ben Gurion believed that Arab groupings would display hostility and expansionist attitudes toward Israel. Accordingly, he proposed to conclude a non-aggression agreement with the Arabs on the basis of the *status quo.* His offer was discarded. See G. Barraclough, *Survey of International Affairs, 1956–58* (London: Oxford University Press, 1962), p. 367.

[64] Cited in Parker T. Hart, "An American Policy Toward the Middle East," *The Annals of American Academy of Political and Social Sciences,* Vol. 390, July 1970, p. 105.

lasting settlement, which included recognition of Israel and its right to live in peace with secure boundaries, no progress towards peace has yet been achieved. This is ascribed to Israel's desire to impose maximum penalties on the Arabs in terms of recognition, territory, waterways, the Jordan waters and the Palestine refugees.

Jordan and the Arab states insist that the U.N. resolution of 22 November 1967, must be the basis for a future peace. Since the resolution dictates relinquishing of territories occupied by Israel in the 1967 War, it was rejected by the Zionist leadership. Dayan on "Meet the Press" on 12 December 1970, verified this policy when he stated that this resolution was "not our Bible."

To Jordan, the return of the Old City represents the main prerequisite for peace, for the question of Jerusalem "is no longer a Jordanian problem, but a Moslem problem, an Arab and a Christian problem."

Although an alien state, existing in the heart of the Arab world, Israel paid remarkably little heed to the necessity of coming to terms with the Arabs. Its attitude did nothing to disarm Arab suspicion. Israel, further, did nothing towards a solution of the Arab refugee problem.

Israel claims that peace is crucial to its continued existence. However, the Zionists demand that such peace be concluded on their own terms. Israel wants recognition to legalize its unjust gains won with the sword, and insists on face-to-face negotiations to achieve this objective.

To the Arab states, direct talks would mean unconditional surrender, tantamount to signing on the dotted line. Israel's consolidation of its grip on the occupied territories made the Arabs apprehensive about such direct talks. Therefore they insist on indirect negotiations through a United Nations mediator.

The Arabs learned a lesson from the Rhodes talks which resulted in devastating consequences to the Arabs. The Arabs fear that mere meetings with the Israelis will confirm recognition. Israel, having secured this important goal, could refuse to concede anything.

Israel's insistence on face-to-face talks seems absurd even to foreign observers. Finding a parallel between the Jewish-Nazi case on the one hand, and the Arab-Zionist case on the other, French Foreign Minister Murville reminded the Israeli leadership that their intense hatred of the Germans prevented them from holding direct talks with West German officials.

Finally, King Husayn also reminded the Jewish people that Zionism, as a colonial system would disappear sooner or later; that Israel should abandon her racist policies and live in association with the people of the region, peacefully.

PART TWO

Jordan and Inter-Arab Relations

CHAPTER EIGHT

JORDAN-SYRIA RELATIONS

THE GREAT SYRIA PLAN

Students of Arab politics consider Syria the backbone of any Arab grouping or union. Throughout its history, particularly, since World War I, Damascus has been the centre of Arab self-determination, while itself being too weak to dominate any Arab bloc. Syria, therefore, became the prize for Arab primacy, and held so central a position that for an Arab state to have an Arab policy came to mean for it to have a plan concerning Syria, either to seek to extend its influence or to prevent a rival from entrenching itself there. The tireless Hashemite solicitude for Syria was matched with determination by Egypt and the Saudis to obstruct a north Arabian federation, with Syria as its centre.

Syria held the balance of power in inter-Arab relations. To Egypt, the loss of Syria meant its moving into a rival sphere of influence, with the consequent emergence in North Arabia of a unit strong enough to challenge it. Thus, for more than a century, Egyptian policy has been to prevent this development. This fact explains Nasser's speedy incorporation of Syria in 1958, when it was ready to go to whomsoever offered her assistance. It also explains the spontaneous creation of the Arab Union to counter the Egyptian move, calculated to take what the Hashemites claimed as their priority right in terms of geography.

For Egypt to take a place commensurate with its size, wealth and development, it must operate in three circles: the African circle, the Muslim circle, and the Arab circle.[1] In the Arab circle, however, Syria, rather than Egypt was considered by the Arabs as the heart and main source of Pan-Arabism.[2] To Egypt, therefore, the only

[1] Gamal Abdel-Nasser, *The Philosophy of the Revolution* (Washington: Public Affairs Press, 1959), pp. 94–98.

[2] The immediate effect of the failure in the Palestine War in 1948 on the Egyptian thinking was outright denunciation of Pan-Arabism. Inter-Arab

agent for its expansion in Asia has always been Syria, which has been regarded as the "Arab Prussia."[3]

Syria is a particularly good observation post from which to view the Great Power politics in the Middle East. It was to a large extent on the plane of internal Syrian politics that the decisive battles over the Baghdad Pact and the Eisenhower Doctrine as well as the Soviet Union's bid to establish a sphere of influence were waged. Consequently discord in Syria is exported to its neighbours and beyond, so that the sources of international crises often are traced to Damascus.[4]

Jordan's relations with Syria have been based on two main factors: one, Faysal's twenty-one-month rule in Damascus and the resolution by the Syrian Congress in 1920 which proposed uniting the Syrian regions; two, in Abdullah's view, Syria was given to the Hashemites. If Faysal lost it to the French, it was Abdullah's duty to restore it. This was the basis for Abdullah's campaign to unify Great Syria.[5]

In order to enforce his scheme, Abdullah made the Great Syria Plan a national programme. Thus, on 1 July, 1941, his cabinet passed the following resolution:

> Syria, in view of its geographic position and natural resources, cannot survive, particularly from an economic point of view, except if united. Previous events have made it clear that any barrier separating parts of this territory will create political anxiety and hinders economic development and prepares the way for intrigues spread by enemy power.[6]

On 6 March 1943, shortly after Eden's speech in which Britain promised to support Arab unity, a number of Transjordanian dignitaries submitted a memorandum to Amir Abdullah concerning the

---

cooperation and solidarity were considered to have failed the vital test. The isolationists saw in Arab weakness and disunity an opportunity to demand that Egypt should abandon the idea of Arab unity and concentrate on Egyptian affairs. Anwar Chejne, "Egyptian Attitude Towards Pan-Arabism," *Middle East Journal*, Vol. 11 (Summer, 1957), p. 260.

3 Musal Al-Alami, "The Lesson of Palestine," *Middle East Journal*, Vol. 3 (October 1949), p. 390

4 Patrick Seale, *The Struggle For Syria: A Study of Post-War Arab Politics, 1945-1958* (New York: Oxford University Press, 1965), p. 3.

5 *Ibid.*, p. 8.

6 *Journal of Middle Eastern Society of Jerusalem*, Vol. I, 1947, p. 109.

Syrian unity. The memorandum stressed that a Great Syria government should be established with the aid of Great Britain and that "His Highness Amir Abdullah Bin Al-Husayn shall be invited to become the head of the Syrian state."[7] Owing to French, Saudi and Egyptian hostility to this plan, Britain was inhibited from promoting it, declaring that the project must wait the return of stable conditions in the region. As the plan was placed in abeyance, a substitute scheme had to be devised. It was the Fertile Crescent Scheme.

THE FERTILE CRESCENT SCHEME

This plan was proposed by the Prime Minister of Iraq, Nuri Al-Sa'ed in 1943, and submitted to the British Minister in Cairo, Richard Casey. The document was secretly circulated among the Arab leaders.[8] The Plan proposed a federation between United Syria and Iraq. It also provided a solution to the Palestine question, since Palestine was to unite with Syria, Lebanon, Transjordan and Iraq.[9]

The Great Syria and the Fertile Crescent Plans had one important point in common: the exclusion of Egypt and the Arabian peninsula from the North Arabian Federation. Although Al-Sa'ed's plan left it open for other Arab states to join, Egypt was left as secondary partner.[10] The politics of both plans created two rival blocs in the

[7] Muhammad Khalil, *The Arab States and the Arab League: A Documentary Record*, Vol. II (Beirut: Khayyats, 1962), p. 13.

[8] *Ibid.*, p. 9; also see Majid Khadduri, "The Arab League as a Regional Arrangement," *American Journal of International Law*, Vol. 40 (October 1946), p. 762. The memorandum was entitled: *Istiqlal Al-Arab Wa-Wahdatuhum: Muthakkirah Fi Al-Qadiyyiah Al-Arabiyyiah*. See Khalil, *op. cit.*, Vol. II, p. 9.

[9] The outcome would have placed the Jews under Arab rule, though given certain autonomy. The Jews would not have been allowed to live in other parts of the Crescent. Sami Hakim, *Mithaq Jami'at Al-Duwal Al-Arabiyyiah Wa-Al Wahdah Al-Arabiyyiah* (Cairo: Anglo Egyptian Press, 1966).

Had this taken place, Zionism would not have been able to strike roots in the Arab homeland, causing instability in the Middle East and endangering its security, with its implication of a dangerous super-power confrontation.

[10] Al-Sa'ed verified this point saying: "I have assumed that these states are not inclined to join an Arab federation or an Arab 'Usbah' from the start. But if

Arab world. This explains why the Egyptian Prime Minister, Mustafa Al-Nahhas initiated the idea of the Arab League to eclipse the Hashemite bloc while insuring Egyptian dominance in the proposed Organization.[11] Thus, the founding of the League doomed Abdullah's Great Syria and Al-Sa'ed's Fertile Crescent Plans.

With unrelenting insistence, Abdullah pursued his Plan. On 18 May 1943, he sent a message to the British Government urging their support for the establishment of a Syrian unity within its natural boundaries. He based his drive on natural and legal rights. He said:

I wish to inform the British Government that my position is not dependent only on being the heir of the Arab Revolt and the trustee for its national principles, but also as head of an independent Syrian regional state. I emphasize that the Syrian unity is an essential principle of the Arab unity idea as well as a basic national demand.[12]

Sensing British coolness towards the project, Abdullah decided to take the initiative.[13] On 8 April 1943, he addressed a message to the Syrian people in which he allayed their fears about the monarchical form of government and urged for a complete union based on the ideas of the Arab Revolt.[14]

---

the union of Iraq and Syria does materialize, it may then very likely be that these states [Egypt, Saudi Arabia and Sudan] may in the course of time show their desire to join the union." *Ibid.*, p. 10.

[11] George Kirk, *The Middle East in the War* (London: Oxford University Press, 1952), p. 336; also Burhan Gazal *et al., Al-Ahdaf Al-Wataniyyiah Wa Al-Dawliyyiah Li Jami'at Al-Duwal Al-Arabiyyiah* (Damascus: The Hashimiyyiah Press, 1953), p. 18.

[12] Sha'ar, *op. cit.* (4th ed.), p. 223.

[13] Musa, *op. cit.,* p. 441: Also Mohammad Izzat Darwazah, *Hawla Al-Qamiyyiah Al-Arabiyyiah*, Vol. I, pp. 90, 92, 101.

Commenting on Britain's attitude towards Arab unity, Iraqi Foreign Minister Jamali said: "The bare fact is that the Western powers never wanted to support Arab unity, for it was the West that divided the Arab homeland for imperialistic interests. Therefore, the West prefers to keep the Arab land divided for the benefit of its child, Israel." Faḍil Al-Jamali, *Thikrayat Wa-Ibar* (Beirut: Modern Book Company), 2nd ed., 1965, p. 182

[14] Sha'ar, *op. cit.,* p. 216.

Abdullah Renews His Campaign

When the Free France promised independence to Lebanon and to Syria in July 1943, Abdullah took the opportunity and addressed a manifesto to the people of Syria in which he urged them to unite according to the decision of the Syrian Congress of 1920. He said:

The First World War resulted in the independence of Iraq, Hijaz and Yemen. Only the Syrian regions remained disunited and in disagreement. Syria, with its natural boundaries is one fatherland united by bonds of nationalism, geography and history. . . . If foreign interests have led to disunity and dismemberment of Syria, the principles of international justice, the right to a natural life and the promises of the Allies to the Syrians, in particular, and the Arabs, in general should certainly prevent the disruption of our own true home, our one fatherland and our one family.

Now the trend is to found some sort of unity between the Arab countries. . . .[15]

[15] *Suriyya Al-Kubra: Al-Kitab Al-Abyad Al-Urduni* (Amman: 1947), pp. 75–77.
Shortly before the outbreak of World War II, France contemplated the establishment of monarchy in Syria. In view of Abdullah's compromising approach to the Palestine problem, his alliance with Britain as well as his good behaviour since the establishment of Transjordan, he appeared to become the King of Syria; *New York Times,* 30 July 1939. However, the coming of the war and the opposition of Saudi Arabia and Egypt, and the disapproval of Iraq—which desired to install Amir Abdul-Ilah in Damascus—forced the abandonment of the plan; *New York Times,* 7 August 1939.
The Plan was envisioned by Gabriel Puaux, the High Commissioner in Syria. He wrote: "What I had to propose to the French government was to amend the Franco-Syrian treaty....A treaty with a king would offer the best chances for stability....But could the French Republic create kings? I would not have dared to present such a plan to a man like Poincare, but to Daladier I had the audacity to submit it. He listened to me attentively....However, the idea of instituting a Syrian monarchy seemed to startle everybody." Gabriel Puaux, *Deux Anne'es au Levant, Souvenirs de Syrie et du Liban, 1939–40* (Paris: n.p., 1942), pp. 40–41.
The Plan centred on a son of Ibn Saud, not Abdullah. Both France and the Saudis had identical goals. The Saudis always objected to a strong Hashemite state which might attempt to reconquer the Hijaz. The French wished to prevent the British or their allies, the Hashemites, from growing strong in which case French influence in the region would be limited. Furthermore, it should be recalled that Abdullah had planned to attack the French in an attempt to restore Faysal's throne in Damascus. Warner Goldner "The Role of King Abdullah Ibn Husein in Arab Politics 1914–1951" (Unpublished Ph. D. dissertation, Department of History, Stanford University), p. 218.

This address coincided with the elections in Syria. His objective was to influence the electorate to pressurize their politicians to support the idea and pave the way for a convention to be held in Amman. The appeal, however, did not succeed, since the dominant National Bloc opposed it firmly. Even Iraq objected because the Plan would endanger the Fertile Crescent idea which she championed. Iraq, also urged Abdullah to desist from his attempts to seize the Syrian throne, for that would antagonize the Syrian nationalists and the Saudi-Egyptian camp.[16]

But to Abdullah, his claims were real, and his drive to achieve this goal seemed limitless. He based his claim on the following considerations.

1. His legally established right to the Transjordan Amirate which is an important section of Greater Syria.

2. His effective assistance to the Allies during the Second World War....

3. His being the first heir to the rights of his father, King Husayn I, to watch over Syrian interests in particular and Arab rights in general.

4. A promise given him in 1921 by Churchill that he would be the head of the Syrian State....

5. The desire of the Syrians for a constitutional monarchy in the event of Syrian unity or a federation of the Arab countries, being realized.[17]

According to Abdullah's plan, the united Syrian state would encompass Syria, Transjordan, Palestine and Lebanon, under a constitutional monarchy, under his rule. To that effect, he communicated with Faris El-Khouri, a prominent Syrian statesman known for his support for the Hashemites. He emphasized that the purpose of unity was a national duty rather than a personal ambition:

The Syrian situation is a national question and not a personal one. It concerns the Syrian group of countries alone. . . . Here

---

[16] George Lenczowski, *The Middle East in World Affairs* (Ithaca, N.Y.: Cornell University Press, 1956), p. 405.

[17] King Abdullah, *Memoirs* (New York: Philosophical Library, 1950), p. 263; also Khalil, *op. cit.*, Vol. II, pp. 13–14.

I want to express my regret that some people believe that I am working for myself. This is not true. Persons like yourself know that. . . . Free France has promised the country its independence and its sovereignty. . . . When this was proclaimed, Transjordan expressed its desire to be annexed to Syria or to annex Syria to it. I approved this for the sake of unity and the security of the home-land. I don't know what the future form of government will be, whether it will be a republic or monarchial, and this is a sacrifice on my part.[18]

The correspondence with Khouri revealed that the aim of the Syrian National Bloc was the maintenance of the republican regime, owing to their underlying fear of Abdullah's personal ambitions and British influence in Transjordan.[19] Thus, his overtures were viewed with disfavour, since the ruling aristocracy tended to support a re-publican Syria within its mandate frontiers, for upon it rested their economic and political power.[20]

ABDULLAH DEFIES THE LEAGUE STATES

In a memorandum to his Prime Minister, Abul-Huda, Abdullah, on 24 August 1943, stressed that while Transjordan whole-heartedly supported all efforts for a comprehensive Arab unity, no strong unity could be attained unless the Syrian region was united.[21] During the talks for the formation of the Arab League, Abul-Huda continued to participate in the discussions with the understanding that it would lead to the unification of Great Syria.[22] On 4 October 1944, only

18 Sha'ar, op. cit., p. 223.

19 According to the Anglo-Jordan Treaty, Transjordan before its indepen-dence in 1946, was not allowed to conduct foreign relations. Consequently, if Syrian unity were to become a reality, Britain's influence would have been inevi-table. Hakim, op. cit.

20 George Kirk, "Cross Currents Within the Arab League," World Today (January 1948), p. 17.

21 Sha'ar, op. cit., p. 211; also Khalil, op. cit., Vol. II, p. 17.

Emphasizing his right to the Great Syria which he made his ultimate objective, Abdullah declared,"...I say today, as I have always said, that any policy which does not include the ultimate union of north and south Syria is sterile...." Ori-ente Moderno (September 1939), p. 504.

22 New York Times, 17 September 1944. For the discussion between Al-Nahhas and Abul-Huda on this issue, see Al-Hayat (Beirut), 1 April 1960.

three days before the signing of the League's Protocol, Abul-Huda suggested to the Council that Syria and Transjordan be given the opportunity to negotiate the Syrian unity before joining the League. While Jameel Mardam, the Syrian delegate, advanced an alternative solution that Transjordan be returned to Syria, he reminded Abul-Huda that the Anglo-Jordan Treaty would preclude such unity.[23] This meant that Abdullah would not become the head of the union. This created a deadlock and forced him to postpone the project.[24]

REACTION IN SYRIA AND LEBANON

When Jordan secured its independence in 1946, Abdullah embarked on an active campaign to realize his ambition. In his speech from the throne on 11 November 1946, he formally proclaimed that the Great Syria Plan was the principle objective of Jordan's foreign policy.[25] Moreover, he envisioned a larger Arab unity revolving around Jordan:"...I offer my throne as a rallying point for that federation."[26]

At the time of Independence, Abdullah stated to the Egyptian periodical, *Akhir Sa'ah*, that he would continue to fight for the creation of Great Syria and added, "my demand for Great Syria is as natural as Egypt's desire for unity of the Nile Valley."[27] Since to Abdullah, partitioning and disunity were unnatural, he was determined to unite the Syrian provinces.

My father fought neither for the independence of Lebanon, nor for that of Syria, nor that of Transjordan.... My policy is clear:

[23] Musa, *op. cit.*, p. 445.

[24] Majid Khaddouri, "Fertile Crescent Unity," *The Near East and the Great Powers*, ed. R.N. Frye (Cambridge, Mass.: Harvard University Press, 1955), p. 143.

[25] Seale, *op. cit.*, p. 13. On 19 November 1946, Jordan's Foreign Minister, Mohammad Al-Shurayqi, said in Parliament: "The Jordan policy will continue to consider the Syrian general unity as the basic and the principle goal of its programme." See Khalil, *op. cit.*, Vol. II, p. 27.

[26] *New York Times*, 26 May 1946; *Palestine Post*, 26 May 1946.

To a German interviewer, Abdullah revealed his passion for Arab unity as he said, "I am convinced that one day an Arab Bismarck will come who will unite these countries...." Geislher Wirsing, *Englander, Juden und Araber in Palastina* (Jena: Diederichs, 1938), p. 235.

[27] *Les Cahiers*, Vol. 5, p. 16.

I want a state which includes Syria, Transjordan, Palestine and Lebanon. Yes, Lebanon....[28]

Such statements were met with hostility in both Syria and Lebanon. It is significant to recognize that splitting the Hashemites between Amman and Baghdad contributed to their ineffectiveness in dealing with the Syrians. Thus, the Damascus leadership would inquire why Amman and Baghdad did not unite first before coming to bother them.[29]

Lebanon was always concerned about its independence, hence suspicious of Abdullah's ambitions. On 13 November 1945, the Foreign Minister of Lebanon, Hameed Faranjiyiah, declared his country's position regarding the Great Syria Plan. He said:

In our view, this question does not exist. The Lebanese government has repeatedly announced its deprecation of such an idea.... The policy of Lebanon is clear....Lebanon enjoys her independence and sovereignty within her present boundaries. She has joined the Arab League on this basis and will accept no alternative to this policy.[30]

Lebanese President Bishara Al-Khouri, declared his country's position on the controversial issue, on 26 November 1946:

The Great Syria project has become a chronic issue. From time to time, the government of Transjordan steps it up, thus producing a counter action in Syria and Lebanon. Some people think that Lebanon is not included in the project. They wonder why the Lebanese government objects to it. Quite contrary to what is thought, every change in the *status quo*, in the Arab countries weakens Lebanon's position. Moreover, in the event of realizing the project, Transjordan desires, as a first step, the reconsideration of the Lebanese boundaries. The second step is that of rounding up the states of the Fertile Crescent. It suffices to point out to those who do not see any danger to Lebanon from this project what is mentioned in the statement of the Foreign Minister of Transjordan in November of 1946. The statement maintained

---

[28] *Kullu Shay'* (Beirut), March 28, 1947.
[29] Vatikiotis, *op. cit.*, p. 14.; Seale, *op. cit.*, p. 14.
[30] Khalil, Vol. II, p. 21.

Page 152

that 'Lebanon controlled some regions and areas which were compelled to join it and accept a particular form of government.'[31]

However, owing to vehement objections of Syria and Lebanon, and the threat by the latter to withdraw from the League—a consequence which Abdullah was not prepared to take the responsibility for—he declared that Lebanon would not be included in Great Syria. In November 1946, he restated his position:

...Nothing will prevent my ascent to the throne of Damascus.... I have received formal and definite promises on that subject; my Greater Syria does not include the Lebanon. I have all intentions to respect the independence and sovereignty of that country. The opposition against my project is not justified....[32]

Abdullah added that he was not seeking a new throne nor wider possessions, but emphasized his right to the Syrian crown. He stated:

I shall never cease my efforts to achieve the unity of Syria.... But...I am not seeking a new throne for myself, nor have I any personal desire for another crown....[33]

Determined to bring about the Syrian unity, Abdullah took up the issue with the League. In August of 1947, he stressed that the League's covenant aimed at preserving the *status quo* and thus obstructing his project, particularly since the League was a major instrument in the hands of Egypt and Saudi Arabia, his major opponents.[34] Accor-

[31] Bishara Al-Khouri, *Haqa'iq Lubnaniyyiah* (Beirut: Awraq Lubnaniyyiah, 1960), Vol. II, pp. 267–77.

[32] *Les Cahiers*, Vol. VII, p. 317; also Seale, *op. cit.*, p. 14. Jamali relates that relations between Syrian President Shukri Al-Quwwatli and King Abdullah were strained over the Great Syria Plan and that he carried a message from the Egyptian ambassador in Baghdad advising King Farouk that the U.N. Partition Plan was very bad for the Arabs who should unite to avert a possible tragedy. "Ask King Farouk to assure King Abdullah that he will be the King of Palestine after uniting it with Transjordan, and Abdullah in return will abandon the Great Syria Plan." Jamali, *op. cit.*, p. 31.

[33] *Middle East Opinion*, 2 December 1946, p. 12.

Seale wrote that Abdullah had enlisted the aid of the Druze in his plan. They live in the region bordering Jordan, and are traditionally resistant to rule from Damascus. Seale, *op. cit.*, p. 133.

[34] Sha'ar, *op. cit.*, p. 275.

dingly, he proposed the convening of a conference of the heads of the Arab countries of North Arabia to meet in Amman on 4 January 1948. By excluding Egypt and Saudi Arabia, Abdullah assumed that he could be more successful once discussions were localized.[35] He sent his Foreign Minister to deliver the invitation personally to the presidents of Syria and Lebanon.[36] Accordingly, Abdullah proposed that the conference should deal with the following questions:

1. To arrive at a decision regarding Syrian unity.
2. To consider Syrian unity as a question that concerns the states in the Syrian region alone and which will be arrived at according to the desires of the Syrian people who are related to this issue geographically, historically, and nationally....

*   *   *   *

4. To determine the position of Palestine with respect to the Syrian unity in order to stop Jewish immigration.
5. To call a federal convention to write a constitution for the union.
6. As soon as the state of Great Syria is established, it will be followed by the formation of the Fertile Crescent in fulfilment of the ideas of the Great Arab Revolt.[37]

Syria and Lebanon vehemently objected to Abdullah's intrusion in their internal affairs and to his violation of their national sovereignties.[38] For this reason, on 27 August 1947, the presidents of the two countries met in Beirut and declared their hostility to "every idea that aimed at changing the *status quo* and the republican form of government in both Syrian and Lebanese countries."[39]

The Jordan project was rejected, especially by the Maronite Christians, who demanded that Lebanon's independence be respected.

[35] Shwadran, *op. cit.*, p. 239. Also *World Today*, Vol. IV, No. 1 (January 1948), p. 21.

[36] Shwadran, *op. cit.*, p. 239.

[37] Musa, *op. cit.*, p. 444. Also George Kirk, "Cross Currents within the Arab League," *World Today* (January 1948), p. 21.

[38] When he visited Turkey in 1947, Abdullah solicited Turkey's support for his Great Syria Plan, and in return he would support Turkey's viewpoint on the Alexandretta question which has been a source of tension between Turkey and Syria. This meddling in Syrian internal affairs detracted from Abdullah's popularity in Syria. *Middle East Opinion*, 20 January 1947, p. 6.

[39] Bishara Al-Khouri, *op. cit.*, p. 140.

Maronite Patriarch Anton Aridah declared his opposition to any
unity plan and demanded that Lebanon's independence be guaranteed by the Great Powers.[40] Lebanese Prime Minister Riyad Al-Sulh
added, "Friendly cooperation between the Christians and Muslims
in Syria and Lebanon was more valuable than building an
empire."[41]

The Maronites objected because they feared the loss of their sovereignty and their republican regime. Unity was viewed as a threat
to their political power and privileges. On 12 February 1947, Lebanon's, Foreign Minister Henry Far'oun said in the Parliament
that such a project encroaches on the independence and sovereignty
of the Arab League states. The Parliament also suggested that a
complaint against Jordan be filed with the League and the U.N.[42]
Lebanon further warned that, if Transjordan continued to raise the
issue, it would withdraw from the League.

Between 1945 and 1952, Lebanon's foreign policy towards the
Arab states revolved essentially round the policies of Transjordan
and Iraq. The basic question was that, despite the formation of the
Arab League, the Hashemite attempts to implement a North Arabian
Federation was not halted. Lebanon's alignment with Syria was
dictated by their mutual interest to safeguard their positions in relation to the inter-Arab rivalry between Iraq and Jordan on the one
hand, and Egypt and Saudi Arabia on the other. However, while
Syria would enter into unity schemes with a republican rule, the
foreign policy of Lebanon was characterized by a reluctance to enter
into formal political alignments.

Syria's position was that it did not wish a monarchial regime.
This official stand was stated by Foreign Minister Khalid El-Azm:

From the beginning of the Arab national movement, Syria has
always striven hard to achieve unity of the Arab countries....
Syria made many sacrifices for her freedom until finally she achieved her independence and sovereignty....

Syria, accordingly, has no desire to join a union which would

[40] Nicola Ziadah, *Syria and Lebanon* (New York: Praeger, 1957), p. 95.
[41] Frye, *op. cit.*, p. 144.
Christians and Muslim ruling families did not desire to see their authority
pass to Damascus. See George Kirk, "Cross Currents...." p. 17.
[42] Lebanon, *Parliamentary Debates* ,12 February 1947, p. 387.

encroach upon the attributes and rights enjoyed by other sovereign states, nor would she accept a constitutional system, which is contrary to her republican regime, as was framed by her constitutional assembly twenty years ago, and which she is still interested in maintaining.[43]

In Syria, President Al-Quwwatli, after his election in July 1947, openly attacked Abdullah and declared: "If Transjordan really wants unity, let her people join the mother country, Syria, as a free republic."[44] This declaration marked a shift in Abdullah's approach; if a union between Syria and the Hashemites were to materialize, it should be with Iraq.[45]

These efforts, however, did not hold Abdullah, who at the end of September 1947, issued another statement expressing his intentions, that he was working actively for the Plan.[46] This alarmed the Syrian Parliament which held a special session on 29 September 1947, and issued a warning to Abdullah to discontinue his efforts.[47]

At the League Council in Beirut in October 1947, Abdullah's project faced great opposition. He was then persuaded to announce on 14 October "that he would refrain from pressing for the Great Syria Plan until the Palestine problem was solved."[48] Faced with the opposition of all the Arab states, Abdullah decided to act unilaterally. To that end, he approached the Palestine problem on a personal basis. This policy dictated reaching some sort of accommodation with the Zionists which culminated in the unilateral negotiations and the ill-famed Rhodes Agreement. The tension in Jordan's relations with the Arab states finally resulted in the annexation of East Palestine on 24 April 1950, as a temporary substitute for a larger Great Syria. Abdullah's strategy was that by winning Arab

---

43 Frye, *op. cit.*, p. 147.

44 *Ibid.*, p. 150.

45 Kirk, "Cross Currents," p. 25.

46 The British opposition on this issue was voiced in the House of Commons by Foreign Secretary McNeil who officially denied British encouragement on the grounds that the Great Syria controversy was an internal Arab problem, and that Britain could take no position on the question for its only interest in the area was the preservation of peace and stability in the Arab countries. Great Britain, *Parliamentary Debates, Commons*, Ser. V, Vol. 400, Col. 9.

47 Musa, *op. cit.*, p. 440. Also Shwadran, *op. cit.*, p. 239.

48 Shwadran, *op. cit.*

Palestine, Syrian monarchists would be encouraged in their support and agitation for his plan.

THE GREAT SYRIA PLAN AND THE SYRIAN COUP D'ETAT

The main obstacle to Abdullah's ambition was the Syrian National Bloc led by Al-Quwwatli. However, on 30 March 1949, the National Bloc lost power to the military, as Colonel Husni Al-Za'im was successful in executing a *coup d'etat* which was backed by the army and the nationalist reformist elements, such as the People's Party, which had been formed in 1948 to promote Syria-Iraq unity.[49] Za'im was primarily concerned with the security of Syria against Israel. An announcement of a Syria-Iraqi agreement would strengthen Syria's hand at the Rhodes Armistice talks.[50] Moreover, since Syria was militarily weak, its union with Iraq would have given her substantial support, particularly, against Israel. Za'im and his army officers favoured a quick union with Iraq.[51] Nuri proceeded with caution and demanded that Syria clarify her foreign policy. The Hashemites had thought that the coup by Za'im and his flirtation with Iraq were, in effect, paving the way for their ambitious plan.[52]

Anxious for an economic alliance with the Arab states, especially, Iraq and Jordan, Za'im "welcomed federation as long as the Hashemite King (Abdullah) does not become supreme ruler."[53] However, Za'im's personal contacts with the French during his visit to

---

[49] After the Syrian coup, in order to show magnanimity, Abdullah extended an invitation to President Quwwatli to come to Amman where he could form a government in exile. Sha'ar, *op. cit.*, p. 277.

For American complicity in the Za'im coup, see Miles Copeland, *The Game of Nations* (New York: Simon and Schuster, 1969), p. 50 ff.

[50] Seale, *op. cit.*, p. 47.

[51] While Egypt withheld its recognition of Za'im's regime, in view of his pro-Hashemite policy regarding Great Syria, Turkey was happy about Za'im's statement and indicated that it would recognize his regime. *London Times*, 13 April 1949.

[52] Although Britain was not publicly promoting unity plans to avoid antagonizing the French, the Saudis and the Egyptians, they probably would have liked to see the plan materialize. A British diplomat comments: "Arab unity is like a train. We shall neither try to push it nor stop it, but if we see it gathering speed, we might even jump on board." Seale, *op. cit.*, p. 82.

[53] *London Times*, 8 April 1949.

Cairo changed his policy and ended, for the time being, any chance for understanding with the Hashemites.

Egypt and Saudi Arabia, in contrast to Iraq and Jordan, were ready to satisfy Al-Za'im's request for recognition and economic aid.[54] France, meanwhile, promised military assistance. Encouraged by his accomplishments, Za'im declared:

My journey to Cairo was an unpleasant surprise to Jordan. The lords of Baghdad and Amman believed that I was about to offer them the crown of Syria on a silver platter, but they were disappointed. The Syrian Republic wants neither Great Syria nor Fertile Crescent. We will pit our forces againt these two projects of foreign inspiration. To counter the military measures taken by the Amman Government, we have concentrated our forces at the frontier, and have decided that all persons, entering into contact with the Government of Jordan or travelling to that country, will be charged before a military court for the crime of high treason and will be sentenced to death. We have decided to call up new draft of 20,000 men. We are awaiting the immediate arrival of large quantities of arms, ammunition and equipment of all kinds. Our army will soon be second only to that of Turkey in the Middle East. Our air force will surpass the Israel and Turkish air forces combined. We will tolerate no threat or pressure, whether it came from Iraq, Jordan or any other country....As for Jordan, which is and remains a Syrian province, she will sooner or later rejoin her mother country and become the tenth Muhafazah [District] of the Syrian Republic. It must not be thought that certain foreign powers support the projects of Great Syria or Fertile Crescent: we have assurances that Great Britain is for the status quo and that the United States and France would never accept any change in the situation.[55]

This shift in policy drew upon Za'im the hostility of pro-Abdullah elements who were working secretly for the creation of a Syria-Iraq-Jordan bloc. Meanwhile, Jordan and Iraq radio and press renewed their attacks on Za'im's regime. In order to enforce Za'im's position vis-a-vis the Hashemites, King Ibn Saud threatened on 16 June 1949

---

[54] Ziadah, op. cit., pp. 99–109.

[55] Journal D' Egypte (Cairo), 27 April 1949, quoted in Seale, op. cit., p. 57.

that he and King Farouk "will not remain with arms folded in the face of attack on Syria."[56]

Most sources agree that the Hashemites, displeased with Za'im's attitude towards them, and with his pro-Saudi-Egyptian policy, "wished to see established in Damascus a government more friendly to them, were ready to pay to bring him down."[57] Thus, on 14 August 1949, Colonel Sami Hinnawi overthrew Za'im's regime in the second coup of the year.

With Hinnawi, the People's Party, which advocated Iraqi-Syrian unity, came to power. In its meeting on 12 December, the Syrian Parliament gave high priority to the question of union with Iraq, and declared it a basic constitutional goal. By uniting Jordan with the Syria-Iraq federation, the Fertile Crescent would emerge under the Hashemites.[58] It looked as if Damascus would have to renounce the republican regime if the scheme were to become a reality. Although the Syrian Parliament declared itself "favorable to the attachment of Syria to Iraq and Jordan," the plan was abandoned.[59] This was a measure to save the League from dissolution or the withdrawal of Saudi Arabia, or creation of two hostile blocs in the Arab world.[60]

With Hinnawi in power, unity seemed imminent. However, the opposition in Syria rallied the army under the leadership of Colonel Adib Al-Shieshakli, who executed the third coup on 19 December 1949. The new regime announced that the coup was justified because the:

> Syrian army had proof that Hinnawi....was preparing a union with a neighboring state....The Syrian army faithful to the republican constitution is resolved that the regime shall be retained.[61]

Under the influence of the anti-Hashemite elements, Shieshakli

---

[56] *Ibid.*, 19 June 1949.

[57] Seale, *op. cit.*, p. 73. Also At-Tall, *op. cit.*, p. 589 regarding a conspiracy to overthrow Abdullah.

[58] While on a state visit to London, only four days after the pro-Hashemite coup, Abdullah stated that Great Syria "is a natural necessity....It will be governed by the Hashemites." New York Times, August 1949.

[59] Dennis Weaver, *Arabian Destiny* (Fair Lawn, N. J.: Essential Books, Inc., 1958), p. 261.

[60] *Ibid.*, p. 262.

[61] *Ibid.*, p. 264.

visited Cairo and Riyadh and concluded commercial agreements, thereby committing Syria to the anti-Hashemite camp, and causing unity plans to lapse.[62]

Observers agree that King Abdullah was a statesman, a good political strategist, but was a poor tactician.[63] The latter trait was manifested in his failure to persuade Arab public opinion of the merits of his plans. Realizing the insurmountable obstacles in swaying the Syrians to agree to his programme, Abdullah, as a last resort, invited Nazim Al-Qudsi, the Syrian Prime Minister, to Amman. The purpose of the visit was "to remove the causes of misunderstanding between Jordan and Syria, and to establish diplomatic representation."[64] In a final attempt to reach an agreement with Syria on the issue of union, even a symbolic one which would serve as fulfilment of his obsession, he declared that he would accept a republican regime as a price for unity. In his portrayal of magnanimity, he added, "you are free to choose a republic which I will accept or the monarchy which I shall not oppose."[65]

With the removal of Hinnawi, the Hashemites feared that their Great Syria project was lost for ever. This fear was verified as the Shieshakli Government declared:

The new Syrian Government is resolved to oppose by all possible means the fusion of Syria and Iraq and the realization of the projects of the Fertile Crescent. . . . We will never consent to be placed under the tutelage of a Hashemite sovereign.[66]

Despite the difficulties he encountered, Abdullah never gave up the idea for Arab unity with Great Syria as its centre. Shortly before

[62] A six million dollar interest-free loan from Saudi Arabia and a five million pound loan from Egypt were secured as the price for underwriting Syrian independence. See Seale, *op. cit.*, p. 92.

[63] Glubb, *A Soldier with the Arabs*, p. 217. As a poor tactician, Abdullah made the Arabs suspicious of his intentions. As a strategist, while for immediate personal ends, his plans may have been crucial to Arab unity. He would make a move only if favourable conditions prevailed. He once said, "Politics is like chess. You cannot rush your pawns across enemy territory, but you must seek favorable openings." *London Times*, 6 February 1948.

[64] Sha'ar, *op. cit.*, p. 271.

[65] Mustafa Kharsa, *Muthakkirat Al-Malik Abdullah* (Beirut: Al-Muktaba Al-Asriyiah, 1960), p. 280; Musa, *op. cit.*, p. 447.

[66] Weaver, *op. cit.*, p. 268, also *Le Monde*, 23 February 1954.

his assassination, he declared: "All my life I have fought for true Arab unity. I shall never give up the struggle until my death."[67] However, the assassination of Riyad Al-Sulh, the Prime Minister of Lebanon on 16 July 1951, in Amman while visiting Abdullah, which was followed by the assassination of the King in Jerusalem on 20 July ended for all practical purposes the project of Great Syria, and the career of a colourful Arab ruler.[68]

CONCLUSION

Jordan's relations with Syria during Abdullah's rule were based on the King's personal aspirations and individualistic policy objectives. The Great Syria idea held a prominent place in plans for Arab unity and was declared to be the major foreign policy objective of Transjordan.

Insisting that Transjordan was the nucleus for his projected united Syria, Abdullah pursued his ambition by urging Britain and the Syrian royalists to accomplish this goal: "my policy is clear. I want a state which includes Syria, Transjordan, Palestine and Lebanon."

Abdullah's foreign policy was unmistakably dictated by personal and dynastic aspirations. While Arab national interest appeared to be a secondary objective, speaking in the first singular, he conveyed this fact, while insisting that what was good for him had to be good for the Arabs in general and the Jordanians, in particular. However, his success in building a Hashemite empire was obstructed by a complicated external setting. His plan was thwarted by the determination of Syria, Lebanon, Egypt, and Saudi Arabia. Added to that was French opposition and Britain's half-hearted support. Preferring a republican to a monarchial form of government, and insisting that unviable Jordan should be annexed to Syria to preclude foreign influence, the Syrian leadership placed an insurmountable obstacle before the King's plan. Although Abdullah devoted his life to the realization of this personal goal, his death in 1951 ended a chapter of Jordan's personalized foreign policy.

[67] *London Times*, 21 July 1951.
[68] Ever since 1957, the Syrians attributed to Husayn the desire and intention to realize his grandfather's ambitions of annexing Syria. Vatikiotis, *op. cit.*, p.162; also Hashim Sharabi, *Palestine and Israel* (New York: Pegasus, 1969), pp. 66-7.

CHAPTER NINE

JORDAN-IRAQI RELATIONS

INTRODUCTION

In the San Remo Conference of April 1920, the peace-makers drew lines on maps that formed the basis of Iraq and Jordan. These two territories were sliced from the defunct Ottoman Empire and entrusted to Britain as mandatory power under the League of Nations. While Western diplomats were sharing spheres of influence in the Arab homeland, the Arabs started setting up kingdoms. By parcelling the Arab territories, the Western diplomats had Balkanized instead of stabilizing the region, thus, contributing to the present instability in the Middle East.[1] While it may be argued that many states in the Fertile Crescent were artificial creation of the European powers who came to control the area at the end of World War I, Transjordan, perhaps, was the most artificial of them all.[2]

As a political force in North Arabia, the Hashemite rulers never enjoyed a strong political base, since they were regarded as "imported" kings, imposed by Britain and functioned under her close direction.[3] Recognizing their status among the Arabs, eager to restore Arab glory under their banner, and aware of their formidable rivals— the Egyptian-Saudi bloc—it seemed logical that the rulers of Iraq and Transjordan should consolidate their front in alliance or in union.

---

[1] Philip Ireland, *The Near East* (Chicago: University of Chicago Press, 1942). This book explains the reasons why Western Powers concluded that mandates and fragmentation were best for the Arabs.

Also see Anis Sayigh, *Al-Hashimiyoun Wa Al-Thawrah Al-Arabiyiah Al-Kubra* (Beirut: Modern Press, 1966).

[2] Vatkiotis, *op. cit.*, p. 7.

[3] "A Study in Contrast: Turbulent Iraq and Jordan," *Wall Street Journal*, Vol. 152, 29 July 1958, p. 10.

Until 1924, the Hashemites were rulers in the Hijaz, the western region of present Saudi Arabia. The conquest of that territory by Ibn Saud placed the Hashemites at the mercy of Britain which had promised them an Arab Kingdom.

EARLY ALLIANCES

After 1941, the two Hashemite rulers of Iraq and Transjordan established closer relations and consulted each other on matters of foreign affairs and other issues of mutual interest.[4] Their representatives held identical viewpoints during the formation of the Arab League. Later, both rulers established relations and entered into treaties with Turkey.

In 1945, continued cordial relations inspired them to discuss the possibility of uniting their countries. In order to coordinate political strategy, Amir Abdullah sent his son, Crown Prince Talal, to discuss the salient points of Abdullah's unification plans. On 4 February 1945, the Regent of Iraq Abdul-Ilah and Prime Minister Nuri Al-Sa'ed met with Amir Abdullah at Shunah, his winter Palace. The British High Commissioner was also invited.[5] An agreement was reached on establishing some sort of union with the knowledge and encouragement of Britain.[6] Amir Abdullah was reported to have declared:

I believe that when a union between Iraq and Transjordan is realized, other Arab countries will follow their example.... I am still working for Syrian unity.[7]

With this statement, Abdullah served notice that he had not abandoned his ambition to become the ruler of a large Arab state without Iraq.

In his speech from the throne dealing with Arab unity, he informed the Parliament of the proposed unity with Iraq, and expressed hope that the proposed Hashemite union would serve as a prototype for future unification agreements in the Arab world:

Please be informed, honorable Deputies, that we are firmly decided on a close unity between ourselves and our sister, Iraq, whose aim is the coordination of efforts and attitudes in the two sister coun-

[4] Majid Khaddouri, *Independent Iraq* (London: Oxford University Press, 1960), p. 343.

[5] *New York Times*, 17 January 1945.

[6] "Transjordan and Iraq, Scheme for Union," *The Times Weekly* (25 September 1946), p. 23.

[7] *New York Times*, 12 February 1946.

tries. The door is not closed between the states of the Arab League and ourselves for any confederal cooperation, brotherly pact, or federation of such nature; for we are, and shall remain, God willing, ready to give advice to all now and in the future.[8]

In Iraq, however, the nationalists viewed the proposed alliance as an instrument to create dissention among the League's members, and feared Transjordan's interference in Iraq's internal affairs in support of Abdullah's expansionist policies. It was also argued that Transjordan's treaty with Britain might lead to indirect British interference in Iraq's internal affairs, a particularly sensitive area in Iraq's thinking.[9]

The plan for full union failed because of the ill feeling and distrust which it had aroused. Although a treaty was finally passed by the Iraqi Parliament on 4 May 1947, by a majority of 83 to 49, with only two opposed, while the rest abstained, the final outcome was a treaty of alliance and brotherhood. It was signed on May 14, and went in force on 10 June 1947. It provided for a ten-year alliance, according to which both countries were to engage in joint military training and stipulated that neither country should become a party to a treaty with a third party in any matter contrary to the interests of the other. In case of aggression or domestic uprising in either country, the other should provide forces to quell disturbances. It further made provisions for unifying diplomatic representations in certain areas.[10]

---

[8] Khalil, *op. cit.*, Vol. II, p. 23. After gaining independence, it was rumoured that Abdullah might become the king of the Iraqi-Transjordan union and that King Faysal II of Iraq would become his successor instead of Abdullah's son Talal. Talal was to be compensated by becoming the viceroy of Palestine. This plan was said to have been approved by the British Foreign Office but was denied by Talal. *New York Times*, 30 March 1946.

[9] *Oriente Moderno*, April 1947, p. 186.

The new Anglo-Jordan treaty put Jordan with Britain "on reciprocal instead of one-sided basis." It was consistent with the League's Charter by denying Britain the right to station its R.A.F. in any part of Jordan. It further provided for an Anglo-Jordanian Defense Board with equal number of military representation charged with "The formulation of agreed plans in the strategic interests common to both countries. . . ." *Keesings Archives*, 1946–48, p. 9175.

[10] English text in Khalil, *op. cit.*, Vol. II, p. 226. Arabic text in Majali, *Qissat Muhadathat Templer* (n.p.: n.d.), p. 29. See also *Transjordan Legislation*, 1947, pp. 102–5.

PRELUDE TO UNION

Undoubtedly, the Arab-Israeli war of 1948 was the most important event in the history of Jordan. On 24 April 1950, King Abdullah annexed Eastern Palestine and, along with the land, Jordan also received hundreds of thousands of refugees who have disrupted the country economically and politically. Until then, Jordan's population was made up mainly of tribes, who remained supporters of the King. Later, however, the Palestinians constituted an entirely new force in the country. With little loyalty to the King, they were more active politically than the Jordanians. This new element was persistently looking for a leader to restore their usurped homes, and thus became an agitative force and a potential threat to the monarchy.

Successful in defying the League in his annexation of Eastern Palestine as recommended by the Jericho Conference, Abdullah felt encouraged to revive his life-long dream, the Great Syria Plan. However, his personal discussions with Syrian Prime Minister Al-Qudsi came to no avail due to the objection of Syria to monarchial regime, Lebanon's refusal to become a part of the plan, and finally due to general Arab suspicion of his personal ambitions.

As all his efforts failed, Abdullah embarked on another scheme in the field of foreign affairs. It was the proposal for union between Iraq and Jordan. It appeared that such a union was motivated as much by his personal ambitions as it was by his attempt to deal with the problem of succession to the Jordan throne. A week before his assassination, Abdullah had invited a major Arab personality, a Lebanese, Riyad Al-Sulh to help realize his plan. On the matter of Jordan-Iraqi unification, he confided to Sulh:

> For some time now, Riyad Bey, I have been absorbed in the issue of the fate of Jordanian throne after me. I do not see in Talal or Naif a suitable man to mount the throne and administer the country. For this reason, I have been turning this subject over in my mind for a long time. To my mind, the best way to solve this problem is an agreement with Iraq on a unification or union of the two regions (al-qutrayn-Iraq and Jordan) under my crown, with the provision that the whole kingdom reverts after me to His Majesty Faysal the Second.[11]

[11] *Al-Hayat*, 18 February 1958; also Nashashibi, *op. cit.*, p. 334. Prime Minister Majali in his memoirs relates that Abdullah discussed with him the

Again, the Iraqi ruling circle favoured a gradual union to be completed at the end of five years. It was to commence with a union of the two crowns, thus, preserving the Hashemite control over both countries. It further provided that only a descendant of the Hashemite dynasty could succeed to the joint throne.[12]

The new government, headed by Huda, appeared to prefer a Jordan-Iraqi union. For this reason, an Iraqi mission came to Amman for the purpose of bringing about unity.[13]

---

question of succession (because he had the premonition that his end was near) because Talal's health had become hopeless. Abdullah further indicated that he wished to have Husayn declared Crown Prince. Abdullah ended by saying: "You are mistaken if you thought that I don't like Talal, but Talal is my son and the father wishes to see his son more successful than he is. I realize that Talal is ill and the interest of the country dictates the resolution of this question before me. However, I do not insist on this but leave it to the Prime Minister. Inform him of this...." Majali adds that Abdullah told him that he depended on him to persuade the Prime Minister to implement this plan. Majali, *Muthakkirati*), p. 106.

Gallman, the biographer of Prime Minister Nuri Al-Sa'ed wrote that Nuri, in order to further cement the Hashemite throne, wanted King Faysal II of Iraq to marry Husayn's sister. This plan did not succeed, as Faysal was about to wed a Turkish princess, but he was killed in the Iraqi coup on 14 July 1958. Weldemar Gallman, *Iraq Under General Nuri* (Baltimore: John Hopkins Press, 1964), p. 136.

[12] This plan was published in *Liwa Al-Istiqlal* (Baghdad), 4 October 1951. The well-informed Egyptian paper *Al-Ahram* reported that King Abdullah had concluded and signed a three-point secret agreement with Abdul-Ilah and Nuri, the authenticity of which was verified after Abdullah's assassination. *Al-Ahram*, 6 June 1952.

During his funeral in Amman, the Iraqi delegation invoked the question of these discussions and claimed that Prime Minister Rifai was informed as correspondence on this question was exchanged. Although the Iraqis were criticized for their conduct—"You came not to console but to take Jordan"—certain discussions were conducted between Huda, Nuri, and Abdul-Ilah (Majali, *Muthakkirati*, p. 108).

Reference was to Regent Abdul-Ilah, Prime Minister Nuri and Saleh Jabre. Majali told them: "We also want unity, but unity can be completed through official discussions of the two countries and not in this manner." Majali, *Muthakkirati*, p. 108.

[13] *Ibid.*, p. 111. During the trials of the People's Court in Baghdad, Mohammad Hasan Salman, the head of the three-man mission disclosed on 13 October 1958, that: The murder of King Abdullah was considered as an opportunity for the realization of a union between Iraq and Jordan....As such a union was one of our national goals, I agreed to undertake this task....We contacted our nationalist colleagues, such as Sulayman An-Nabulsi, Hikmat

However, following Huda's visit to Saudi Arabia, his thinking changed. He appeared to defend the right of Talal to the throne and thus preclude the union with Iraq.[14]

FOREIGN POLICY UNDER TALAL

On both banks of the Jordan, there was a strong feeling for the maintenance of Jordan's sovereignty under the leadership of King Talal. Talal's extreme popularity was based on his pure nationalism and his long opposition to the policies of his father and to Britain.[15] His popularity was further strengthened in view of the popular belief that his illness, which was used as a pretext for depriving him of the throne, was merely a fabrication staged by the British, and an "invention of political intrigues."[16] Britain was believed to be favouring the idea of unity with Iraq, which meant Talal's loss of the Jordan throne. But, since public opinion supported Talal, Britain abandoned the idea.[17]

In foreign affairs, Talal stressed Arab cooperation, that Jordan was an independent state and the Jordan people were a part of the

---

Al-Misri, Abdullah Ar-Rimawi, Anwar Al-Khatib, Mamduh Sukhan, Zuhayr Darwazi, Dr. Shawayhat, Akram Zuayter and others. The idea of the mission was that, in the event of the nationalist candidates' victory, those members could be persuaded to work for union with Iraq. Muhakamat Al-Sha'ab, *Mahadir Jalsat Al-Mahkamat Al-Askariyyiah Al-Ulya Al-Khassah,* Baghdad: Wizarat Al-Difa'a, 1959, IV, p. 1255-6. See also Ann Dearden, *op. cit.,* p. 96 ; and Majali, *Muthakkirati,* pp. 110-11.

[14] Majali, *Muthakkirati,* p. 111. In a secret session of the Parliament on 18 December 1951 (after Abdullah's death and the traditional change of government), Huda told the Parliament: .... If the proposed union aimed at the unification of defense or the army, or at any other practical joint action, we would have considered it useful and fruitful. But the written and unequivocal plan is confined to the unification of the crown provided the army continued to receive foreign aid as before, and provided it preserves its present status and composition for another five to ten years after which time, the question of what may be done concerning the army or any other real co-operation in economic matters will be considered. Khalil, Vol. II, pp. 46–7. Also *London Times,* 20 December 1951.

[15] Majali, *Muthakkirati,* p. 112.

[16] *Ibid.,* also *London Times,* 4 July 1952.

[17] Abidi, *op. cit.,* p. 89.

Arab nation. He began to bring Jordan's policy in line with Syria, Egypt, and Saudi Arabia and away from Iraq and Britain.[18] The establishment of the Arab Collective Security Pact in January 1952, which Jordan joined, verified Talal's Arab policy.[19]

During Talal's 340-day rule, public opinion became apprehensive about the poor economic conditions of the country, the lack of material resources and the political stability of the state. Accordingly, a consensus of opinion was that Jordan's present viability could not maintain it as a separate state for long. Although the West saw that Jordan's economy would inevitably be connected with that of Israel, the Arabs instead saw that annexation of Jordan by any of its Arab neighbours could solve its chronic economic problems.[20] Despite its shaky position, however, Jordan's geographical location made it of far greater importance to the League and to the defence of the Middle East.[21]

Pursuing a policy of Arab cooperation, Talal deemed it more appropriate to seek financial aid from the Arab states even if such dependence could lead to an economic union with them. Foreign aid was deprecated. At this point, the government was urged by the Deputies to state its position on the question of a Jordan-Iraqi union.[22] To discourage a union with Iraq, to which he objected earlier, Huda, on a radio broadcast on 12 January 1952, said that a political unity with Iraq was primarily aimed at the unification of the crown and such a union would not alleviate economic conditions.[23]

The interest of Iraqi ruling circles to absorb Jordan had not diminished. Thus, Abdul-Illah and Nuri continued their visits to Amman and to Lausanne, Switzerland, where Talal was hospitalized. Although these talks were secret, Abdul-Illah in an effort to make such a union feasible insisted that a member of the Hashemite house, Prince Zayd (Abdullah's brother), should be appointed as head of the Advisory Council. However, Huda refused this demand on the

---

[18] Talal visited Saudi Arabia from 8–19 of November 1951 at the insistence of Prime Minister Huda. Majali, *Muthakkirati*, p. 117.

[19] Musa, *op. cit.* p. 565.

[20] Plans for the development of the Jordan River Valley, such as the Johnson Plan during the Eisenhower Administration, were based on this idea.

[21] "Jordan and its Legion," *The Economist*, Vol. 59, No. 14 (15 July 1950), p. 128.

[22] *Middle Eastern Affairs*, 3 February 1952, p. 53.

[23] *Ibid.*

basis that the Jordan Constitution does not allow it.[24]

A medical board concluded that Talal was suffering from schizophrenia. On this basis, the Parliament met in a secret session on 11 August 1952, whereupon Huda declared Talal's son, Prince Husayn, to be the constitutional king. A Regency Council was appointed to rule the country since Husayn was not of age.

The first question to be discussed by the Council was the issue of Jordan's continued existence as a nation. A series of articles appeared in *Falastine* newspaper discussing this very issue. The authors argued that the economic and financial capabilities of Jordan were not commensurate with the great responsibilities which she inherited as a result of the Palestine tragedy. Since complete dependence on foreign aid involved many dangers, the only solution to this dilemma was the establishment of a union between Jordan and another Arab state, such as Iraq, whose resources would be sufficient for the needs of the union. Furthermore, a federation was viewed as a national necessity and such a limited union would expedite a fuller Arab unity.

Iraq was chosen due to its abundant resources compared to the other Arab countries. In addition, foreign ties of both countries were indentical and both countries were ruled by the same dynasty.[25]

This proposal was met with approval by the public opinion of Jordan, particularly in the West Bank, where it was received with enthusiasm and support in view of their fear from Zionist expansionism.[26] However, due to Huda's resolute opposition to any form of union with Iraq this idea was abandoned, to the displeasure of the Iraqi leadership.

There was little, if any, sentiment in Nuri's approach to Jordan. He viewed the country in a factual way, and always considered Jordan as:

...an artificial political entity and inevitably bound to become linked in time with a neighbouring Arab country. If Jordanians were given free choice, the majority would opt for union or for federation with Iraq.[27]

[24] Majali, *Muthakkirati*, p. 120.
[25] *Ibid.*, p. 123.
[26] *Ibid.*
[27] Gallman, *op. cit.*, p. 137.

Nuri was concerned about Jordan's political position in the face of pressures from other Arab countries. The army was unable to stabilize the internal situation and, at the same time to meet the Zionist aggression. Under the Arab Solidarity Pact of 1950 and the Jordan-Iraqi Treaty of 1947, Jordan had the right to call on Iraq for help in case of an external aggression. Further, in case of internal upheaval, Iraq also reserved the right to "free and wider movement within Jordan, should disorder become widespread."[28]

Nuri always kept in mind the possibility of Iraqi intervention in Jordan, because he espoused the policy that rich and powerful Iraq was the guardian of poor, unstable and weak Jordan which could at any time be swallowed by its neighbours. Thus, on 20 September 1956, he sent supplies to three points along the route to Jordan under the pretext that "Iraq's sole aim in anything undertaken in the military field was to save Jordan from Communism."[29]

During the tripartite aggression on Egypt, Husayn proposed opening a new front from the Jordan side against Israel. But the cabinet advised caution for two reasons: one, hostilities could mean gambling with the West Bank and the possibility of losing it; and two, under the Jordan-Iraq treaty, if Jordan became involved in the conflict, the Iraqi army would also march into Jordan.[30] This the government sought to prevent in view of the serious differences with Iraq's foreign policy, particularly on the question of union. In any event, at the invitation of Husayn, Syrian and Iraqi forces entered Jordan on 3 November 1956. When the Jordanian Prime Minister demanded that Iraqi troops be placed under the Jordan-Saudi-Syrian joint command, the Government of Iraq refused and declared that its forces had entered Jordan at the personal request of Husayn and that their presence in Jordan was specifically in accordance with the Jordan-Iraqi Defense Treaty.[31] In any event, at the insistence of the cabinet, the withdrawal of the Iraqi troops was secured.

[28] *Ibid.*, p. 140.

[29] *Ibid.*

[30] Majali, *Muthakkirati*, p. 205. An Iraqi delegation arrived in Amman to decide on a united military plan. According to the plan, an Iraqi division entered and camped in East Jordan. It was agreed that the Jordan General Ali Hayari would command the combined forces. However, the Iraqi Government refused to place its forces under the command of the Egyptian General Amer who was the head of the Arab command. *Ibid.*, p. 206.

[31] *Ad-Difa'a*, November 5, 1956.

KING HUSAYN'S REIGN

Husayn assumed his constitutional powers on 2 May 1953. In his letter of commission to Prime Ministeı Mulqi, Husayn instructed:

> We hope that the program of your cabinet will aim at strengthening the national sovereignty and safeguarding of the Arab rights through cooperation and understanding with all Arab states. Further, one of our objectives is to preserve the cordial relations with the allied and friendly states.[32]

Although the Prime Minister agreed to abide by the King's wishes in developing strong bonds between Jordan and the Arab countries, it was clearly understood that Jordan was not prepared to establish political union with the Arab states or to sever its traditional relationship with Britain. Due to popular agitation relating to internal affairs and to the position of Jordan in relation to the foreign states, particularly Israel and Britain, Mulqi resigned and Abul-Huda was asked to form the next cabinet.[33]

Abul-Huda's foreign policy was based on his preference for preserving the Jordan sovereignty. To that end, he clearly rejected the idea of a larger Arab federation which might result in the loss of the independent status of Jordan.[34]

Up to this period, Jordan had never known ideological political parties. Among the newly established political parties was the Al-Hazb Al-Watani Al-Ishtiraki (the National Socialist Party) organized in Amman on 7 July 1954. The Party's most important objective was the call for an Arab union. The first step to be taken was to unite Jordan with Iraq, considering that Iraq was the only country which possessed large material capabilities, and the fact that the

---

[32] Musa, *op. cit.*, p. 580. By contrast, Talal's address did not include the term "allied" states. This indicated the course of his policies towards Britain.

[33] The government was asked to hold meetings of the Cabinet and the Deputies in Old Jerusalem, but the request was denied.

Two reasons were given for Mulqi's resignation. According to *Al-Bina'a* (Damascus) of 15 May 1954, Mulqi had received a note from the British Government directing that Jordan should hold meetings with the Zionists to discuss outstanding questions. Another possible reason was cabling a message of thanks to Andre Vyshinski by the Deputies for supporting Jordan in the Security Council. Abidi, *op. cit.*, p. 115: also Musa, *op. cit.*, p. 595.

[34] Abidi, *op. cit.*, p. 115.

foreign relations of both countries were identical; both countries were ruled by the same dynasty ; furthermore, the strength and training of the Iraqi army would supplement the Jordan army. All of these factors would improve Jordan's position *vis-a-vis* Israel. Later on, after the abrogation of the Iraqi-British and Jordan-British treaties, Syria would join the union. This postponement was preferred in view of the fact that Syria did not have any international obligation outside the Arab states and that Syria should not be burdened with Jordan-Iraq-British treaties.[35]

Husayn's first effort was to build the country's economy without Western assistance. In September 1953, a Jordanian delegation visited Saudi Arabia and Iraq to seek financial assistance. Influenced by the Queen Mother Zayn to develop closer relations with the wealthy Saudi family, Husayn met King Saud, whereupon the Prime Minister of Iraq declared that Jordan could not be viable unless it united with Iraq.[36] Iraq's declaration was received unfavourably in Jordan and, perhaps, more in the various Arab countries. Shieshakli, then in power in Syria, worked with Saud to prevent an Iraqi-Jordan union. Husayn's cousin, King Faysal II, exerted more pressures and succeeded in pulling Jordan to his side, thus, saving it from becoming a victim of economic pressures from other neighbours.

In February 1955, during the discussions in Amman regarding Jordan's joining the Baghdad Pact, an economic delegation from Jordan visited Iraq for the purpose of obtaining a loan to finance a number of developmental plans. The Iraqi government made one important condition for their approval of the loan, namely, Jordan's joining the Turkish-Iraqi alliance, known as the Baghdad Pact.[37] This condition was refused by the delegation on the basis that a loan should not be connected with any political conditions. However, the intervention of Husayn secured a loan of 1,600,000 dinars.[38]

MOTIVES FOR THE JORDAN-IRAQI UNION

On 1 February 1958, Presidents Gamal Abdel Nasser of Egypt and Shukri Al-Quawwatli of Syria signed a communique announcing

[35] Majali, *Muthakkirati*, p. 143; and Musa, *op. cit.*, p. 600.
[36] Shwadran, *op. cit.*, p. 213.
[37] Majali, *Muthakkirati*, p. 167.
[38] *Ibid.*, p. 168.

the formation of the United Arab Republic. It was the first political union between two Arab states in modern times.

The U.A.R. was a peculiar union between two states; one in Africa and the other in Asia. In some respects, it was an unnatural union, since Syria has always been considered a constituent part of the Fertile Crescent region whose population had closer relations with northern Arabs than with the Egyptians.[39]

By 1957, the Ba'ath Party and President Nasser had become the two most dynamic forces in Syrian politics. Both held similar views on Arab unity and were in agreement on the question that a Syria-Iraq union amounted to extending British influence into Syria. These were the basis for the Ba'ath alliance with Cairo which resulted in the creation of the U.A.R.[40]

Michael Aflaq, the Party theoretician, came to the crucial conclusion that Arab union must start with Egypt, not because she was the Prussia of the Arab World, uniting it by force, but because Egypt could and would successfully obstruct any unity movement which excluded her.[41]

Nasser's Arab "unity" plan did not involve territorial mergers as a first step. Egyptian Foreign Minister, Mahmoud Riyad verified this policy as he declared: "We never asked for union with Syria. We always argued that it was premature. ... Our policy was, in fact, to avoid union."[42] Instead, Nasser wanted Arab solidarity on foreign issues under Egyptian direction. To that end, he wished to control the foreign policies of the Arab states. Since the Syrians have always been especially responsive to any appeal for Arab solidarity or unity, control of Syria appeared crucial if Egypt's idea were to triumph throughout the Arab World.[43] Though a hazardous venture, Nasser was attracted by the magnitude of the enterprise. While it appeared that the merger would be beneficial to Egypt as well as to Arab unity, Syria, in the meantime, was engulfed in unusual circumstances which rendered its security, even continuation, as a viable state, doubtful. For one, Syria was gradually

[39] Salah Al-Din Al-Bitar, a leading Syrian Ba'athist said: "...the ordinary Egyptian does not yet feel Arab," that the Arab idea never went very deep in Egypt. Cited in Seale, *op. cit.*, p. 311.

[40] *Ibid.*

[41] *Ibid.*, p. 311.

[42] *Ibid.*, p. 314.

[43] *Ibid.*, p. 313.

being brought under Communist influence. The Union had, in fact, caused the Communists to lose a decisive round. Ex-Prime Minister, Faris Al-Khouri, though a Hashemite loyalist, had declared:

> Although I did not approve of the union, I did not openly oppose it. I thought at the time it was the only way to check the progress of Communism in the country.[44]

Thus, the virtual collapse of the Syrian state dictated direct intervention by Nasser, for to him and the Ba'ath subservience to Russian influence was as much an offence to the Arab nation as was their subjection to Western influences and policies.[45] For another, Nasser and the Ba'ath feared the formation under Western sponsorship of an Arab bloc consisting of Iraq, Jordan, Saudi Arabia, and Lebanon, designed to close the ring around Syria and in the long run, force it to join that bloc.[46]

Syria occupied a key position in the Fertile Crescent: it was the centre of the most pro-Western group of states in the Middle East— bordering on Lebanon, Turkey, Iraq and Jordan. Thus, Syria's political orientation had immediate bearing on Western plans—the Eisenhower Doctrine and the Baghdad Pact. When the Syrian Minister of Defence concluded an economic agreement with the Soviet Union in September 1957, the situation in Syria was viewed by the West as leading to "Communist control." Since the United States had decided to refrain from carrying out her plans, an alternative was devised:

> Syria was to have been declared under Communist control....Iraqi and Jordanian armies would invade Syria .... Later, however, King Husayn, the key figure in the plan, changed his mind....[47]

To the Hashemites, the U.A.R. represented Egyptian expansion in the area designated for the Hashemite-sponsored Fertile Crescent.

[44] *Ibid.*, p. 324.

[45] "Pan-Arab Challenge to Ankara," *The Economist*, Vol. 56, 1 February 1958, p. 379.

[46] George Kirk, "The Syrian Crisis of 1957—Facts and Fiction," *International Affairs*, Vol. 36, p. 58.

[47] Hashim Sharabi, *Palestine and Israel; The Lethal Dilemma*, New York: Pegasus, 1969, pp. 66–7.

It was understood that the Egyptian type of Arabism could not strike roots in North Arabia,[48] while Iraq was the natural backbone for Arab unity movements in view of its potential economic wealth, geographic position as well as history. Only Iraq could give permanence to it. But Iraq was occupied with its role in the Baghdad Pact which prevented it from taking an effective leading position in Arab affairs, and, consequently, was looked upon as de-Arabized. However, Iraq's absence from the Arab arena created a vacuum which had to be filled by its counterpart, Egypt.[49]

In the Arab World, the creation of the U.A.R. had a spontaneous effect, as the wave of Nasserism seemed to herald the dawn of the long-awaited unity, particularly to the younger generation that was brought up in the spirit of this idea. In Jordan, mass sympathy with the Republic seemed dangerously possible, especially among the Palestinians.[50]

The wave of exuberance that swept Syria at the start of the union, signified by the triumphant crowds that welcomed Nasir to Damascus, and widely shared by Arab opinion in the surrounding Arab states, reflected a conviction that the tables had been turned that the initiative in the Middle East had passed to the revolutionary Pan-Arab movement.[51]

Less than two weeks after the U.A.R. was proclaimed, the Hashemite rulers announced that they were forming an Arab Federation. The motive was clearly evident. It was a spontaneous move to counteract Egypt's expansion in Syria which placed it in a stronger position vis-a-vis the Hashemites by successfully preserving Syria from possible absorption by Iraq or Jordan. The Hashemite kings decided to act immediately to halt the spread of Nasserism and Communism and

[48] Salah Al-Din Al-Bitar, a leading Ba'athist said: "Abd Al-Nasir's mind was awakened to Arabism in 1953 or 1954. It was the first time an Egyptian ruler started to think about the Arab World in terms other than the mere desire to dominate. But the Arab idea never went very deep in Egypt; the ordinary Egyptian does not yet feel Arab. We in the Ba'ath always hoped that a union would foster in Egypt the same nationalistic sentiments that fired us." Cited in Seale, *op. cit.*, p. 311.

[49] "Political Trends in the Fertile Crescent," *World Today*, Vol. XII (June 1956), p. 215.

[50] *Ibid.*

[51] Husayn, *Uneasy Lies the Head*, p. 234.

ironically to save Jordan from falling within the U.A.R.'s sphere of influence. Husayn stated the Hashemite strategy, in view of the fact that both Iraq and Egypt had "intensified efforts to win Jordan over as an exclusive ally."[52] Accordingly,

The new Arab Union with a common defense program, had a frontier stretching from Sinai to Kuwait. Nasser might have hoped to swallow up Jordan one day and so form a land link between Syria and Egypt, but now that Jordan was united with Iraq it was not possible.[53]

The Arab Federation was, therefore, urgently needed to save Husayn's Jordan from becoming swallowed by the U.A.R., to keep the country running on lines approved by Iraq, to preserve the Hashemite and to extend its authority to Jerusalem monarchy with its combined military might against Israel.[54]

The Federation gave prominence to the Palestine question. King Husayn said:

On this day we turn our hearts toward Palestine and we promise before God to work as before to achieve our rights, which were stolen by the enemy. We will not lay down our arms until we have achieved our aims.[55]

These were the immediate reasons, others justified the move: both rulers felt that it was their duty to make a gesture of Arab unity which

---

[52] *New York Times*, 18 March 1956.

[53] Husayn, *Uneasy Lies the Head*, p. 233. In their meeting on the frontier, Faysal told Husayn, "The Iraqi financial support for Jordan...will constitute a clear snub to Egypt, Saudi Arabia and Syria, who have offered to take the place of the British subsidies...." *London Times*, 16 March 1956.

[54] Israel protested the presence of Iraqi troops on its frontiers, the truce line. Iraq did not sign a truce agreement with Israel, as other Arab states have. Musa, *op. cit.*, p. 689; also Ionides, *op. cit.*, p. 237.

[55] Cited in M. Pearlman, "Fusion and Confusion: Arab Mergers and Realignments," *Middle East Affairs*, Vol. IX (April 1958), p. 128. The two unions involved imminent danger to the existence of Israel. Premier Ben Gurion was among those who believed that the Arab Union and the United Arab Republic might result in a desire for expansion and a display of hostility towards their neighbours, Sudan and Israel. Under these conditions, he offered to conclude a non-aggression agreement with the Arab states on the basis of territorial *status quo*, but his offer was disregarded. See. G. Barraclough, *Survey of International Affairs* (1956–1958), p. 367.

was sparked by their great grandfather, Husayn I, and to which they claimed leadership.

The union seemed more natural than the United Arab Republic. Geographically, both countries had a common frontier. Internally, there was a marked similarity in the areas of sterling currencies, law and courts, and the administration of the armies. In addition, Jordan which had been in urgent need of financial help would get it by allying itself with the oil-rich Iraq.[56]   Iraq would pay eighty per cent of the budget, taking into consideration national incomes and the chronic annual deficit in Jordan's budget.   The opening of trade and removal of customs, would relieve Jordan of pressures for food-stuffs which would be brought from Iraq to supply the economically inviable Jordan with its half a million turbulent refugees who had been living under the auspices of the United Nations.

Since the treaty provided for domicile and freedom to work in either country, Iraq would benefit by absorbing needed labour in its agriculture and various public works projects which consumed seventy per cent of its oil revenues as well as the economy in general.[57] Thus, Jordan's union with the oil-rich Iraq meant a boom for her.

Previously, when Jordan accepted an Arab subsidy, Iraq shied away to avoid assuming the economic burden which poor Jordan would impose on her. The picture, however, changed in 1958, when Iraq contemplated annexing Syria to gain an outlet on the Mediterranean. When Syria became unavailable, Iraq rushed to join with Jordan.

THE JORDAN-IRAQ FEDERATION

The kings of Jordan and Iraq opened a series of discussions which climaxed in the promulgation of the Arab Federation on 14 February 1958.   King Husayn believed in Arab revolutionary nationalism and identified himself with it. To save his throne and the state which his grandfather built, he was forced to revert to his grandfather's

---

[56] The Federation would reduce, if not completely eliminate Jordan's dependence upon the United States' aid.   It would ease American responsibility, as it would remove the stigma from Jordan for being an American dependency.   See S. H. Longrigg, "New Groupings among the Arab States," *International Affairs,* Vol. 34 (July 1958), p. 316.

[57] Expended for reclamation and dam projects.

type of nationalism, the principles of which can be summarized as follows:

Whereas: the Great Arab Revolt led by His Majesty the great saviour Al-Husayn Ibn Ali was a proclamation of a new dawn for the Arab nation. . . .

Whereas: the mission of the Arab revolt, for which its leader has striven, passed to the sons and grandsons. . . .

Therefore: the two Hashemite states decide to form a federation between themselves. . . .[58]

The Hashemite confederacy was opened to all interested Arab states that wished to join by agreement with the Federal Government.[59] While Member states would retain their independent, national status and international personality, currency, customs, law and education, armed forces, diplomatic representation and foreign affairs were to be unified. King Faysal would be the head of the federation and King Husayn, his deputy. When other states joined the federation, the question of the head would be reviewed according to circumstances. The federal capital would alternate between Baghdad and Amman, and the federation flag would be the flag flown during the first Arab revolt.

The federation legislative authority rested with the Union Council and the President of the Union. The Council would be composed of forty members, half of whom represented each kingdom. The cabi-

[58] Muhammad Khalil, *The Arab States and the Arab League: A Documentary Record*, Vol. 1: *Constitutional Developments* (Beirut: Khayats, 1962), p. 79.

[59] *Ibid.*, p. 80. Also See Pearlman, *op. cit.*, p. 128. In an effort to support the union, it was reported in Baghdad on 6 May 1958, that Britain had informed Iraq of its willingness to give up its treaty arrangements with Kuwait, if the Shiekhdom joined the federation. *Middle Eastern Affairs*, Vol. 9, (June-July, 1958), p. 237; also Ionides, *op. cit.*, p. 235.

Although the Hashemites feared that Saud would become the head of the federation, if he joined, they, nevertheless, sought to include him in a three-king front. Saud, however, maintained strict neutrality for two reasons: One, his fear that a strong Hashemite union would inevitably destroy him; second, his fear of Egyptian expansion. Saud remembered that Mohammad Ali had conquered the peninsula in 1818 and Nasser might have been operating against that background. Keith Wheelock, *Nasser's New Egypt* (New York: Praeger, 1960), p. 259. Also Great Britain, *British and Foreign State Papers*, 1957-58, 163 (London: Her Majesty's Stationery Office, 1966), pp. 933-36.

net was small, comprising only three portfolios: foreign affairs, finance, and defence. Each kingdom would have a minister of state, a Prime Minister and a Deputy Prime Minister. The Iraqi Prime Minister was appointed first Premier of the union; Jordan's Prime Minister his deputy. Article 62 enumerated matters within the jurisdiction of the union government:

1. Foreign affairs and diplomatic and consular representation.
2. Negotiation of treaties, pacts and international agreements.
3. Protection of the states of the union and preservation of their security.
4. Establishment and management of the armed forces under the name of "The Arab Army." No member state may maintain armed units other than police and internal security forces.[60]
5. Organization of the Supreme Defense Council, military service and military recruitment.
6. Customs and customs legislation.
7. Coordination of financial and economic policy.
8. Currency and financial affairs.
9. Highways and communications.
10. Unification of educational policy; programmes and curricula.[61]

Being a federation, with central powers delegated to the central government, all other affairs and powers would remain under the authority of the Member States. From a political and international viewpoint, the federation strengthened Jordan's position, since Iraq's military diplomatic, financial and economic resources became available to it, as it became an equal partner.

DISSOLUTION OF THE UNION

Despite its long range programme, the Federation was unofficially ended on 14 July 1958, the day of the Iraqi *coup d'etat,* only a few

---

[60] The army of Transjordan was called "Al-Gaysh Al-Arabi Al-Urduni," while other states called their armies after their countries, i.e. the Syrian Army.

[61] Arab Information Center, *Basic Documents of Arab Unification,* p. 39; also Khalil, Vol. I, p. 88.

Although Jordan joined the Union, it did not become party to the Baghdad Pact. Husayn, *op. cit.,* p 187.

months after its announcement.[62] It was most easily disposed of, partly because of Husayn's voiced hostility to the Iraqi Republic. On 15 July 1958, one of the first decisions of the Iraqi cabinet was the Iraqi withdrawal from the Federation, and the annulment of all measures connected with it.   The reason given was that the union had not been a true one with the interests of the people as its objective. The proclamation signed by the Prime Minister and issued on July 23, read:

> The federation between Iraq and Jordan, in the manner it was affected under the previous regime, was not a real union aimed at (realizing) the interests of the people in the two countries. It was rather (meant) to consolidate the corrupt monarchial system as well as to disrupt the unity of the emancipated Arab (people) and to realize the interests of a clique of rulers who did not come to office through (the choice of) the people and who did not work for the realization of their aspirations.
>
> Accordingly, the Government of the Iraqi Republic declares its immediate withdrawal from this Federation....[63]

Since King Faysal II was murdered during the coup, King Husayn became the head of the federation. The Constitution of the Union stipulated that either State could intervene to quell internal uprising inside the other.   On that assumption, Husayn could declare, "We might still have to take military action."[64] The Jordan Cabinet urged

[62] See Khalil, Vol. 1, pp. 32-7 for Qassim's speech to the congress of Arab lawyers at Baghdad on 26 November 1958, in which he disclosed the conspiracy by the Arab Federation to "attack our sister Syria," causing the Iraqi coup. To verify the "conspiracy," see Seale, *op. cit.*, pp. 263-82.

The revolution came as a complete surprise to the world, particularly, since the representatives of the Western powers in Baghdad were not aware of the possibility of such an uprising.   Commenting on the revolution, Eisenhower remarked "This was the country that we were counting on heavily as a bulwark of stability and progress in the region." Dwight D. Eisenhower, *The White House Years: Waging Peace,* 1956-61 (Garden City, New York: Doubleday, 1965), p. 269.

For an excellent detailed discussion of the Iraqi revolution see Majid Khadduri *Republican Iraq* (New York: Oxford University Press, 1969).

[63] Khalil, *op. cit.,* Vol. 1, pp. 91-2.

[64] Husayn, *Uneasy Lies the Head, op. cit.,* p. 205.

The Jordan ambassador to London declared in this connection that "It was the prerogative of King Hussein to decide on the measures to counter the revolt in Iraq," *Parliamentary Debates,* 591, Col. 1516.

Husayn to oppose the new Iraqi regime with force and to restore order, but Husayn refused.[65] His decision was influenced by several factors: one, marching on Iraq would mean fighting other Arab population who had taken no part in the revolution;[66] two, Husayn was worried about the threat to Jordan from an Israeli attack; therefore, he could not leave the frontier unguarded. There was genuine fear that Israel might seize the moment for a thrust into the West Bank;[67] three, it was possible that he received no encouragement or support to restore the Federation.

. . . . Was there an idea of invading Iraq by a combined attack from Turkey, Iran and Jordan? (Husayn had legal grounds for such action, as he was co-sovereign of the newly formed Arab Federation of Jordan and Iraq). If there was any such intervention, it did not materialize. For one thing, Husayn's position was too shaky for him to trust his own army; in late July 1958, he had to call on British troops to protect his throne.[68]

In any event, although the new Iraqi revolutionary government antagonized outside powers as little as possible, "Western intervention could not yet be completely ruled out as an eventuality."[69]

In answer to a question in the Commons, whether British troops would keep order inside Jordan while the Jordan army proceeded to Baghdad, Prime Minister McMillan said, "That will not be its function...movements from Jordan to Baghdad are quite difficult on either side." *Ibid.*, 1443.

[65] Husayn, *Uneasy Lies the Head, op. cit.*, p. 199.

[66] *Ibid.*

[67] *Ibid.*

[68] Sharabi, *Palestine and Israel, op, cit.*, p. 70.

During the debates in the House of Commons, the leader of the Opposition, Hugh Gaitskell, raised the question, whether "Husayn made his appeal to us or to the U.N. as King of Jordan or as King of Jordan and Iraq—the Federation; whether we have given him any assurance that we will assist him, should he try to re-assert his authority over Jordan and Iraq." McMillan replied : "As far as I know, it will be in his name and title as King of Jordan." Great Britain, *Parliamentary Debates* (Commons), Vol. 591, 1958, Col. 1439-1440.

McMillan also added: "I should make it clear that it is to the kingdom of Jordan that we are sending our help in this time of need, not the union. I must add that in making their request, the Jordan King and Government said that they had no intention that the British troops should be used to release Jordan forces to attack Iraq. The obligation remains with them and it is upon this basis that we have decided to send our help." *Ibid.*, Col. 1511.

[69] Uriel Dann, *Iraq Under Qassem* (New York: Praeger: 1969), p. 52.

The precipitate landing of American marines in Lebanon was thus occasioned in reality not by what was going on in Lebanon but by the military coup in Iraq. It was not. . . because Lebanon had accepted the Eisenhower Doctrine and hence was in a position publicly and internationally to invoke it that the United States intervened. Dulles wanted to demonstrate to foe and friend alike that the U.S. was capable of more than only words—that it was not afraid of the Soviet Union. . . . That we were afraid of Soviet reaction if we attempted military action. American credibility was at stake; intervention after the Iraqi coup, seemed necessary.[70]

The American landing demonstrated American determination to act militarily in the Middle East. Intervention may have prevented the Baghdad Pact from collapsing, since Iraq, the main partner withdrew.[71] It was also accredited for the survival of Husayn's regime and probably for re-enforcing the Saudi monarchy.[72]

Immediately after the revolution had succeeded, radio Baghdad announced: "A revolution has started in Iraq and one in Lebanon, and tomorrow, another revolution will start in Jordan."[73] Fearful of

[70] Sharabi, *Palestine and Israel*, p. 69.

[71] The passions released by Iraq's joining the Baghdad Pact eventually destroyed the regime which manipulated it. "A Baghdadless Baghdad Pact was to become in 1959, a living symbol of boomerang," for it resulted in removing the Cold War from the Arab World. Fayez Sayegh, *Dynamics of Neutralism in the Arab World* (San Fransisco: Chandler, 1964), p. 182.

[72] Sharabi, *Palestine and Israel*, p. 69.

In answer to a question whether British troops were to prevent external aggression McMillan said: Our sole purpose and indeed our only purpose is to try to stabilize the position and to prevent a repetition in Jordan of the events which took place last Monday in Iraq." Great Britain, *Parliamentary Debates* (Commons), *op. cit.*, Col. 1444.

Justifying the immediate response by Britain and the U.S., McMillan stated in the Parliament: "But the immediate result of refusing this request might well have been the overthrow of yet another small and independent country. . . . With the end of Jordan's independence what other countries in the Arab World could have maintained their freedom ? I do not believe that Honourable Members on either side of the House really wish to see a dictatorship established in the name of Arab nationalism and stretching all across the broad lands of the Middle East. To preserve Jordan's independence was, perhaps, a limited objective but there is reason to hope that by achieving this aim we may at least, reassure the other independent Arab countries and states." *Ibid.*, Col. 1509. See also Khaddouri, *Republican Iraq, op. cit.*, p. 56.

[73] Great Britain, *Parliamentary Debates* (Commons), Vol. 591, 1958, Col. 1508.

an imminent revolution which would certainly end the Hashemite dynasty, Husayn's last resort was to request direct intervention by his Western allies. It was expected that British troops would be sent to Jordan due to Britain's long association with the King, its familiarity with the country, government and the people.[74] Accordingly, the request was made, as Husayn wrote:

> The Cabinet met and decided to ask the United States and Britain to send us troops. Not so much physical as moral help. A token force would be enough, something to take some of the load, at least for a short while. . . . We do not mind which countries send troops. We need them for a limited period only. I look upon this move as a symbol of the ties that bind free peoples in times of crisis.[75]

In his biography, Husayn alludes to the possibility of a plot against Jordan's monarchy saying: "We could do nothing but wait and see what steps would next be taken by the latest Pharoah across the Nile."[76]

[74] In the House of Commons, Prime Minister Harold McMillan said that the Government of Jordan had made a similar request for help to the U.S. Government, who were considering it urgently in the light of their commitments in the area. The U.S. had sent reconnaissance flights over Jordan to precede the landing of British troops. He added that the British Government's decision was taken after full consultation with the U.S. Government. *Ibid.,* Col. 1509.

[75] Husayn, *Uneasy Lies the Head,* pp. 204-05; also Robert Murphy, *Diplomat Among Warriors* (Garden City, New York: Doubleday, 1964), p. 397.

Prime Minister McMillan told the House of Commons that the action by Britain and the U.S. was a moral one:

> By intervention at the request of President Chamoun and of King Husayn of Jordan, Her Majesty's Government and the U.S. Government have acted quite rightly on moral, legal and strategic grounds to keep both the Lebanon and Jordan outside Nasser's fold. *Ibid.,* Col. 1521.

[76] Husayn, *Uneasy Lies the Head,* p. 200. See also *Parliamentary Debates,* 549, 1956, Col. 1714.

In the House of Commons, Prime Minister McMillan agreed with Husayn on blaming Nasser for the unrest:

> In making this request, the King and the Prime Minister said that Jordan was faced with an imminent attempt by the U.A.R. to create internal disorder and to overthrow the present regime on the pattern of recent events in Iraq....

On that basis, British Prime Minister Harold McMillan acted quickly in order "to protect a small and independent country which had appealed for help against the threat of aggression and subversion stimulated from without."[77] Britain and the United States realized that unless they intervened, Jordan and Lebanon would be lost to the revolutionary regimes and the situation in the Middle East would deteriorate to threaten other conservative governments and Western interests. Accordingly, while the American forces landed in Lebanon, British troops were flown into Jordan immediately.[78] They were withdrawn on 2 November 1958.

Having lost hope of restoring the federation, Husayn announced the formal dissolution of the union on 1 August 1958, because the new Baghdad government made Iraq "incapable of performing its share of responsibility in the union."[79]

Jordan's territorial integrity was threatened by the movement of Syrian forces towards her northern frontier. They had information that a coup organized by the U.A.R. would be attempted today. . . .

The purpose of this military assistance is to stabilize the situation in Jordan by helping the Jordan Government to resist aggression and threats to the integrity and independence of their country. *Ibid.*, Col. 1438.

[77] A letter from Prime Minister McMillan to Premier Khrushchev dated 22 July 1958, quoted in Great Britain, *British and Foreign State Papers,* Vol. CLXIII, 1957-1958, p. 591.

The British troops were flown over Israel, without prior permission explaining why it was so urgent for them to reach Amman. Husayn, *Uneasy Lies the Head,* p. 207; see G.B., *Parliamentary Debates,* Vol. 591, Col. 1556.

Protesting his government's action, a British Socialist member of Parliament said that instead of sending troops to Amman, "would not the King be safer here in London—where he could be looked after by a couple of policemen?" Husayn's remark to this statement: "It was not me or my country those British troops came to protect, it was freedom." Husayn, *Uneasy Lies the Head,* p. 208.

[78] Khadduri, *Republican Iraq,* p. 56.

In diplomatic communications to Prime Minister McMillan dated 19 July 1958, Premier Khrushchev called the Western action a "military invasion" at the request of an irresponsible monarch who does not enjoy the support of the people and acts against the will of the people. He demanded the immediate withdrawal of British and American troops from the Middle East, declaring, "The Soviet Union . . . cannot be indifferent to what is happening in the Middle East, which is in direct proximity to its frontiers." G.B., *Parliamentary Debates,* Vol. 597, pp. 587 ff.

[79] *Middle Eastern Affairs,* Vol. 9 (October 1958), p. 326; for the text of Jordan Cabinet decree, see G.B., *British and Foreign State Papers,* 1957-1958, Vol. 163, pp. 937-38.

Husayn feared that in the absence of the balancer, Iraq, his regime would be swept by the U.A.R. However, the new Iraqi regime did not seem to constitute a threat to Jordan itself, as Qassem concentrated on consolidating the position of his regime inside Iraq. He manifested respect for all the Arab states: even Jordan was mentioned with goodwill or, at least, without malice. He was not interested in annexing Jordan or in the political character of the regime in Amman.[80] He even regarded the British landing in Amman following the Iraqi coup as Jordan's internal affair,[81] and went so far as to suggest that any attack on Jordan would be considered an attack on Iraq.[82]

In an attempt to enhance his position, Husayn quickly renewed relations with Qassem's government. He even "nursed hopes for re-establishing the Jordan-Iraqi federation with himself as head."[83] Consequently, he recognized the revolutionary government on 1 October 1960, and resumed diplomatic relations with it on 12 December 1960.[84]

Conclusion

Despite their claim to Arab leadership, the Hashemites lacked a popular political base. Abdullah's failure to unite the Syrian region testifies to this crucial point. Although Iraq and Jordan had more in common than any other two Arab states, particularly the dynastic

---

The Republic of Iraq signed an agreement of cooperation and solidarity with the U.A.R. on 19 July 1958. G.B. *British and Foreign State Papers, op. cit.,* p. 930.

Jordan ended diplomatic relations with the U.A.R. on 20 July 1960, because it recognized the Iraqi revolutionary regime. Musa, *op. cit.,* p. 692.

[80] Dann, *op. cit.,* p. 67.

[81] *Mid East Mirror,* 3 August 1958, p. 24.

[82] Hans Tutsch, "A Report from Jordan," *Swiss Review of World Affairs,* Vol. X, No. 11 (February 1961), pp. 6-10.

[83] *Middle Eastern Affairs,* Vol. 9 (October 1958), p. 405.

[84] *New York Times,* 12 December 1960.

As a gesture of goodwill, Qassem ordered reburial of Faysal II in the Royal tombs. Hans Tutsch, *op. cit.*

Britain and the United States recognized the new regime on 1 August 1958, while Turkey, a member of the Baghdad Pact extended its recognition on 31 July 1958. See Khadduri, *Republican Iraq,* p. 58.

aspect, no union had taken place until the advent of the U.A.R.

Egypt's intrusion in north Arabia was a clear challenge to the Hashemites who hitherto considered the Fertile Crescent region as their domain. The U.A.R. not only presented a clear threat to the Hashemite plans, but Jordan would become a part of the U.A.R. sooner or later. Husayn's evaluation of the situation proved accurate. The majority of his subjects were Palestinians whose consensus hailed the U.A.R. as the dawn for a comprehensive Arab unity, and Nasser as Saladin, the leader and unifier. Husayn, thus, was placed in a precarious position as he could not ignore popular pressure for joining the U.A.R. It was a political crisis of grave consequences. Joining the U.A.R. meant forfeiting his claim to leadership while assuming a secondary role, perhaps, even fading into oblivion. One alternative was open to Husayn: immediate unity with Iraq.

Husayn's decision was dictated by internal as well as external forces. One, a Hashemite union would not be considered wholly repugnant, for, although it was an obvious response to the U.A.R., it, nevertheless was a form of Arab unity. Two, it was the only way by which the Hashemites could preserve their political independence by precluding the loss of Jordan to Egypt, their competitor for Arab leadership. Such a development would have been detrimental to Iraq's position of leadership. Three, establishing the Arab union may have been a tactic by which the U.A.R. would collapse, thereby eliminating Egypt's challenge. Four, such a union would ease the chronic economic crisis in Jordan, as Iraq's economy would absorb Jordan's unemployed manpower and budgetary deficit. Five, the union would strengthen Jordan's military capability in facing the Israeli threat, as Iraq's army would share in its defence.

Jordan held a pivotal position in Arab unity. Had it joined the U.A.R., a comprehensive unity would have been forthcoming. However, the establishment of the Hashemite union emphasized the schism between the conservative and the progressive regimes, as it did emphasize the Hashemite-Egyptian rivalry. By declining to join the U.A.R., Husayn and Faysal stressed their dynastic interests rather than their concern for an Arab unity in which they assume secondary roles.

CHAPTER TEN

JORDAN AND THE ARAB LEAGUE

FORMATION OF THE LEAGUE: BACKGROUND

The Great Syria and Fertile Crescent schemes were Hashemite in content, designed to prevent Egypt and Saudi Arabia from extending their influence into the North Arabian regions.   However, the feeling that it would be "unwise to found a League on the Fertile Crescent from which Egypt was not a member from the start," made its implementation impractical.[1]

Motivated by tangible advantages, Egypt developed immense interest in Arab unity movement.   To that end, she took the initiative in playing the role of a builder and unifier of the Arab World.[2] Thus, on 30 March 1943, Mustafa Al-Nahhas, Prime Minister of Egypt, presented a tentative proposal for creating an Arab League to the Egyptian Parliament.   Nahhas was motivated by three considerations: first, he could not reject the Fertile Crescent scheme without being accused of opposing a form of Arab unity.   He had to submit an alternative.   Second, he believed that an Egyptian dominated League would serve Egyptian politics.   Third, he acted out of motives of personal ambition.[3]

While there was manifest support for the idea, there was also suspicion about its practical application. Amir Abdullah had indicated that a "loose federation" was all that could be achieved, and added: "as long as the Syrian countries remained without sovereignty, without unity, and under foreign rule, cooperation between them and Egypt and Iraq would be ineffective."[4]   Recognizing Egypt's leading role in Arab politics, he agreed to support the plan and urged

---

[1] Albert Hourani, *Syria and Lebanon* (New York: Oxford University Press, 1946), p. 5., Also Seale, *op. cit.,* p. 200.

[2] Boutrus Ghali, "The Arab League, 1945-1955," *International conciliation* (May 1954), p. 389.

[3] Lenczowski, *The Middle East in World Affairs, op. cit.,* p. 403.

[4] Graves, *op. cit.,* p. 254.

the Arab governments to "aim first and foremost at achieving the union of Syria."[5] However, during the conferences of the Arab Prime Ministers in Cairo, Syria emphatically rejected Abdullah's Great Syria project preferring a comprehensive Arab union instead and declaring that "Syria will refuse to have raised in her sky any flag than her own save that of an Arab union."[6]

THE PACT OF THE ARAB LEAGUE

The Pact recognized the independence and sovereignty of the League members and their right to secede from the Organization.[7] While membership was limited to the Arab countries, only those with independent status were qualified to join.[8] Furthermore, the Pact differed from the Alexandria Protocol in one, particularly important aspect. The Protocol stipulated that "in no case will the adoption of foreign policy which may be prejudicial to the policy of the League or any member state be allowed." The Pact, not only omitted this provision, but specifically denied such unity in foreign policy matters by stating that "treaties and agreements already concluded, or to be concluded in the future between a member state and another state, shall not be binding or restrictive upon other members."[9] Thus, while the Pact emphasized the sovereignty of the members, it rendered the Organization ineffective and reduced it to a mere meeting-place.

---

[5] *Ibid.*, p. 255.

[6] Khaddouri Majid, "Toward an Arab Union: The League of Arab States," *American Political Science Review,* Vol. 40 (February 1946), p. 95.

[7] Lebanon was given specific guarantees for her independence.

[8] Burhan Ghazal, *Al-Ahdaf Al-Qawmiyyiah Wal-Dawliyyiah Li-Jami' at Al-Duwal Al-Arabiyyiah* (Damascus: Hashiyyiah Press, 1953), pp. 23-4.

Because of their colonial status, the membership of north African Arab states was suspended. Jordan, however, was considered a full member since Britain had promised its independence in 1946. Bevin declared in the U.N., "Regarding Transjordan, it is the intention of His Majesty's Government to take steps in the near future for establishing this territory as a sovereign, independent state and for recognizing its status as such." *London Times,* 18 January 1946.

Amir Abdullah signed the League Charter on 2 April 1945. It was published in the *Official Gazette* on April 19, and became effective on May 10, Musa, *op. cit.,* p. 397.

[9] See Article 9 of the Covenant of the League of Arab States, Khalil, Vol. II. p. 59; and Ghazal, *op. cit.,* p. 49.

THE GREAT CHALLENGE: ABDULLAH ANNEXES ARAB PALESTINE

JORDAN'S VIEW OF THE LEAGUE

The Arab League was an idea conceived by Iraqi Prime Minister Nuri Al-Sa'ed, adopted by Mustafa Al-Nahhas, Prime Minister of Egypt and approved by Britain's Foreign Secretary Anthony Eden.[10] Lacking direction and orientation, and armed with minimum previous political experience and association, certain Arab states were brought together into the Organization which King Abdullah described as "a quiver containing seven heads."[11] Except for Najd and Yemen, all other Member states were directly or indirectly under foreign control.[12] As an inter-Arab organization, the League served as a front for promoting political ambitions of some founding states.[13]

The Arabs viewed the League as a primary medium for inter-Arab relations, or as a foundation for Arab solidarity only when Egypt's own interest required it.[14] Jordan considered the League as having lost its purpose as an instrument of collaboration among the Arab

[10] Lord Altrincham, the British Minister of State in the Middle East, said that if the White Paper had not been issued, the whole Arab world would have been against the Allies in the most serious and dangerous years of the war. The way to safeguard Western interests in general and British in particular was to act with the Arabs assembled in their own League. Cited in Elli Kedouri, "Pan-Arabism and British Policy," *Political Quarterly*, Vol. 28 (April-June 1957), p. 145.

[11] Sha'ar, *op. cit.*, p. 238.

[12] Notice Abdullah's reference to Saudi Arabia as comprising only the eastern part of the Saudi Kingdom. Hijaz, the western part, was conquered by Ibn Saud in 1924, causing the Hashemites to lose their kingdom. However, Abdullah and Ibn Saud signed a treaty on 27 July 1933, in which Abdullah recognized Saudi control over Hijaz. Khalil, Vol. II, p. 212; also Musa, *op. cit.*, p. 346.

[13] Reference to Saudi and Egyptian opposition to the Great Syria-Fertile Crescent Plans. See *L' Orient*, 28 March 1947; Seale, *op. cit.*, p. 312.

[14] Kerr, *The Arab Cold War*, p. 128. Jordan believed that as long as the League Secretary-General is an Egyptian, the organization would continue to be an "arm of the Egyptian foreign policy." See Sha'ar, *op. cit.*, p. 239. See also Mustafa Kharsa, *Muthakkirat Al-Malik Abdullah*, (Beirut: Dar Al-Tali'ah, 1965). Seale, *op. cit.*, p. 200.

John Philby, adviser to the late Ibn Saud, said of the Arab League: it is "frustrated by the jealousies and dissensions, corruption, and incompetence of its Member States". . . . Whether the Arab League "can survive the internal stress of house divided against itself is very much open to doubt." John Philby, *Arabian Jubilee*, (New York: Day Company, 1953), cited in *Security and the Middle East*, A report submitted to the President of the U.S., April 1954, p. 22.

countries, because it had become an integral part of the Egyptian foreign ministry. The League was a victory for Egyptian diplomacy against rival Hashemite plans for the Fertile Crescent and Great Syria. As long as the League continued to be "a tool in the hands of the Egyptian government" and as long as its headquarters continued to be in Cairo, Jordan would not consider it an effective instrument to serve all states on an equal footing. To that end, on 15 January 1963, Jordan asked that the League Headquarters be officially transferred to either Beirut or Damascus.[15]

THE ALL-PALESTINE GOVERNMENT

Abdullah 's entry into the Palestine War of 1948 was based on earlier plans for annexing the Arab part of Palestine.[16] Thus, when Britain contemplated ending the mandate, Abdullah began to toy with the idea of uniting Palestine with Transjordan. His intention violated the League Political Committee resolution of 12 April 1948, which was unanimously passed and which provided that:

The entry of the Arab armies into Palestine for the purpose of saving it should be viewed as a temporary measure free from any of the characteristics of occupation and division of Palestine, and that following its liberation it should be handed to its owners so that they might rule it as they please.[17]

To counter Abdullah's claim and to keep the name of Palestine alive, the Arab League authorized the Arab Higher Committee to proclaim at Damascus on 29 September 1948, an All-Palestine Government (Hukumat' Umum Filastin) with headquarters in Gaza.[18]

---

[15] *Middle Eastern Affairs,* XIV (April 1962), p. 123.

[16] Nashashibi, *op. cit.,* p. 77.

[17] Khalil, Vol. II, p. 166.

[18] On 10 July 1948, the Secretary-General of the Arab League announced that the Political Committee had approved the establishment of:

a provisional civil administration shall be set up in Palestine (whose function shall be to manage the public affairs and (to provide) the necessary services on condition that it shall not have competence at present over the higher political affairs . . . .

A congress of Palestine Arabs assembled at Gaza on October 1. The congress called itself the National Assembly and by acclamation elected Amin Al-Husayni as its president and resolved that:

> On the basis of the natural and historical rights of the Arab people of Palestine to freedom and independence. . . . we, the members of the National Assembly of Palestine meeting at Gaza, declare on this day, October 1, 1948, the sovereign independence of all Palestine which borders Syria and Lebanon in the north, Syria and Transjordan on the east, the Mediterranean Sea on the west, and Egypt on the south, and proclaimed the establishment of a free and democratic state working for the realization of the freedom and rights of the people. . . .[19]

To Abdullah, installing the All-Palestine Government was a design to prevent the realization of his own plans, while Egypt and Saudi Arabia, his main rivals, were in agreement that a union with Palestine must be prevented at all costs.[20] To this, Abdullah reacted violently and exchanged telegrams with Ahmad Hilmi, the Prime Minister of the Gaza Government. On 16 September 1948, he cabled:

> The Government of the Hashemite Kingdom of Jordan will not allow the formation of any administration which deprives the people of Palestine of the freedom of choosing their government after the present conflict is concluded. This government will not allow the formation within its security zone, which extends from the borders of Egypt to the borders of Syria and Lebanon, of a military organization which gives allegiance and benefits to certain personalities. . . .[21]

In another telegram on 20 September he said:

Third, the jurisdiction of the Civil Administration Council shall extend to all the areas, at present occupied by the Arab Armies or which may be occupied by the whole Arab Palestine is included . . . .

Khalil, Vol. II, p. 566.
[19] Ari Al-Arif, *Al-Nakbah* (Beirut: n. d.), p. 703.
[20] Lenczowski, *op. cit.*, p. 406.
[21] Ahmad Tayi' a *Safahat Matwiyyiah'an Filistin* (Cairo: Al-Shaab Publishing House, n,d.), p. 150.

What has been organized under the name of All-Palestine Govern-ment, whether decided by the League or those who aspire to rule, turns the clock back to pre-May 15 conditions. . . . This means that the partition which you fought against would occur. The soldiers of the Arab Legion who died trying to prevent it would not like tampering with the destiny of the land. The government of the Hashemite Kingdom is determined to keep under its control the pacified territory which extends from the borders of Egypt to the Lebanese-Syrian frontier. . . .[22]

In a third cable to Abdul-Rahman Azzam, the League's Secretary-General, Abdullah said:

Ahmad Hilmi Pasha in his reply said that the formation of the All-Palestine Government was decided by the Arab League. The Jordanian delegation denies this. Anyhow. . . since the Jordan army is still fighting in Jerusalem alone. . . we refuse the introduction of another authority into territorial jurisdiction of our military government, particularly those personalities who wish to govern. . . . . Thus, to preserve the League, we announce that we shall not accept any changes inside the security zone controlled by Jordan. The creation of such new authority compels the Palestinians to accept something they did not choose. To this we do not agree, and we will attempt to prevent it. However, if this government were formed and accepted by the United Nations, as it did the Jewish claims, then the League would have agreed to the partition against which it fought.[23]

In a letter to Prince Faysal Bin Saud, dated 30 September 1948, Abdullah stated:

I would like to remind the representatives of the Arab states in Paris that we (Jordan) did not deny the existence of a Palestine government, but opposed denying the Palestinians the right to choose for themselves the form of government following the victory. If I had accepted a state encompassing all Palestine before then I would have been made the laughing-stock. My fear is that

22 *Ibid.*, p. 151.
23 *Ibid.*, p. 152.

following victory, the United Nations would recognize this government (All-Palestine), as they accepted the Jewish claims; thus, partition would take place....[24]

Furthermore, in another letter to Riyad Al-Sulh, Prime Minister of Lebanon, Abdullah complained:

> ...While we in Transjordan have been carrying out our military operations and bearing the heaviest of military burdens alone. the League decided to set up in Gaza a feeble state for all Palestine in order to get rid of its responsibilities....[25]

The proclamation of the Gaza government was of little attraction to the Palestinians under Jordan's control whose immediate need was safety rather than independence. Furthermore, Gaza was geographically separated from East Palestine by the Zionist forces, and while the Palestinians were not allowed to live in Egypt, they were integrated in Jordan. As the Palestine question crystallized, the Gaza Government fell into oblivion. This situation augmented Abdullah's authority to claim absolute control of East Palestine. This was accomplished by popular conferences staged with this end in mind.

CONFERENCES AND UNITY

Abdullah's opposition to the All-Palestine Government was based on the fact that his army was in control of Eastern Palestine whose population enjoyed safety under Jordanian administration. Second, these people wanted a settlement to normalize their lives, and Abdullah was considered the only leader who could accomplish such results. Third, since Jordan contributed most to the Palestine conflict, saving the Arab part would be possible under the King's direction.[26]

Responding to the Gaza National Assembly, a conference was held in Amman on the same day, 1 October 1948, and adopted the

---

[24] Sha'ar, 4th ed., *op, cit.,* p. 243.
[25] Sha'ar, Ist ed., *op. cit.,* p. 282.
[26] *London Times,* 4 January 1949.

following resolution: "We shall not accept any solution brought about by the previous leaders of Palestine whose bad behavior precipitated the present tragedy."[27]

The conference authorized Abdullah to speak on their behalf, to negotiate and to deal with the problem as he saw proper. "While the other Arab leaders sat waiting, watching, hoping, blaming each other, Abdullah acted."[28]

On 1 December 1948, another conference was held in Jericho. It called for the unity of Palestine and Transjordan with Abdullah as King.[29] The resolutions of the conference were cabled to the Arab governments and to the Arab League. After discussion by the Cabinet, a resolution was passed:

> The Government of Jordan appreciates the desire of the Palestine people represented at the Jericho Conference for the unity of Transjordan and Palestine. This desire coincides with the wishes of the Government of Jordan and we will proceed to take the necessary constitutional steps.[30]

In its meeting on 13 December the Parliament declared its endorsement of the Government's policy with regard to annexing Arab Palestine.[31]

Abdullah's activities were met with indignation by most of the Arab states, and the League itself. Abdullah, who did not believe in the power of the League, boycotted its meetings. "The absence of the Jordan delegate was promptly exploited by Nahhas who moved that Hilmi be invited to attend the session."[32] In response to this motion, Abdullah instructed his minister in Cairo to appear at the Council meetings but to refrain from participating, in case the territorial disposition of Palestine was discussed. On 27 March 1950, Abdullah informed the league that he would not send a delegation until Egyptian press attacks were stopped, and "until certain points are clarified."[33] He accused the League of inventing the Gaza

---

[27] Musa, *op. cit.,* p. 535.

[28] Husayn, *Uneasy Lies the Head,* p. 124.

[29] Musa, *op. cit.,* p. 536.

[30] *Al-Difa'a,* 25 April 1950.

[31] Musa, *op. cit.,* p. 536.

[32] Lenczowski, *op. cit.,* p. 410.

[33] *Ibid.*

Government to oppose his ambitions, and stated also that the Organization was being dominated by those who opposed unity, namely, Egypt and Saudi Arabia. Abdullah further presented three conditions for returning to the League: one, that no delegation from the Gaza Government attended the meetings; two, no discussion of annexation should be carried on; and three, Egypt should apologize to Jordan for press attacks on Abdullah.[34]

In an attempt to prevent uniting both banks of the Jordan, the representative of Lebanon presented on 29 March 1950, a proposal calling for automatic expulsion of any League member who signs a treaty with Israel. By that time, it became common knowledge that Abdullah had carried on secret negotiations with the Zionists in search of peace, in violation of the League Resolution No. 292 of 1 April 1950.[35] This resolution was approved by all states except Iraq and Yemen.[36] This resolution, which censored Abdullah, failed for lack of a unanimous vote. Expulsion would merely have deepened the conflict among the states, and, at the same time, it could have encouraged Jordan—which at the time was conducting secret negotiations—to come to an agreement with Israel.[37] Thus, the failure of the League to dissuade Abdullah from annexing Palestine emphasized the Organization's inability as an instrument of leadership.

Abdullah, however, attacked the League's objection to unity and welcomed expulsion. "If the League ostracized us for annexation, welcome."[38] He was of the opinion that it would not be in Jordan's interest to withdraw from the League but declared that if Jordan's interests were in contradiction with the League's policy, he would protect the interests of Jordan, even if that would result in leaving the League. He further stated that Jordan was no longer bound by the League Resolution of 1948, on the grounds that the Arab armies had not liberated Palestine and that the Arab states had concluded armistice agreements with Israel, thereby accepting the U.N. Partition Plan. To Abdullah, annexation was best for the Arabs. By annexing

---

[34] *London Times,* 28 March 1950.

[35] Khalil, Vol. II, p. 165.

[36] Frye, *op. cit.,* p. 168. Iraq supported Jordan on account of Hashemite dynasty in both countries; Yemen to pay a debt. Abdullah had supported Iman Ahmad's legitimacy against a rebellion. Sha'ar, *op. cit.,* p. 240.

[37] Frye, *op. cit.*

[38] *London Times,* 10 April 1950.

the West Bank "we protected the remaining part from being lost to
the Jews."[39]

In his speech from the throne on the occasion of unity, Abdullah
declared:

> The Jordan [River] is like a bird whose wings are its east and west
> banks. Its natural right is to unite and merge....The unity of
> the two banks is an indisputable fact which evolved from the
> establishment of strong ties ever since 1922. Such visible ties
> include: unity of currency, common defense, common ports, faci-
> litation of travel and customs exchange of cultural and legal
> programs. All these endowed each bank with a most favored
> position by the other .... The difference of opinion which resulted
> after the armistice stemmed from misunderstanding of the Jordan-
> Palestine relationships which my government has been trying to
> explain.
>
> My government considers the decision of the Political Commit-
> tee of the Arab League on 12 April 1948, as null and void, since
> the other Arab states had accepted the Armistice, which, in effect,
> implicitly meant their approval of the United Nations Partition
> Plan.[40]

Tension caused by the Palestine question endangered inter-Arab
relations and threatened to break up the Organization. The situation
dictated a reversal with respect to Jordan's expulsion. As a compromise measure, it was proposed that the West Bank be considered a
trust in Jordan's hands. Jordan qualified the annexation by announcing that its policy was not to divide Palestine, but to restore it as
a unit and to give it back to its original owners.[41]

On 24 April 1950, the United Parliament adopted the following
resolution which provided for the unification of the two banks but
without prejudicing the final settlement of the Palestine question:

> ...Therefore, the Jordanian Parliament representing both banks
> ...resolve and declare the following:

---

[39] Sha'ar, op. cit., p. 244.

[40] Ibid., p. 246.

[41] Husayn, Al-Urdun Wa-Al-Qadiyyiah Al-Filistiniyyiah Wal-Alaqat Al-
Arabiyyiah, (Amman: Ministry of Foreign Affairs, n.d.), p. 32.

First, the upholding of the complete unity of the eastern and western banks of the Jordan and their merging into one state—the Hashemite Kingdom of Jordan—headed by his Hashemite Majesty the Exalted King 'Abdullah Bin Al-Husayn,' (a state) based on a parliamentary, constitutional regime, and on equality of rights and duties among all citizens.

Second, the affirmation of (the determination) to preserve all the rights of the Arabs in Palestine and the protection of these rights by all lawful means—and with the full right (to do so) without prejudice to the final settlement of the just cause (of Palestine) and within the framework of national aspirations, Arab cooperation and international justice.[42]

The Joint Defence And Economic Cooperation Agreement

After the 1948 War, it was natural for the Arab governments to emphasize military matters and to coordinate their future military policies for common defence of their states and to safeguard peace and security of the area. Another immediate reason was to prevent the Hashemites from realizing their ambitions in North Arabia.[43]

---

[42] On 21 April 1950, a new cabinet was formed with representatives from both banks. The annexation resolution was signed by Abdullah the same day. Musa, *op. cit.*, p. 538; *Al-Difa'a* 25 April 1950. English text in Khalil, Vol. I, p. 54.

Britain recognized the unity of both banks in a letter dated 24 April 1950. While Britain indicated that it would extend its protection to the new Jordan territory under the 1948 Treaty, the Old City of Jerusalem was excluded in deference to the United Nations internationalization plan of 9 December 1949.

Israel protested against the British approval but Britain replied that "this was the concern of Britain and Jordan alone and that Israel should not fear Britain unless it attacks its neighbors." Musa, *op. cit.*, p. 545; Shwadran, *op. cit.*, p. 297.

[43] During their meeting in 1949, President Bishara Al-Khouri of Lebanon and President Husni Al-Za'im of Syria revealed their opposition to the Great Syria-Fertile Crescent Plans, and presented their policies as follows:

1. Lebanon and Syria are two independent countries and the one supplements the other economically and supports it politically. . . .

2. As far as our relations with the sister Arab states are concerned we know that some of them have ambitions in our two countries and that some others do not. In spite of that, we should preserve the balance between them and in their conflict assume the role of mediator. What prompts this role is the presence of Arab kingdoms with ambitions.

The Egyptian-Saudi camp, in support of Syria and Lebanon, and in order to obstruct possible Iraqi and Jordan expansion, proposed a more grandiose scheme which no responsible Arab could possibly reject: the Collective Security Pact of 1950.[44] Although Iraq and Jordan disliked it, they could not oppose it. This explained, Jordan-Iraq reluctance in signing the Pact.[45]

Ironically, the Pact was advocated by King Talal and the Chamber of Deputies, while the Cabinet was cool towards it. The accession of Jordan to the Pact on 16 February 1952, indicated Talal's triumph over the Cabinet.[46]

The Collective Security Pact preserved the *status quo* in the Arab world, and represented a victory for the Egyptian-Saudi camp against the unity of North Arabia for it forbade any acts of aggression against the territorial integrity, independence and security of any Arab state.[47]

The Arab states agreed that an armed attack on any member would be considered an attack on all.[48] Article 2 relates specifically to this

---

3. We should attempt to strengthen the Arab League and oppose within its framework every plan that aims at establishing the Great Syria Project or the Fertile Crescent scheme. Moreover we should show deference to the rulers of both Iraq and Transjordan. for it is not wise to challenge them. It is enough to defend ourselves without provoking anyone. (Bishara Khouri, *Haqa'ia Lubnaniyyiah* (Beirut: Awraq Lubnaniyyiah, 1960), Vol. II, p. 232.

In a debate in the Egyptian Parliament a question was raised: "What action would be taken in the case of the unification of two states such as Iraq and Jordan?" The Foreign Minister replied that "If unification were by force of arms other Arab states would be entitled to thwart it." Quoted in *Security and the Middle East,* p. 23.

[44] Tom Little, "The Arab League: Area Assessment," *Middle East Journal,* X, No. 2, (April 1956), p. 143.

[45] Lenczowski, *op. cit.,* p. 410.

[46] Talal devoted great attention to closer relations with the Arab states but made no mention of "The friendly and allied states," particularly Britain in his address to the Parliament (Jordan, *Chamber of Deputies Debates, The Official Gazette,* 15 November 1951, pp. 12-4).

[47] J. C. Hurewitz, *Diplomacy in the Near and Middle East,* Vol. II (Princeto Van Nostrand, 1956).

Cairo accused Abdullah of smuggling arms to the Druz and warned Jordan that Syria, Egypt, and Saudi Arabia were opposed to the Great Syria Plan, that they were interested in " maintaining the balance in the Arab orient and putting an end to Hashemite ambitions." *London Times,* 29 January 1949.

[48] Article 1 states: "Being anxious to maintain and stabilize security and peace, the Contracting States hereby confirm their determination to settle their

point, and Article 5 provided for creating a permanent military commission in order to organize the plans of joint defence and to prepare their means and methods.[49]   Article 8 provided for the creation of an economic council to be concerned with economic and financial affairs such as unifying currency and creating an Arab Common Market.[50]

Conclusion

Jordan's relations with the League have been far from cooperative. This was caused by Abdullah's belief that the Organization had been the major obstacle to achieving his personal ambitions in the Fertile Crescent.

Abdullah's hostility to the League appeared to derive from personality conflict. Compared to the other Arab states, Jordan lacked the fundamental criteria for statehood: its foreign relations, economy and army were, until 1956, exclusively in the hands of Britain. Accordingly, Abdullah's claim to leadership lacked viability.

---

international disputes by peaceful means whether in their mutual relations or in their relations with other states." Khalil, Vol. II, p. 102.

[49] The absence in this treaty of explicit obligations to use their armed forces to defend other Arab states was the main reason for the reluctance of some of the Arab countries to aid Egypt during the 1956 tripartite aggression. Mahmoud Khattab, *Al-Wahdah Al-Askariyyiah Al-Arabiyyiah* (Cairo: Modern Technical Press, 1969), p. 38.

[50] Aisha Ratib, *Al-Alaqat Al-Dawliyyiah Al-Arabiyyiah* (Cairo: Dar Al-Nahdah Al-Arabiyyiah, 1968), p. 72; and Khalil, Vol. II, pp. 101-05.

The Pact was signed by Egypt, Lebanon, Syria, Saudi Arabia and Yemen on 17 June 1950. Iraq and Jordan signed it with reservations on 2 February 1951, and 16 February 1952, respectively. It came in force in August 1952. Iraq requested more power in the hands of the Joint Chiefs of staff to coordinate training programmes and supply problems of the armed forces of each Member state. It also reserved the right not to be bound by the League in financial matters. Jordan made the following stipulations: one, the provisions that a two thirds majority binding on all members should be replaced by a clause stating that execution of any decision should be the responsibility of only those who voted for it. Two, "aggression" should be defined and referred to an act by a non-League member. Three, the general mechanism of the Pact should be further revised and simplified. Four, the Pact should not affect treaties between League members and other states. Five, an authority should be appointed to define the "threat of war." Harry Howard "Middle Eastern Regional Organization: Problems and Prospects," *Proceedings of the Academy of Political Science*, Vol. 24, (January 1952), p. 546.

Although Jordan was given special permission to become a founding member of the League—since Transjordan was not independent in 1944—and had become signatory to all resolutions, Abdullah was never at ease with the Organization. He held that it was an instrument for advancing Egypt's interests; thus it was of no value since his policies were for the most part contrary to those of Egypt. Anticipating Egypt's drive for leadership under the guise of the League, he dismissed the idea that the League could be the catalyst for Arab unity.

Abdullah's challenge to the League was manifested in his violation of its resolutions pertaining to the annexation of Arab Palestine. Determined to eliminate any rivals, he defied the League's plan to install the All-Palestine Government of Gaza by unilaterally annexing Eastern Palestine and disbanding the former's para-military organizations. His challenge exposed the League's weakness, thereby establishing a dangerous precedent. Accordingly, Abdullah always stressed that if Jordan's interests and the League's policies were contradictory, he would sacrifice the League and protect the interests of Jordan.

This policy has been pursued. Thus, bilateral alliances and agreements rather than all-League coordinated policies were entered into. King Husayn's espousal of Arab policy proved beneficial to Jordan. He took advantage of the League as an all-Arab Parliament to establish better relations with the other Arab heads of state. Under the auspices of the Organization, Jordan called summit conferences and received financial subsidies. Paramount was the Arab financial aid which Jordan has been receiving as budgetary support since 1967, replacing the American subsidy.

CHAPTER ELEVEN

JORDAN'S ARAB POLICY

The Arab Solidarity Pact

The Arab policy of King Abdullah may be characterized by almost complete lack of cooperation with the other Arab heads of state, except Iraq. His disregard of the League and animosity towards most Arab rulers resulted in his alienation, which, in turn, caused him to adopt parochial Jordanian nationalism. However, this situation changed somewhat, after Husayn II became the King.

Upon becoming the ruler, King Husayn stressed the policy that Jordan's bonds with the sister Arab States should be preserved and strengthened. "Jordan is nothing but a part of the Arab nation and the Arab Legion is but one of its armies."[1] This policy was reiterated by his first Prime Minister, Fawzi Al-Mulqi, in his statement to the Parliament on 24 May 1953.[2] The same policy was followed by Abul-Huda, as directed by Husayn in his letter of commission: "The foreign policy of Jordan is based on complete understanding and absolute cooperation with the Arab states."[3] Husayn continued:

As to foreign policy, Jordan's relations with all Arab states must always be on the best terms just as if they were between different parts of one nation. The unchanging policy of Jordan takes into consideration the interests of the Arab states as an indivisible unit....[4]

On that basis, following the Qibya incident, Husayn requested the aid of the Arab states. The League's Political Committee, meeting in Amman, promised to pay to Jordan two and a half million dinars. While the army was supported by the British subsidy, it became the

---

[1] George Harris, *Jordan*, (New Haven: HRAF Press, 1958), p. 104.
[2] Jordan, *Official Gazette*, 6 May 1953, p. 191.
[3] Musa, *op. cit.*, p. 596.
[4] *Husayn Ibn Talal*, (n.p.: n.d.), p. 17.

duty of the Arab states to equip and maintain the National Guard. Thus, on 5 July 1954, Husayn wrote to the heads of the Arab states that "owing to limited resources, Jordan cannot face the Zionists alone," and added that "unless the Arab states aid the Jordan National Guard soon, it will be too late."[5] The Arab states immediately donated one million dinars of the promised two and a half.

Since the Arab states did not send large military aid, Husayn decided to open negotiations with Britain, aiming at increasing the British subsidy to be paid as rents for the British bases in Jordan, not as charity. However, these negotiations did not yield the expected results, particularly when Britain was revising its Middle East policies, which included the establishment of a Turkish-Iraqi alliance. Thus, Britain wished to postpone the negotiations until talks with Iraq on the Baghdad Pact were concluded, aiming at enticing Jordan to accede to the Pact.

From 1955 onward, friction ensued between the United States and Britain on the one hand and Arab Nationalists on the other. The West desired that the Arab League states be included in Western alliances.[6] However, Egypt espoused neutralism while Iraq responded approvingly to Western plans for a Middle East Defense Organization because it felt threatened by Soviet closeness to its territory and believed that the Kurdish minority in Iraq might be incited to revolt by the U.S.S.R.[7] Furthermore, Iraq's association with Britain dictated such cooperation. Most importantly, however, was Iraq's realization that a union between Jordan and Iraq, then perhaps, with Syria and Lebanon, could not materialize, due to the opposition from Egypt and Saudi Arabia. Therefore, Iraq began to break away from the League and declared its intention of joining the Baghdad Pact, which it signed on 24 February 1954.

Fearful of Iraq's supremacy and possible annexation, Syria consulted with Egypt and Saudi Arabia and signed the Arab Covenant on 2 March 1955.[8] The main features of the alliance were: federation of all the Arab states which repudiated the Baghdad Pact; maintenance of the *status quo* and friendly relations among the Arab states; and

---

[5] Musa, *op. cit.,* p. 608.

[6] *Ibid.,* p. 610.

[7] John C. Campbell, *Defense of the Middle East* (New York: Praeger, 1960), p. 53.

[8] Text in Khalil, Vol. II, p. 239; also *Al-Ahram,* 7 March 1955.

the coordination of foreign, economic, and cultural policies of the states acceding to the alliance.[9]   This step rendered Jordan a victim of inter-Arab political struggle.   It was reported that Husayn was in favour of the Baghdad Pact, but the army officers were sharply divided.

In view of these developments, Jordan was approached by Britain as Abul-Huda declared that his government contemplated the revision of the Anglo-Jordan Treaty of 1948.[10]   Simultaneously, Jordan was evading the Arab Covenant and appeared to be more inclined to the Western approach of joining the Baghdad Pact.[11]   The Arab offer of the Arab Covenant was politely rejected as "premature" since Jordan was still tied to Britain by the Treaty of 1948, and because Husayn did not wish to provoke further dissension among the Arab states.[12]

Cognizant of the deep apathy between Egyptian-Syrian-Saudi bloc on the one hand, and Iraq on the other, Husayn exploited the situation by presenting a counter plan, thereby sealing the fate of the Arab plan.   He always insisted that the other Arab countries must share in defence responsibilities with Jordan.   In a letter to the Arab heads of state, he wrote:

I invite the heads of state to plan for future events [Israeli aggression] with one united idea.   Jordan is your country and your first line of defense and the front line of attack. I hope for your agreement, for there is no strength except in unity and in sacrificing our persons for (Arab) unity.[13]

[9] Abidi, *op. cit.*, p. 123.

[10] The British Foreign Secretary announced in Parliament that his government would grant £ 350,000 annually to Jordan for the maintenance of the National Guard. In addition, Britain gave Jordan a gift of 12 Vampire fighters in 1955. (Great Britain, *Parliamentary Debates*, (Commons), Vol. 537, 16 February 1955, col. 51; also Anthony Eden *Full circle: The Memoirs of Anthony Eden* (Cambridge: Houghton Mifflin Company, 1960), p. 383.   Egypt also approached Jordan with similar aid when Salah Salim, a member of the Revolutionary Council, visited Amman.   *Al-Difa'a*, 4 March 1955.

[11] *Al-Difa'a*, 4 March 1955.

[12] *Filistin*, 12 January 1956.   The Arab offer was announced in Damascus on 11 January 1956.   It provided for a payment of 100 million Egyptian pounds over ten years; establishment of an Arab bank for economic development; financing development projects;   sale of Jordanian bonds in other Arab countries.   *Al-Ahram*, 12 January 1956.

[13] *Al-Husayn Ibn Talal, op. cit.*, p. 75.

THE JORDAN-SYRIA ALLIANCE

Following the dismissal of Glubb, Husayn was invited to visit Syria where he was welcomed as an Arab liberator.[14] On 11 April 1956, the King, President Al-Quwwatli and their Prime Ministers agreed on the following:

1. Since Israel follows an aggressive policy while discarding U.N. resolutions, thereby creating a state of tension and insecurity along the truce line ... the two parties agree to coordinate their defence plans and to improve cooperation between the two armies to repel Zionist aggression.
2. That both parties confirm that their policies are based on joining no foreign alliances.[15]

Since the Arab Collective Defence Pact of 1950 proved ineffective, the Arab countries entered into bilateral and multilateral agreements with each other.[16] Syria and Egypt concluded a special alliance which in effect combined both armies under one command. On 24 October 1956, Jordan joined the alliance and placed its army under the united command.[17] This alliance may have been the immediate cause for the Israeli invasion of Egypt five days later.[18] As the Tripartite Aggression was under way, Husayn, in fulfilment of his obligations under the alliance, proposed opening the Jordanian front, but Nasser declined

[14] *Ibid.,* p. 99.

[15] *Ibid.,* p. 101. In May, Quwwatli visited Amman and signed an agreement with Jordan which provided for actual unification of war efforts by creating a war council. Other provisions of the agreement included:

a.   elevating diplomatic representation to the rank of Embassy;
b.   eliminating passports;
c.   facilitating transit through Syria; and
d.   admission of more Jordanian students to Syrian colleges.

Ibid., p. 103.

[16] Jordan-Lebanon, 21 May 1956; Jordan-Iraq, 13 June 1956; Jordan-Saudi Arabia, 7 September 1956. Syrian, Iraqi, and Saudi Arabian troops entered Jordan on 7 November 1956 and 15 November 1956., respectively. *Filistin,* 17 November 1956; Musa, *op. cit.,* p. 647.

[17] *Al-Husayn Ibn Talal, op. cit.,* p. 107; Hasan Mustafa, *Al-Ta'awun Al-'Askari Al-Arabi,* (Beirut: Dar Al-Tal'ah, 1965), 2nd ed., p. 53.

[18] Eden, *op. cit.,* p. 579.

the offer since it was Britain and France who attacked Egypt.[19] But Husayn cabled Nasser declaring, "We are with Egypt in her distress. With all my resources and forces, we will join the fight on your side to the end."[20] While Jordan broke diplomatic relations with France, Husayn warned Britain's ambassador saying, "My forces will demolish British airfields and bases inside Jordan if these bases were used in attacks against Egypt."[21]

Two important steps were taken by Jordan following the Suez War: the conclusion of the Arab Solidarity Pact, signed on 19 January 1957;[22] and ending the Anglo-Jordanian Treaty of 1948.

[19] *Al-Husayn Ibn Talal,* p. 110.   Placing the blame on his Prime Minister Nabulsi, the King stressed his determination to help Egypt:

> I was determined to help Egypt from the first moment by entering the battle before the British-French ultimatum.   But I was discouraged by Nabulsi and some of his ministers and the Chief of staff, who sent an ambassador of a great power to alter my decision.   Had I encountered sincere determination in that Cabinet before the ultimatum and we entered the battle at the beginning it would have been possible to change its results .   I stood by Egypt since the nationalization of the Canal burdening myself with great responsibilities.

Ibid., p. 232.   Following the attack, Husayn, invited the Arab heads of state to a meeting in Beirut to discuss the tripartite aggression and "to reach an accord on what should be done to support Egypt. . . ."   See U.S. Dept. of State, *United States Policy in the Middle East,* September 1956-June 1957   (New York: Green wood Press, 1968), p. 220.

[20] *Ibid.,* p. 110.

[21] *Ibid.,* p. 232.   In his public speeches Husayn attacked the aggressors, while declaring Arab support to Egypt.   He said:

> . . . We say to the Jews and their supporters that the present battle is not the battle of Egypt alone, but it is the battle of the entire Arab nation.   History will hold those responsible who have helped the aggressor and failed the international Organization in pursuit of their unholy goals.   Instead of stop- ping the Jewish invasion, they supported that aggression, and instead of solving the conflict by peaceful means in support of the United Nations and its Security Council, they rejected international principles and endangered peace and security in this land....I call upon the Arab nation to share her struggle....

Ibid., p. 113.

[22] Text in Khalil, *op. cit.,* Vol. II, p. 287; Arabic text in *Al-Husayn Ibn Talal,* *op. cit.,* pp. 138-40.

THE ARAB SOLIDARITY PACT

Following the dismissal of Glubb, the British treaty with Jordan became worthless. Furthermore, the participation by Britain in the Suez attack ended all understanding between her and the Arabs. In Parliament, many urged ending the subsidy to Jordan by cancelling the treaty, and they were supported by the British press. Meanwhile, in Jordan, the country's position can be summarized in two points: one, the British subsidy was part of the treaty according to which Britain was obligated to pay; two, only through this subsidy could the expenditures of the Jordan army be covered.

In the meanwhile, King Saud, Presidents Quwwatli and Nasser met in Cairo and sent Sa'ed Al-Ghazzi, Syria's Prime Minister on 8 March 1956, carrying a message to King Husayn, inviting him to discuss Arab problems.[23] Husayn's reply was that an invitation was previously issued by him personally; that replies were received from Quwwatli and Saud, but not from Nasser;[24] and that only Faysal and Chamoun agreed to meet. In his negative reply, Husayn said:

> I cannot agree to any diversion from the idea which I have already expressed....Taking a new stand, as proposed in your message— a stand to be limited to the four of us only—does not in my opinion, agree with the noble aims which we all wish to accomplish, nor does it serve the interests which we all attempt to realize for the future of the nation, the defense of its dignity, and the guarantees of its destiny.[25]

Husayn's reaction was for self-preservation. He always preferred a joint aid to Jordan by all the Arab states. Thus, any summit meeting should include his faithful friends, his cousin, Faysal of Iraq and Lebanese President Camile Chamoun.[26] This policy con-

---

[23] Khalil, *op. cit.*, Vol. II, p. 245.

[24] *Al-Husayn Ibn Talal, op. cit.*, p. 76.

To Egypt, the inclusion of Iraq could achieve little except to provide another occasion for expressing Arab disagreements. In the meantime, Egypt denied that its lack of reply implied non-cooperation on the Palestine question. *Survey of International Affairs*, 1955-56 (London; 1960), p. 205.

[25] *Al-Husayn Ibn Talal, op. cit.*, p. 146.

[26] *Ibid.*, p. 105.

tained the shrewd realization that the more Arab states he could involve in the deliberations, the less likelihood of their reaching   an
agreement.   Meanwhile, he clung to the British subsidy.   Husayn's
diplomatic drive for a wider Arab Collective Security Pact was meant
as no more than a smoke screen. Ideally, he felt that a new arrangement with Britain was the best course.[27] To Husayn, his security and
salvation lay in association with Iraq, not with the anti-Hashemite
camp, regardless of the enticing offers.

Insisting on isolating Husayn from Faysal and Chamoun, and in
an attempt to break the pro-Western bloc, the three leaders wrote
again on 12 March 1956, offering:

> Aid to Jordan to replace the British subsidy to the Arab Legion and
> the National Guard in the event of the stoppage of the   British
> subsidy.   The aid to the Hashemite Kingdom of Jordan would
> continue for a period of not less than ten years.[28]

Also, they expressed their readiness to conclude military agreements
coordinating the military relations with Jordan.[29]

While Jordan preferred association with and friendship to Britain,
it was at the same time, under public pressure to terminate the 1948
Treaty and to replace the British subsidy with that offered by the Arab
states on condition that Jordan's army be included in the United
Arab Command.[30]   Tactfully avoiding the Arab offer, King Husayn
refused replacing the British subsidy.   However, he indicated his
acceptance of a secondary aid.   He wrote:

> The subsidy which the Hashemite Kingdom obtains from Britain
> in accordance with the provisions of the existing treaty   between
> the two countries, is a part of Britain's commitments according to
> the treaty.   On this basis, Jordan has the full right to request the
> British side to fulfil them so long as the treaty remains in force, but
> I welcome any aid you offer to my country. At the same time, my
> country declares that she is ready to coordinate military plans
> among ourselves in the face of the common enemy....[31]

---

[27] Vatikiotis, *op. cit.*, pp. 124-25.
[28] Khalil, *op. cit.*, p. 246.
[29] *Ibid.*, p. 247.
[30] *Ibid.*, 640; also *Al-Husayn Ibn Talal*, p. 129.
[31] *Ibid.*, p. 247; *Al-Husayn Ibn Talal, op. cit.*, p. 129.

Prime Minister Rifa'i echoed Husayn's position on the question of subsidies as he told the Parliament:

> If someone claims that the Government should abandon this aid and that it should be replaced by Arab aid, this means that Jordan's Government must exempt Britain from an obligation while retaining Jordan's obligation.[32]

Husayn's rejection of the Arab offer appeared to have been caused by his suspicion of their ulterior motives which could endanger Jordan's sovereignty. He declared:

> Jordan welcomes aid from every Arab country which discharges its duty for strengthening our forces to resist the common enemy. We, however, would reject any aid which is not given with good will or has ulterior motives.[33]

Thus, the British treaty continued in effect, and with it the Legion's subsidy. With the coming to power of the pro-Nasser group, the treaty was cancelled in March 1957.

THE RISE OF PRO-NASSER NATIONALISTS: THE NABULSI GOVERNMENT

The policy of the Jordan monarchy supported progressive socialist regimes and ideologies in the Arab world provided that they were not violent in nature, employing military force to attain their goals.[34] However, fearing the end of the monarchy, as was the case in Egypt and Iraq, Husayn was never at ease with the revolutionary regimes. Nasser's plan to build his policy on revolutionary ideology resulted in unrelenting attacks on the conservative regimes, including the Jordan monarchy. Since Nasserism had a great appeal with the majority of the Jordanian population, particularly the Palestinians, the pro-Nasser leadership succeeded in attaining power under the

---

[32] *Documents on International Relations,* 1956, p. 46.

[33] *Al-Difa'* 2 October 1956; Shwadran, *op. cit.,* p. 347.

[34] Jordan, *Al-Urdun Wa Al-Qudiyyiah A-Filistinyyiah Wa Al-Alaqat Al-Arabiyyiah, op. cit.,* p. 26.

leadership of Prime Minister Sulayman Al-Nabulsi, who made
unprecedented changes in Jordan's foreign policy by adopting the
Egyptian foreign policy line.[35] Since Jordan's policies, until that
time, were in line with those of the West, it became the landmark of
Egyptian policy to attack and criticize Jordan in almost every
action.

As Prime Minister desiring changes in his government's policy,
Nabulsi, on 27 November 1956, made an elaborate exposition of
Jordan's foreign policy. He said:

...The Government considers it a national duty to greet the
struggle of Egypt against the British, French and Israeli enemies.
The aggressors must abide by the United Nations resolutions and
withdraw from the Arab land. The Government declares that the
action against Egypt is an attack on the Arab nation, the world
public opinion, the United Nations and world peace. Its result
would be a continuation of Imperialism and Zionism.

The Government will work in cooperation with free Arab states
in order to eradicate imperialism and all its facets from the Arab
homeland. This can be accomplished by the freedom, unity and
strength of the Arabs. In this respect, the Government will
endeavour to promote relations with the free Arab countries in the
political, economic and cultural fields as a first step toward a
federal union. The Government will abide by the military agreement with Egypt, Syria and the joint command. Following this,
the Government announces that it will accept the financial aid
offered by Egypt, Syria and Saudi Arabia in order to replace the
British subsidy, given to the army and to the National Guard.

The Government reiterates that the Arab nation is one, and so
also is the Arab homeland. The Hashemite Kingdom of Jordan is
a part of the Arab Homeland and the Jordanian people are a part
of the Arab nation. The present Government is determined to
lead the people under the leadership of His Majesty the King, to
the path of unity, freedom, strength and honor....

The foreign policy of the Government emerges from the fundamental national interest. It is the assertion of our rights, sovereignty and freedom. The foreign policy would be free from any

[35] Jordan, Chamber of Deputies, *Al-Risalah Al-Rasmiyyiah* (*Official Gazette,*
9 December 1956), p. 1; *New York Times,* 17 December 1956.

consideration or condition inconsistent with it. There would be coordination with the foreign policies of the free Arab countries. The national interest requires the establishment of diplomatic, economic and cultural relations with all those countries which have sincerely stood with the Arabs in all their disputes and demands. In the light of this factor, the Government is considering the recommendations of your sovereign chamber to establish diplomatic relations with the Soviet Union and other countries.

...The Government considers all the imperialist pacts, with varying names and natures, and among them the Baghdad Pact, a great danger to the Arab nation and homeland. The Government denounces them and is determined that Jordan will not join them or associate herself with any of their subsidiaries.

The Anglo-Jordanian treaty was signed in a set of specific conditions. When the treaty was signed, there was no equality between the contracting parties. It is unsatisfactory. Britain has contravened and violated its spirit and letter. Since its conclusion, fundamental, international, internal and Arab changes have taken place rendering the treaty out of date. The Government, after acceptance of the Arab financial aid and after determining other diplomatic, international, financial and economic arrangements, will terminate the Treaty and will ask for the withdrawal of the British forces from, and liquidation of their bases in the Jordanian lands.[36]

Nabulsi's statement was a bold departure from previous policies of Jordan.[37] While he advocated Arab union, he declared that Jordan... "cannot live forever as Jordan.... It must be connected militarily,

---

[36] *Ibid.*, pp. 1-5.

[37] The Speaker of the House sent on 7 November a telegram of protest to the Speaker of British House of Commons and the Speaker of the Iraqi Chamber of Deputies. He asked that Iraq withdraw from the Baghdad Pact. *Ibid.*, 25 November 1956, p. 3. Furthermore, the Foreign Relations Committee proposed establishing diplomatic relations with both the U.S.S.R. and Red China, and the termination of the British treaty. These recommendations were approved by the Chamber of Deputies on 20 November, *Ibid.*; see also *Al-Husayn Ibn Talal*, pp. 193-94.

The chamber, in response to a rally, called for investigating the causes which led the Jordanian ambassador to the U.N., A.M. Rifa'i to abstain from voting for the admission of Red China, although he was instructed to join Syria and Egypt in voting for admission. *Ibid.*, p. 1. He was dismissed on 10 April 1957.

economically and politically with one or more Arab states."[38]
In pursuance of his new policy, entailing the severance of all ties
with Britain including the subsidy, and of bringing Jordan into the
Arab fold, Nabulsi declared that Jordan would accept the Arab aid.

> The Government declares that it was decided as a matter of princi-
> ple to accept the Arab subsidy offered by Egypt, Syria, and Saudi
> Arabia to replace British aid to the Army and National Guard and
> will take positive steps to realize this decision.... The Government
> will be in contact with its sister states that offered Arab subsidy to
> take all the diplomatic, international, financial, and economic pro-
> cedures which insure its determination to end the Anglo-Jordan
> Treaty.[39]

At the request of Husayn, the four heads of state met in Cairo and
signed the Arab Solidarity Pact on 19 January 1957.[40] According to
the agreement, the three states pledged to pay the total amount of
12,500,000 Egyptian pounds annually or their equivalent to Jordan
under the heading "Arab obligation."[41] This amount was to be
devoted to the army and the National Guard. The agreement was
valid for ten years and could be automatically renewed unless the

[38] *New York Times,* 16 December 1956.; Hisham Sharabi, *Government and
Politics of the Middle East, op. cit.,* p. 187.

[39] *Al-Husayn Ibn Talal,* p. 133. This declaration comforted the British side,
for it relieved Britain from paying annual subsidy. The Arab side, on the other
hand, were faced with a matter of fact. The Egyptian ambassador in Amman met
with three cabinet members and warned them against the consequences of the
"dangerous game" as enunciated in the Government statement, and added that
Egypt preferred postponing the abrogation of the treaty. *Ibid.,* pp. 133-34;
Musa, *op. cit.,* p. 653.

[40] For the text of the Pact, see Great Britain, *British and Foreign State Papers*
1957-1958, Vol. 163, p. 398; Khalil, Vol. II, pp. 287-88; *Al-Husayn Ibn Talal,* p.
138; Musa, *op. cit.,* p. 649; Jordan, *Chamber of Deputies* 27 January 1957, p. 2.
Sabri Al-Asali signed for Quwwatli who was visiting Russia. Musa, *op.
cit.,* p. 649.

[41] Syria was to pay two and a half million, Saudi Arabia five million, and
Egypt five million. Only Saud paid in full for the first year; Syria and Egypt
did not. Jordan exempted Saud from his obligation when the Arab Union went in
to effect. Musa, *op. cit.,* p. 651; Husayn, *Uneasy Lies the Head,* p. 161. Majali
wrote that the Syrian ambassador to Amman had stated that the Arab subsidy
was merely a promise aimed at threatening Britain so that it would not take
advantage of Jordan's economic needs, and impose on Jordan conditions to
follow a certain policy. Majali, *Muthakkirati,* p. 207.

parties agreed to terminate it.

Criticizing the Arab subsidy to Jordan as valueless, Burhan Eddin Bashyan, Foreign Minister of Iraq, said on December 30:

The Anglo-Jordanian treaty cannot be terminated by the mere giving of annual financial aid to Jordan in place of Britain's aid. Any such aid would relieve Britain of the aid it gives annually to Jordan, without affecting in the least the Anglo-Jordanian treaty. It would, in fact, be aid to Britain more than aid for Jordan.[42]

Immediately after the signing of the agreement, Britain sent a memorandum requesting that Jordan clarify its position regarding the treaty in the light of Arab subsidy, and also to open the negotiations to end the Anglo-Jordan Treaty of 1948.[43] The negotiations were conducted at Amman, and on 13 February 1957, the treaty was abrogated. The agreement was unanimously approved by a joint session of Parliament on 3 March 1957.[44]

However, the honeymoon of the nationalists was shortlived. It may be noted that, until the advent of the Nabulsi government, the King and Cabinet used to have identical views on foreign policy, and together held the opposition in the Parliament at bay. With Nabulsi as Prime Minister, the Cabinet became a part of the opposition and elbowed the King into isolation. Meanwhile, both the Cabinet and the King looked for support inside the country and outside it. It was, however, clear that Husayn could not turn the balance in his favour without external support.[45]

The opposition wanted to change the British-Jordan alliance with Egypt, Syria and Saudi Arabia, but Husayn showed little enthusiasm. If Husayn needed a strong ally in his battle against the pro-Egyptian Nabulsi government, the United States was also desirous of isolating Egypt. While the Cabinet's policy was encouraged by Nasser, the uncompromising attitude of Husayn was also directly encouraged by the United States. The Eisenhower Doctrine supplied Husayn with assurances against the opposition who

[42] "Nasser and Arab Unity," *Editorial Research*, 1958, p. 85.

[43] Majali, *Muthakkirati*, p. 210.

[44] Musa, *op. cit.*, pp. 651–60; *Al-Husayn Ibn Talal*, pp. 151–52; for correspondence, termination of the treaty and annexes, see G.B., *British and Foreign State Papers*, 1957–1958, Vol. 163, pp. 39–49.

[45] Abidi, *op. cit.*, p. 165.

were branded as Communist-inspired.[46]

While Jordan's relations with other Arab countries were secondary, its Egyptian foreign policy was pivotal, as it, more often than not, affected and guided inter-Arab politics. The major policy disagreement revolved around Husayn's attempts at wresting Arab leadership from Nasser. Husayn's success was conditional upon non-Arab support, while Nasser's triumph was dependent upon his espousal of an all-Arab policy which appealed to the overwhelming majority of the Arab people including the Jordanian subjects.

In this cold war, Saudi Arabia seemed to hold the balance in view of its wealth and its shifting policy from one grouping to another. It sided with Egypt and Syria when rivalries with the Hashemites were in question; and with the Hashemites when the conservative regimes were being threatened by the progressive rulers.[47] Thus, while the Saudis opposed Jordan's entry into the Baghdad Pact, for that was tantamount to strengthening their traditional rivals, they welcomed the Eisenhower Doctrine from which Saudi Arabia would receive financial, military and political support.[48] Accordingly, the Saudis joined Husayn's semi-official endorsement of the American Plan, which was viewed as beneficial to the monarchial regimes. This was disappointing to Egypt, whose policies stressed opposition to all Western schemes in the Arab World, viewed as detrimental to Egypt's leadership in particular and to Arab unity in general.[49]

---

[46] *Ibid.*, p. 166.

Hanson Baldwin, *New York Times* correspondent, observed on 10 March 1957, that the differences between Husayn and the Cabinet grew "with American encouragement." See also the "Zarqa Affair" in *Al-Husayn Ibn Talal*, pp. 136ff; also Majali, *Muthakkirati*, pp. 217ff; also Musa, *op. cit.*, pp. 661ff. For the statements of Nabulsi and General Hayari, C.G.S. see *Al-Hyah*, 21 April 1957; *New York Times*, 24 April 1957; *Filistin*, 23 April 1957; Seale, *op. cit.*, p. 289.

[47] During the Zarqa incident, when Husayn accused the army high command of plotting to overthrow him, King Saud told Husayn, "You can always count on the support of my country, my army, my fortunes and myself." *Al-Husayn Ibn Talal*, p. 190; also *London Times*, 23 June 1967.

[48] J.S. Raleigh, "The Middle East in 1956: A Political Survey," *Middle Eastern Affairs*, IX, March 1958, p. 93.

[49] Fisher, *op. cit.*, p. 175. Islamic ideology still plays a decisive role in sustaining the structure of the state in Jordan, Saudi Arabia and Iran. Islamism provides the necessary justification for combating Communism. Ironically, the

The Qassem-Nasser difficulties erupted as a result of the creation of the U.A.R. which facilitated Egypt's control of Syria, and partly because Nasser's plan to bring Iraq's revolutionary government within Egypt's orbit had not succeeded. The outcome of the conflict was a rapprochement between Egypt on the one hand, Saudi Arabia and Jordan on the other.[50] As Nasser sought to isolate Iraq, he flirted with conservative regimes. However, "the price for Jordan and Saudi Arabia was a form of assurance of respect for the integrity and independence of their regimes."[51] Thus, after interruption, Jordan-Egyptian diplomatic relations were restored in August 1959.[52] A year later, following the assassination of Prime Minister Majali, enmity broke out again.[53] Moreover, because Jordan and Turkey recognized the secessionist Syrian regime with haste, followed by the great powers, it seemed that Turkey and Jordan must have been "privy to the plot." Nasser's reply was the immediate breaking off relations with Ankara and Amman.[54] When the secessionist Syria flirted with Iraq to form a union, Egypt opposed the move. This even had a significant impact on Jordan's foreign policy which resulted in

---

conservative regimes are committed to pro-Western policies, partly due to Islamic conservatism. Sharabi, *Palestine and Israel,* p. 99.

[50] George Kirk, *Contemporary Arab Politics* (New York: Praeger, 1961), p. 146–47.

[51] Kerr, *The Arab Cold War,* p. 25.

[52] *Ibid.* This was the result of the visit by the League Secretary-General who visited Amman and conducted talks with the Jordan government. Musa, *op. cit.,* p. 699.

[53] Haza'a Al-Majali became Jordan's Prime Minister with the objective of joining the Baghdad Pact. Popular opposition compelled him to resign. His assassination was connected with Egyptian intrigues. At the U.N. General Assembly, Husayn accused the U.A.R. of "incitements to overthrow our Government and assassinate our leaders...." The Arab League, meeting at Shtoura, Lebanon in 1958, passed a resolution calling upon its members "to refrain from all activities that would disturb 'Fraternal Relations." See Husayn's speech in *Khalil,* Vol. II, p. 985.

[54] Kerr, *The Arab Cold War,* p. 30. Husayn could not send a committee to Damascus to congratulate Syria for its independence for fear of being implicated. Mohammad Faraj, *Al-Ummah Al-Arabiyyiah Ala Al-Tareeq Ila Wahdat Al-Hadaf* (Cairo: Dar Al-Fikr, 1964). When the Republic of Iraq signed a unity treaty with the U.A.R. in 1962, the Jordanian Parliament met for nine hours and urged the government to join the treaty. Faced with a vote of no confidence, the government fell. *Ibid.*

Jordan's rapprochement with Egypt, for Jordan was threatened by the consolidation of the Ba'ath Party in Syria and Iraq.[55]

Nasser's decision to build his policy on revolutionary ideology led him to the intervention in Yemen, which to him seemed a golden opportunity. His army intervened as the champion of revolutionary progress while Saudi Arabia and Jordan felt compelled to support the royalists out of dynastic solidarity, and were put in an ultra-reactionary light in the eyes of their own people.[56]

When the Iman of Yemen was ousted Husayn sent him a message of support in which he declared, "We confirm to you that we shall do our national duty fully in all fields and in every respect to halt aggression."[57] This declaration was followed by an attempt by Jordan and Saudi Arabia to bomb the republican-held territories, but this threat was never carried out because the Yemeni Republican Government of Abdullah Al-Sallal threatened to declare war on both countries if that ever took place.[58]

Husayn's alliance with Saud on the Yemeni war against Egypt further widened the gulf between the progressive ideology and conservatism in the Arab world. To confirm their alliance, Husayn and Saud met at Ta'if, Saudi Arabia in August 1962 and agreed to establish a unified military command, thereby weakening the Arab Solidarity Pact.[59]

---

[55] Kerr, *The Arab Cold War*, p. 122.

[56] *Ibid.*, p. 54. While Nasser could have had extra-territorial ambitions, in the Peninsula, his move into the Yemen was unavoidable and was not dependent upon Soviet support. He told the American Ambassador: "What I am doing in Yemen and elsewhere I would be doing even if the U.S.S.R. did not exist." Copeland, *op. cit.*, p. 276. Egypt's involvement in Yemen was opposed because Saudi Arabia viewed it as establishing foothold on the Peninsula, as it was viewed in the light of the Egyptian invasion of Saudi Arabia in 1820. By supporting the republicans against the royalists, the monarchists in Saudi Arabia and Jordan would be threatened by similar revolutions. Thus, the two monarchs opposed Nasser in Yemen by sending troops and arms to the royalists. Even the Shah of Iran became involved. In addition to troops dispatched on 13 September 1961, Husayn sent one-half of his air force to Yemen. However, the pilots defected to Cairo instead. Later, when relations improved, Husayn gave amnesty to the pilots while Nasser, at Husayn's request, released the aircraft. Faraj, *op. cit.*, p. 474.

[57] *New York Times*, 22 October 1962.

[58] *Ibid.*, 13 November 1962.

[59] Mustafa, *op. cit.*, p. 60; also *Middle Eastern Affairs*, Vol. 14, (1963), p. 44.

By late 1963, Husayn was no longer able to count on Western support as a reward for his anti-Communist policy. The U.S. became convinced that its policy which was adopted in 1958, had been unsuccessful in isolating Egypt from the Arab people.[60] Instead, the events in the Arab World resulted in the U.S. losing its supporters following the Iraqi revolution and the subsequent removal of Lebanese President Chamoun. Only King Husayn was left tied to the Western alliance. This situation signalled to both the U.S. and Husayn that their policies should be changed to accommodate Arab relations. Accordingly, the U.S. adopted a policy of "disengagement" from inter-Arab disputes in an attempt to avoid confrontation with Arab nationalism.[61]

As a result, the U.S. recognized the Yemeni Republic, and extended economic aid to Eygypt.[62] Meanwhile Nasser's exchanges with Khruschev over Communist influence in Egypt, made him America's "chosen instrument" in the Middle East.[63]

Husayn, on the other hand, had to depend on his own resourcefulness in re-establishing his popularity. He increased his visits to the West Bank, and on 16 January 1960, he announced that Jerusalem would be the second capital where the Cabinet and Parliament would meet from time to time.[64] The emphasis on the unity of the two banks was, in fact, a belated response to President Qassem's as well as Egypt's call for the creation of a "Palestine Entity," which Jordan had opposed earlier.

By reconciling with Nasser, it was hoped, Husayn would enhance his position in the Arab World.[65] While such approach would help relax the Arab Cold War, it would also minimize the Nasserite pressures in Jordan.[66] However, by claiming that his differences with Nasser were insignificant and not deep-rooted, Husayn might have been responding to American policy of strengthening Arab nationalism

[60] John Badeau, "U.S.A. and U.A.R. : A Crisis of Confidence," *Modernization of the Arab World, op. cit.,* p. 216.

[61] Campbell, *Defense of the Middle East, op. cit.,* p. 154.

[62] *Ibid.,* p. 155.

[63] Richard Nolte, "United States Policy in the Middle East," *The United State and the Middle East,* ed. Georgiana Stevens (Engle Wood Cliffs, N.J.: Prentice Hall, 1965), p. 171.

[64] *Filistin,* 17 January 1960.

[65] Kerr, *The Arab Cold War, op. cit.,* p. 151.

[66] *Ibid.*

in the face of Communism. Furthermore, Husayn came to realize that Jordan's stability depended, to a large measure, on closer relations with Egypt. He declared:

> There is no doubt that Egypt loses a great deal when Jordan draws away from it. While I am speaking to you from the bottom of my heart, Jordan loses more and more as Egypt draws away from it.[67]

Thus, when Nasser called for an Arab summit, Husayn accepted the invitation on the same day. The Cairo Conference gave Jordan an opportunity to emerge from its isolation, particularly in relation to the Arab republics. At the Alexandria Summit, also in 1964, Husayn did, in fact, bring Jordan's policy in line with those of the other Arab states. Accordingly, he joined Iraq and Egypt in supporting the idea of a Palestine entity, and agreed to the creation of the Palestine Liberation Organization.[68] Having recognized the Yemeni Republic on 23 July 1964, Husayn acted as mediator between Nasser and King Faysal Ibn Saud on the Yemeni question. Moreover, Husayn affirmed his abandonment of neutralism, declaring that Jordan would accept Soviet aid, and that American aid could be exchanged with aid from the Arab states.

Following the Cairo Summit, King Husayn visited the U.S.A. not to reaffirm his loyalty to Washington, as he did in 1959, following the implementation of the Eisenhower Doctrine, but as an ambassador of all the Arab States to verify Arab solidarity in the face of Israeli aggression, and its plans to divert the Jordan River.[69] The Arab summits resulted in almost a turn about policy by Jordan, as it expressed indentification with the non-aligned bloc. Having established closer relations with Nasser, Husayn visited India on 3 December 1963, and headed the Jordanian delegation to the conference of the neutralist nations in Cairo on 5 October 1964. Moreover, Jordan continued the policy of exchanging diplomatic relations with the East European states. Husayn's previous activities did

---

[67] *Middle Eastern Affairs*, Vol. 12, No. 5, May 1961, p. 145.

[68] Egypt never did acknowledge Jordan's annexation of Arab Palestine, and considered the West Bank as "occupied by the Jordan army." *Ibid.*, Vol. XI (December 1960), pp. 330ff.

[69] *New York Times*, 17 April 1964.

not involve the U.S. directly, although Jordan's policy had veered away from a strictly pro-West orientation. However, in June 1965, Jordan joined other United Nations members in censoring the American action in the Dominican Republic.[70] This unprecedented involvement in international questions appeared as an act of defiance of the United States which gained for Husayn a new position with the non-aligned bloc.

Thus, improved relations with Egypt restored Husayn's prestige which he lost in 1957. While he began to speak for the Arabs rather than against them, Faysal Ibn Saud and Husayn welcomed the era of Arab summitry because it provided for peaceful coexistence with the Arab republican regimes, hence an assurance for their conservative thrones.[71]

The summits were an approach to stand united against a common enemy and to concentrate on economic development by suspending the Arab Cold War. In this period Husayn acted as his own Foreign Minister. Ironically, in 1964, Husayn implemented the Nabulsi platform of 1956, which called for closer relations with Egypt and the other Arab states, espousing neutralism, and recognizing the U.S.S.R.[72]

The era of reconciliation lasted until 1966, then collapsed. This change was caused by the Yemeni War, the Egyptian sensitivities, and the Syrian prodding. The Soviet Union, Britain and the United States, by giving encouragement to rival proteges, contributed to this collapse which resulted in sharply divided blocs: a Syria-Egyptian axis confronting a Jordan-Saudi one. In January 1967, Husayn was prepared to withdraw his recognition of the Yemeni Republic in view of the latter's attitude towards Jordan. Thus, Husayn threatened that until the Yemeni Republic changed its relations with the U.A.R. and its attitude towards the monarchies, recognition would be withdrawn.[73]

The rivalry between Nasser and King Faysal Ibn Saud led the latter to organize an alignment of Muslim states, which he called the Islamic Conference, ostensibly, to "stop Communism," but in fact, to "stop Nasser."[74] Viewing the Conference as political rather

---

[70] *Ibid* , 8 June, 1965.
[71] Kerr, *The Arab Cold War*, *op. cit.*, p. 146.
[72] The U.S.S.R. recognized Jordan in 1964.
[73] *Al-Ahram*, 26, 27 January 1967.
[74] Copeland, *op. cit.*, p. 271.

than spiritual, Cairo and Damascus labelled it "the Islamic Pact."[75] Displeased with Husayn's endorsement of the Saudis American-inspired alliance, Nasser accused Husayn as having "wagged his tail."[76] Two months later, when Nasser publicly described Husayn as a "debauched King, the adulterator of Jordan." Husayn, meekly protested by withdrawing his ambassador to Cairo.[77]

However, shortly before the 1967 War, Husayn decided to normalize relations with Egypt. On 30 May 1967, he signed the defence pact, about which General Amer, in the name of the Egyptian army commented, "We are glad that you are once again in the family picture. It strengthens our confidence."[78] Compared to pre-1967 period, Jordan's relations with the Arab states have been closer and more friendly. Perhaps, fighting a common war and taking an anti-Western stand contributed to this situation.

Following the war, the Arab leaders met at Khartoum from 29 August to 1 September 1967, to study the Arab situation and to smoothen inter-Arab relations. Among the resolutions taken at the

[75] Kerr, *The Arab Cold War*, p. 146. King Faysal visited Jordan, Iraq, Iran, Turkey, Tunisia, Pakistan, Sudan, Mali, and Guinea to invite their leaders to meet at Mecca and to discuss the creation of an Islamic solidarity as opposed to progressive secularism.

His father, King Ibn Saud, considered Arabism as second to Islamism. His idea was spiritual rather than political in content. Mohammad Rifa'at, *Al- Tawjih Al-Siyasi Lilfikrah Al-Arabiyyiah Al-Hadithah*, (Cairo, Dar Al-Ma'arif, 1964), p. 298. See an elaborate discussion on the Islamic union in Mohammad Hasanein Heykal, "Tareeq Al-Malik," *Al-Ahram*, 13 February 1967. Also Ahmad Kamel Tubji, *Al-Quwwat Al-Musallahah Al-Arabiyyiah Wa Al-Salam Fi Al-Yaman* (Cairo: Al-Dar Al-Qawmiyiah Lil-Tiba'ah Wa- Al-Nashr, 1966), pp. 87–91.

[76] Kerr, *The Arab Cold War*, p. 155. At the Casablanca Third Arab Summit, the heads of states agreed to "respect the sovereignty of each Arab state...and non-interference in their internal affairs," and "revision of press laws... to prohibit any discussion outside constructive criticism, which would worsen Arab inter-relations or does harm to the heads of states, directly or indirectly." Ratib, *op. cit.*, p. 91.

[77] *Ibid.* See a brilliant commentary by Heykal in *Al-Ahram* entitled, "Asl Al-Hikayah," 6 January 1967. King Husayn accused the U.A.R. of "tampering with Jordan's security and misleading the citizens," *London Times*, 24 February 1967.

[78] Vance and Lauer, *op. cit.*, p. 48. With the signing of the Pact, Cairo Radio ceased its attacks on Husayn and the Jordanian Government, and Nasser addressed Husayn as "Dear Brother." "Research Report, The Arab-Israeli Conflict, the 1967 Campaign," Keesings Archives (New York- Scribners, 1968), p. 22.

conference was an agreement that provided for indefinite financial aid to Jordan and the U.A.R. The resolution stated:

> The kings of Saudi Arabia, the state of Kuwait, and the State of Libya, resolve to be obligated to pay the following amounts annually and at the beginning of every three months starting the beginning of October until the erasing of all traces of aggression: Saudi Arabia fifty million pounds; Kuwait, fifty million sterling and Libya, thirty million sterling.[79]

CONCLUSION

Except with Iraq, the policies of King Abdullah were characterized by lack of cooperation with the Arab states. In order to avoid Abdullah's dangerous course and for tactical reasons required to cope with the new circumstances that engulfed his regime, King Husayn adopted a policy based on "complete understanding and absolute cooperation with the Arab states."

This policy seemed to be a continuation of King Talal's plan to bring Jordan back into the Arab fold, for the era when Abdullah thought that he was an island unto himself had ended. Husayn came to realize that he could best preserve his throne by pursuing a middle of the road policy. Accordingly while he stressed cooperation with the Arab states, he also emphasized Western friendship. This was an escape route which Abdullah refused to provide for himself, and which ultimately resulted in his demise. The difference between the two kings may lie in their personalities and to the internal and external settings during their respective reigns. Husayn's youthfulness and Western education, together with the new political atmosphere in the Arab World, had great impact on his behaviour and policies. On the other hand, Abdullah's autocratic mentality and superiority complex rendered him inflexible, hence, scornful of others, as he pursued an independent personalized policy. By contrast, Husayn adopted a flexible policy which enabled him to exhibit cordiality and cooperation when it was in Jordan's interest. Accordingly, it became a landmark in Husayn's foreign policy to associate with one state or a bloc, Arab or Western,

---

[79] Ratib, *op. cit.*, p. 91.

when such action provided him with economic, political or military advantages. Thus, Husayn's foreign policy could be described as neutral, permitting him to manoeuvre without limitations.

Husayn's fluid policy derived from his quest for the security of his regime. He was never at ease with the Arab revolutionary regimes which he believed to have constituted the major threat to his throne, even more than Israel. This attitude inevitably resulted in the Jordan-Arab states cold war.

For one thing, Husayn differed from Nasser on the issue of Arab nationalism. While Nasser's policy stressed comprehensive unity— that is liquidation of states—, Husayn wanted unity based on the equality of member states. Accordingly, he accused Nasser of imperialism since his plan, according to Husayn, would subjugate other states to Egyptian domination. Thus, agreement with Nasser meant capitulation which he resisted.

One concludes that Husayn would agree to a comprehensive Arab unity provided that he is its leader. Barring that, he approved of a confederation whereby each state preserved its own leadership. Such policy proved harmful to Jordan since Arab public opinion yearned for full unity rather than parochialism. Furthermore, to become a leader, one must secure the trust, allegiance and the consensus of the population. While Husayn could have achieved such stature, by espousing parochialism and emphasizing dynastic interests, he alienated Jordan while placing obstacles to unity.

PART THREE

Jordan : Great Powers Relations

CHAPTER TWELVE

JORDAN-BRITISH RELATIONS

INTRODUCTION

Transjordan was a British creation which came as a result of the compromise reached between Amir Abdullah and Churchill at the Jerusalem Conference on 27 March 1921.[1] The Anglo Jordan relationship was governed by the terms of the Palestine Mandate.[2] The Mandate was an attempt to establish European influence instead of direct colonialism which could create national reaction in the colonial nation. However, the creation of the Amirate was a step in the direction of fulfilling Britain's obligation to the League of Nations to encourage self-government. The Amirate was an administrative unit under the Mandate with Abdullah as Britain's agent: its financial, military, and political relations were entirely in the hands of Britain. Thus, in effect, the territory of Transjordan was a colony except in name,[3] since it was administered indirectly through the British Resident.[4]

The Hashemites did not see in the mandate system any evil. They only saw in it a method of ruling which would allow them through cooperation with Britain to preserve their thrones. Abdullah considered Britain as a private and personal friend under whose protection his dynastic interests would be preserved.[5] In return, the Hashemites chose to advance British policies in their territories at the expense of nationalist demands.

---

[1] Sha'ar, lst ed., op. cit., pp. 176–82.

[2] Until 12 August 1927, The Mandate for Palestine and Transjordan was one.

[3] Glubb, A Soldier With the Arabs, p. 64.

[4] London Times, 28 March 1928. Commenting on this point, Abdullah said, "This is my problem with all the Prime Ministers....They could do nothing before they consulted the British Ambassador." Majali, Muthakkirati, p. 97. This state of affairs continued even during Husayn's reign, See Husayn, Uneasy Lies the Head, p. 152.

[5] Anis Sayegh, op. cit., p. 251.

Britain recognized the Amirate of Transjordan in the Anglo-Transjordanian treaty of 25 May 1923, when the principality attained autonomy.[6] A second agreement with Britain was signed in 1928. It provided for the creation of a political system with limited constitutional characteristics. The Treaty of 1928 "was imposed without consultation or negotiations with the Transjordan people."[7] It also undermined Abdullah's sovereignty, as Toynbee related:

It made no express recognition of Transjordan independence except in the technical sense in which the term was used in British treaties with trucial chiefs in the Persian Gulf.[8]

Accordingly, the treaty gave Britain a great degree of control over "all matters concerning the foreign relations of Transjordan," military affairs, and more importantly, Transjordan's finances.[9] It was incompatible with independence.

From 1921 to 1956, Jordanian politics were greatly influenced by its relations with Britain. This influence was the source of contention between the Arab nationalists and the Hashemites which was a factor in the uncertainty of political life in Jordan.

Abdullah's pro-British policy earned him the respect of the Western world. Supported by British relationships, a major source of his legitimacy and authority, and by controlling the Arab Legion, Abdullah secured for himself the separate statehood of Transjordan.[10]

After World War II, British-Jordanian relations were extraordinarily cordial. The 1928 Treaty was revised in March 1946. The new treaty recognized the independence of Transjordan which became the Hashemite Kingdom of Jordan.[11] Abdullah's ability to obtain independence was a reward to an ally. For example, he declared war on Germany and the Arab Legion shared greatly in

[6] The British High Commissioner of Palestine informed Abdullah of his independence in a public ceremony on 25 May 1923. Musa, *op. cit.*, p. 201.

[7] Musa, *op. cit.*, p. 279.

[8] Royal Institute of International Affairs, *Survey of International Affairs*, ed. Arnold Toynbee (London: Oxford University Press, 1928), p. 323.

[9] Musa, *op. cit.*, p. 280.

[10] Vatikiotis, *op. cit.*, p. 48.

[11] For the text of the treaty, see Khalil, Vol. II, pp. 379–84; G.B., *British and Foreign State Papers*, 1946, p. 461.

the Allied war effort.[12]

While the Amirate became independent, Britain retained the right to station troops anywhere in the country to protect its vital strategic military interests in the region. Furthermore, while the provisions of the new treaty changed much of the legal terminology of the state's institutions, it did not alter the nature of rule and authority.[13]

The 1946 Treaty was superseded two years later by the Treaty of 1948. Although the new treaty limited British presence inside Jordan to three airstrips only, Jordan's military and financial affairs continued to be under the direct British authority. Although Abdullah became very active in the field of Arab nationalist politics, his foreign relations were unequivocally in line with those of Britain. To some extent Abdullah's ability to conclude the 1948 Treaty was "due to the revived political opposition in the country."[14] Although the Treaty was an improvement over that of 1946, opposition inside the country was manifested.[15] The press attacked Prime Minister Abul-Huda for yielding to Britain and for including many reservations.[16] The treaty was not sent to Parliament because the constitution dictated that King and the Cabinet were responsible for treaty-making.[17]

After the conclusion of the 1948 Treaty, relations with Britain became cool due to the Arab policy in general and to British support of the Zionist state. While the Treaty obligated Britain to come to

[12] The Arab Legion was assigned to the security of the vital communication lines in the Middle East, particularly, the oil pipelines. Furthermore, units were given guard duties for British installation in the Middle East theatre. In addition, the Legion units participated in quashing the Rashid Ali Al-Kilani revolt in Iraq, and in fighting against the Vichy French in Syria and Lebanon in 1941. Musa, *op. cit.*, p. 400; Vatikiotis, *op. cit.*, p. 73.

[13] Vatikiotis, *op. cit.*, p. 49.

[14] *Ibid.*, p. 50.

[15] Opposition centred on the following points:

1. The people were not consulted because the constitution prohibited it.
2. The treaty placed Jordan in a subservient position, particularly, in connection with finances.
3. National aspirations dictated the abrogation of the treaty and prevention of the conclusion of any other which limits national sovereignty. Musa, *op. cit.*, p. 432. For the text of the treaty, see Khalil, Vol. II, pp. 386–89; G.B. *British and Foreign State Papers*, 151, II, 1948, p. 90–100.

[16] Majali, *Muthakkirati*, p. 64; Musa, *op. cit.*, p. 432.

[17] Majali, *Muthakkirati*, p. 64; Vatikiotis, *op. cit.*, p. 50.

the aid of Jordan in case of outside aggression, the treaty was not sufficiently and plainly enunciated. This made the British press and politicians who sympathized with Zionism suggest that Britain would never go to the defence of its ally against Israel. This enabled hostile Arab opinion to doubt British sincerity.[18] This suspician was verified on several occasions.[19]

The Treaty would expire in 1968. However, it could have been revised after fifteen years and its duration reduced "if a complete system of security agreements under Article 43 of the Chapter of the United Nations is concluded before the expiry of this period."[20]

This provision served as the basis for the Huda negotiations in 1954, and the subsequent demand by Britain that Jordan accede to the Baghdad Pact in return for abrogation of the treaty.

On 7 November 1954, Prime Minister Huda declared that his government wished to amend the 1948 Treaty. This was occasioned by the changes in the international situation in general, and in Egypt and Iraq in particular. Britain had concluded an agreement with Egypt to evacuate the Suez Base and negotiations were made with the Iraqi Government regarding the revision of the Anglo Iraqi Treaty to be replaced by the Baghdad Alliance. "Iraq has made my government think of amending our treaty with Britain and negotiations in this regard will start shortly."[21]

Negotiations for the revision of the Anglo-Jordan Treaty were

---

[18] Glubb, *A Soldier with the Arabs*, p. 301. Britain made it clear that it would defend East of the Jordan proper, not the West Bank.

[19] One example was when Britain failed to come to the aid of Jordan when Zionist forces, in violation of the truce, occupied Eastern Negeb and the Gulf of Aqaba. The British were in an extremely awkward position; "they decided not to comply with Transjordan's request for assistance. This meant that they were giving up their hope of obtaining the Negeb for Transjordan, and indirectly for themselves." Shwadran, *op. cit.*, pp. 275–78. Britain justified her action by stating that her decision was in deference to the U.N. Another was in 1956 when the British declined Husayn's demand that the British air force help Jordan in central Palestine when Zionist attacks were being conducted on peaceful border villages by air and large infantry forces supported by armour. Glubb, *A Soldier with the Arabs*, p. 302; Musa, *op. cit.*, p. 530.

[20] Article 7. Text of treaty is in Khalil, Vol. II, p. 387.

[21] *London Times*, 8 November 1954. The termination of the treaty was welcomed by Britain. "No longer did Britain find it advantageous to be associated with an Arab state on terms that might involve Britain against Israel." M.A. Fitzsimmons, *Empire By Treaty* (Notre Dame: Notre Dame University Press, 1964), p. 197.

linked with the success of the Baghdad Pact and Jordan's accession to it. However, Jordan's failure to join the alliance together with nationalist pressure resulted in the dismissal of Glubb and the subsequent termination of the treaty which formally ended Jordan's financial dependence on Britain in March 1957.

THE BAGHDAD PACT

Background

The objective of British policy in the Middle East was the security of a broad belt of territory stretching from the Mediterranean to the Arabian Gulf containing the oil fields.[22] For more than two hundred years, Britain regarded the free access to these lands as its vital interest for its transit. Yet, "Britain had no interests in these countries themselves."[23] British negotiations with Husayn I, in December 1915, were to create a unified Arab state friendly to Britain to replace the Turks. But the introduction of the Zionists into Palestine and the French conquest of Syria ruined the plan. The creation of the Arab League in 1945, however, aimed at creating similar conditions with a bloc of Arab states.

Strategically Britain considers the Middle East as most vital for the security of Europe and was ready to accept Arab friendship, and guaranteed to keep Palestine an Arab territory if the Arabs agreed to enter into security alliance with the West.[24] British Prime Minister Ernest Bevin's statement verified this point: "The Arab friendship is more precious to Britain than military bases or armies stationed in the Middle East."[25]

The outbreak of the Korean War was the catalyst that produced a frenzy of Western activity directed at strengthening defences throughout the world. It was hypothesized that the U.S.S.R. would expand its borders if it found Western defences weak. Secretary of State Acheson said:

The only way to deal with the Soviet Union ... is to create

---

[22] Glubb, *A Soldier with the Arabs*, p. 224.
[23] *Ibid.*, p. 361.
[24] Jamali, *op. cit.*, p. 58.
[25] *Ibid.*

situations of strength. . . . Whenever the Soviet Union detects weakness or disunity, it exploits them to the full.[26]

Since World War II, colonial people everywhere have risen against white-man rule. The United States had generally lived up to its promises to support their independence. While pressing for emancipation, the U.S. had to make sure that it would have the cooperation of those nations in its international policy. Consequently, the task of the American post-war policy in the colonial world has been to encourage the liquidation of colonialism while simultaneously integrating the newly emancipated people into its security system.[27]

Extending N.A.T.O. to the Bosphorus made it imperative to consolidated Middle East regional defences.[28] Thus, the West planned to create the Middle East Defence Organization (M.E.D.O.) to serve as a corollary to N.A.T.O.[29]

Following the 1948 War, the Arab states were anxious for Western aid to prevent Zionist expansion. This led to the formation of the Arab collective security Pact in 1950, which was met with favour in London and Washington. But Western policies met with a dilemma: supplying the Arabs would mean limiting Zionist ambitions, and would have been contrary to British-American attitudes toward Israel. An alternative decision was to take a stand favourable to Israel. Thus, on 25 May 1950, Britain, France and the U.S.A. issued the Tripartite Declaration which limited arms imports into the Middle East to keep the Palestine conflict under control, thereby emphasizing the *status quo* in favour of Israel. The Declaration read:

The three Governments recognized that the Arab states and Israel all need to maintain a certain level of armed forces for the purpose of assuring their internal security and their legitimate self-defence and to play a part in the defence of the area as a whole. All applications for arms or war material for these countries

---

[26] United States, *Department of State Bulletin,* Vol. XII (20 February 1950), p. 472.

[27] Peter Fliess, *International Relations in the Bipolar World* (New York: Random House, 1968), p. 108.

[28] *London Times*, 30 July 1952.

[29] *New York Times*, 17 March 1949, p. 3.

will be considered in the light of these principles.[30]

However, while Egypt rejected the M.E.D.O., the Western governments declared their intention to continue their plans despite Egypt's objection.

British withdrawal from the Middle East was seen as a constructive step towards improving Arab relations with the West. American concern for the security of the Middle East, following the withdrawal of the British was occasioned by the power vacuum theory. Relaxation of the British authority was interpreted by the U.S.A. as an indication of the need to defend her own interests directly. Thus, the American position was that Britain should be replaced by an institution that serves the West. Having emerged as the leading power, the U.S.A. felt the urge to oppose Communism. The vital interests of the U.S. in western Asia have become of politico-strategic character, thus, its policy aimed at preventing the region from falling into the hands of the U.S.S.R.

Secretary of State John Foster Dulles was concerned about the absence of adequate defence arrangements in the Middle East. While he affirmed American support to the Tripartite declaration, he stressed the advisability of anti-Communist defence arrangements, backed by the U.S.A. Dulles gave his views of M.E.D.O., stating:

I believe that there should be established an original defence organization in the Middle East. It is too costly for these countries individually to have adequate defence establishments of their own. A collective system is much cheaper and is more reliable. . . .[31]

Dulles added that an all-Arab defence system was unattainable, since the Arabs did not see the Communists threat. The Arabs,

[30] United States, *Department of State Bulletin*, XII (5 June 1950), p. 886. Prime Minister Nuri Al-Sa'ed of Iraq indicated that the Tripartite Declaration was an aggression against the Arabs, since Western policies aimed at maintaining a balance of arms in favour of Israel. See Al-Sa'ed's speech on Radio Baghdad, 16 December 1956, cited in Khalil, *op. cit.*, Vol. II, pp. 255–78. Patrick Walker, Member of Parliament in charge of foreign affairs in the Labour Party's foreign policy said: "We in Britain have one foreign policy. The Labour Party foreign policy centres on maintaining a balance of power in the Middle East." Quoted in At-Tall, *Khatar Al-Sahyouniyiah Al-Alamiyiah Ala Al-Islam Wa Al-Masihiyiah* (Cairo: Dar Al-Qalam, 1964), p. 377.

[31] *London Times*, 23 May 1953; also Ionides, *op. cit.*, p. 92.

however, were concerned with the Zionist threat and that Western sponsorship of Israel had destroyed Arab hope for cooperation with the West.[32] However, the Arab states, in an effort to stabilize the region, stipulated that an acceptable solution to the Palestine conflict would be a precondition to their cooperation.[33] But Zionist influence in the U.S.A. and Britain precluded such solution.

The Arab demand was dictated more by their desire to halt Zionist aggression than their fear of Communism as Pierre Rondott observed:

> The Arab world became more and more obsessed with the Arab-Israeli conflict. In its eyes, this was the only topic that mattered. The East-West conflict did not interest the Arabs nor would they listen to the Free World's anti-Soviet propaganda. Nothing counted with them except the threat from Israel. They refused to regard the U.S.S.R. as, in any way, an enemy. Soviet domination which would, they imagined, humor Arab suscepti-bilities seemed a lesser catastrophe (should it ever come to pass) than Israeli domination with its inevitable commitment, the expiration of Pan-Arabism.[34]

In this light, Dulles's attention was, therefore, focused on the countries in close proximity to the Soviet border, for he believed, "In general, the Northern Tier of nations show awareness of the danger."[35]

In the early 1950's the Middle East was the only region adjacent to the Soviet territory which remained unattached to a Western collective security system. Britain and the United States were eager to associate Middle Eastern states with their global cold war policy including the negotiation of pacts.[36] Their eagerness was based on

---

[32] Glubb, *op. cit.*, p. 376.

[33] *Ibid.*

[34] Pierre Rondott, *Changing Patterns of the Middle East* (New York: Prae-ger, 1959), p. 136. The Arab population do not fear Communism because they have never had any contact with Russia. "...Russia is an unknown quantity, since it has never been in the Arab World. Many Arabs, consequently, are speculating about Russia and Communism." *Security and the Middle East: The Problem and Its Solution*, Proposals submitted to the President of the United States, April 1954, p. 110; Ionides, *op. cit.*, p. 92; Rondott, *op. cit.*, p. 137.

[35] U.S., *Department of State Bulletin*, XXVIII (15 June 1953), p. 831.

[36] Vatikiotis, *op. cit.*, p. 121.

their calculation that the value of this territory in fighting limited wars ranked high. Thus, cultivating friendship, promoting stability and securing peace time agreements were essential to the policy of containing Soviet expansion.[37]

In early 1953, Dulles visited the Middle East. He came to the conclusion that any defence alliances against Soviet aggression must spring from the desire of the people and the governments, and that the states of the northern tier due to their closeness to the Russian frontiers would be willing to form a regional defence organization. This was the origin of the Baghdad Pact.[38]

It was logical to have as the founding states of such pacts those which immediately border on the U.S.S.R., namely, Turkey and Iran. Although Pakistan and Iraq did not share frontiers with the U.S.S.R. nevertheless, they were included.[39] To the West, the position of Turkey was decisive in the Near East. Thus, Turkey was the catalyst of the Pact.[40] Accordingly, the Turkish Foreign Minister had without difficulty included the Shah of Iran who was anxious to secure new weapons to please his army.[41] The Western bait of economic aid as

[37] Elizabeth Monroe, *Britain's Moments in the Middle East,* 1914–1956, (Baltimore: Johns Hopkins, 1963), p. 182. While Britain declared that the Member states of the Baghdad Pact became partners "to protect themselves against any possible aggressive expansion," presumably against the U.S.S.R., the British Government reaffirmed the "defensive nature of the Pact," and allayed the fears of Moscow that the Pact members have "no aggressive intentions whatever against the Soviet Union or any other Country." G.B., *British and Foreign State Papers*, Vol. CLXIII (1957–1958), p. 70. In a memorandum to the British Government, the U.S.S.R. declared that the Baghdad Pact was a part of the "closed aggressive military blocs," *Ibid.*, p. 58. Its true character is "demonstrated by the fact that one of its organizers and members [Britain] carried out an attack on Egypt, while another member contributed to this action by making its territory available for use by the bombers of the attacking party." *Ibid.*, p. 67.

[38] John Foster Dulles, "Report on the Near East," *Department of State Bulletin*, XXVIII (15 June 1953), pp. 831–35.

[39] The U.S.S.R. concluded non-aggression pact with Afghanistan and sent an economic mission to establish a foothold and to prevent it from joining the Baghdad Pact. Thus, Afghanistan, though a Muslim country, served as a wedge between Pakistan and Iran.

[40] Fuad Koprulu, Turkish Foreign Minister, was inspired by the vision that all Muslim states would come under Turkey's leadership. Cited in Seale, *op. cit.*, p. 208.

[41] Iran's entry into the Pact was welcomed by the U.S. The Soviet Union alleged that the Baghdad Pact was an extension of N.A.T.O. and a violation of

well as armaments also attracted Husayn's attention who declared his interest in joining the Pact in order to improve Jordan's defences against Israel.[42]

The British Government was neutral about the Hashemite plans, but, in the mid-1950's, the inhibiting factors ceased to carry weight and Britain decided to lend Iraq its support. Due to the difficulties it encountered in Iran and Egypt, and in an attempt to save its position throughout the Middle East, particularly in Jordan and Iraq, Britain decided to embark on the creation of the Baghdad Pact. In establishing the Pact, Britain envisioned an Arab World under Iraqi leadership harnessed to Britain through the alliance.[43]

The creation of the Baghdad Pact was mainly for British interests. Campbell wrote:

> With Suez being evacuated and with only Egypt's promise on which to depend for its use in case of war, Britain looked all the more to its position in Iraq as a means of protecting the security of Britain's interests in the Middle East, especially in the Persian Gulf area. Membership in the Baghdad Pact seemed the best available means of protecting the oil supplies so necessary to Britain's economy, it might also check the erosion of British position throughout the Middle East especially if Jordan were brought in.[44]

British policy was still based on the premise that her Middle Eastern interests could best be defended by retaining political and military

---

Soviet-Iranian treaties. The U.S.S.R. said in a note on 26 November 1955:

> The Soviet Government believes that essential to confirm the fact that Iran's accession to the Baghdad military grouping is incompatible with the interests of strengthening peace and security in the Near and Middle East and is contrary to Iran's good neighbour relations with the Soviet Union and to certain of Iran's treaty obligations." *Current Digest of Soviet Press*, 11 January 1956, p. 22.

[42] Monroe, *op. cit.*, p. 188.

[43] Anthony Eden, *op. cit.*, p. 244. Beal, biographer of Dulles, claimed that Dulles was surprised at Iraq's joining the Pact. Robinson Beal, *Dulles* (New York: Harper, 1957), p. 248. The Soviet Union stressed that such foreign military bases in the Middle-East are "being used to undermine the sovereign rights of these countries." G.B., *British and Foreign State Papers*, 1958, p. 66.

[44] Campbell, *op. cit.*, p. 58.

supremacy in the area and by an unyielding attitude towards local nationalism. It must be remembered that Eden always considered Arab nationalism as non-existent. By severing Iraq from the other Arab states, Eden was implementing this theory; thus, Britain set herself against the current popular feeling, driving the nationalists into alliance with the Communists.[45]

Iraq's Position

Iraq viewed its position as different from other Arab states in regard to defence arrangements. It was "in special circumstances due to its proximity to the U.S.S.R., and its common frontier with Turkey and Persia."[46] The Egyptian estimate was different: "Iraq derived a guarantee more than adequate from the Arab Collective Solidarity Pact."[47]

Iraq, however, disliked the Arab Collective Security Pact and the League which seemed to be the instrument for Egyptian opposition to the Hashemite plans in North Arabia.[48] In fact, Nuri described the Arab Collective Security Pact (A.C.S.P.) as "mere ink on paper; therefore another means of defence must be found."[49]

In a meeting with Nasser, Nuri declared his lack of faith in the Arab Collective Security Pact, and stated:

I cannot depend on the Arabs to defend my country. If I tell my people and my foreign friends that I am going to depend on Syrian, Saudi Arabian, and Lebanese armies to defend my country, they will say, 'Nuri, you are a fool!' The only way to defend my country is to make an alliance with the West. I will understand your suspicion of the British but I am going ahead right away.[50]

To Iraq, the Baghdad Pact was a means to an end: to secure its

---

[45] Seale, *op. cit.*, p. 264.

[46] Monroe, *op. cit.*, p. 181.

[47] *Akhbar Al-Yawme* (Cairo), December 1954.

[48] Seale, *op. cit.*, p. 200.

[49] *Ibid.*, p. 208.

[50] *Ibid.*, p. 207. The Arab rulers made it clear that if Iraq or Jordan were attacked by Russia, it would be because both serve as Western bases. Therefore, no obligation would rest upon the League members to come to their rescue. *Security and the Middle East, op. cit.*, p. 24.

interests as well as Arab interests. By joining the Pact, Iraq would get rid of the British treaty which was a stigma.[51] Another advantage would have been enhancing Iraq's role in Arab politics, as it would have been supported by Britain and the United States as well as the Pact members.[52] A third advantage would be receiving new armaments. A fourth would be an alliance on equal footing with the other Member states. This new position would have brought Iraq to the leading position in the Arab World for having a large army and powerful allies.[53]

Although the Baghdad Pact appeared to be a Western alliance, it still could have brought advantages to the Arab World. Turkey, which had been a supporter of Israel, started to change its policies towards the Arabs and promised to help solve the Palestine problem in the United Nations. Turkish Prime Minister Adnan Menderes assured Nuri that Turkish-Israeli relations were shrinking, trade had diminished and that Turkey had withdrawn its ambassador to Israel.[54]

In January 1955, Nuri insisted that the Pact be used to solve the Palestine question. In Parliament, on 2 February 1955, Nuri declared:

I explained to the Egyptians that we have two foes: the first is Israel, the second is Communism. As regards the first, Iraq's policy is to seek assistance of as many Muslim combines as possible.... I always placed first the Zionist danger and the need

---

[51] Eden took this point into consideration. He stated:

There was another reason why we should support and may join the Pact. The Anglo-Iraqi Treaty of 1930 would expire in 1957, and we had to take account of nationalist feelings, even in the most friendly countries. It was important to get rid of any taint of patron and pupil. An attempt by the Labour Government to negotiate a new treaty had ended in riots and disappointment. Eden, *Full Circle*, p. 244. A special agreement was signed on 4 April 1955, replacing the Treaty of 30 June 1930, and constituted Britain's accession to the alliance. Seale, *op. cit.*, p. 226.

[52] Eden, *Full Circle*, p. 243.

[53] Nuri argued that if Iraq were to become a lynchpin in the Baghdad Pact, it would benefit from the flood of Western arms, money, and equipment. Other Arab states would follow her lead. Egypt would be faced with the choice of isolation or joining as a junior partner. Seale, *op. cit.*, p. 201.

[54] Jamali, *op. cit.*, p. 116.

to secure the support of the world in order to eliminate that danger.[55]

The Iraqi-American military assistance agreement of 21 April 1954 constituted the crucial point of departure in gaining Iraq's willingness to take part in the regional arrangements.[56]   Despite enticements, Iraq wavered in the early stages of the discussions.   This attitude was ascribed to three considerations: first, the desire to make a better bargain, thus, increasing the benefits that might be offered; second, the instability of the Iraqi Government in the first half of 1954; third, the severe criticism of Iraq by the Arab states for contemplating a non-Arab alliance which would be damaging to the Arab cause while increasing political instability in the Arab World.[57]

The Arab Response

The signing of the Pact brought an immediate reaction that "Britain, because of its vast oil interests in the area, and influence, had "'got at' Iraq."[58] Nasser, due to internal reasons centering around anti-Western feeling, had to move slowly towards alliances with the West.   On the other hand, Nuri for external factors focusing upon Anglo-Iraqi relationships and in quest for Arab leadership, wanted to move fast.[59] Iraq's initiative infuriated Egypt because it was bypassed, thus, it branded the Pact as the "catspaw of imperialism."[60] While King Husayn described Egypt's feelings in this matter as "intolerable," he remarked that the Western nations made a fatal

---

[55] Monroe, *op. cit.*, p. 185.   There was an agreement within the Pact that the Palestine problem would be discussed at the U.N. General Assembly, and attempts be made to implement the U.N. Resolutions, and force Israel to obey them.   Jamali, *op. cit.*, p. 116.

[56] U.S. *Department of State Bulletin*, 31 April 1954, p. 772.

[57] In his radio speech on 16 December 1956, Nuri revealed that the Egyptian attacks on Iraq had started "before the existence of the Baghdad Pact, had even before we had thought of concluding this Pact....The attacks had started in March 1954, and the Pact was signed only at the end of February 1955." Khalil, II, p. 268.

[58] Husayn, *Uneasy Lies the Head, op. cit.*, p. 102.

[59] Monroe, *op. cit.*, p. 182.   Shortly after Nasser signed the Anglo-Egyptian Agreement of 1954, the Muslim Brotherhood made an attempt to assassinate him. Cited in Fitzsimmons, *op. cit.*, p. 130.

[60] Husayn, *Uneasy Lies the Head*, p. 103.

mistake by rushing into an agreement with Iraq alone.[61]

Nasser had taken the bold step of making Arabism Egypt's major foreign policy objective. The Arab solidarity was wedded to non-alignment. Thus, the policy which the Egyptian leadership urged the Arabs to adopt was: the Arabs must unite only with Arabs.[62]

The Egyptian opposition was based on the following premises: one, associating with the imperialist powers would eventually bring back colonialism in a disguised form.[63] Two, by joining the Pact Iraq would assume leadership position in the Arab World, replacing Egypt. Three, Iraq would emerge so powerful that Syria, Lebanon and Jordan would inevitably be annexed, thereby, in effect, recreating the Fertile Crescent Plan, causing the isolation of Egypt.[64] Accordingly, the Arab League was convened to discuss Iraq's decision to join the Pact.[65]

The Arab countries have never disagreed on a foreign policy issue as they did on the Baghdad Pact and the policy of positive

---

[61] Ibid., p. 102. Husayn told the Turkish Prime Minister Menderes that any agreement would have to include most of the Arab states at once, "for if any Arab states formed a pact without prior consultation and agreement with the other Arab states, it would be a disaster." Ibid.

[62] Seale, op. cit., p. 197. In a meeting with Major Salah Salem, Nasser's personal envoy at Baghdad, Nuri told him: "I am not a soldier in Abdul-Nasser's army. Please tell him that I will never obey his orders." Ibid., p. 217. Barely, a month after the conclusion of the Pact, Israel attacked an Egyptian outpost in the Gaza area killing over thirty soldiers. "This event was considered by the Arab public opinion as the West's answer to the Egyptian opposition to the Baghdad Pact." Fayez Sayegh, op. cit., p. 116. Furthermore, Egyptian opposition to the Pact resulted in Western denial of military and financial aid. Egypt's request for a loan to build the Aswan Dam from the World Bank did not materialize since the Bank sought to impose conditions which would have subjected the Egyptian economy to Western control. "The American offer of funds had been withdrawn for the political reasons that Egypt was opposed to the Baghdad Pact." Anthony Eden, The Suez Crisis of 1956 (Boston: Beacon Press, 1968), p. 53.

[63] Hafez, op. cit., p. 215.

[64] Although Turkey was always opposed to Arab unity, it agreed to an Iraqi-Syrian union since Iraq had joined the Baghdad Pact. Jamali, op. cit., 116. The traditional rivalry between Egypt and Iraq had for centuries constituted the basic elements of the region's politics, while the rest of the smaller countries were merely incidental. The relationship resembled Belgium, Holland and Luxemburg when France and Germany were at war. Glubb, Soldier with the Arabs. op. cit., p. 377.

[65] Seale, op. cit., p. 212.

neutrality.   Article 10 of the Treaty of Joint Defence and Economic
Cooperation stated:

> Each of the contracting states undertakes not to conclude any
> international agreement which may be inconsistent with this treaty,
> and not to adopt in its international relations any course which
> may be contrary to the aims of this treaty.[66]

The Arab states, except Jordan and Iraq, disapproved of the Pact,
and considered it a trick to help Israel, and believed that Jordan
would eventually be tricked into signing a treaty with Israel.[67]
Egypt declared that the objective of the Pact was to break up the
Arab Collective Security Pact, and was tantamount to the return of
imperialism which ignores the interests of the Middle East, while,
at the same time frustrating the work of the League.[68]

The attitude of Saudi Arabia was outright hostility to the alliance
because it aimed at strengthening the Hashemite position which the
Saudi had always obstructed.   Furthermore, the Pact involved
Britain with whom Saudi Arabia had outstanding disputes over the
Burami Oasis and other territories.   A third reason for Saudi opposition was that, by enticing Jordan to join the alliance, the League
would collapse leaving Egypt and Saudi Arabia isolated.   In an
interview with King Saud, he replied to the question why he was
critical of the Baghdad Pact:

> Saudi Arabia is an independent country. She has a policy dictated
> by its own interests. Her view of the Baghdad Pact agrees
> with that of Egypt, Syria and other Arab countries based upon a
> thorough study of the Pact which was concluded in secret.
> The participation of Turkey, the intimate friend of Israel, increases
> Arab suspicion of the Pact. Moreover we all believe that the

---

66 Khalil, Vol. II, *op. cit.*, p. 103.

67 Although Article 5 of the Pact gave Iraq a veto against the admission of
Israel, and while the Pact was not designed to take sides in the Arab-Israeli issue,
however, by preserving the *status quo* in the region, the Pact was interpreted as
guaranteeing the frontiers of Israel. *People's Court Proceedings*, Baghdad, 1959,
Vol. VI, p. 2360. Testimony given by Fadil Al-Walid of the Iraqi Foreign Ministry
on 30 October 1958.

68 Alexander DeConde, *A History of American Foreign Policy*, (New York:
Scribner, 1963), p. 751.

purpose of the Pact is to do away with the Arab League and to work indirectly for bringing about peace with Israel and the insurance of Zionist objectives.[69]

The attitude of Syria was no different. The mood of the Syrian people had already been expressed by Foreign Minister Ma'rouf Al-Dawalibi earlier, when the issue of Western alliances arose. To the Syrians, Western pacts aimed at entrenching Israel at the expense of the Arabs. Dawalibi declared to the Egyptian daily, *Al-Misry*:

Should the U.S. pursue their present policies and should the Arab countries be forced to choose between becoming a Soviet republic or a part of a Jewish state, the Arabs would rather be a Soviet republic.[70]

However, the Syrian reaction to the Pact was voiced by Prime Minister Sabri Al-Asali in the Chamber condemning all pacts and embracing the Egyptian foreign policy theme:

December 1954, witnessed the last Byzantine discussions inside the Arab League, for then they evolved around the questions: shall the Arabs join alliances or not? Would they accept help and assistance? Must a decision among the Arab states be taken unanimously? The purpose of this discussion was to impose the logic of subservience and surrender in all Arab States

[69] *Sunday Times.* In his biography, Eden accused the Saudis of undermining the Pact. He wrote:

The agents of King Saud, their pockets bulging with gold, were cooperating everywhere with the communists against Western interests.... Unlike ourselves, they [the Americans] did not feel any responsibility for insuring that these oil revenues were wisely invested. King Saud, at liberty to spend his money as he wished, chose palaces for his family at home and subversion for his policies abroad, in Jordan, the Lebanon, and Iraq. Eden, *op. cit.*, p. 382.

The Christian Science Monitor, in its editorial on 12 January 1956, commented: "The Soviet Union would like nothing better than to see revolts which would, perhaps, overthrow the Government of Jordan, carry the country into the Cairo camp, and pay its troops with Saudi Arabian royalties from American-developed oil."

[70] Walter Z. Lacqueur, *Communism and Nationalism in the Middle East* (New York: Praeger, 1956), p. 256; *New York Times* 12 April 1950.

and to make of Iraqi policy the example to be followed. From that month on, imperialist maneuvering has been liquidated in Egypt and Syria. No government could come to power in Syria except by emphatically declaring "No alliances." Previous governments used to say "No alliances if they derogate from our sovereignty." The difference between the two stands is enormous. The latter means nothing else but alignment.[71]

The Dilemma of Jordan

Jordan was reluctant to join the Pact due to popular pressure and the sharp criticism of Iraq.[72] It, therefore, was in no mood to accept further involvement with Western military pacts, particularly, since the Palestinian majority in Jordan was responding to the Egyptian-Saudi Arabian anti-pact campaign, and held that the West was responsible for creating and sustaining the Zionist state.[73] Campbell observed:

...The great unsettled questions of Palestine stood as a mountain barrier in the way of all Western efforts to win the cooperation and support of the people of that part of the Middle East.[74]

The League was called for an emergency meeting to discuss Iraq's entry into the Baghdad Pact. Egypt and Saudi Arabia saw in the Baghdad Pact a violation of the League Covenant. Abul-Huda counselled taking a moderate stand because Jordan's position was based on a good-neighbourly policy, since it needed help from all Arab states. He cautioned against taking any action against Iraq and declared his intention to conciliate.

Against this background, Abul-Huda proposed to the League the formation of a joint peace command which could be expanded as a general command during a war, as an alternative to joining the Baghdad Pact.[75] This proposal placed Jordan on the side of Egypt and Saudi Arabia whose policies aimed at isolating Iraq.[76]

[71] Fayez Sayegh, op. cit., p. 134.
[72] Eden, Full Circle, p. 384.
[73] Vatikiotis, op. cit., p. 117.
[74] Campbell, op. cit., p. 47.
[75] Documents on International Affairs, 1955, p. 324.
[76] Seale, op. cit., p. 216.

However, when Iraq threatened to withdraw from the League if this resolution was adopted, a milder resolution was approved by the majority including Jordan. It stated:

> The foreign policy of the Arab states is based on the Arab League Charter and the treaty of Joint Defence and Economic Cooperation between the Arab states. This policy does not approve of concluding other alliances.[77]

Jordan's problem was that it needed both Egyptian and Iraqi help against Israel. Furthermore, Saudi Arabia had an eye on Aqaba, Jordan's only port. And lastly, if the Arab states continued to fight, Israel would take advantage of the confusion to occupy the West Bank.[78] Thus, in the summer of 1955, Husayn tried to create better understanding between Cairo and Baghdad. His mission to Iraq failed when Nuri, "the actual ruler of Iraq," told him: "Sir, we are in the Baghdad Pact. That is that, and we are certainly not backing out of it."[79] Husayn's meetings with Nasser on the issue led him to believe that "if Nasser had been consulted in the preliminary stages, the result might have been very different."[80] This is supported by Nasser's statement: "I do not like the way it was done. I have nothing against the Pact as such, but we should have been consulted properly."[81]

But Husayn had to make a stand. His ties with Iraq were dynastic, and, economically, Jordan was dependent on British support. Thus, Jordan was in a dilemma as *The Economist* explained:

---

[77] *Documents on International Affairs,,* 1955, p. 325.

[78] Husayn, *Uneasy Lies the Head,* p. 105.

[79] *Ibid.*, p. 105.

[80] *Ibid.* Nasser charged Eden of bad faith on Britain's part, since the treaty negotiations of 1954 implied that Nasser "was to be aided in organizing Middle Eastern defence on an Arab foundation." Fitzsimmons, *op. cit.*, p. 129.

[81] *Ibid.*, p. 106. At the end of 1954, Nuri had arranged a meeting with Menderese and Nasser, but the latter was opposed to Turkey's leadership in the Middle East and refused a meeting with Menderese. He, however, was ready to receive the mayors of Ankara and Istanbul, and a group of Turkish journalists. At this point, Menderese visited Baghdad instead, and signed the Iraqi-Turkish alliance on 24 February 1955. Monroe, *op. cit.*, p. 182; Kirk, *Contemporary Arab Politics*, p. 33. For the text of the agreement, see G.B., *British and Foreign State Papers*, Vol. XLI, 1955–1956, p. 1; *Parliamentary Papers*, Cmd. 9859, 24 February 1955.

The political pressures of the Arab World fall so heavily on troubled Jordan that it had little choice but to take cover in neutrality between Egypt and Iraq. Geographically it is in a triangle of the bilateral pacts extended by Egypt to Syria and Saudi Arabia, but economically it lives on British money and Britain supports the Iraqi defence policy.[82]

The revision of the Anglo-Jordan Treaty of 1948 was aimed mainly at changing the manner in which the subsidy was paid. Husayn and Abul-Huda demanded that payments be made directly to the government instead of to General Glubb, for this would be consistent with national dignity while it would reduce Glubb's influence. Furthermore, the negotiations aimed at exchanging the subsidy for rents of the British military bases in Jordan.[83] However, Britain refused Jordan's demand, but agreed to pay additional funds for the National Guard. Thus, negotiations came to a halt pending certain developments which were expected to occur in the Middle East.[84]

Britain's objection to the revision of the treaty before its expiration in 1968, was due to the evacuation of the Suez Base, and Britain's desire to secure new defence organizations.[85] However, as the Baghdad Pact alliance was concluded, and to which Britain adhered on 30 March, Abul-Huda was approached to join the Pact in return for the revision of the Anglo-Jordanian treaty.[86]

Caught in the struggle between Cairo and Baghdad, "Jordan had to do something." Britain supplied the answer. Eden wrote:

---

[82] *The Economist*, 24 December 1955.

[83] *Al-Husayn Ibn Talal, op. cit.*, p. 43.

[84] *Ibid.*; Majali, *Muthakkirati, op. cit.*, p. 152. Abul-Huda who was considered Britain's "man" in Jordan, was attacked in the British press, while in London, negotiating the revision of the treaty. He was called dictator, and one who had rigged the elections. The British had conducted talks with Nuri Al-Sa'ed and arrived at two plans: one, the Arab League would conclude a defence alliance with the West, thus, the need for bilateral treaties would end; two, if the Arab League did not take this step, Iraq would end its treaty with Britain. Thus, the future of the Jordan-British treaty depended on the future talks with Nuri, which ended in signing the Baghdad Pact in March 1955. Majali, *Ibid.*, p. 153.

[85] *Documents of American Foreign Policy and Relations, 1954*, pp. 391–95.

[86] Majali, *Muthakkirati, op. cit.*, p. 152.

It was reported that Britain offered to double the financial assistance to Jordan if it joined. *New York Times*, 23 December 1955, p. 2.

Jordan was a country for which we had special responsibilities:
we had brought it into being. . . . Early in November of 1955, our
ambassador, Mr. Duke, reported a conversation with King Husayn.
The Jordan Government were ready to join the Baghdad
Pact, the King said, provided they received 'the necessary backing'
from us. A court minister spoke in the same sense and General
Glubb reported like information to the War Office. All these
sources agreed that this was the moment of opportunity. If the
Jordan Government did not act now, they would waver indefini-
tely. . . . MacMillan was encouraged by his meeting at Baghdad
and judged this to be the moment to get some other Arab states
to join the Pact. Iraq felt isolated as the only Arab present.
The first new member, he considered, should be Jordan.[87]

On 2 November 1955, the President of Turkey, Jalal Bayar, accompanied by his Foreign Minister, Fateen Zorlo, visited Jordan, ostensibly to return the visits of Kings Abdullah and Husayn. However,
talks were conducted relating to the desire of Turkey to have Jordan
join the Turkish-Iraqi alliance. The Jordan Government explained
to Bayar that the Palestine war "had all but ruined Jordan's economy"
and demanded economic and military aid as a price for Jordan's
entry in the Pact.[88]

On 16 November, Prime Minister Sa'ed Al-Mufti sent a message
to the British Government requesting commencement of negotiations
for the revision of the treaty. While the memorandum detailed
Jordan's economic, military and financial needs, it also explained the
policy of Jordan:

1. Preservation of the Arab Solidarity Pact to enable Jordan to
   fulfil its obligations under it.
2. Supporting Jordan in realizing its demands and rights in
   Palestine and defending Jordan from any threat regardless
   of the sources.

---

87 Eden, *Full circle*, pp. 381–82.
88 Husayn, *Uneasy Lies the Head*, p. 108. Following Bayar's visit, a
delegation headed by Hazza' Al-Majali arrived in Baghdad for the purpose of
securing a loan to finance a number of economic development projects. The negotiations for the loan were hampered since the Iraqis insisted, as a condition for the
loan, that Jordan should join the Pact. Majali, *Muthakkirati, op. cit.*, p. 167.

3. Establishment of the following as minimum defence forces for Jordan:
   (a) an infantry division
   (b) an armoured division
   (c) heavy artillery
   (d) paratroopers
   (e) commando groups
   (f) an air force which includes bombers and fighters, and
   (g) a naval force in Aqaba and the Dead Sea.[89]

On 5 December, Britain announced that Sir Gerald Templer, Chief of the Imperial Staff, had been sent to Amman to consult with the Government of Jordan on military matters concerning the Arab Legion, and to conduct negotiations for the revision of the treaty.[90] Britain's action seemed to have been caused by the fact that the British General Staff were seriously disturbed about the security of Jordan and the future of the Arab Legion, considered as the "lynch-pin of our Middle East defence plans."[91]

Accordingly, the Jordan Government communicated with the British Government requesting her suggestions. This was done in an

---

[89] Majali, *Qissat Muhadathat Templer, op. cit.*, p. 4; *Al-Husayn Ibn Talal, op. cit.*, 44.

[90] In the House of Commons, a question was raised as to "why was a military man sent to undertake an extremely delicate diplomatic mission? Was it thought that he could bulldoze the Jordan Government into joining the Baghdad Pact? Will [Mr. Nutting]...confirm the report that Sir Gerald Templer told the Jordan Government that they had better make up their mind within 48 hours or take the consequences?"

Mr. Nutting replied, "There is no truth whatsoever in this statement. As to the selection of Sir Templer, he went because there were military matters to be discussed with the Jordan authorities." G. B. *Parliamentary Debates*, Vol. 548, 1956, Col. 594.

[91] Noel Monk, "Trouble Builds upon the Middle East," *Daily Mail*, 7 December 1955, p. 2; Glubb, *A Soldier With the Arabs,* p. 427. Other reports were that top Arab Legion officers had convinced King Husayn that it would be advisable to allow Egyptian-trained Palestinian commandos to carry on attacks against Israel from Jordan's territory. Husayn agreed to a plan of admitting five hundred commandos. The plan was to be kept from Glubb. This would have undermined Britain's position in the Midddle East, since for the first time military action would be conducted without Glubb's approval and direction. However, when Glubb became aware of the plan, he advised the War Office in London of the need for vigorous action. The result was the dispatch of General Templer. Shwadran, *op. cit.*, p. 326.

official memorandum on 11 December 1955, which included:

1. The Government of Jordan will sign the Baghdad Pact.
2. After signing the Pact, the British government will decide on the following: to increase the Jordan army by 65 per cent and to supply heavy and medium arms valued at six and one half million dinars; Britain will support Jordan's military requests from the Baghdad Pact; immediate commencement of negotiations to exchange the Anglo-Jordan treaty for a special agreement under Article 1 of the Pact; to help in the defence of Jordan which would require the increase of the British subsidy; in return, the Jordan government will give every assistance to the British forces stationed in Jordan.
3. Britain will cooperate in the building and the maintenance of the Jordan air force.
4. Jordan shall not enter in agreements or obligations outside the jurisdiction of the Pact.
5. The British government will agree to come to the aid of Jordan in case of armed aggression.
6. The duration of the agreement shall be twelve years.[92]

According to this memorandum, the Jordan government decided on the following as the minimum demand, and it was sent to the British delegation:

The Government of the Hashemite Kingdom of Jordan agrees to join the Baghdad Pact on the following conditions:

1. Her Majesty's Government should provide the following military units:
   (a) Increase by 65 per cent of the Arab Legion forces.
   (b) Various heavy and medium arms valued at six and one half million dinars.
2. Her Majesty's Government should support Jordan's viewpoint at the Military Commission regarding its needs in order to carry its defence responsibilities according to a military plan drawn for that purpose.

[92] Musa, *op. cit.*, 614. Regarding item 4, the counter proposal indicated that Jordan would not be obligated outside its borders. Majali *Qissat Muhadathat Templer*, p. 8.

3. Her Majesty's Government should commence negotiations with His Majesty's Government for changing the 1948 Anglo-Jordan Treaty with a special agreement.... The agreement should include the following:

(a) The strengthening of friendship between the two parties.

(b) Ending the Treaty, its annexes, and communications connected with it.

(c) The cooperation of both countries in the defence of Jordan including drawing military plans, common training, and assistance which included:

1. Her Majesty's Government should pay Jordan a financial assistance to be spent on Jordan forces.

2. The Hashemite Kingdom of Jordan should facilitate the establishment of British air force units in Amman and Mafraq.

3. The new arrangement shall not obligate Jordan outside its borders.

(d) Her Majesty's Government will immediately come to the aid of Jordan in case of an armed aggression.

* * * *

(g) This agreement shall be in force as long as both parties belonged to the Pact.[93]

In addition, Jordan insisted that the parties to the Pact should support Jordan's position on the Palestine question according to the U.N. Resolution of 1947, and to reject Israel's entry in the alliance.[94] Jordan also stipulated that its entry into the Pact would not in any way affect its obligations toward the Arab States under the Arab Solidarity Pact.[95] More importantly, the Pact nations promised to help the economic development of Jordan and to supply arms in addition to those secured from Britain.[96]

---

[93] *Al-Husayn Ibn Talal, op. cit.*, pp. 46–9; Also Majali, *Qissat Muhadathat; Moman, op. cit.*, pp. 9–10. Regarding (3-c-1), the financial aid shall not be less than fourteen million annually, *Ibid.*, p. 9. As to Arabization of the army, Majali, seemed assured that it was possible for Jordan to assume full command of its forces after four years instead of thirteen, under the 1948 Treaty. *Ibid.*, p. 22.

[94] *Falastin*, 14 December 1955.

[95] *Ibid.*, p. 10. The Member States cabled their support for the demand.

[96] *Ibid.*, p. 22.

Count Jordan Out

Four Palestinian Cabinet members raised the question of whether the Jordan proposal to the British Government would be shown to the Egyptian Government. But Jordan wanted to consult Egypt and other Arab states after the plan had been submitted to Britain. A compromise, however, was reached according to which both Britain and Egypt would receive the agreement simultaneously.[97]   Complicating the matter for Jordan, four ministers resigned the following day, a development which led to the resignation of the entire Cabinet. Their action was taken "through patriotic motives," and in support of Egypt's policy which stressed that Israel would, sooner or later, be included in the alliance.[98] Cognizant of Nasser's influence in Jordan, Husayn declared that Jordan would not join the Pact without Cairo's approval.[99]

Nasser's campaign against Iraq's entry into the Pact was futile. Thus, after losing the battle with Nuri, Nasser decided to score a victory in Amman by preventing Jordan from joining the Alliance, thereby ensuring that Iraq would be the lone Arab state in the Pact. Thus, from the Egyptian point of view, according to Glubb:

> The prospect of Jordan joining the Baghdad Pact meant another Arab country renouncing her leadership and placing itself under that of Iraq. She accordingly concentrated all her efforts on preventing Jordan's adherence. Passionate appeals were directed

---

[97] *Ibid.*, p. 11.

[98] Husayn, *Uneasy Lies the Head*, p. 110. Although the possibility of Israel's joining the alliance existed, Iraq's veto would prevent such a possibility, if invoked:

> This pact shall be open for accession to any member of the Arab League or any other state, actively concerned with the security and peace in this region and which is fully recognized by both the High Contracting Parties. Khalil, *op. cit.*, II, p. 370; Majali, *Muthakkirati*, p. 178.

Israel was not asked to join the Pact, but its supporters in the House of Commons questioned Eden, who replied that the stability in the Middle East is actually to the advantage of Israel, for it creates a better atmosphere for it to become more secure and added that: "It is impossible that any alliance in which Britain is a member would be aimed at Israel," and expressed his hope that "Israel should join the Pact in happier days." *Parliamentary Debates,* 30 March 1955, and 4 April 1955; Eden, *op. cit.*, p. 223.

[99] Husayn, *op. cit.*, p. 109.

to the people of Jordan, particularly the Palestinians. The fact that Egyptian propaganda stated that the Baghdad Pact was primarily intended to help Israel, gives some idea both of the gullibility of the Arab public and of the distortion of facts which was practised by the Egyptian radio stations. So effective was the campaign that crowds rioted in the cities of Jordan, and the government in alarm abandoned its intention of joining the Pact.[100]

Following the resignation of the Cabinet members, riots broke out in Jordan against the Pact and Templer had to leave Amman. Afraid that other Arab states, and Jordan, in particular, would join the Pact, Cairo seized the initiative: "The Baghdad Pact is an imperialist plot."[101] Capitalizing on the issue of British influence in Jordan through the army, Cairo urged the people to "get rid of the British officers in the army.... Get rid of the King who is keeping Jordan as a tool of the West."[102]

A flurry of state visitors to Jordan in 1955, including Turkish President Jalal Bayar, and Generals Templer and Amer, clearly indicated the involvement of Jordan in alignments and alliances in the Midle East.[103] Jordan's position towards the Baghdad Pact, its

---

[100] John Bagot Glubb, *Britain and Arabs* (London: Hodder and Stoughton, 1959), p.321.

[101] Husayn, *Uneasy Lies the Head,* p. 111.

[102] *Ibid.*, p. 107. Husayn's response to Arab pressure was to dismiss Glubb which was largely aimed at satisfying Jordan's demand to command their army, the most 'powerful single force in the country, and to keep the army on his side. Monroe, *op. cit.*, p. 189.

"With Communism filtering into the Middle East and Cairo branding Jordan as an imperialist power, there was no alternative, Glubb had to go." Husayn, *op. cit.*, p. 138.

[103] In the wake of suspicions aroused by Bayar's visit, General Amer was sent at the head of a military mission to Amman in December. In the Officers' Club visitors' book he wrote: My visit to the Club which represents the youth of the army impressed upon me that I was in the company of young officers who wished to elevate the standards of the army of the sister state of Jordan. My visit has strengthened my faith in the Arabs and Arabism. Vatikiotis, *op. cit.*, p. 122; *Al-Difa'a,* 3 December 1955.

Amer's visit and the people's enthusiastic response to it increased the anxiety of the Jordan Government. The inscription was interpreted as an appeal to the ambitious officers who favoured Arabization of the army and to galvanize any resistance among them against a re-negotiated British-Jordanian agreement, but, most importantly, to encourage their opposition to Jordan's entry into the Baghdad Pact. *Ibid.*

relationship with Britain, its internal explosive Arab nationalism placed it in an unenviable position. The nationalist groups, such as the Ba'ath, and the Socialists, were vociferously demanding that Jordan take an Arab nationalist course which meant an anti-Iraq, anti-Pact position. Husayn, however, chose involvement with the West and requested the resignation of Abul-Huda's government for its failure to join the Baghdad Pact. On 28 May, Husayn accepted Abul-Huda's resignation and Sa'ed Al-Mufti was asked to form a government. Abul-Huda's resignation was attributed to his desire to uphold neutrality in inter-Arab struggles. External and internal pressures were being exerted for closer associations with Iraq. Meanwhile, the nationalists who were influenced by the Bandung Conference favoured non-alignment and were actively working for the Egyptian-Syrian-Saudi line-up. This upset Iraq, and the King had to remove Abul-Huda.[104]

In view of the Cabinet's inability to force the Pact on reluctant public, the King decided to assume entire responsibility for signing the Pact.[105]

[104] Shwadran, *op. cit.*, pp. 324-25. In his memoirs, Majali indicated that even the ardent nationalists favoured joining the Pact. The pro-Egyptian Nabulsi group met with Iraqi Prime Minister Nuri As-Sa'ed at Baghdad and urged him to intervene with Husayn to have Abul-Huda resign so that they could form a government. In return they promised Nuri that "when they assume power, they would work to have Jordan join the Baghdad Pact, for in their opinion it was the only way to salvation." *Al-Husayn Ibn Talal*, p. 165. Paramount in Nabulsi's mind was the desire that Jordan join the Baghdad Pact during his term in office. His first request was to ask the King to direct the Government to espouse a policy of rapprochement with Iraq in line with the Baghdad Pact. *Ibid.*, p. 165.

[105] According to Glubb, signing the Pact represented a unique opportunity to Husayn who was eager to reap the following benefits: one to increase the military capability of his army which seemed to reflect his personal ambition to be the commander of a larger and stronger army. This would improve his position internally as well as externally. Two, by joining the Pact, he would be assured against Israeli aggression. Three, financial assistance would be forthcoming for development plans which Jordan needed most since its problem was mainly economic. Four, it would strengthen his association with the West, particularly, with Britain, thus, insuring continued subsidy. Five, because of psychological reasons, Husayn was eager to clarify the question of subservience to Britain. By entering the Pact, not only Jordan would become an equal partner in the alliance, but also the treaty relations with Britain would be altered in Jordan's favour as it was to be replaced by a special agreement. Glubb, p. 395; Eden, p. 384: Hafez, *op. cit.*, p. 215; Majali p. 22.

According to Glubb, Husayn wanted to sign the Pact without the consent of the Government, but General Templer advised him against such a step: "His Majesty is a constitutional monarch....He would expose himself to intrigue."[106]   Husayn wrote:

> I realized that if Jordan joined, the free world would gain an enormous victory.   I felt that if we joined, we should receive more arms and economic aid, and the Anglo-Jordan Treaty should be changed and its duration shortened so that Jordanian officers would have more opportunities to rise in the Arab Legion.[107]

Due to the disagreement in the Cabinet and the refusal of some ministers to sign the document of accession, Templer communicated with the Jordanian Prime Minister on 12 December 1955, allaying the fears of these ministers that Jordan's accession to the Pact would weaken its position regarding the Palestine question:

> It has become clear to me and the Ambassador within the last 24 hours that the main disturbing point is the fear of some Cabinet members that joining the Baghdad Pact would somehow weaken Jordan's position in regard to any future settlement of the Palestine question.   I am authorized by Her Majesty's Government to inform you that as far as my Government is concerned, Jordan's entry into the Pact shall not affect in any form the position of Jordan as to the final solution of the Palestine problem.
> Assurance to that effect may be added, if you wish, to the agreement plan which I sent you last night.[108]

The Templer-Jordan discussions and airing of issues toppled the Mufti Government, since the Palestinian ministers would not cooperate with, let alone support, it.   On 13 December, Husayn asked Hazza'a Al-Majali to form a new government with the express purpose of joining the Baghdad Pact.[109]   To the Associated Press on 20 December 1955, Majali stated:

---

106 Glubb, *op. cit.*, p. 396.

107 Husayn, *op. cit.*, p. 108; Majali, *op. cit.*, p. 22.

108 Majali, *op. cit.*, p. 12.

109 Vatikiotis, *op. cit.*, p. 123. Majali demanded that Templer return to Britain as a condition for forming a new government. Majali, p. 172. Majali wrote *Qissat Muhadathat Templer* (*Story of the Templer Talks*) in an attempt to convince the people of the advantages to Jordan in joining the Pact.

I fully realize the peculiar position of Jordan and the great benefits which Jordan would reap according to the demands submitted in the memorandum signed by the previous government which also constituted the basis for the foreign policy of my government....

...I consulted more than thirty representatives, and a large number supported my viewpoint regarding the benefits which would accrue to Jordan: to conduct its own affairs, to improve its military and economic situation. At the same time, Jordan's obligation to the Palestine question and to the Arab states would not be affected....[110]

Owing to the insurmountable nationalist pressure, the Majali Government resigned on the 19th, and the King ordered the dissolution of the Parliament.[111] Because of the demonstrations, frequent changes of government, and the fear that Israel might attempt to invade the West Bank, the Pact idea was abandoned in favour of neutrality. At this point, Husayn felt that continued negotiations meant continued attacks from other Arab states and that would not help inter-Arab relations. Jordan's entry into the Baghdad Pact was no longer practical politics because Jordan could never afford to incur the resentment of the other Arab countries.

Until 18 December, Husayn and his government had been determined to enter the Pact at all costs. Now the affirmed policy was, on no account, to enter it.[112] At this point, Husayn declared: "No pacts."[113]

Opposition to the Baghdad Pact was based on the idea that joining it was tantamount to dividing the Arab front. But others did not appreciate Jordan's particular position. Majali said:

I say frankly: if I were an Egyptian, Saudi, or Syrian, and if the

[110] Majali, *Ibid.*, p. 19.

[111] Vatikiotis, *op. cit.*

[112] Glubb, *A Soldier With the Arabs,* p. 422.

[113] *Al-Husayn Ibn Talal,* p. 56; Musa, *op. cit.,* p. 627. Husayn expressed to the United Kingdom Ambassador that "in time the question of Jordan joining the Baghdad Pact could come up again." Britain decided not to press the matter for the time being for "we might spoil all." Eden, p. 385.

On the B.B.C., Alec Kirkbride, former British Resident and Ambassador to Amman, said on 10 June 1956, that it was a mistake to bring Jordan into the Pact because it had no border with the U.S.S.R., while it had bilateral treaties with Iraq and Britain. *Middle East Mirror,* 16 June 1956, p. 26.

interests of my country dictated such action, I would have refused joining the Pact.

But I am a Jordanian who is fully aware of my position....I realize that the capabilities of my country differ to a large extent from those of Syria, Egypt and Saudi Arabia....As a loyal Jordanian, I realize fully the delicate circumstances of Jordan which could not be ignored under any conditions....[114]

Prime Minister Majali was succeeded by Ibrahim Hashem, whose government lasted for two weeks only. He was followed by Samir Al-Rifa'i. In his letter of commission to Rifa'i, Husayn directed that the policy of the new government should follow the following lines:

1. The preservation of friendly relations with all Arab states, taking into consideration the interests of Jordan and its number-one question: the problem of Palestine.

2. The preservation of friendly relations with all friendly and allied states.[115]

The policy of the Rifa'i Government was submitted to the Chamber of Deputies on 26 January 1956. Its main feature was that Jordan's policy would be not to join any foreign alliances:

There are two currents of opinion in the Arab world today: one aims to organize defense on the basis of alliances extending beyond the Arab sphere, and the other seeks to establish defense arrangements within an independent Arab framework. And whereas the Hashemite Kingdom of Jordan was committed to the sister Arab states by multilateral agreements within the framework of the Arab League and the Mutual Cooperation Pact, I have declared in a statement delivered upon the formation of this Cabinet, which I am honoured to head, that it is not our policy to join or be tied in any way to any new alliances, and to work for the consolidation of Arab solidarity.[116]

114 Majali, *Qissat Muhadathat Templer,* p. 1. Since Jordan's problem was mainly economic, the Pact-nations promised to give economic assistance for economic development plans. *Ibid.,* p. 22.

115 *Al-Husayn Ibn Talal,* p. 57.

116 Jordan, *Proceedings of the House of Representatives,* 26 January 1956, p. 244; *Al-Husayn Ibn Talal,* p. 58.

Rifa'i encountered a warm welcome in Jordan and outside, since he adopted a policy which was anti-Baghdad Pact. It also necessitated neutrality in the struggle between Cairo and Baghdad. However, the Egyptian and Syrian presses continued their attack on Jordan because Egypt wanted Jordan to be on its side.[117] Though a reversal of the Majali policy, the Rifa'i statement to steer clear of foreign alliances did not imply neutralism, since it indicated that Jordan would persist in respecting its agreements with Britain and Iraq.[118]

Opposition to the Government was expressed in the streets. Opposition leaders were arrested, public pressure was too strong to be ignored. Thus, a major shift of policy was the only alternative and the Government was put on the defensive even after it renounced the Pact. Elizabeth Monroe observed:

> The disastrous Templer mission to Jordan in December 1955, exposed the degree to which Arab unity and Arab nationalism must now be taken into account in any successful Middle Eastern policy....The Templer incident was proof that the force of public opinion in the Middle East, though it may be volatile, was henceforth powerful, and that its impulses were all against the policy of a few sedate politicians who thought a pact with the West a price worth paying for stability.[119]

And *The Observer*, critical of Britain's policy commented:

> There was a brief honeymoon, then Britain plunged into the Baghdad Pact Plan which she knew in advance was, in our opinion, a threat to our vital interests. It was also against the genuine desires of the Arabs. Any policy in this area must recognize nationalism....Arabs are not now able to accept themselves as a tail to British policy....I believe that by attempting to keep this area as a sphere of influence, Britain will lose her real interests.[120]

[117] Majali, *Muthakkirati*, p. 182.   Egypt and Syria told Rifa'i that the purpose of the proposed Arab subsidy was to remove British pressure off Jordan. Both countries promised "in the event the British subsidy was ended, they would be ready to pay a substitute to Jordan." *Ibid.*, p. 181.

[118] Jordan, *Proceedings of the House of Representatives, op. cit.*, p. 245.

[119] Monroe, *op. cit.*, p. 188.

[120] *Ibid.*, p. 191; *Sunday Times*, 25 March 1956, *The Observer*, 25 March 1956.

The Role of the United States in the Baghdad Pact

The Baghdad Pact was inspired by Secretary of State, Dulles, and implemented by Eden. Dulles contemplated a flexible series of bilateral assistance treaties with Middle Eastern States. In his Northern Tier Plan, the stress was on American military aid, and the regional forces.[121] Dulles's conception of the Northern Tier Plan assumed the bypassing of the Arab-Israeli conflict and the disentangling of the United States from association with British Middle East policies, which had faced unpopularity.[122]

By contrast, Eden's Baghdad Pact reintroduced Western power and represented the continuation of the imperialist policy of stationing foreign troops in the Arab countries. It also aimed at aligning the Arab people with the West, a policy which intensified inter-Arab rivalries which Dulles hoped to avoid.

Dulles was unwilling to recognize, unreservedly, Eden's interpretation of the primacy of Britian's responsibility in the Middle East which constituted the basis for Britain's central role in the Baghdad alliance.[123] This difference in viewpoint represented a lack of Anglo-American coordination on the highest level which proved to be calamitous.

The United States had supported the Baghdad Pact in its early stages but refrained from joining it as a full-fledged member.[124] Eden was critical of American abstention and accused the U.S. of venturing on a course of "uncertain diplomacy" in inspiring the alliance and then holding back.

Having played a leading part to inspire the project, the United States Government held back while Britain alone of the Western powers joined it. Worse still, they tried to take credit for this attitude in capitals like Cairo, which were hostile to the Pact. Then, by a series of hesitant steps, they drew nearer the Pact, sending

---

[121] Fitzsimmons, *op. cit.*, p. 134.

[122] *Ibid.*

[123] *Ibid.*, p. 135.

[124] At the Bermuda Conference on 24 March 1957, Eisenhower and MacMillan agreed that the U.S. would be active in the Military Committee: "Willingness of the United States, under the authority of the recent Middle East United Joint Resolution to participate actively in the work of the Military Committee of the Baghdad Pact." *U.S. Policy in the Middle East,* p. 421; G. B., *British and Foreign State Papers,* Vol. 163, p. 80.

an observer and spending money, but still not joining it. An ounce of membership would have been worth all the wavering and saved a ton of trouble later on.[125]

While the Americans would not join, they were prepared to give the alliance "moral support."[126] For a time, the Pact stimulated diplomatic activity that made it appear as a successful plan. Efforts were initiated to link many Middle East countries in a series of alliances that might form a defense system.[127] Thus, by the end of 1955, "the Baghdad Pact was proving a firm stabilizer."[128]

The reluctance of the United States was due to the Egyptian and the Saudi opposition to the Pact and the desire of the U.S. to avoid endangering its interests in Saudi Arabia.[129] Moreover, Israel had opposed the alliance because it would not be permitted to join it, as a result of the Iraqi veto. Israel feared that the West would change its attitude towards her as well as the Palestine question, and thus, Western aid would become commensurate to its size. At the same time, the armies of the Arab States would be strengthened and could enter a battle against her.

However, Eden's speech in the House of Commons on 30 March 1955, allayed the fears of the Zionists:

> I take the view that when this agreement comes to be studied, it will be seen that from the viewpoint of Israel it is likely to be a desirable development because this is the first time an Arab state is looking in another direction than simply toward Israel.[130]

---

[125] Eden, *Full Circle*, p. 375.

[126] *Ibid.*, p. 374.

[127] Fitzsimmons, *op. cit.*, p. 128. It was announced that the Prime Minister of Pakistan and the President of Turkey had been working on a project that might include Jordan, Syria, Lebanon, Yemen, and Iran. *London Times,* 21 February 1955.

[128] Fitzsimmons, *op. cit.*, p. 128. A writer in *Round Table* concluded: "By and large the Middle East seems in a better shape for defending itself in 1954 than at any time since the end of the war." *Round Table,* XLV, 1954, p. 133.

[129] In an attempt to appease the Saudis, the U.S.A. offered to mediate in the British-Saudi dispute over the Buraimi Oasis. Hafez, *op. cit.,* p. 216; Also M. Perlman, "The Turkish-Arab Diplomatic Tangle," *Middle Eastern Affairs,* Vol. VIII, January 1955, p. 16.

[130] Monroe, *op. cit.,* p. 184.

Moreover, because of the Palestine problem, the United States decided not to join, since American membership would very likely result in an Israeli request for a treaty with the U.S.A., and such an eventuality would inevitably worsen Western relations with the Arab States. In addition, the Congress had insisted on making permanent the borders in Palestine but Dulles refused this request.[131] Thus, the fears of Israel echoed in Washington. The State Department was reluctant to put the treaty of the Baghdad Pact before Congress because that would have meant the initiation of a debate over the whole Middle East policy, a debate in which the Zionists and local party politics might have played a great role in deciding its outcome.

The Anglo-Egyptian agreement for the evacuation of the Suez Canal Zone drastically reduced Britain's presence in the Middle East. Her attempt to restore lost influence through the Baghdad Pact alliance further undermined her prestige, since the Arabs opposed it as being a direct attack on their unity. Britain's participation in the Suez affair of 1956, on the side of Israel, further diminished its influence in the Arab World. However, the dismissal of General Glubb from his powerful position as the commander of the Jordan armed forces and sole director of the army's budget, had entirely eliminated British presence and prestige in the Arab countries.

The Dismissal of Glubb and the Arabization of the Jordan Army

The inability of the Jordan Government to join the Baghdad Pact lowered its prestige and forced it to reach an accommodation with the nationalists. During the period when Jordan was contemplating joining the Pact, Cairo was inciting the Jordan people to pressurize their government to "get rid of the British officers in the army . . . . Get rid of the King who is keeping Jordan as a tool of the West."[132]

---

[131] Jamali, *op. cit.*, p. 115.

[132] Husayn, *Uneasy Lies the Head, op. cit.*, p. 107. In the House of Commons, the leader of the Opposition, Gaitskel said, "I think that the Baghdad Pact. . . has itself contributed very materially to this development." *Documents on International Affairs*, 1956, p. 15. Legge Bourke, Member of Parliament, added: "The decision taken by the King of Jordan was the lesser of two evils and may be the responsibility of another state altogether. Can we have an assurance that in examining this problem, Her Majesty's Government will bear in mind that the real culprit in this matter may well be Egypt?" (G.B. *Parliamentary Debates*, Vol. 591, Cols. 1714-1715).

Husayn's response was to dismiss Glubb, who was regarded by Arab public opinion as the last vestige of imperialism.[133] This measure was largely aimed at satisfying Jordan's demand to command its own army as well as to keep the armed forces on his side.[134]

The Role of the Army in Jordan

While Jordan has been an independent state only since 1946, its army dates back to 1921. One could, therefore, argue that the army created the state.[135]

In its earlier history, the Legion's function was mainly a "praetorian guard" to establish the authority of Amir Abdullah over a divided and unstable society.[136] With the expansion of the kingdom and the infusion of new population, the political role of the Legion acquired new dimensions: to prevent any successful challenge to the authority of the King and to protect the dynasty, its regime and establishment from any external or internal threats.[137] In Jordan, the Palace system of power has survived longer than elsewhere in the Arab World. This is due to the loyalty of the army to Western military and economic aid and to the role of Israel in the politics of the region. Until the end of 1961, Jordan was a garrison state in so far as the Palace used force for the maintenance of its rule.[138]

---

[133] The Templer Mission contributed to the erosion of British prestige. In his biography, General Glubb wrote that Prime Minister Samir Al-Rifa'i had visited Egypt shortly before the dismissal, and that he had settled it with Egypt to Arabize the Army.   Glubb, *op. cit.,* p. 427.

[134] Monroe, *op. cit.,* p. 189; Ray Allan, "Jordan: Rise and Fall of the Squirarchy," *Commentary*, Vol. 13, March 1957.

[135] "In Jordan there is an army which owns the state." *The Armies of the Arab States in the Context of Their Environment* (Hebrew), Tel Aviv, 1948. This publication was intended to acquaint the Zionist soldier with the Arab defence forces.   Cited in Vatikiotis, *op. cit.,* p. 5.

[136] Vatikiotis, *op. cit.,* p. 6.

[137] *Ibid.*

[138] *Ibid.,* p. 12. Although the period (1950-1957) was generally turbulent, as it was dangerous for the monarchy, post-1967 war period proved to be the most dangerous in the history of the country. This was essentially due to the increasing power and activities of the Palestine Liberation Organization, with whom King Husayn made various agreements. However, due to difference in their policies regarding Palestine and peace with the Zionists, confrontation between the P.L.O and the Jordan army was inevitable, as was the case in September 1970.

In Jordan, the army is not only the instrument for defence and stability, but a part of everything.[139] To a large extent, the Jordan army today continues to be one of the most important factors in the country's economy.[140]

Reasons for the Dismissal

In his biography, King Husayn indicated that dismissing General Glubb was the only alternative to appease the opposition and to regain his position, following the eclipse of the Government as a result of the Baghdad Pact controversy. Husayn wrote:

> One thing led to another. With Communism filtering into the Middle East and Cairo branding Jordan as an imperialist power, there was no alternative, Glubb had to go.... I would say that if Glubb had been in command of the army a year longer, it would have been the end of Jordan.[141]

On the other hand, General Glubb suggested the underlying reasons for Husayn's action. He said:

> ...The King had been enthusiastically determined to enter the Baghdad Pact, and he had, thereby incurred the hostility of Egypt and of the Jordan extremists. The policy had failed. It was pointed out to him that he could regain his popularity with these extremely vocal enemies at one stroke. To perform some act of defiance towards Britain and to dismiss me would immediately re-establish his popularity.... The King was probably influenced partly by the illusion that I had neglected to provide ammunition, partly by a desire to exercise authority himself, unfettered by a middle-aged and cautious adviser. He also believed that to defy Britain would restore his popularity and, finally, his imagination was fired by the idea of being the hero of his country.[142]

[139] Husayn, *Uneasy Lies the Head,* p. 133.

[140] Vatikiotis, *op. cit.,* p. 12. In the period (1950-57), the largest item of Jordan's budget was that of the army whose expenditure exceeded the combined budgets of all other departments. *Ibid.,* p. 10.

[141] In denying the accusation that the dismissal was the result of emotionalism as it was spontaneous, the King answered: "Let it not be thought that I dismissed an old and trusted friend in a fit of emotional pique." *Ibid.,* pp. 43-6.

[142] Glubb, *A Soldier with the Arabs,* pp. 425-26.

There are, however, various interpretations for Glubb's dismissal: one, Glubb represented Jordan's subservience to Britain.[143] Jordan was dependent for its political and economic existence on British support and subsidy which was paid directly to an account controlled by Glubb.[144]   Thus, Britain which paid the annual subsidy to Jordan also supplied officers to train its army, and in fact ran it.[145]   In the political sphere, this meant that Jordan's policies could not deviate from established policy lines drawn in London.   According to Glubb, Jordan, of all the Arab states, discovered the secret of success that "the Arabs could not progress without European help."[146]

Two, the role of the British officers and Glubb, in particular, regarding the strategy and defence of the country, was viewed as a danger to the army and the homeland.[147]   Despite his long service in Jordan, Glubb persisted in giving allegiance to Britain first and thus, placed its interests before those of Jordan.[148]   It appeared that in receiving his orders from White Hall, Glubb's strategy was based on defensive plans.   To Husayn, this was a damaging strategy which could cost Jordan dearly and result in defeat:

To my way of thinking, a purely defensive strategy invited disaster. If the enemy knew we would hit them as hard as they hit us where

[143] Don Peretz, *The Middle East Today* (New York: Holt, 1963), p. 313.

[144] Husayn, *Uneasy Lies the Head*, p. 131; Gerald Sparrow, *Hussein of Jordan* (London: George G. Harrap & Co. Ltd., 1960), p. 119.

[145] Husayn, *ibid.*, p. 131. In 1949, Prime Minister Abul-Huda reached an agreement with Britain to replace Glubb with another Chief of the General Staff, but Abdullah disagreed saying: "A face you know is better than one you do not know.   As long as the C.G.S. would have to be a Britisher, Glubb is better than any other Englishman."   Majali, *Muthakkirati*, p. 94.

[146] Glubb, *A Soldier with the Arabs*, p. 64.

[147] *Filistin,* 4 March 1956. Brigadier Ashton, Glubb's second in command, was dismissed from the service for dereliction of duty during the Qibya massacre which took place on the night of 14-15 of October 1953. *Al-Husayn Ibn Talal,* pp. 19-20; Vatikiotis, *op. cit.,* p. 120.   The opposition leader, Hugh Gaitskell, said in the British House of Commons that the dismissal of Glubb: increases the danger of a war between the Arab states and Israel. . . . The reason why there has been such general agreement on this is that we know. . . that General Glubb and his fellow officers have exercised a restraining influence upon the Arab Legion and upon the policy of Jordan.   I can vouch for that because the Foreign Secretary of Israel himself told me that three years ago. *Documents on International Affairs,* 1956, p. 15.

[148] Husayn, *Uneasy Lies the Head*, p. 135.

it would hurt the most, it would make them think twice before attacking.[149]

Husayn felt that Jordan should answer force by force. However, Glubb's policy, which invited border incidents, created a gulf between the army and the people.[150] This was due to the fact that what happened on the Jordanian-Israeli frontier could affect the political equilibrium of the state of Jordan. Often it led to serious disturbances in Jordan, particularly, when Israeli raids inflicted extensive damage to life and property. Thus, political demonstrations against the regime were directed against the inability of the army to give adequate protection against the Israeli raids which would be attributed to a lax command.[151]

Three, since Jordan depended completely on British weapons and in view of Glubb's theory of defensive strategy which did not require large stores of ammunition, the stock was inadequate for any prolonged confrontation. Thus, Jordan's security would be endangered and Glubb's "very presence in our country was without doubt an important factor in the trouble. We were in the hands of foreigners."[152]

---

[149] *Ibid.* As an example, in March 1949, when the Zionist forces advanced eastwards across the Negeb, Glubb withdrew the Jordan forces well inside the Jordan frontier, thus, allowing the Zionists to occupy a substantial area in the eastern Negeb as well as the port of Elat. Musa, *op. cit.,* p. 529.

[150] The most devastating exercise by Glubb was in exceeding his authority on many occasions. In his lecture to army officers he asserted that, since Israel was stronger than the Arabs, it was unwise to fight on the frontier.

"In vain I pointed this out to Glubb. . . . He advocated at first a withdrawal in the event of an attack and withdrawal would end up on the East Bank. Thus, the defensive strategy of Glubb meant losing a lot of territory before a battle even started." Husayn, *Uneasy Lies the Head,* pp. 135-38.

[151] Vatikiotis, *op. cit.,* p. 16.

[152] Husayn, *Uneasy Lies the Head,* p. 137. Husayn declared: "This was not a matter of theory, it meant a margin that separates victory from defeat." *Ibid.,* p. 135. In his memoirs, Glubb revealed that, although the Arab Legion was essentially a part of the British defence forces, it was not supplied for offensive action. Perhaps Britain's plan was to prevent Abdullah from undertaking an offensive action and occupying a larger part of Palestine, thereby endangering the existence of the Zionist state in whose creation Britain had played a crucial role. Glubb commented: "the British refused to give us ammunition but they agreed to send us barbed wire." Glubb, *A Soldier with the Arabs,* p. 213.

Four, the role of the Arab officers in the army was one of secondary nature. The British dominated the Jordan military affairs while no Arab officers were given important responsibilities.[153] Husayn observed:

Around me I saw junior Arab officers who would obviously never become leaders. Some of them were men lacking in ability and force, men prepared to bow to White Hall's commands transmitted by senior British officers. Men who had no spark. Men without initiative and who could be trusted not to cause any problems. These were officer material.[154]

In his biography, Husayn expressed his disagreements with Glubb in connection with preparing Arab officers to assume high commands, but Glubb's "British policy" did not take into consideration Jordan's national aspiration to Arabize its army.[155] Husayn wrote:

I was determined to build up strong, well-balanced armed forces

---

During the war of 1948, complaining about the shortage of ammunition, Glubb told Abdullah: "We have very little ammunition and the depots are empty. I cannot fight for more than five hours." Nashashibi, *op. cit.,* p. 151. Minister of Defence, Falah Al-Madadhah, gave his view:

"The army secrets were all with Glubb. . . . Treasury secrets were all with Glubb. Political plans were all with Glubb. As for us [Ministers], we knew only what he wanted us to know." Nashashibi, *op. cit.,* p. 151.

[153] In an answer to a question whether the dismissal of the British officers would create new incidents along the Israeli frontier, Eden replied in the House of Commons:

As regards the effect of these dismissals upon the international situation and upon Israel, the House must judge and can judge as well as her Majesty's Government—as to the effect of the presence or absence of these officers I would have thought that many would realize that the effect upon the military value of the Legion would be very serious indeed. G. B., *Parliamentary Debates,* Vol. 549, Col. 1711.

[154] Husayn, *Uneasy Lies the Head,* p. 131; see Husayn's speech to the Cabinet on 9 April 1955, in *Al-Husayn Ibn Talal,* p. 62. In the Qibyah incident, the garrison commander, an Arab army officer, refused to answer questions of the ministerial investigating commission. He said: "If it were not for Glubb, I would be a shepherd. Therefore, I refuse to talk unless my master [Glubb] orders me to." Nashashibi, *op. cit.,* p. 149.

[155] Husayn was told that Arabization could not be accomplished before 1975 and that "the Royal Engineer of the Arab Legion would have an Arab commander by 1985." Husayn, *Uneasy Lies the Head,* p. 132.

...and since this was not possible with Glubb, our self-respect demanded that we fight our battles alone.[156]

To Husayn, Glubb's attitude seemed to reflect the British policy to dominate the Jordan army through slow change. To his Prime Minister he expressed:

Since I assumed my constitutional powers, I have been trying to correct these conditions in a manner which suits the dignity of Jordan....However, I have not detected any positive results of these attempts.[157]

Arabization of the army which meant eliminating foreign influence and transforming the Arab Legion into a genuine national Arab army, ranked high in Husayn's calculations. At the time, he ordered his Prime Minister to dismiss Glubb, the army commander, Patrick Coghill, Chief of Intelligence, and Brigadier Hutton, Chief of Operations, Husayn revealed to the Cabinet that it was time to save Jordan from further catastrophe. He said:

...I believe that if matters were left to the mood of the Chief of General Staff, it is very probable that we would find ourselves face to face with a catastrophe similar to that of 1948, even worse. Therefore, I decided to end the services of the C. G. S. together with other British officers who assist him in implementing his policy and ambitions. I also decided that this order be executed without hesitation or delay, and ordered him to leave the country today.[158]

Five, another important problem was Glubb's interference in the politics of the country. By controlling the finances of the army, Glubb was incapable of divorcing himself from politics, particularly since the security forces were under his command. "He operated from a position of such strength that our political leaders tended to turn to him or to the British embassy before making the slightest

---

156 *Ibid.,* p. 138.
157 Husayn, *Al-Husayn Ibn Talal, op. cit.,* p. 83.
158 *Ibid.,* p. 85.

decision."[159]   Although Jordan became independent in 1946, virtually, all policy decisions had to be cleared with the British Ambassador.   This was possible, since the finances and the military in Jordan were at the mercy of London.   Thus, while the political leaders ceased to think of Jordan as an independent country, it also became axiomatic to come to the British embassy for advice.[160]

Husayn's action must have been contemplated years earlier. His statement at a top-leadership military meeting on 9 April 1955, in which the Cabinet and Glubb were present revealed his future plans regarding the Arabization of the army, the position of Glubb, the sovereignty of Jordan, and the general internal conditions:

It is impossible for any military force today to fulfil its duty unless certain conditions are met.   The army's high command must possess high qualifications to accomplish its goals....A number of senior officers in our army and the National Guard in particular have not attained an academic level but were promoted according to seniority rather than ability.

...I believe that loyalty to one person is a mistake....Loyalty should be to the country and to the national interests, not to certain personalities.

The army machinery in the Legion is in need of change and revision and reorganization.   The apparatus which was adequate in the past cannot do the job today....To the military man, is a certain function and to the politician another.

[159] Husayn, *Uneasy Lies the Head,* p. 139.   In his biography, Husayn revealed that Glubb had refused to promote, even dismissed senior Arab army and police officers because they were nationalists or ambitious. *Ibid.,* p. 140.

[160] *Ibid.,* p. 152. Glubb's interference in political affairs led to differences with Prime Minister Rifa'i. A group of army officers, formed on the lines of the Egyptian "Free officers," were reported to have visited the King and handed him a British newspaper with the heading, "The Uncrowned King of Jordan." They asked him to dismiss Glubb because by so doing, Husayn would compensate for popular unrest caused by the Baghdad Pact episode and thus, would become a nationalist hero while ending Glubb's dictatorship. The King responded: I wish what happened in Amman on 3 March 1956 had taken place ten years earlier....The army got rid of its commander before the catastrophe took place, and Palestine was lost. Nashashibi, *op. cit.,* p. 139.

Glubb was reported to have described the politics of the Middle East in the following terms,..."We have given them self-government for which they are totally unsuited. They veer naturally toward dictatorship. Democratic institutions are promptly twisted into an engine of intrigue...." Quoted in *Golden Carpet,* p. 106, and cited in *Security and the Middle East,* p. 51.

The Hashemite Kingdom of Jordan is an independent sovereign country with a treaty with Britain.... We must devise a military plan according to which there will be no retreat from any position ...A military plan must mean a counterattack.

Our internal position today does not correspond to the reality. We are in a state of war with the Jews. Our ammunitions are inadequate....[161]

The British Response

From Jordan's official viewpoint, Glubb was a civilian employee whose dismissal should not affect Anglo-Jordan relations. To convince the British Government of this policy, Husayn issued a statement in Amman emphasizing Anglo-Jordan friendship:

Nothing was further from my thoughts than to terminate the friendship but it was essential to prove our country independent, free to speak its mind and free to act without outside influence or dictation.[162]

From the British viewpoint, the dismissal of Glubb and other command officers was against the spirit of the Anglo-Jordan treaty.[163] However, in spite of Jordan's assurances, Eden, personally, cabled Husayn asking him to change his mind. The British Ambassador in Jordan also threatened:

You must be aware, Sir, that the step you have taken has caused a tremendous uproar in London....I must advise you, Sir, that Her Majesty's Government feels that unless you change your decision immediately on this matter, unless Glubb Pasha is permitted to continue his work here, and we are given a chance to clear this whole matter up, the consequences, Your Majesty, could be very serious as far as you, yourself, the monarchy, and the whole future of Jordan is concerned.[164]

[161] *Al-Husayn Ibn Talal*, pp. 62ff.

[162] Husayn, *Uneasy Lies the Head*, pp. 138-39.

[163] It meant the end of British as well as Western influence in the region. Emphasizing this development, *The Economist* commented: "The political life in the Middle East has escaped from Western control." 10 March 1956.

[164] *Al-Husayn Ibn Talal*, p. 145.

King Husayn replied:

> I believe, Mr. Duke, that what I have done is for the good of my
> country, and I am not going to alter my decision regardless of any
> consequences.   I would rather lose my life than change my mind.
> The monarchy belongs to the people, I belong to this country. I
> know that I am doing this for the best, come what may.[165]

In spite of this announcement, indignation in Britain seemed to
swell into new hysteria, even Eden's statement in the House of
Commons in which he said:

> The House will have heard with resentment and with regret of the
> summary dismissal of General Glubb and two other senior British
> officers of the Arab Legion. The lifetime of devoted service which
> General Glubb has given to the Hashemite Kingdom of Jordan
> should have received more generous treatment.
>
> It is right to tell the House that the King of Jordan and the
> Jordanian Prime Minister have told Her Majesty's ambassador
> that they don't want any change to take place in Anglo-Jordan
> relations, and that they stand by the Anglo-Jordan treaty.
>
> Her Majesty's Government have given due weight to Jordan's
> Government statement regarding the officers. They feel that in
> view of the treatment meted out to the British officers who have
> been dismissed, it would be wrong for British officers in the Arab
> Legion to be left in an uncertain position. In our opinion,
> officers in the executive commands cannot be asked to continue
> in positions of responsibility without authority. We have there-
> fore asked that such officers should be relieved of their commands.
>
> It is clear from the treaty that its whole spirit is based on the
> need for consultation to ensure mutual defense, and in this sense,
> General Glubb's dismissal is in view of the Government against
> the spirit of the treaty.[166]

The British protest did not move the King to rescind his order. In
a joint session of the Jordan Parliament on 3 March 1957, Husayn
declared that Arabization of the army was a necessary step to ending

[165] *Ibid.*
[166] Husayn, *op. cit.,* p. 148.

subservience to Britain. Husayn stated:

...We arabized the army. Arabization was a reply to a threat which I had received, that our very existence and the throne would not survive longer if I did not follow the policies desired by a certain great power. This was the practical answer. But the reply which the representative of that power received was that this throne is a part of this country, as it is its symbol. I am ready to leave if it symbolizes anything else. Its value equals the power it gives to the sons of Jordan and Arabism....But my position was not shaken and I have been successful....[167]

Conclusion

Jordan's relations with Britain were essentially the personal connections of Kings, Abdullah and Husayn with London, for, with her protection, funds and direction, they became rulers and contenders for Arab leadership. In the political sense, both owed their political survival to Britain. For this reason, the Hashemites did not see evil in the Mandate system nor in their personal association with the British. In return they advanced British interests in their territories in spite of Arab nationalist opposition.

In the mid-fifties, Britain's declining influence in the region seemed to endanger Western economic, political and military interests. An alternative was the establishment of the Baghdad Pact through which Western interests would be protected without Western physical presence.

[167] *Al-Husayn Ibn Talal, Uneasy Lies the Head, op. cit.,* p. 153.
The *London Times* made the following observation after Glubb's departure: Amman is still *en fete* in celebration of General Glubb's departure and it must be recorded that the pleasure seems both to be universal and genuine. Young Arab Legion officers claim to believe, it will take politics out of the army on the grounds that General Glubb refused promotions to officers not sympathetic to Western policies.
There are a few who even think it will help rather than hinder good relations with Britain and many who are convinced that if Britain had voluntarily withdrawn her officers long ago, perhaps, incorporating them in a military mission, such an unhappy event would never have occurred.
...The whole trend of Arab policy for years has been toward the removal of such symbols of Western influence (cited in Husayn, *Uneasy Lies the Head,* p. 1497.

Husayn was personally enthusiastic about joining the Pact. His policy was based on sound reasoning, as he was confronted with complex situations. The internal setting in Jordan was an explosive one. Husayn was under increasing nationalist pressure to end treaty relations with Britain. Simultaneously, he was faced with an external pressure, Britain would refuse to revise or end the treaty unless Jordan became a member in the defence alliance. Secondly, Jordan suffered from instability and Husayn's policies appeared to lack consensus of his subjects. This situation rendered his regime on the brink of collapse. Thirdly, Jordan stood in dire need for economic as well as military aid while Husayn needed the political support of a great power.

Five main factors influenced Husayn's decision to join the Pact. First, the U.S. and Britain had promised to equip and expand his army. To Husayn such development meant personal fulfilment, for he desired to lead a strong army. Second, strengthening his army would minimize Israeli attacks. Further, membership in the Pact would in all probabilities preclude any Israeli attempt to invade Jordan's territory, thereby insuring the security, independence and integrity of the country. Also, Husayn was promised the large economic aid sorely needed for developmental projects to alleviate the chronic unemployment. Such aid could have minimized internal upheavals, since it might have kept thousands engaged in other employment than in politics. Finally, membership in such defence system under the protection of two major powers would have enhanced his personal stature among the Arab leaders, while it could have enabled him to conclude a separate peace with Israel which Abdullah strove for, and which Husayn desired.

Viewing this reasoning from Husayn's personal and dynastic looking glass, the logic for his enthusiasm is evident. However, from the popular point of view, such policy seemed dangerous and had to be stopped. Since the King was suffering from lack of popular base, the only alternative was to submit to the popular will; no pacts.

Husayn's venture worsened his status with the nationalists, particularly, with the army officers. Since the army was considered the most loyal institution to the Palace, his course had grave consequences. Thus, in order to avoid the collapse of this regime, and to restore the confidence of the nationalists, he decided on a major act of defiance against Britain. Such course appeared to have been the most potent weapon in the arsenal of the nationalists. Arabization of the army was the goal. Overnight, Husayn's image changed into that of a nationalist hero. However, Husayn may have been considering such action earlier, since external as well as internal factors made such action imperative.

To enhance his personal stature in the Arab world, the King had to command his army, for the presence of the British commanders made the army a point of controversy. Another was Glubb's involvement in politics which the King considered unwarranted curtailment of his personal prerogatives. As to Jordan's military capability, ever since 1948, it was defensive one, simply because General Glubb and London wanted it so. This strategy has always encouraged Israeli aggression. Lack of retaliation by Jordan's army— having been commanded by British officres—had always aggravated the Arab officers and placed Husayn in uncomfortable position which he desired to avoid.

In any case, the Arabization of the army and ending treaty relationships with Britain pacified the nationalists and preserved the regime for only a few months, as Husayn, again, embarked on a similar venture: adherence to the Eisenhower Doctrine.

CHAPTER THIRTEEN

JORDAN-UNITED STATES RELATIONS

BACKGROUND

American-Jordan relations went through three stages. In the first period, 1946–1949, relations were not close in spite of the fact that Amir Abdullah had declared war on Germany on the side of the Allies. The American attitude may have been influenced by many factors, paramount among which was the pro-Zionist groups which demanded that Transjordan should be opened for Jewish immigration and colonization. Thus, the United States did not recognize Jordan when it became independent in 1946. When informed of its independence, a telegraphic reply acknowledged that the message had been noted by the United States Government.[1] On 31 January 1949, however, the United States extended *de jure* recognition to Jordan, almost three years after her independence.[2]

The second period, 1950–1956, stressed Western interests in Jordan, due to its strategic importance, between the Mediterranean and the Gulf of Aqaba, its inclusion of most of the Holy Places, its long boun-

---

[1] *Department of State Bulletin,* Vol. 14, No. 357, 5 May 1946, pp. 765-66. Senator F. Myers championed the idea that Jordan should be opened to Zionist colonization instead of being given statehood. In a letter dated 23 April 1946, Secretary of State James Byrnes refuted Myer's claim that Jordan was a part of Palestine. He said that the Department... has found nothing which would justify it in taking the position that the recent steps taken by Great Britain with regard to Transjordan violated any treaties existing between Great Britain and the United States, including the Convention of 3, December 1924, or deprived the United States of any rights or interests which the United States may have with respect to Transjordan, the Department of State considers that it would be premature for this government to take any decision at the present time with respect to the question of recognition of Transjordan as an independent state. U.S. *Congressional Record,* 79th Cong. 2nd Sess., 1946, XCII, Part 7, 8130. See Myer's charges on the State Department and his attacks against Britain, *Ibid.,* 8128-8132.

[2] By contrast, the U.S.A. recognized Israel within a few hours of its establishment on 15 May 1948.

dary with Israel, and its involvement with the Palestinian refugees. The multiplicity of Jordan's problems made financial assistance imperative to keep the kingdom stable and independent, and the West was willing to pay the price. Jordan, during this period, was supported by Britain with the United States playing a secondary role. However, in April 1957, the United States, in replacing Britain, played the major role in supporting Jordan after the abrogation of the Anglo-Jordan treaty.

A third period, 1957 on, manifested United States' intervention to restore Husayn's position which was eclipsed by the Nationalists. Friendly U.S. relations were strengthened, while British relations normalized and improved considerably after the summer of 1958.

Up to 1957, American policy in the Middle East had evolved through two phases, neither satisfactory to U.S. interests. Truman's policy of open partiality for Israel was followed by Dulles' efforts to punish Nasser for having accepted Communist arms and for rejecting Western offers of protection.[3] It may be said that by 1957, the United States was entering the history of the Middle East, and by 1958, in order to contain Communism, a policy of even-handedness was adopted. The U.S., generally, adopted a policy of neutrality in Arab disputes.[4] The United States had rejected unilateral pledges to Israel and promised to defend victims of aggression in the Middle East, including Jordan.[5] While this policy guaranteed the protection of Israel, it also stressed the maintenance of Jordan's government, for the overthrow of King Husayn would react immediately on the Arab-Israeli dispute.[6] For example, Israel's opposition to Jordan's

[3] Harry Ellis, "The Arab-Israeli Conflict Today," *The United States and the Middle East* (Englewood Cliffs, N.J.: Prentice Hall, 1964), p. 117.

[4] George Lenczowski (ed.), *United States Interests in the Middle East,* (Washington, D.C.: American Enterprise Institute, 1968), p. 25.

[5] Ellis, *op. cit.,* p. 116. When the U.S.A. pressed Israel to withdraw from Sinai after the Suez War, a delegation of American Zionists met Dulles and protested the U.S. action and argued that the U.S.S.R. did not withdraw from Hungary. Dulles replied: "Israel has an ambassador who can defend Israel's viewpoint. You are U.S. citizens, and I am not going to accept your protest." Jamali, *op. cit.,* pp. 135-38. President Eisenhower said, "I assure you that I will not bend before Zionist pressure and the Arabs will not be injured by my policies. As to the mistakes of previous administrations, I cannot erase." *Ibid.,* p. 11.

[6] Ellis, *op. cit.,* p. 118. King Faysal Ibn Saud also said that he wished, the U.S.A. would make greater effort to sustain Husayn. His reason was that if internal pressures toppled the moderate King Husayn, Saudi Arabia

engulfment by the Arab Solidarity Pact in 1956 led Ben Gurion to declare that Israel retained freedom of action to occupy the West Bank of the Jordan. To this pronouncement, the United States reacted by delivering a warning to Israel against any preventive move into Jordan.[7]

Until 1957, Jordan depended upon Britain for its survival. After the Suez crisis, British influence in the Arab World, including Jordan, had diminished. To keep Jordan within the West's sphere of influence, the United States replaced Britain as the political guardian of Jordan and assumed its financial burden. Prior to 1957, American aid was largely to head off social unrest and to meet urgent needs. While military aid was small, the assistance was spent for long-range economic development.[8]

American foreign policy in the Middle East stressed the maintenance of pro-Western conservative monarchial regimes. Accordingly, the survival of Jordan as a viable independent state became of "vital concern" to the U.S.A. This policy was given official backing by the proclamation of the Eisenhower Doctrine, which served as the basis of Jordan-American relations since January 1957.

---

would be the only important state friendly to the U.S. and would eventually come under pressure to alter that position.

[7] *Ibid.*, p. 115.

[8] U.S.A.I.D., *U.S. Economic Assistance to Jordan,* 1952-1962 (Amman, 1962). A major example was the "Jordan TVA Project." Another was the Jordan East Ghor Canal Project. In 1953, President Eisenhower sent Eric Johnston to negotiate a peace plan with the Arab states and Israel. It was based on utilizing the Jordan River waters to benefit both sides and to contribute to the resettlement of the Arab refugees. However, due to the political reasons, the Plan never materialized. The Arabs viewed it as a measure to liquidate the Palestine question through economic measures, that it would have meant the recognition of Israel through collaboration in the common project and rehabilitating the refugees. Edward Rizk, *The River Jordan* (New York: The Arab Information Center, 1962), p. 20. Nonetheless, Israel embarked on its water projects according to the Johnston Plan. These projects were largely financed by the United States. Simultaneously, the U.S.A. financed a small-scale water project in Jordan, the East Ghor Canal Project. This was a unilateral move by Jordan, since the Arab states had rejected the Johnston Plan. The project had economic significance for Jordan, as it could irrigate one third of all potentially cultivable land in the country. Joseph Dees, "Jordan's East Ghor Canal Project," *Middle East Journal,* Vol. 13, No. 4, (Autumn, 1959), p. 370.

The Eisenhower Doctrine

Introduction

In 1956, the British and the French governments declared that the issues of the Middle East required forthright Western intervention. Dulles, however, did not share their use-of-force approach, and insisted that the United States would not "shoot its way through the Suez Canal," and advised the use of moral force instead. While the tripartite aggression of 1956 curtailed, to a large measure, the influence of France and Britain in the Arab World, the growth of the nationalist movement further hindered imperialist penetration in the region. From the viewpoint of the West, a vacuum was created which had to be filled by the United States to guarantee the security of Western interests.[9] Thus, the Doctrine was an outcome of the Anglo-French-Israeli fiasco at Suez.[10]

The United States' stand on the Suez issue was interpreted by the Arab nationalists as acceptance by the U.S. of their policy, that of neutrality. But they soon found that a dialogue with the West could not be fruitful, since Western policy aimed at hindering Arab unity, interfering in inter-Arab affairs, and isolating Nasser who was viewed by the Arab people as a "mystical sort of savior."[11]

The idea of Pan-Arabism had Soviet support. The U.S.S.R. aimed at eliminating the Western position in the Middle East. To that end, it found Nasser's neutralism a valuable ally. Such alliance was based on superficial grounds. In 1964–65, the Government of the Soviet Union communicated with Israel that:

The Soviets and Arabs did not really have much in common, but the Arabs, as the Soviets had discovered a decade earlier, were determined to eliminate Western interests and influence in the Middle East. On this basis, the Soviets and the Arabs could make common cause. But the Israelis did not have to worry and should not get excited. The Soviets intend to be a moderating influence in the Arab-Israeli conflict. Nasser was merely the best means for

[9] Mishil Kamil, *Al-Mu'amarah Al-Amrikiyah fi al-Urdunn* (Cairo: Dar al-Fikr, 1957), p. 19.

[10] Copeland, *The Game of Nations*, p. 214.

[11] Husayn, *Uneasy Lies the Head*, p. 107.

getting the West out of the entire region.[12]

Nonetheless, Nasser's arms deal secured for the Eastern camp a foothold in the region. In an effort to dissociate the United States from Nasser without abandoning the other Arab states to his leadership, the U.S. embarked on a policy of active anti-Communism in the Middle East.[13]

Preoccupied primarily with the global task of containing the Communist advance by erecting alliances around it, the United States policy was neither concerned with British interests nor with Hashemite ambitions. To the Eisenhower Administration, the difficulty had been that the Middle East was becoming exposed to increased danger of international Communism. In his statement before the House Committee on Foreign Affairs, Secretary of State Dulles said:

I can assure you that the leaders of International Communism will take every risk that they dare to take in order to win the Middle East. Already, they have made that clear.[14]

He, therefore, was convinced that "basic U.S. policy should now find expression in joint action by Congress and the Executive."[15]

In attempting to counter Communist expansion in the Middle East, American policy had to work with the remains of British influence in Iraq and Jordan. Earlier attempts to build a position of strength for the West, namely, the Middle East Defense Organization and the Baghdad Pact, foundered on the rocks of local politics and Arab nationalism.[16] Accordingly, on 5 January 1957, President Eisenhower proposed a third attempt, the Eisenhower Doctrine, which was the major American response to the post-Suez growth of

---

[12] Draper, *op. cit.,* p. 34.

[13] Paul Hammond, *The Cold War Years: American Foreign Policy Since 1945* (New York: Harcourt), p. 117. At the height of the Lebanese crisis in 1958, the U.S. ambassador reported to the State Department that: America's prestige in Lebanon was deeply involved and...the State Department should be prepared either to support the current regime in resisting subversion or to cut its losses and learn to live with a great Arab nation presided over by Nasser. Charles Thayer, *Diplomat* (New York: Harper, 1959), p. 8.

[14] *U.S. Policy in the Middle East,* 1956-57, p. 38.

[15] U.S., *Department of State Bulletin,* 36, 21 January 1957, pp. 83-7.

[16] John C. Campbell, "From Doctrine to Policy in the Middle East," *Foreign Affairs,* Vol. 35, No. 3 (April 1957), pp. 2141-2142.

Soviet and Communist influence on radical Arab nationalism.[17]
Eisenhower appealed to anti-Communism as a way to reconstruct
the American position in the Middle East.[18]   He declared that:

> The Middle East has abruptly reached a new and critical stage in
> its long and important history.... Our country supports without
> reservation the full sovereignty and independence of each and
> every nation in the Middle East.[19]

However, the United States failed to recognize that Arab nationalism
and Islam on the one hand, and Communism on the other, could not
mix. It also failed to acknowledge that by 1960, "Nasser had proved
to be a relatively competent nationalist leader who was not at all
inclined to become a tool of either Soviet or American policies."[20]

To certain Arab leaders, fear of Communist infiltration in the
Middle East was a theory rather than a fact. However, Western intervention through the Baghdad Pact and Eisenhower Doctrine, ostensibly to check Communist expansion, was carried out despite public
declarations to the contrary by responsible Arab statesmen as well
as by American officials. President Nasser stated:

> They [the Americans] say Nasser is turning to the East and wants
> to put his country under Eastern domination, but dealing commer-
> cially with Russia is not the same thing as turning Communist.
> We aim at equal relations with all nations.   To say we are encour-
> aging Communism is completely untrue. We have our own
> philosophy.[21]

In 1958, a leading American authority on the Middle East, Harold
B. Minor, told the Senate Foreign Relations Committee:

> We should avoid the erroneous and easy assumption that there
> is a deliberate trend in any Middle Eastern country toward Com-
> munism.   There is an ideological gulf between Islamic and other

---

[17] Lenczowski, *The United States Interests in the Middle East,* p. 20.

[18] Hammond, *op. cit.,* p. 174; Seale, *op. cit.,* p. 285.

[19] *U.S. Policy in the Middle East,* 1956-57, p. 15.

[20] Hammond, *op. cit.,* p. 175.

[21] Quoted in Cecil Crabb, *American Foreign Policy in the Nuclear Age*
(2nd ed.; New York: Harper, 1965), p. 242.

Middle Eastern cultures...and Communism.[22]

When the Soviet Union supported Egypt during the Suez crisis of 1956, the Kremlin had made an expediential decision in the hope of gaining "an opportunity of having a legitimate place in the Arab community."[23]   But Egypt, bluntly warned the Kremlin:

> Contrary to what was then given wide currency, this policy [of expelling Western colonialism from the Arab world] was not meant to open the doors of the Middle East to Soviet Communism.... The Middle East and Afro-Asian world will be closed to all alien principles, be they Communist or otherwise.[24]

Furthermore, when ex-Vice-President Richard Nixon (now President of America), visited the site of the Aswan Dam in 1963, he observed that while Egypt was relying heavily upon Soviet technicians to build it, there was "no possibility of infiltration" of the Egyptian Government by Communism because of this fact.[25]

In Syria, the situation was identical to that of Egypt. Following a trip behind the Iron Curtain, the Syrian Minister of State Khalid Al-Azm, publicly declared:

> The U.S.S.R....does not want to interfere in our affairs nor does it want to interfere with our political or social systems. It wants Syria to have a strong economy to support Syria's political independence....The U.S.S.R. has given us political support and supplied us with arms, which we were completely unable to obtain from countries other than the U.S.S.R.[26]

However, despite Nasser's public declarations that the Arabs, in general, and Egypt, in particular, were not interested in changing Western imperialism for an Eastern one, he, nevertheless, continued hostilities towards Israel. This attitude, rather than association

---

[22] U.S., Congressional Hearings *Review of Foreign Policy*, 85th Congress, 2nd Session 1958, p. 565.

[23] *Egyptian Mail*, 16 December 1961.

[24] "Communism and Us," *The Scribe* (Cairo), Vol. 2, May-June, 1961.

[25] *New York Times*, 4 June 1963.

[26] *Documents on International Affairs, 1957* (London: Oxford University Press, 1960), p. 322.

with the Soviet bloc led Congress to view him in a negative light, and over President Kennedy's protest passed an amendment to the Foreign Assistance Act of 1963 which "denied aid to Egypt if she engaged or prepared for 'aggressive military efforts' against other recipients of American aid."[27]

In the House hearings, Dulles described the proposed Eisenhower Doctrine as a policy of containment similar to the Truman Doctrine, since both aimed at preventing Soviet moves in advance. The objective of the United States, therefore, was to warn the Soviet Union "to stay out, and to build up the vitality of these countries."[28] Dulles insisted that the U.S.A. can promote peace in the area by "making clear our position in advance," thus, preventing "miscalculation by a would-be aggressor."[29] Dulles also insisted that best results could be attained if Congress has spoken, "for that would make the Soviet rulers more deterred, while the target people would also feel more secure."[30]

The Eisenhower Doctrine was the last link in the Western-sponsored defence alliances for the containment of the Soviet Union's expansion. It was to provide a protective screen against Russian penetration, behind which the U.S.A. could work diligently to strengthen the internal security and economic stability of the indigenous states.[31]

[27] Hammond, *op. cit.,* p. 175.

[28] House *Hearings,* on the Eisenhower Doctrine, p. 41.

[29] U.S. Congress, House Committee on Foreign Affairs, *Hearings,* of H.J. Resolution 117, 85th Cong., Ist Sess., p. 3. Hereafter cited as House *Hearings* on the Eisenhower Doctrine.

[30] U.S. Congress, Senate, Committee on Armed Services and Foreign Relations, *Hearings,* on S.J. Res. 19, and H.J. Res. 117, 85th Cong., Ist Sess., pp. 9-10.

[31] The Soviet Union viewed the Doctrine as detrimental to both the U.S.S.R. as well as to these states. In a diplomatic note to the British Government dated 3 September 1957, the Soviet Government characterized the Doctrine as . . . put forward by monopolistic circles in the United States and approved by the British Government which aims at United States interference in the Middle East to bolster up the crumbling colonial system and place obstacles in the path of the peoples of the region toward independent development and deprive them of national independence. G.B. *British and Foreign State Papers,* Vol. CLXIII (1957-1958), p. 72. By contrast, the Soviet policy was characterized by non-interference in the internal affairs of the host countries. In his study of Communism in the region, Laquer wrote: "Soviet and Communist propagandists could point to the stark contrast between Moscow's policy of 'hands off' and Western imperialist attempts to 'organize' the area. To draw the various countries into all kinds of suspect

On 9 March 1957, the Congress approved the Eisenhower Doctrine, which authorized the President to undertake "military assistance programs with any nation or group of nations of that area desiring such assistance."[32]   The joint resolution further declared that the "United States regards as vital to the national interest and to world peace the preservation of the independence and integrity of the nations of the Middle East."[33]   With this, the U.S.A. issued a "unilateral warning to the world that the United States would defend the whole Middle East against Soviet attack."[34]   However, when President Eisenhower referred to "any nation controlled by International Communism," he probably had Egypt in mind.[35]

The critics pointed out that the danger was subversion not "covert armed aggression."   But Dulles replied that the United States "could not protect the Middle East through defense treaties without becoming involved in local disputes not connected with Communist action."[36]   This policy did, in fact, permit the U.S.A. to interfere in the internal affairs of the host nations, and became the main target for attacks by the Soviet Union as well as the states which opposed American domination.

By assuming the entire responsibility for Western defence of the Middle East, it became apparent that "No power—friend, potential enemy or 'neutralist' Arab State—could now assume that the U.S. would not fight for the Middle East."[37]   By guaranteeing the security of the area, the Doctrine had implicitly guaranteed the safety of Israel through maintaining the *status quo*. This was confirmed by President Kennedy in 1963, when he declared that the U.S.A. supports the security of Israel and its neighbours, and would take necessary action if needed to stop any aggression that might erupt in the

---

'defense' blocks. These Western activities tended to fan smouldering anti-Western resentment and to antagonize most of the Arabs who were psychologically quite unprepared; the Soviet danger was in their eyes some mythical invention or perhaps a clever stratagem of American and European 'imperialists' desirous of perpetuating their rule in the Middle East.   As a result, Soviet prestige grew." Laquer, *op. cit.*, p. 261.

32 *U.S. Foreign Policy in the Middle East, September 1956 to June 1957*, Documents (New York: Greenwood Press, 1968), p. 45.

33 *Ibid.*

34 Deconde, *op. cit.*, p. 755.

35 Copeland, *op. cit.*, p. 216.

36 Deconde, *op. cit.*, p. 756.

37 *Ibid.*

Middle East.[38]

Neither S.E.A.T.O. nor the Baghdad Pact has been as exclusively directed against International Communism as was the Eisenhower Doctrine, because it provided for economic and military assistance with special provisions for prompt implementation of such assistance.[39]

Jordan and the Eisenhower Doctrine

As the Eisenhower Doctrine went into effect on 9 March 1957, Jordan became the centre of the next Middle East crisis. The coming of the pro-Nasser revolutionary nationalists to power in Jordan resulted in a split with the Palace, since the Government's policies displeased the King, as they were diametrically opposed to those adopted by him. The Nabulsi government had recognized Red China and indicated interest in exchanging diplomatic relations with the Soviet Union.[40] At the same time, the King was denouncing Communism. Supported by the Parliament and many army officers, the Nabulsi government succeeded in diminishing the role of the King who decided that this trend had to be stopped.[41] The only pretext that King Husayn could devise was cautioning of increased Communist activities inside the country.[42] In February 1957, the King sent a letter to Prime Minister Nabulsi, asking him to curb Communist infiltration:

[38] Mohammad Ghanim, *Al-Alaqat Al-Dawliyyiah Al-Arabiyiah* (Cairo: Nahadat Misr, 1965), p. 313.

[39] Hammond, *op. cit.,* p. 117.

[40] Majali, *Muthakkirati, op. cit.,* p. 211.

[41] Kamil, *op. cit.,* p. 25. Also Musa, *op. cit.,* 663.

[42] On 31 December 1956, Nabulsi permitted the Communists to issue the weekly, *Al-Jamaheer.* To Husayn, this action was in defiance of the established anti-Communist law which declared: Article 3: A person will be penalized by temporary hard labour if he:

1. became a member of a Communistic organization for the purpose of propagandizing,
2. became a member of a Communistic organization, occupied an office or funtioned as its agent,
3. urged people to become Communists by speech, writing, or photography,
4. distributed a Communist document with the purpose of propaganda, and
5. possessed a Communistic Document. Musa, *op. cit.,* pp. 664-65; *Al-Husayn Ibn Talal,* p. 175.

...During the Cold War between the two camps, foreign doctrines began to seep into our land. Those doctrines contradict our principles and beliefs which, unless stopped, will adversely affect our nationalism, for we might substitute the high principles which elevated our nation for materialistic doctrines which contradict the basics of our nation. Also we might exchange one form of imperialism for another from which we would never liberate ourselves if it rooted its foundations. The Arab nation has not forgotten that the Eastern camp which exports its attractive doctrines was a major supporter of our enemy, as it assisted it to expropriate a precious part of the Arab homeland—Palestine. International Zionism found effective asssistance with the Eastern camp as well as imperialistic nations of the West.

...At this time we see the danger of Communist infiltration into our homeland.... If we permit the Communist doctrine which unites the Arab Communists and the Zionist Communists to infiltrate our ranks, we will have lost our heritage as a nation.... We believe in the rights of this homeland.... We want a strong structure based on the Arab legacy and a hope in the future insulated from Communist propaganda and the ideas of Bolshevism....[43]

The letter revealed the widening gulf between the Cabinet and the Palace.[44] The King's message was broadcast at the same time, it was handed to Nabulsi.[45] With strong external support, the Palace decided to challenge the Cabinet at the moment when the latter decided to exchange diplomatic representation with the U.S.S.R.[46] The crisis became acute on 10 April, when Husayn dismissed Nabulsi.[47]

[43] *Al-Husayn Ibn Talal*, pp. 177-80; English text in Khalil, Vol. II, pp. 916-19.

[44] Majali, *Muthakkirati*, p. 212.

[45] *Ibid.*

[46] *Ibid.*, p. 213. Majali wrote that C.G.S. Nuwar had met with the Russian Ambassador at Damascus. Upon his return to Amman, the Cabinet met and decided to exchange diplomatic relations with Soviet Russia. This decision was a clear reply to Husayn's message. Majali added that Nuwar had negotiated with the Americans regarding a treaty between the two countries to replace the Anglo-Jordan treaty. *Ibid.*, p. 214.

[47] Nabulsi's resignation was submitted with the phrase "by order of your Majesty." Husayn, *Uneasy Lies the Head*, p. 163.

Husayn wrote that on 10 April, a telegram from Nasser to Nabulsi was inter-

In making his move, the King was betting on his life and the life of Jordan, as the weeks following the dismissal were filled with uncertainty, turmoil, and suspense.[48]

Some sources believe that one main reason for the Cabinet-Palace differences was that Husayn was willing to accept American aid even if it meant agreeing to the Eisenhower Doctrine. Accordingly, he contacted the American Embassy and consulted with old politicians.[49]

More significantly, Husayn's fear of the Communists coincided with the basis for the Eisenhower Doctrine. His letter seemed a direct appeal to the assistance clause of the Doctrine.[50]   Campbell wrote:

> What is significant is that a test of strength took place in what was ostensibly a Jordan domestic affair, that was also a test of alignments in the Middle East and especially of American policy. As early as February 1957, King Husayn was publicly denouncing Communism as if to make Jordan eligible for American aid under the Eisenhower Doctrine, while Nabulsi was preparing to establish diplomatic relations with the Soviet Union.[51]

Thereafter, Husayn's relations with the Cabinet were dependent upon the attitude in Washington.   He also received support from Saud whose visit to Washington signalled his acceptance of the Eisenhower Doctrine.[52]   In a letter on March 31, he assured Husayn of support:

---

cepted which read, "Do not give in.   Remain in your positions." *Ibid.,* p. 162; Shwadran, *op. cit.,* p. 348.

One year later, Rifa'i, at the U.N. General Assembly stated that Nabulsi was acting under instructions from Egypt and was instructed to comply with the King's demand for his resignation.   U.N.G.A., *Official Records,* 3rd Emergency Special Session A/PV.735, 14 August 1958, p. 25.

[48] In Israel it was decided that if the pro-Nasser Nationalists win in Jordan, then the Israel forces would enter Jordan.   Foreign Minister Meir declared: "Israel would not stay with hands tied if foreign forces entered Jordan."   After the dismissal of Nabulsi, however, Israel's position changed suddenly and the United Press reported that Ben Gurion had declared that "the situation in Jordan is no longer dangerous and that he would not take any steps to complicate the efforts by Husayn and his Prime Minister Khalidi."   Cited in Kamil, *op. cit.,* p. 32.

[49] Shwadran, *op. cit.,* p. 347.

[50] Tutsch, *op. cit.,*

[51] Campbell, *op. cit.,* p. 128.

[52] Saud received $50 million in military aid, and renewed the agreement of the Dahran A.F.B. for another five years.

We should cooperate to oppose all destructive principles which contradict our religion, our traditions, and our customs. You will always find me by your side in my person, my soldiers, my money, my country—working for the victory of Islam and the Muslims.[53]

In Jordan, popular and governmental attitude towards foreign pacts including the Eisenhower Doctrine was negative. The Speaker of the House, Hikmat Al-Masry, declared that "the Baghdad Pact and the Eisenhower Doctrine are twins, one complements the other."[54] The Chamber also rejected the Eisenhower Doctrine in the following statement:

1. The United States Government regarded the Doctrine as part of a larger scheme aiming at the restoration of Western influence in the Middle East. The Doctrine was designed to replace the Baghdad Pact.

2. The aim of the United States Government was to create division among the Arab governments and to woo Arab leaders who were opposed to nationalism in the hope of isolating Egypt and its friends.

3. Jordan, which was engaged in discussions to bring the abrogation of its treaty with Britain had no intention of selling itself to a higher bidder despite its limited resources.[55]

Furthermore, the Secretary of Foreign Affairs, Abdullah Al-Rimawi affirmed the stand of the Chamber and the Government's commitment to the policy of positive neutralism and declared that the Arab states were capable of defending themselves.[56] He added:

It is an essential element in Jordan's foreign policy that the vacuum theory should be utterly rejected. Jordan does not believe

---

[53] Royal Institute of International Affairs, *Documents on International Affairs,* 1957, p. 1645. The *New York Times* reported on April 17 that a Saudi plane brought sufficient gold to Amman as a reward to the loyal troops and Bedouin chiefs who supported Husayn at the Zarqa Affair. Help came from Saud "who placed the Saudi Arabian troops then in Jordan under Husayn's personal command." Campbell, *op. cit.,* p. 129.

[54] Kamil, *op. cit.,* p. 21.

[55] Jordan, *Proceedings of the House,* 6 January 1957, p. 2.

[56] *Ibid.*

that the disappearance of British and French influence has left a vacuum that somebody else ought to fill....Jordanians will not agree to one foreign influence directly or indirectly replacing another. Defense of the Arabs should solely be the responsibility of the Arabs.[57]

To enforce the stand of the Government and the Parliament, a national congress was convened in Nablus on April 22 and adopted a resolution demanding that the Government reject the Eisenhower Doctrine and expel the United States Ambassador and his military attache. These demands were presented to the Cabinet with the threat of demonstrations if the Government failed to respond. However, while the Cabinet agreed, the King rejected the demands. Thus, demonstrations took place and caused the Khalidi Government to resign.[58]

On April 24, the King asked Ibrahim Hashim to form a new Cabinet of old conservatives and those loyal to the Palace. He dissolved the Parliament, abolished political parties, suspended the constitution, and declared martial law.

The United States Responds

Husayn's control of the situation was attributed to the loyalty of certain Bedouin army units and the placing of Saudi troops in Jordan under Husayn's command, but, most importantly, due to the support of the United States Government. This fact was confirmed by Dulles in a speech before the Senate declaring that: "Husayn had

[57] *Al-Difa'a,* 3 January 1957; this attitude was shared by the Syrian Government which on 1 January 1957, issued a statement rejecting the Vacuum Theory and denying that Communism presented any immediate threat to the Arab World. Seale, *op. cit.,* p. 289.

[58] Musa, *op. cit.,* p. 675; *Al-Difa'a,* 23 April 1957. It was reported that the United States Ambassador in Amman had told Husayn on 24 April that, unless he took stern measures against nationalist elements in the Khalidi Cabinet, intervention of Israel would be inevitable and that the U.S. would not stop this. Accordingly Husayn ordered the formation of a new Cabinet under Hashim. Cited in Kamil, *op. cit.,* p. 43; Musa, *op. cit.,* p. 675.

Supporting this point, Majali wrote: "The reasons for the Zarqa Affair were to prevent [thwart the attempts], for installing a Cabinet to succeed the Nabulsi Government. Also, to pressure the King to restore the Nabulsi group to office." Majali, *Muthakkirati,* p. 218.

derived from the Eisenhower Doctrine the power to face the difficult stuation in his country."[59]

Certain army units at the Zarqa army base were supposed to have
been involved in an attempted coup.[60] During the Zarqa Affair,
the Sixth Fleet was permitted by Lebanon to stand by in Beirut while
Husayn carried out his *coup d'etat* in Jordan.[61] As Cabinet instability became the order of the day, the United States decided to come
openly to the support of Husayn. Thus, on April 23, Dulles in a
press conference said:

> We have great confidence in and regard for King Husayn because
> we really believe that he is striving to maintain the independence
> of his country in the face of very great difficulties and he does not
> want to see Jordan fall under the domination of other countries
> which have indicated a desire to work contrary to what the King
> considers to be in the best interests of his country. It is our
> desire to hold up the hands of King Husayn in these matters to
> the extent that he thinks that we can be helpful. He is the judge
> of that.[62]

[59] Cited in Kamil, *op. cit.*, p. 35.

[60] *Al-Husayn Ibn Talal*, p. 206; Shwadran, *op. cit.*, p. 349; Musa, *op. cit.*,
p. 669. General Ali Al-Hayari declared that there was no plot against Husayn,
and that the Palace invented the idea of the coup because the army officers refused
to strike against the people for resisting the formation of a new government "willing to cooperate with imperialism and accept schemes which forced Jordan out
of the Arab liberation policy of Egypt and Syria," Shwadran, *op. cit.*, p. 351;
see *supra* footnote 58.

[61] Kirk, *Contemporary Arab Politics*, p. 121. At the Bermuda Conference,
Jordan was selected as a testing ground for the Eisenhower Doctrine. At that
conference on 24 March 1957, Prime Minister Macmillan said: "The U.S. and
Great Britain are in agreement on new methods to solve any Middle East
problem if present solutions fail....Jordan constitutes the major source for war
in the Middle East." Cited in Kamil, *op. cit.*, pp. 25-6. The Associated Press
commented on Macmillan's statement that "there is an agreement for combined action in case of a sudden collapse, such as the collapse of the Jordan
Government." Cited in *Ibid.* The aim of the U.S. Sixth Fleet which was given
permission for flights over Israeli territory was to frighten the nationalists in
Jordan as well as other Arab states supporting them. It was reported that
Nasser and Ben Gurion were told that the U.S. would not let Jordan's cry
for help go unanswered. *Newsweek*, 25 April 1958.

[62] *U.S. Policy in the Middle East*, 1956-1957, p. 69; U.S., *Department of
State Press Release*, 237, 23 April 1957.

As the struggle between the Palace and the Nationalists persisted, it became evident to the United States that Jordan could no longer rely on the Syrian and Egyptian subsidy, nor could it survive merely with Saudi Arabian aid. At this point, Husayn won his victory with the support of the United States which was willing to extend help as long as Husayn was willing to maintain his independence and fight Communism. James P. Richards, Eisenhower's special assistant for Middle Eastern affairs and former chairman of the House Foreign Affairs Committee, embarked on a visit to Middle East. Husayn, however, faced with nationalist pressure decided not to invite him to Jordan. At the same time, Husayn decided to enjoy the benefits of the Doctrine without subscribing to it. Washington, cognizant of this fact, expressed its understanding:

....It was realized that for Husayn to embrace the Eisenhower Doctrine in the present circumstances would be equivalent to the kiss of death. Mr. Dulles, therefore, deliberately played down the Eisenhower Doctrine, but announced that the U.S. would give Husayn its full support in whatever he considers to be in the interest of his country.[63]

On April 24, at Augusta, Georgia, Press Secretary James Hagerty said that he had been authorized to say that "both the President and the Secretary of State regarded the independence and integrity of Jordan as vital."[64] An explicit application of the Eisenhower Doctrine to Jordan was stated in an announcement by Lincoln White of the News Division of the State Department on April 25. He said:

I can only say with respect to Jordan that the statement issued in Augusta yesterday afternoon represented a reminder to the world by the President that a finding had been made in the Joint Resolution of the Congress on the Middle East that the preservation of the independence and integrity of the nations of the Middle East was vital to the national interest of the United States and to world peace. This reminder was appropriate because of the threat to the

[63] Barraclough, *op. cit.*, p. 173.
[64] Cited in *U.S. Policy in the Middle East*, 1956-1957, p. 69; Magnus, R.H., *Documents on the Middle East* (Washington: American Enterprise Institute, 1969), p. 95.

independence and integrity of Jordan by international Communism, as King Husayn himself stated.[65]

On the same day, elements of the Sixth Fleet including the carrier Forestal, were dispatched to the East Mediterranean to implement the Eisenhower Doctrine. In the meantime, martial law was established and hundreds of opposition leaders were either sent to jail or fled the country.[66]

To the West, Jordan occupied an important military and strategic position in the heart of the Middle East. It constituted a bridge connecting Syria, Iraq, Saudi Arabia, Israel, and, in a technical sense, Eygpt. Commenting on Jordan's position in this regard, Ben Gurion said:

Occupation of Jordan territory by Israel will not result in geographic division of the Arab States only, but will be the beginning of the end of the spiritual unity among the Arabs.[67]

The justification for supporting Husayn to preserve his throne and the sovereignty of Jordan was that it provided a convenient buffer between Egypt and Syria on the one hand, and Israel on the other, thus, minimizing the probability of a second round in Palestine.[68]

Eisenhower's offer of American aid was implicit in his statement of April 24, in spite of Husayn's reluctance to invite Ambassador Richards to visit Jordan. Marguerite Higgins observed that:

the United States will not, for instance, embarrass the King by demanding that he receive Richard's mission as the price of getting financial aid. If the King wants that aid from us, he can get it in other ways. We are prepared to furnish assistance via Saudi Arabia.[69]

In a radio speech on 25 April 1957, Husayn justified the dismissal of the Nabulsi Government as Communist inspired:

[65] *U.S. Policy in the Middle East,* p. 69; *New York Times,* 26 April 1957.
[66] Musa, *op. cit.,* p. 677.
[67] Kamil, *op. cit.,* p. 40.
[68] Kirk, *Contemporary Arab Politics,* p. 111.
[69] *New York Herald Tribune,* 29 April 1957; Shwadran, *op. cit.,* p. 356; Abidi, *op. cit.,* p. 165.

...You all know that the Communist Party in Jordan is illegal, not only because international Communism is opposed to our religion and beliefs as well as the elements of our nationalism, but because the Communists in Jordan were and still are in consort with Communists inside Israel from which they received directions since the latter is the bastion of Communism in the Middle East.

...The Communists and their supporters in Jordan have shown contempt to our religion by accusing those who respect the doctrines of Islam and protect it of being reactionary elements. They aim at disintegrating the unity of the nation and to eradicating its progress....

As to the stand of that Cabinet with regard to the Eisenhower Doctrine and American financial assistance....I want to assure my people that it is not our policy to invite the American envoy [Richards] to visit our country and we deny that we will accept the Doctrine. Jordan's policy is purely Arab which derives from the decisions of the Cairo conference. I would like to add and declare that Jordan under no circumstances will separately consider this Doctrine and will not take any step in that regard without agreements with the Arab states. This [the dismissal of the Cabinet] is an internal matter unrelated to our foreign policy. We, therefore, will not allow outsiders to interfere in our local and private matters....[70]

Husayn's statement that the internal crisis of Jordan was "the responsibility of international Communism and its followers"[71] acted as the magic phrase which quieted the American conscience and loosened the American purse strings. The United States shouldered the financial subsidy promised by the Arab states and within two years was aiding Jordan to the tune of some $70 million a year.[72]

Only Lebanon and Libya formally approved the Eisenhower Doctrine.[73] Saud, however, was in full agreement with its provisions

---

[70] *Al-Husayn Ibn Talal*, pp. 229-34.

[71] *New York Times*, 25 April 1957, p. 13.

[72] Kirk, *Contemporary Arab Politics*, p. 111.

[73] In Lebanon, the Eisenhower Doctrine was considered as treasonable behaviour of the Government and a distinct breach of its National Covenant which recognized Lebanon as an Arab state that should never seek assistance from any European power to the detriment of another Arab state. The Eisenhower Doctrine implied that the Christians were calling upon the U.S. to

although he did not formally adhere to it. When Saud returned from his visit to Washington following the declaration of the Eisenhower Doctrine, Husayn flew to Riad and, after consultation on April 29, both kings issued a communique emphasizing friendship and co-operation.[74] On the following day, Husayn formally requested financial aid from the United States State Department which was immediately approved—perhaps, the first time in history, such aid was sanctioned in a few hours. Jordan was granted $10 million "in recognition of the brave steps taken by His Majesty King Hussein and the Government, and the people of Jordan to maintain the integrity and independence of their nation."[75]   Furthermore, the American Ambassador added that the United States would "maintain a continuing review of Jordan's problems with His Majesty's Government to determine what further steps can be required."[76]

Although Husayn had no intention of adhering to the Eisenhower Doctrine, "the speed with which the U.S. responded to his needs suggests that there was, nevertheless, an understanding."[77]   This also indicated the extent to which the United States was willing to go in order to break the pro-Nasser front in Jordan. Since the date, Jordan continued more than ever to side with the West.[78] The *Manchester Guardian* wrote that: "It is no longer a secret that Husayn had reached an agreement with the U.S. before changing the policy of Jordan."[79]

In Jordan, Husayn put down his Left-leaning army opposition in an encounter in April 1957. Washington sealed its victory by sending the Sixth Fleet to the East Mediterranean and adding $30 million in economic assistance to Jordan.[80]   In responding to Husayn's anti-

---

replace France as their protector and to intervene in Lebanon on their behalf. Cited in *Ibid.*, p. 121; K.S., "The Lebanese Crisis in Perspective," *World Today*, No. 74 (1958), p. 372; Ionides, *op. cit.*, p. 240.

[74] *American Foreign Policy*, Current Documents, 1957, p. 1024.

[75] *New York Herald Tribune*, 29 April 1957; Shwadran, *op. cit.*, p. 356; *London Times*, 30 April 1957; *Department of State Bulletin*, Vol. 37, No. 945, p. 260.

[76] *American Foreign Policy*, *op. cit.*, p. 1025.

[77] Shwadran, *op. cit.*, p. 356.

[78] Georgiana G. Stevens (ed.), *The United States and the Middle East* (Englewood Cliffs, N.J.: Prentice-Hall, 1965), p. 167.

[79] Cited in Kamil, *op. cit.*, p. 35.

[80] Hammond, *op., cit.*, p. 118. Foreign Minister Rifa'i declared that Jordan would need about $50 million annually in U.S. aid for the next five to ten

Communist appeals, Washington was able to use the Eisenhower Doctrine to shift the key political issue in the Middle East from Western imperialism to Soviet imperialism, but only at the cost of severely limiting the U.S. influence in the area.[81] Furthermore, Husayn's policy of suppressing nationalist feelings through the use of Bedouin army units and his unofficial adherence to the Eisenhower Doctrine, resulted in worsening of inter-Arab relations and placed Husayn in a negative light to a degree which the Eisenhower Doctrine did not ask for.[82]

EVALUATION OF THE EISENHOWER DOCTRINE

In putting the Doctrine to the test, the United States was rendering aid to the ruling group while defying the will of the population.[83] In the opinion of Senator Ralph E. Flanders, to be effective, any American formulation of a new foreign policy should take into account the realities of the conditions and the needs of the people of the region. American foreign policy should take into consideration seriously the aspirations of the people rather than the unpopular governments. Flanders remarked:

> ...Our whole policy is based on the endeavor to form alliances with persons, ...that to trust in rulers and governments is vain compared with trust in people. Governments come and Governments go....The people remain.[84]

Sharing this view, a student of the area politics, John Campbell, commented:

> Yet the American diplomatic victory had some angles worthy of

---

years to develop her economy and maintain the armed forces; Jordan was counting on the U.S. "not to let us down." In order to vindicate his country in the eyes of the Arab World for accepting American assistance, Rifa'i stated that the American aid must be given without strings attached. Shwadran, *op. cit.*, p. 369.

[81] *Ibid.*

[82] Hafez, *op. cit.*, p. 151.

[83] *Ibid.*

[84] Senator Ralph E. Flanders, "We Are off the Summit—Let Us Strengthen the Foundation," *Congressional Record* (Senate), 85th Congress, 2nd Session, CIV, part 13, 6 August 1958, p. 16324.

future thought. Its permanence was open to question....Hussein had no guarantee of a long and quiet reign. The United States had taken sides in what was basically an inter-Arab struggle ....It had supported its friends, but also raised cries against 'gunboat diplomacy' and in doing so it had placed itself in a position hardly distinguishable from that which the British had just been forced to relinquish.

Henceforth, Jordan was to be kept alive by American instead of British guarantees, by dollars instead of pounds. Would America be any more successful over the long run in combating Arab nationalism by these methods than the British?[85]

Various positions were taken on the subject. While Elizabeth Monroe described the situation as "a former British protege had changed protectors,"[86] the *New York Times* held that the American move to aid "embattled Jordan" was a "landmark in American foreign policy," and insisted that the United States had acted "as a great power in defense of our vital interest."[87] On the other hand, the Soviet Union accused the United States of manipulating the Government of Jordan as the country was brought into the American sphere of influence. The *New Times* of Moscow wrote appealing to Arab patriotism:

Today it is no longer Glubb Pasha but Ambassador Mallory who directs the reprisals agaignst Jordanian patriots and forms the Governments of Jordan. It is no longer Britain but the United States which subsidized the Arab army from which the patriotic officers were expelled.[88]

The American move involved military protection, political support and financial assistance. Commenting on Jordan's complete dependence on the United States, particularly, from the subsidy point of view, the *New York Herald Tribune* wrote that the American assistance to Husayn would be disasterous:

[85] Campbell, *op. cit.*, p. 131.

[86] Monroe, *op. cit.*, p. 208.

[87] *New York Times*, 28 April 1957.

[88] Y. Bochkaryov, "The Jordan Events," *The New Times* (Moscow), 9 May 1957, p. 12.

One of the main dangers which threaten Husayn was his adoption by the United States Government because this adoption is the kind which will inevitably lead in the end to death by strangulation.[89]

The United States took these steps, once King Husayn charged that the army attempted a coup to dethrone him and to federate Jordan with Egypt and "to make Jordan a vassal state of Soviet Russia."[90] But most importantly, because Husayn played the American game of charging that the internal crisis in Jordan "was the responsibility of International Communism."[91]

---

[89] Cited in Kamil, *op. cit.*, p. 49. This prediction was fulfilled following the 1967 War, when the Johnson Administration suspended the budgetary assistance which had sustained Jordan's economy ever since 1957. It is ironic that Jordan's survival has depended upon the policies of other nations. King Husayn's biographer, Sparrow, revealed that Jordan could be a rich state if its mineral wealth were developed. He wrote:

...I was handed in Britain a document dealing with the secret mineral wealth of Jordan unexploited in the days of the Mandate. The document was never published, but was compiled by experts in their field. The allegation is made that the British oil interests, as a matter of policy, were opposed to the development of Jordan oil. Very detailed and convincing figures are given in this document still in my possession, of the location of oil and mineral wealth in Jordan, with estimates of the amount and quality of each locality. Sparrow, *op. cit.*, p. 124.

[90] Husayn, *Uneasy Lies the Head*, p. 183.

[91] *New York Times*, 25 April 1957, p. 13. General Ali Abu-Nuwar, C.G.S., was accused of engineering the so-called coup, but permitted to leave Jordan. He went to Damascus. Nuwar was succeeded by General Ali Al-Hayari, who requested the King to head an investigating commission of the Zarqa Affair and the coup. This was denied. Hayari then went to Syria and telephoned his resignation on April 20. In a press conference he declared: I proclaim to the Arab and international public opinion that there was no plot for a coup against King Husayn. The whole thing is an imperialistic plot aimed at certain objectives—particularly that of forcing Jordan out of the Arab liberation policy of Egypt and Syria. *New York Times*, 24 April 1957.

Al-Ahram reported that Radio Damascus accused the American Embassy of creating the convulsion in Jordan through direct interference in her affairs. *Al-Ahram*, 21 April 1957.

Stevens also commented: Indeed, at least one Western authority (and many Arabs) believed the alleged plot was fiction and the April crisis was an American contrivance from start to finish. Stevens, *op. cit.*, p. 167. For an account of the plot, see *Husayn Ibn Talal*, pp. 206f; Majali, *Muthakkirati*, pp. 213f; Abidi, *op. cit.*, p. 164.

The Doctrine did serve a more immediate purpose. As it abandoned Nasser and constructed a pro-American, anti-Nasser, anti-Communist bloc, forcing the Middle East states to choose between the Moscow-Cairo axis on the one hand and Washington on the other.[92]

Although the Eisenhower Doctrine was manifestly anti-Communist in scope, its application verified the fact that it aimed at involvement in inter-Arab affairs, specifically in Lebanon and Jordan. The Doctrine did not allow for inter-Arab disputes while ignoring Arab unity covenants. It appeared to have the goal of isolating certain Arab states according to the axiom, "divide and rule."[93] However, this policy found adverse reaction inside the Arab world for it pushed the nationalists and the Communists towards each other. Patrick Seale observed:

This alliance between Nationalists and Communists was cemented by the West's failure clearly to distinguish between them. Faced with the Ba'ath-Communist front in Syria, and with evidence of Abdul Nasser's growing dependence on the Soviet Union, Western diplomats tended to overlook the fierce anti-Communist record of the Ba'ath Party and Nasser's treatment of his local Communists. The truth is that Communists and Nationalists were exceedingly wary of each other and were united only in opposing Western pressures: it had been a gross tactical error to push them into each others arms.[94]

Although Jordan offered the first case of the application of the Eisenhower Doctrine and accepted American aid and protection, it could never officially adhere to the American Doctrine. In this situation the Eisenhower Doctrine was interpreted to have worked for the preservation of Husayn's throne, as he reverted from anti-Western Arabism to cooperation with the United States.[95] The crux of the matter was that there had not been a single Arab leader who

[92] Hammond, op. cit., p. 118.

[93] Ionides, op. cit., p. 240. The Arab nationalists in Lebanon—mostly Muslims—saw Chamoun's acceptance of the Eisenhower Doctrine as "the Americans ganging up with the Christian Chamoun against the Arab nationalists of Syria." Ibid.

[94] Seale, op. cit., p. 287; Ionides, op. cit., p. 243.

[95] Fitzsimmons, op. cit., p. 198.

could lead his country into an alliance with the West, without eventually running into a head-on collision with the nationalists—a collision that might threaten his throne or his office.[96] Thus, when the United States sought open support for the Eisenhower Doctrine, its new policy encountered the same difficulties that beset the Baghdad Pact:

> Mass opinion still tends to become very easily anti-West because colonial memories are so recent. To build alliances with the ex-colonial powers can easily be twisted to look like falling once again under their imperial control. This twist it need hardly be said, is stable Communist propaganda. The real government in Iraq fell in part because of its readiness to work with the West and Middle East military alliances.[97]

Although the Eisenhower Doctrine was resisted by the host countries, it nevertheless, persisted to be the backbone for American involvement in the region. In his progress report to Congress in 1960, President Eisenhower stated:

> The Middle East Resolution remains as a safeguard in reserve available to any country of the region desiring outside assistance against a possible threat to its independence and stability from external forces of International Communism.[98]

The Husayn-American understanding was of a reciprocal nature. In return for placing Jordan under the American umbrella, the King reaffirmed his anti-Communist policy.[99] Accordingly, he accused Nasser of making possible Communist infiltration in the region. By contrast, he characterized Jordan "as a model state" representing true Arab nationalism, which could never coexist with a foreign

---

[96] The case of Lebanese President Chamoun is a good example. By inviting American intervention, he, in fact, split the country. See Kirk, *Contemporary Arab Politics*, pp. 120–34.

[97] Barbara Ward, *The Rich Nations and the Poor Nations* (New York: W.W. Norton and Co., Inc., 1962), p. 128.

[98] Richard Stebbins, (ed.), *Documents on American Foreign Relations* (New York: Harper, 1961), p. 401.

[99] Seeking to consolidate his unofficial alliance with the West, the King, accompanied by Prime Minister Rifa'i, visited Formosa, South Korea and the United States in March 1959. Husayn's tour signified his affirmation of his pro-Western position in return for American commitment to preserve Jordan's independence.

ideology such as Communism.[100]   In a Washington speech at the Press Club, he declared that his anti-Communist stand "brought us not only the enmity of the Communist camp but also created serious misunderstanding with some Arab states."[101]

Pursuing his pro-Western, anti-Communist stand, the King further declared, "There is no life or future for Arabism if it departs from the camp of the free world and embraces Communism."[102]   Husayn's anti-Communist campaign which was either tailored by him to please the United States or programmed by the West for pronouncement by an Arab Muslim leader, was not restricted to the Arab World, but took an international scope.   At the United Nations General Assembly, on 4 September 1960, he said:

... The nations of the world are being offered a choice. . . . It lies between becoming a part of the Soviet Empire subservient ulti-mately to the dictates of the Supreme Council of the Soviet Union or standing as a free nation with sole external allegiance to the United Nations itself.   That is the choice. . . . May I say at once and with all the strength and conviction at my command that Jordan has made its choice.   We have given our answer in our actions and I am here to reaffirm our stand to the nations of the world.   We reject Communism.   The Arab people will never bow to Communism.   Communism will never survive in the Arab world because if it ever did, it would have replaced Arab nationalism.   There would cease to be an Arab nation and an Arab world. . . .

... It is my firm belief that all nations which believe in God should meet in counter attack against the common challenge to their very existence represented by Communism. . . .   Not until those who honestly believe in God and His dictates of love, equality and social justice unite to translate their ideal into action, will Communism be defeated and peace restored to earth.   In the great struggle between Communism and freedom there can be no neutrality.[103]

100 Husayn, *Uneasy Lies the Head, op. cit.*, p. 234.

101 *New York Times*, 29 March 1959.

102 Husayn, *Al-Qawmiyiah Al-Arabiyyiah* (Amman: Bureau of Information, 1960).

103 Khalil, *op. cit.*, Vol. II, pp. 982–87.

To the American and British public, the West was defending freedom and democracy against Communist aggression. However, since the Arab nationalists were neither Communists nor even communistic, the more the West pursued its policy of using the reactionary rulers to perpetuate its neo-colonial position, the more material they gave to Nasser and the Russians to swing Arab popular opinion against the West.[104]

For Husayn, identification with the West has been a "matter of personal conviction."[105] In the councils of Arab leaders, he dauntlessly, would declare: "We were, we are and we will be friends of the United States. We have faith in the United States."[106] Thus, Husayn's acceptance of American policies secured for Jordan an annual subsidy of fifty million dollars.[107] He also was assured by President Eisenhower that "Jordan was not alone." In expressing his appreciation for American "adoption," Husayn rejected the idea of neutralism, and pledged to fight on the side of the West in the event of a major war.[108]

The King's insistence on receiving equipment from the West was another way by which he maintained his independence from Egypt and Syria.[109] Furthermore, maintenance of Jordan's ties with the West was considered a way by which Arab-Israeli conflict could be prevented from becoming an East-West question.[110] Israel wanted an East-West polarization because that would effectively ensure American ties with her. The Russians, too, wanted such polarization to take place because that would render the Arabs completely dependent on the Soviet Union.[111]

The United States has been interested in maintaining Husayn's regime because it was more kindly disposed towards her and relatively less hostile towards Israel than the rest of the Arab states.[112] "This has been the reason why the United States has been providing most amounts of military assistance to Jordan since 1957."[113]

[104] Ionides, *op. cit.*, p. 243.
[105] *New York Times*, 24 September 1968, p. 2.
[106] *Ibid.*
[107] *Ibid.*, 23 March 1959.
[108] *Ibid.* 17 April 1959.
[109] *Ibid.*, 24 September 1968, p. 22.
[110] *Ibid.*
[111] *Ibid.*
[112] *New York Times*, 28 February 1965, p. 3.
[113] *Ibid.*

The Jordan army, until the 1967 War, was viewed by the American officials as a stabilizing force in Jordan. By partly satisfying the appetite of the army for modern weapons, the United States had hoped to strengthen the military support of the Government of King Husayn.[114]

The impact of American economic assistance on Jordan, since the inception of the U.S. Aid Program in 1952, can hardly be exaggerated.[115] Without such assistance, Jordan, in all probability, would have perished in the cross-fire of politics in the turbulent Arab World. Thus, before 1957, the United States felt that Jordan's collapse would very likely set in motion a chain of events which could all but destroy prospects of peace in the region. Added to that was the probability of resumption of the Arab-Israeli hostilities and intensification of East-West conflict. Thus, in view of the United States foreign policy, the preservation of Jordan was important to the security of the West.

[114] Secretary of Defense Robert MacNamara said that arms were given as gift to friendly nations, such as Israel, Jordan and Iran. *London Times* 31 January 1961. To qualify for such grants, a Middle Eastern country must assent to the goals of the Mutual Security Act—the security of the U.S. and the free world being implicitly against the Soviet Union. *Security and the Middle East,* A report submitted to the President, April 1954, p. 113.

[115] Expenditures from the inception of the programme in February 1951, to 30 September 1968, totalled $569,939,184 for economic assistance. Military assistance totalled an additional $68 million. The United States began to provide budget support assistance to the Government of Jordan in 1957, following the termination of the Anglo-Jordan Treaty. Until then, Britain contributed substantially to the budget through support of the army. The level of the United States assistance has been decreasing continuously from a high of almost $46 million to $32 million in 1966. The total amount of budget support payments from March 1957 to 30 September 1968 was $373,900,317. These funds were given to Jordan to make up its annual budget deficit and to provide the foreign exchange.

Although the economic assistance given to Jordan after 1967 was viewed by the United States as necessary "to help King Husayn maintain political control," the war of June 1967 required adjustment in the U.S. economic assistance programme. The U.S. budget support payments have been stopped. "We decided to suspend direct budgetary payments, the largest increment of our pre-1967 aid program, when Jordan began to receive the Khartoum subsidies" (From a letter to the author from the Jordan Desk Officer, U.S. Department of State, dated 2 December 1969). The preceding figures were derived from U.S.A.I.D., *United States Assistance to Jordan,* published on 24 December 1968; also *New York Times,* 12 June 1967.

...We have national interests of the highest importance in the Arab World... to encourage and strengthen the moderate Arab states in order to weaken the radical potential and to avoid a polarization of power relationships in which the United States would have no friends in the Middle East except Israel, while the Soviet Union would gain uncontested influence and possibly control throughout the vast and populous Arab World.[116]

The United States policy for the Middle East following the 1967 War was announced by President Johnson on 19 June 1967. Paramount among his principles for peace was the "respect for political independence and territorial integrity of all states in the area."[117] This was a reiteration of his statement of 23 May 1967:

To the leaders of all the nations of the Near East, I wish to say what American Presidents had said before me—that the United States is firmly committed to the support of the political independence and territorial integrity of all nations of that area. The United States strongly opposes aggression by anyone in the area, in any form, overt or clandestine. . . .[118]

However, this policy is viewed by Jordan as mere empty promise, because its territorial integrity was violated while the U.S. has been either reluctant or unable to implement its policy.[119] Accordingly, after the 1967 War, Husayn's talks with Johnson were unproductive, since Washington's dictates were not always obeyed in Israel.[120] However, while the U.S. resumed arms sales to Jordan

---

[116] Letter from Townsend Hoopes, Deputy Assistant Secretary of Defense for International Security Affairs, to Chairman Mendel Rivers of the House Armed Services Committee. Quoted in the *New York Times*, 18 August 1967, p. 7.

[117] Magnus, *op. cit.*, p. 205.

[118] Lenczowski, *United States Interests in the Middle East*, p. 30.

[119] Dismemberment of the Jordan territory by continuous Israeli occupation poses a threat that the kingdom may disintegrate. The collapse of Jordan is viewed as adverse to the U.S. policy in the region, since the latter has been trying to uphold the independence and territorial integrity of that country since the proclamation of the Eisenhower Doctrine. This was because the country was considered an element of stability in the region, as a state friendly to the West, and because it resisted Communist infiltration by rejecting Soviet offers of aid. Lenczowski, *op. cit.*, p. 11.

[120] For example, Johnson's message to Eshkol regarding the status of Jerusalem was not given any attention as Israel decided to annex the Old City.

after the conflict, the Johnson Administration attempted to "per-suade Husayn to settle with Israel on a piecemeal basis without following the other Arab states into a blind alley."[121] But Husayn's refusal to attempt a separate peace treaty—which to him was a political impossibility—resulted in U.S. retaliation when it informed Jordan not to expect any more budgetary assistance. The United States Government also threatened that it would not sink more money into Jordan's war-shattered economy "unless the King took a more realistic position."[122] While this decision was ostensibly based on Jordan's acceptance of Arab subsidy, many observers believe that Husayn "was being punished for declaring war on Israel and for refusing to accept the realities of defeat."[123]

Although the United States has no public treaties with Israel, nevertheless, unofficial commitments for its defence and economic development have been a substitute. Consequently, Israel has been enjoying almost unlimited American political support, particularly at the United Nations.[124] Furthermore, Israel has been the recipient of large amounts of military equipment as well as foreign aid.[125]

Financial Times, 21 November 1967. Expressions by prominent Americans had been usually deferential to Israel in her dispute with the Arab states. Shortly before his inauguration, President-elect John F. Kennedy, for instance, told Ben Gurion; "I was elected by the Jews of New York, and I would like to do some-thing for the Jewish people" (C.L. Sulzberger, *New York Times,* 31 July 1968; Ben Gurion was quoted as commenting: "I was shocked. Why should he say such a thing to a foreigner?" Cited in Lenczowski, *United States Interest in the Middle East,* p. 31).

In their television debate on 1 June 1968, Senators Robert Kennedy and Eugene McCarthy—then presidential aspirants—both spoke of American "commit-ment" to Israel, as an exception to their general views. *Ibid.,* p. 31.

[121] Hodes, *op. cit.,* p. 160.

[122] *Ibid.,* p. 161.

[123] *Daily Telegraph,* 9 January 1968; George Lenczowski, "Arab Bloc Realignments," *Current History* (December 1967), p. 346.

[124] On 7 June 1967, C.L. Salzburger of the *New York Times,* refuted the idea that the U.S. policy in the Arab-Israeli dispute was even-handed. He, instead, characterized it by saying, "Washington is about as neutral on Palestine as Peking on Vietnam." The *New York Times,* on 29 June 1967, reported that the U.S.A. had given "diplomatic support" to Israel throughout the 1967 crisis.

[125] In answer to a question, Eban said that the U.S. "should strengthen Israel to the maximal degree. There is progress in that." *Issues and Answers on A.B.C. Television Network,* 4 October 1970. In December 1970, the U.S. Congress appro-ved a $500 million aid bill to Israel. By contrast, on December 10, following King Husayn's visit to President Nixon, Jordan was given a $30 million in military aid.

Until June 1967, Husayn's relations with the United States were friendly and cooperative. However, a drastic change took place as the U.S. policy towards the Arabs became hardened regarding a peace settlement. This placed Husayn in a precarious position. He explained:

Due to the indifferent attitude of the United States and her one-sided policy up to now in terms of support to Israel, the constant question I am asked by the leaders of the Arab World is, "As a friend of the United States, what has the U.S. done for you in Jordan in your present crisis?" and I find it exceedingly difficult to answer that, unfortunately.[126]

CONCLUSION

Essentially, American-Jordanian relations assumed significance with the implementation of the Eisenhower Doctrine. Although Husayn had failed to officially adhere to the American plan, Jordan reaped the political, military and economic benefits provided by the Doctrine.

King Husayn was, perhaps, more determined to recognize the Eisenhower Doctrine than the Baghdad Pact, since American aid and protection became more urgent than during his confrontation with the nationalists in 1954. The crystallization of the nationalists' opposition to the Palace posed significant danger to the regime, particularly, when the Cabinet under pro-Nasser Prime Minister Nabulsi and a few high-ranking army officers including the C.G.S., General Ali Abu Nuwar, himself a Jordanian, adopted an all-Arab policy and recommended establishing diplomatic relations with the Communist bloc.

---

[126] Husayn, interview on A.B.C.'s "Issues and Answer," 3 May 1970.
The Arabs charge that Israel's preemptive strike in 1967 was with knowledge and approval of the U.S.A. Haykal added that "the American Sixth Fleet in the Mediterranean is a military and a strategic reserve for Israel if matters became critical." M.H. Haykal: "This is the Real Crisis," *Al-Ahram*, 19 June 1970.
In a television conversation with reporters from the three networks on 1 July 1970, President Nixon revealed the true pro-Zionist, anti-Arab U.S. policy as he said: "...The other Arab countries do want to drive Israel into the Sea.... We will do what is necessary to maintain Israel's strength *vis-a-vis* its neighbors..."

Realizing that the first was aimed at placing him in an inferior position to Nasser, and the second would have isolated Jordan from the West, Husayn concluded that his salvation lay in Western protection through adhering to the Eisenhower Doctrine. Since the American policy aimed at crushing the pro-Nasser nationalists as well as halting Communist subversion in the region, the objectives of Husayn and the Eisenhower Doctrine appeared to coincide. By recognizing the Doctrine, Husayn would receive American political support to quell the tide of nationalist danger, thus, preserving his throne, and the independence of Jordan. Furthermore, he would secure a more dependable financial aid to replace the Arab subsidy. Husayn's pro-Western attitude was a matter of personal conviction. While dependence on the Arab subsidy might eventually result in ending Jordan's political independence, the American aid would perform the opposite. Thus, to Husayn, association with the West became more valuable than Arab cooperation.

Aside from Husayn's personal desires, the external setting also dictated his positive response, for failure to do so could have been even more devastating to Jordan. Jordan was faced with the threat of a military attack from Israel which the country's military capability could not possibly prevent. The American ambassador warned that unless Husayn took stern measures to eliminate the nationalist elements from the Cabinet, the Parliament and the Army, intervention by Israel to prevent the pro-Nasser group from taking over would be inevitable and that the United States would not stop it. Realizing that the United States was using Israel's military to enforce its policy in the Arab world, Husayn had no alternative. Thus the Zarqa incident was staged to provide the Palace with a pretext for the dismissal of the nationalist army officers and the quelling of public clamour for restoring the pro-Nasser Cabinet led by Prime Minister Nabulsi. Therefore, Husayn carried his revolution under the protective shadow of the Sixth Fleet and the threat of an Israeli invasion and appointed General Habis Majali, a loyal conservative, as C.G.S. and restored to the Palace the powers which the Nabulsi group had monopolized.

For a decade, Jordan was placed under the United States protective umbrella, because King Husayn played the American game of curtailing the Arab revolutionary progress as well as minimizing Communist influence in the region. It appeared that Jordan was chosen as the testing ground for Western policies, as all requirements were present. While the King benefited significantly, the United States' gains were greater. The success of Western strategy secured American influence in the region for a decade.

The United States policy in the Arab World has, ostensibly been aimed at stopping the Soviets. However, behind this facade was the policy of protecting the oil. This policy aimed at preventing the control of Arab oil by the revolutionary regimes which might nationalize it, or by the Soviet Union *per se*. Thus, Nasser's victory in the Yemen War was interpreted as a prototype for revolutionary trend, aiming at eliminating the conservative regimes. Elaborating on this point, the *New York Times* wrote on 17 April 1967:

> The glittering prize on the horizon is the oil of the Arabian Peninsula and the Persian Gulf . . . . A part of the prize could be command of the Middle East. . . .

The United States policy has emphasized non-direct involvement in the Middle East. Its instrument has been Israel which has been the receiver of the eternal American economic and military aids. The *New York Times* of 11 June 1967 reported:

> The United States. . . must rely on a local power, the deterrent of a friendly power as a first line to stave off American direct involvement. Israel feels that she fits this definition . . . .

But if the American policy aimed at humiliating Nasser, thereby stemming the tide of the Arab revolution, while keeping the Arab oil out of Nasser's grip, why a "friend" as Husayn was made to suffer immensely as a result of the 1967 War ? A logical explanation may be found in the fact that the West considered Jordan as having served its purpose, and that friendship with Israel was considered more valuable as well as more permanent.

CHAPTER FOURTEEN

CONCLUSION

The foreign policy of Jordan has been the product of the dynamics of the interaction between its internal setting and the geopolitical environment. Several factors have influenced the substance and the process of foreign policy. They include (1) geography, (2) the monarchy, (3) the economy, (4) the role of Israel, and (5) the role of the Arab states.

Though small in population and productivity, Jordan had held a pivotal position in the game of nations, both locally and international-ly. Jordan's geographical circumstances have shaped its foreign policy. Its geographic location has endowed it with strategic impor-tance rendering it a pawn, both in the inter-Arab and the inter-national struggle to dominate the Middle East. This situation may have been based on the assumption that, whoever controls Jordan, controls the Arab East, and in turn whoever controls the Arab East, controls the Middle East. On the local level, Jordan has been the object of control by Egypt and Iraq because of its central position in the Arab World, as was the case with the U.A.R. and the Arab Union in 1958. It links Saudi Arabia, Iraq, and Syria on the one hand, and on the other, it links the Arab East with Egypt. Furthermore, control of Jordan's territory is strategically crucial to the containment of Israeli expansion. In this regard, Ben Gurion declared that, without Jordan, there would not be an Arab unity, and that Israel's occupation of Jordan would also end the Arabs' spiritual unity. On the inter-national level, however, Jordan has been and will continue to be coveted by both camps.

Throughout its history, the Palace in Jordan had a virtual mono-poly of all powers in the state. Thus, in spite of the efforts of the Cabinet and Parliament, particularly in 1956, the making of the foreign policy rested almost exclusively in the hands of the King, whose character and personality were of crucial significance in deter-mining the foreign policy of Jordan.

The characteristics of the political culture during Abdullah's reign were a decisive factor in his monopoly over the conduct of Jordan's foreign relations. His autocratic outlook and patriarchal rule precluded political opposition and rendered democracy and parliamentary institutions a mere facade. Held by coercive cohesion, the population was, for the most part, precluded from political participation. The King tolerated no opposition, as he suppressed all ideological groups at both ends of the spectrum. He only approved of traditional, pro-monarchial Transjordan parties which accepted his autocratic rule.

The union with Palestine, however, brought with it the problems of integrating the socially, culturally, economically, and politically different populations. The situation developed into a Palestinian-Transjordan, Muslim-Christian problem. The Transjordan population represented a factor of stability and the Palestinian, a force of instability. While the Muslim majority looked for union with other Arab states and desired an end to all connections with Britain and the West, the Christian minority, on the other hand, preferred the continuation of influence in Jordan through which they secured better government positions as well as the protection. Consequently, adaptation and assimilation of the different groups caused friction which inevitably became a significant factor influencing the conduct of Jordan's foreign relations.

The introduction of the politically involved Palestinians into the Jordan polity brought untold problems to the monarchy. The articulate Palestinians attacked Abdullah for his autocratic rule, for suppressing political opposition and for his alliance and subservience to Britain. They demanded liberalization and clamoured for republicanism. Having become Jordanian subjects, they demanded representation in a truly representative government. They placed the monarchy under fire, for hitherto the country's politics had been oligarchic in nature since the Cabinet was the King's personal instrument and the Legislature was powerless. Abdullah, however, fought these manifestations with vigour and determination.

Until annexation, Abdullah, who believed in and practised patriarchal rule, was not concerned with such problems as constitutional reforms, fundamental rights, and parliamentary sovereignty which the Palestinians began to question. He was determind not to sacrifice his royal prerogatives to appease the new articulate opposition. Instead, he considered their attacks as subversive, aimed not only at the monarchy but at the separate existence of the state. He declared their action to be open treason and treated it accordingly. In the meantime, Abdullah took advantage of the division among the Palestinian leadership. Most appointments of the Palestinians to senior posts were based more on consideration of loyalty to him than on merit.

The Jordan polity was tranquil until the annexation. The Palestine issue brought fresh challenges to Abdullah as instability was caused by factors of agitation. These were his relations with Britain, his attitude towards Israel, and the economic situation.

Despite the fact that an assault on the Jordanian monarchy was made by Abdullah's assassination, his regime faced insignificant problems compared to Husayn's. In the main, Abdullah's encounter with Arab nationalists centred on the fact that Jordan's politics was greatly influenced by the country's relations with Britain. Even independence, when granted in 1946, was largely theoretical, since the country lacked the economic, military, and political requisites for statehood. As these manifestations gained momentum and became explosive issues, Husayn was confronted with more violent attacks, which compelled him to Arabize the army in 1956 and to end the treaty relationship with Britain. British influence was the bone of contention between the nationalists and the Hashemites, and persisted to be a significant factor in the uncertainty of political life in Jordan.

The dissatisfaction of the Palestinians centred on the discrepancy between the provisions of the constitution and the practices of the state. Whereas Abdullah was autocratic by nature, his son, Prince Talal (the father of Husayn) had the making of a democratic king. Annexation and the assassination of King Abdullah as well as the desire of King Talal to end the autocratic rule, required the revision of the constitution. This took place in January 1952, thus partially satisfying the demands of the opposition. Although the new instrument stressed Cabinet's responsibility to the Parliament instead of to the Palace, the powers of the King were not reduced. They remained substantially strong. The King continued to appoint the Prime Minister and the House of Notables, to dissolve the Parliament and to veto legislation.

During King Abdullah's reign, the Palace bore the Arabic-Islamic impact, which emphasized unquestioned allegiance to the King, thus, facilitating his autocratic paternalistic rule. By contrast, Husayn's British training instilled in him the Western ideas of democracy: political parties and parliamentary sovereignty. However, despite the differences in orientation, Husayn followed in Abdullah's footsteps. He relied on the elder statesmen who were trained in

Abdullah's service to implement his policies.   Ruling the country riddled with crisis, Husayn applied all his powers, and until 1967, when the P.L.O. challenged his authority, he was a strong ruler.

During the last two decades, the Palestinian majority wanted to dominate the politics of Jordan.   They were, for the most part, not loyal to the Hashemites whom they considered selfish and an obstacle to Arab unity, a unity which they favoured to Jordanian parochial nationalism.

To appease the opposition, the 1953 law permitted the establishment of political parties.   In theory, any party could be allowed to operate but, in reality, only the conservative and moderate parties were in fact licensed.

In his encounter with the nationalists, Husayn sensed that opposition to Abdullah was of a different nature.   After the rise of Nasser to Arab leadership, popular allegiance to the Hashemites was determined by one factor alone—Jordan relationship with Egypt.   King Husayn enjoyed full support of both, the army and the subjects, as long as he maintained cooperative relations with Nasser.   He realized that sixty-five per cent of the population were attracted to Pan-Arabism represented in Nasser's leadership.   Since this popular force appeared potentially dangerous to the security of the state, his solution was to integrate politically the leaders of the opposition into the elite of the state.   Although he limited their influence by refusing to appoint them in the major organs of the state—which remained exclusively for the Transjordanians—his liberalization and integration policy may have been his greatest achievement, since it narrowed the gap between the pro-monarchial Transjordanian leadership and the emerging West Bank leadership.   However, this policy almost cost him his throne, as the pro-Nasser nationalists controlled the Cabinet and the Parliament, and tried to alter the direction of Jordan's foreign policy to a purely Arab one.

Suppressing the opposition, regardless of the method, gained for Jordan the description of a garrison state, because coercion, rather than consensus for political action and for ruling, appeared to dominate.   This attitude was made possible as both kings were supported by the army—the backbone of the monarchy.   Having exercised *de facto* control of the state, the army became the final arbiter of political power in the country.   Subsidized and patronized by the kings, it became the ally of the Palace and the guardian of the throne. In particular, the kings have depended upon the Bedouin elements who believed that since the Hashemites were the direct descendants of the Prophet, disloyalty was a sinful act. With such unswerving loyalty, the kings ruled fairly autocratically, as they felt safe against revolutionary thinking in the military establishment.

Before annexation, the army was not involved in politics. With the infusion of new population and by offering all groups the opportunity to serve, the army's political role acquired a new dimension. The Palestine question brought instability to Transjordan in the form of two related factors—Israeli aggression and the dissatisfaction of the Palestinians. Border incidents had their immediate effects inside the country, as the population blamed the government for its inability to defend its citizens. This inevitably caused the loyalty of the officers to waver. Consequently, solidarity was diluted as the army officers and personnel came to hold divergent political views ranging from the support of the monarchy to advocacy of republicanism.

King Abdullah was a "statesman" in the sense that he was a leader who thought of the future generations. His vision was to head a large Arab state. Although he was a competent strategist, he was also a poor tactician. However, he seemed unaware of the real political and power aspects of the situation. His autocratic mentality ignored Arab nationalism except on his own terms and the force of public opinion as both factors rejected autocratic rule and preferred representative democracy and republicanism. Nonetheless, his personality and political drive were factors to reckon with, as General Glubb related:

> When King Abdullah was alive, Syria and Saudi Arabia lived in fear of Jordan, and Egypt, with fourteen times her population, viewed her with anxiety as a rival. So immense can be the power and influence of one man.[1]

Abdullah's motives to create a Great Syria revolved round his personal ambition to rule an Arab kingdom as promised by Britain. Such a kingdom would provide sufficient economic and manpower capabilities to enable him to secure freedom from British dictation. At the same time, he would be able to compete effectively with the other Arab rulers. His dream may have been a reflection of the

---

[1] Glubb, *A Soldier with the Arabs*, p. 438.

idea of a Muslim Middle East bloc which would place him in a
respectable role in both Arab and Islamic worlds. Thus, his eagerness
to annex Eastern Palestine may have been due to his view that this
would be a first step to the realization of his political aspirations.

"Unrealism" appeared to be an important factor which Abdullah
did not take into consideration. Although Jordan's economic and
military capabilities were exceedingly inadequate for supporting his
political aspirations, he persisted in his efforts to realize a Hashemite
domination over Great Syria. Furthermore, the external environment
opposed, rather than eased, his programme. Thus, while it was practical to annex Arab Palestine which had no actual state or effective
leadership, it was impossible to sway the Syrians to his programme.
It must be recalled that the major obstacle had been his insistence on
monarchial and dynastic interests. Abdullah never won the initiative
in Syria, for splitting the Hashemites had contributed to their
ineffectiveness. His continued claim to Syria had done the Arabs
grave injury. While his policy revived enmity, it divided the Arabs
where it sought to unite them.

Safeguarding the security of the state is a paramount foreign
policy goal. A foreign policy is never totally divorced from security
considerations. The formation of the U.A.R. in 1958 heralded a new
dawn for Arab unity. The Egyptian extension in North Arabia, the
irresistible tide of Arab nationalism, and the clamour of the majority
of the Jordan population to join the U.A.R. presented Husayn
with a problem of significant consequences. Joining the U.A.R. meant
sacrificing the Hashemite claim to leadership as well as to his throne.
In order to preserve the Jordan entity, the Hashemite kings, in
response to the U.A.R. and their dynastic interests, established their
own union. One might surmize that the collapse of the United
Arab Republic might have been caused by the absence of Jordan.

Neither Abdullah nor Husayn was ever at ease with the other
Arab leaders. Having espoused Jordanian parochial nationalism
both suppressed opposition which appeared to be a potential threat
to their regimes and their monarchy. This sheds light on Abdullah's
disagreements with the Arab League which he considered an instrument to block his personal plans. Husayn, too, has never been at
ease with the Arab revolutionary regimes which he believes to have
constituted the major threat to Jordan's conservative monarchy.
This state of affairs inevitably resulted in the Arab cold war which
was tantamount to a contest for Arab leadership between the con-

servative and progressive regimes.

Both Kings, Abdullah and Husayn, have claimed Arab leadership as heirs of the Arab revolt of World War I and have considered Jordan the nucleus for a comprehensive Arab unity. Accordingly, they would agree to such a unity if they were to lead it. Contrariwise, they insisted on the preservation of the independence of monarchial Jordan against outside attempts at Arab unity, such as the U. A. R.

King Abdullah had developed his own brand of Arab nationalism, namely, Jordanian or Hashemite nationalism. Like Abdullah, Husayn considered Jordanian nationalism as true Arab nationalism, and declared that Jordan would be the "model Arab state." Thus, Husayn differed with Nasser on the issue of Arab nationalism. Nasser equated comprehensive Arab unity with Arab nationalism. To avoid sacrificing Jordan to an Arab unity in which the Hashemite monarchy would disappear, Husayn stressed local nationalism and, on many occasions, requested foreign intervention to achieve this goal. In this regard, he accused Nasser of using Arab unity as a pretext for Egyptian imperialism. To Husayn, acquiescence to Nasser's policies meant capitulation which he resisted.

Another aspect of Jordan's foreign policy under Husayn has been flexibility which enabled him to exhibit cordiality when it was in Jordan's interest. While Abdullah's policy was to trust no one except Iraq, it became a landmark in Husayn's foreign policy to associate with one state or a bloc, Arab or Western, when such action provided him with security of the monarchy. Husayn would associate with the Arab revolutionary regimes, such as Israel, to gain support against external threats, as was the case on 30 May 1967. On the other hand, he would associate with the conservative monarchial, Saudi Arabia and Yemen against the progressive regimes, as was the case in the Yemeni War.

One of Jordan's chronic problems has been that of the economy. Since the state has been unviable economically, its dependence on external assistance has, to a large degree, influenced the direction of its foreign relations. The subservience of King Abdullah and Husayn to Britain was, in the main, occasioned by Jordan's dependence on British subsidy which had been the basic factor in the survival of the state.

Abdullah's peace negotiations with Israel had begun even before hostilities erupted in 1948, and continued during and after the war. His rationale was that Jordan's military and economic capabilities could not sustain prolonged hostilities. Jordan's economy depended on peace with Israel, for hostilities meant economic blockade of land-locked Jordan. Traditionally, Jordan's trade was received at ports on the Mediterranean Sea. In the absence of peace, Jordan was left with two alternatives: to pay transit duties to Lebanon and Syria, or to use its southern port of Aqaba through the Suez Canal. In both cases, Jordan's economy would suffer. Thus, peace talks with Israel became an urgent matter. Abdullah's peace proposals included giving Jordan port privileges on the Mediterranean Sea and the concluding of a non-aggression pact. Furthermore, Abdullah had other motives. By finalizing peace, Israel would recognize his control of Eastern Palestine. Once this goal was accomplished, Jordan would be recognized by foreign powers and would be admitted into the U. N. Thus, economic assistance would be forthcoming, particularly from the U.S. and through the U.N.

When Britain decided to restore its political influence in the Arab World through the Baghdad Pact, Husayn became determined to join the alliance through which large amounts of economic assistance, sorely needed for developmental projects, were promised. However, the violent opposition, Arab nationalism, and anti-British feeling forced Husayn to abandon the idea.

The termination of the British subsidy in 1957, left Jordan at the mercy of the Arab states. Husayn dreaded dependence on them, for such dependence would inevitably put the monarchy and the country's destiny in the hands of the Arabs. His foreign policy would have to be in line with the contributing states. Accordingly, he preferred dependence on Britain instead. He might have been of the opinion that while Britain would share his interest in preserving the independence of the Hashemite dynasty, the Arabs—Saudi Arabia, Egypt, and Syria (traditional rivals of the Hashemites)—might well bring to an end Jordan as a state.

To free himself from his critical situation, Husayn played the American game by declaring that the Nabulsi Cabinet and Parliament as well as the army had been infiltrated by Communists, and that Communism was the major cause for instability in Jordan. Under the protective eye of the U.S.A., Husayn executed his coup against the nationalists and the army, thus bringing Jordan within the American sphere of influence. Although Husayn encountered the same opposition when he planned to adhere to the Eisenhower Doctrine, he nonetheless, became the recipient of an American subsidy replacing the Arab aid. At the same time, the independence and territorial integrity of Jordan were preserved, but at the cost of perpetual internal instability, for the Arab nationalists interpreted such an association as the return of Western colonialism in other forms, aiming at dividing the Arabs when they needed unity most.

The future of Jordan remains uncertain. Its independence is being permanently threatened by external as well as internal pressures: the threat of an Israeli invasion and Arab nationalism, both aiming at destroying Jordan's sovereignty. Significantly, the major Arab protagonists on the one hand and Israel on the other are not convinced that Jordan, as a buffer state, has outlived its usefulness. The Palestine Fedayeen Movement has developed into a significant political and military force challenging Husayn's regime and has become his main concern and worry.[2] Ironically, while the Arab nationalists and Husayn consider Israel the main threat to the Arab World, the existence of Jordan as an independent state has been contingent upon the continued survival of the state of Israel. Fearing that a change in Jordan's political identity would increase the threat to its security, Israel often threatened to intervene.

Despite the varied negative factors governing its survival, Jordan continues to exist. This may be attributed to the personality, courage, determination and political finesse of King Abdullah and King Husayn. However, the course of events in Jordan will be determined by the general conditions in the Middle East and the world situation. So long as Israel continues to hold the military and the political balance in the region and the Arabs remain disunited, Jordan's political status is not likely to change.

[2] The events of September 1970 resulted in eliminating all Fedayeen activities inside Jordan.

BIBLIOGRAPHY

BIBLIOGRAPHY

Primary Sources

DOCUMENTS

JORDAN

Al-Husayn Bin Talal (Collection of King Husayn's Speeches, Messages and Communications), Publisher, 1957.

HUSAYN, KING OF JORDAN, *Al-Qawmiyiah Al-Arabiyiah* (Arab Nationalism), Amman: Ministry of Information, 1960.

——, *Al-Risalah Al-Malakiyiah*, The Royal Message, Amman: Ministry of Information, 1968.

——, *Speech at the U. N. General Assembly Emergency Session, June 26, 1967*, Amman: Ministry of Information, 1967.

——, *Speech at the Press Club, Washington, D. C., November 7, 1967*, Amman: Ministry of Information, 1967.

——, *Speech at the Press Club, Washington, D.C., April 9, 1968*, Amman: Ministry of Information, 1969.

JORDAN MINISTRY OF INFORMATION, *Al-Urdun Wa-Al-Qadiyiah Al-Filistiniyiah Wa Al-Alaqat Al-Arabiyiah* (Jordan, the Palestine Question and Arab Relations), Amman: no publisher, no date.

——, *Kalimat Al-Husayn: July 1967 to July 1968* (The Words of Husayn), Amman: Al-Mutba'ah Al-Hashimiyiah, 1968.

JORDAN CHAMBER OF DEPUTIES, *Al-Jaridah Al-Rasmiyiah* (The Official Gazette), 1947-1968.

Muthakkirat Majlis Al-Nuwwab (Proceedings of the House of Representatives), 1947-1968.

Suriyya Al-Kubra: Al-Kitab Al-Urdani Al-Abyad (Greater Syria: The Jordanian White Paper), Amman: 1947.

JORDAN MINISTRY OF INFORMATION, *Yawm Al-Naksah* (The Day of the Setback), Amman: Al-Mutba'ah Al-Wataniyyiah, 1969.

ISRAEL

EBAN, ABBA, *Speech in the General Assembly, June 1967.*

——, *Speech in the General Assembly, September 25, 1967.*

——, *Speech in the General Assembly, October 8, 1968.*

——, *Speech in the General Assembly, September 19, 1969.*

——, *Speech in the Security Council, June 6, 1967.*

——, *Speech at the Security Council, November 13, 1967.*

Israel Government Year Book, 1951, 1952, 1956, 1958, and 1959.

Jerusalem and the United Nations, Washington, D. C.: Office of Information, July 1953.

ISRAEL: MINISTRY OF FOREIGN AFFAIRS, *The Arab Plan to Divert the Headwaters of the River Jordan*, April 1965.

THE JEWISH AGENCY FOR PALESTINE, *Statistical Handbook of Jewish Palestine*, 1947.

MEIR, GOLDA, *Speech before the Israel Parliament, May 5, 1967*.
——, Interview on "Meet the Press," September 28, 1969.

GREAT BRITAIN
BUTLER, ROHAN AND WOODWARD, E. L., (editors), *Documents on British Foreign Policy*, 1919-1939, London: H. M. Stationery Office, 1952.
British and Foreign State Papers, Vol. CLXIII (1957-1958).
British and Foreign State Papers, Vol. CXLVI (1946).
British and Foreign State Papers, Vol. CLI (1948).
British and Foreign State Papers, Vol. CLXI (1955-1956).
Parliamentary Debates (5th series, Commons), Vol. CCDXIII.
Parliamentary Debates (5th series, Commons), Vol. CD.
Parliamentary Debates (5th series, Commons), Vol. CDLI.
Parliamentary Debates (5th series, Commons), Vol. DXXXVII.
Parliamentary Debates (5th series, Commons), Vol. DXLVIII.
Parliamentary Debates (5th series, Commons), Vol. DXLIX.
Parliamentary Debates (5th series, Commons), Vol. DXCI.
Parliamentary Papers (Correspondence of the Colonial Office with the Palestine Arab Delegation and the Zionist Organisation), Cmd. 1700. 1922.
Parliamentary Papers (Palestine Royal Commission on Report, Peel), Cmd. 5479. 1937.

ROYAL INSTITUTE OF INTERNATIONAL AFFAIRS, *Documents on International Affairs*, 1955, 1956 and 1957, London: Oxford University Press, 1960.

UNITED NATIONS
General Assembly Official Records, 1956.
General Assembly Official Records, 1958.
General Assembly Official Records Annexes, "United Nations Emergency Force Report of the Secretary-General," Agenda Item 21, Document A/6406, 1966.
General Assembly Official Records, Document A/6730, 1967.
General Assembly Official Records, "Introduction to the Annual Report of the Secretary-General on the Work of the Organization," Document A/7201, June 16, 1967.
General Assembly Official Records, 5th Emergency Special Session, Supplement 1, Annexes.
Report to the General Assembly, Special Committee on Palestine, Vol. I, Document A/364, 1947.
Security Council Official Records, 301st meeting, No. 72, 3rd year, 1948.
Security Council Official Records, Document S/801, 1948.

Security Council Official Records, Document S/1058, October 26, 1948.
Security Council Official Records, Supplement for July, August and September, 1967, Document S/8229.
Security Council Official Records, Document S/7879, 1967.
Security Council Official Records, Document S/7893, 1967.
Security Council Official Records, Document S/8052, 1967.
Security Council Official Records, Document S/8109, August 3, 1967.
Security Council Official Records, Document S/8247, 1967.
Security Council Official Records, Documents S/8549, April 18, 1968.
Security Council Official Records, Document S/8650, June 21, 1968.
Security Council Provisional Verbatim Record, October 14, 1966.
Trusteeship Council Official Records, Annex I, 4th year, 6th session, Document T/431, January 5, 1950.
Trusteeship Council Official Records, Annex 1, 4th year, 6th session, Document T/487, March 4, 1950.

UNITED STATES

DULLES, JOHN FOSTER, "Report on the Near East, " *U. S. Department of State Bulletin,* XXVIII, June 15, 1953.

FLANDERS, SENATOR RALPH E., "We are off the Summit—Let Us Strengthen the Foundations," *Congressional Record,* Senate, 85th Congress, Second Session, CIV, Pt. 13, August 6, 1958, 16324.

STEBBINS, RICHARD (ed.), *Documents on American Foreign Relations,* New York: Harper & Brothers, 1961.

U.S. A. I. D., *U. S. Assistance to Jordan,* Published, December 24, 1968.
——, *U. S. Economic Assistance to Jordan,* 1952-1962, Amman: 1962.
Congressional Record, 1947-1968.
U. S. DEPARTMENT OF STATE, *American Foreign Policy: 1950-1955, Basic Documents,* Washington, D. C.: United States Government Printing Office, 1957.
——, *Digest of International Law,* Vol. I, Washington, D. C.: United States Government Printing Office, 1963.
——, *Issues in U.S. Foreign Policy,* No. 1: *The Middle East,* Washington, D. C.: United States Government Printing Office.
——, *United States Policy in the Middle East, September 1956-June 1957,* New York: Greenwood Press, 1968.
Department of State Bulletin, XIV, No. 357, May 5, 1946.
Department of State Bulletin, XXII February 20, 1950.
Department of State Bulletin, XXVIII, 1953.
Department of State Bulletin, XXXI, 1954.
Department of State Bulletin, XXXV, July, 1956.
Department of State Bulletin, XXXI, 1954.
Department of State Bulletin, XXXV, July, 1956.
Department of State Bulletin, XXXVI, January 21, 1957.
Department of State Bulletin, XXXVII, No. 945, 1957.

Department of State Press Release, No. 237, April 23, 1957.

U. S. SENATE, *The President's Proposal on the Middle East*, Hearings before the Committee on Foreign Relations and the Committee on Armed Services. U. S. Senate, 85th Congress, First Session on S. J. Res. 19 and H. R. Res. 117, 1957. Washington D. C.: United States Government Printing Office, 1957.

——, *The President's Proposal on the Middle East*, Hearings before the Committee on Foreign Relations and Committee on Armed Services, 85th Congress, First Session on S. J. Res. 19 and H. J. Res. 117, Part II, February 5, 6, 7, 8 and 11, 1957. Washington D.C.: United States Government Printing Office, 1957.

——, *Review of Foreign Policy*, 1958, Hearing before the Committee on Foreign Relations, United States Senate, 85th Congress, Second Session on Foreign Policy (February 3–March 10, 1958), Washington, D. C.: United States Government Printing Office, 1958.

——, *Situation in the Middle East*, Hearing before the Committee on Foreign Relations, 84th Congress, Second Session, February 24, 1956, Washington, D.C.: United States Government Printing Office, 1956.

GENERAL

KHALIL, MUHAMMAD, *The Arab States and the Arab League: A Documentary Record*, 2 Vols., Beirut: Khayats, 1962.

HUREWITZ, J. C., *Diplomacy in the Near and Middle East*, Vol. I, Princeton, N. J.: Van Nostrand Co., 1956.

MAGNUS, RALPH H. (ed.), *Documents on the Middle East*, Washington, D. C.: American Enterprise Institute, 1969.

Parliamentary Debates (Lebanon), February 12, 1947.

MEMOIRS

ABDULLAH BIN AL-HUSAYN, *Al-Amali Al-Siyassiah* (Political Aspirations), Amman, n.p., 1939.

ABDULLAH, KING OF JORDAN, *My Memoirs Completed*, Washington, D. C.: American Council of Learned Societies, 1954.

ABU-AL-SHA'AR, AMEEN, *Muthakkirat Al-Malik Abdullah* (Memoirs of King Abdullah), Sao Paolo: n.p. 1953.

——, *Muthakkirat Al-Malik Abdullah Bin Al-Husayn* (Memoirs of King Abdullah), 4th ed. Amman: Al-Mutba'ah Al-Hashimiyyiah, 1965.

AL-TALL, ABDULLAH, *Karithat Filistin: Muthakkirat Abdullah Al-Tall*, Cairo: n.p. 1959.

BAR ZOHAR, MICHEAL, *The Armed Prophet: Biography of Ben Gurion*, London: Arthur Baker, Ltd., 1967.

BEAL, ROBINSON, *John Foster Dulles: A Biography*, New York: Harper, 1957.
BERNADOTTE, FOLKE, *To Jerusalem*, London: Hodder-Stoughton, 1951.
BURNS, E. L. M., *Between Arab and Israeli*, London: Harrap, 1962.

EDEN, ANTHONY, *Full Circle*, Cambridge: Houghton Mifflin, 1960.

HUSAYN, KING OF JORDAN, *Uneasy Lies The Head*, New York: Geis, 1962.
HUTCHINSON, ELMO, *Violent Truce*, New York: Adair-Devine, 1956.

AL-JAMALI, FADHIL, M., *Thikrayat Wa Ibar* (Recollections and Lessons), Beirut: Dar Al-Kitab Al-Jadid, 1965.

KHARSA, MUSTAFA, *Muthakkirat Al-Malik Abdullah* (Memoirs of King Abdullah), Beirut: Dar Al-Talayi'a, 1965.
KIRKBRIDE, ALEC, *A Crackle of Thorns: Experiences in The Middle East*, London: John Murray, 1965.

LAU-LAVIE, NAPHATALI, *Moshe Dayan: A Biography*, London: Valentine, Mitchel, 1968.

AL-MAJALI, HAZZAA', *Muthakkirati* (My Memoirs), n.p., 1960.
——, *Qissat Muhadathat Templer* (The Story of the Templer Talks), n.p., n.d.
McDONALD, JAMES, *My Mission in Israel*, New York: Simon and Schuster, 1951.

AL-NASSER, GAMAL ABDEL, *Falsafat Al-Thawrah* (The Philosophy of the Revolution), Cairo, 1954.

SYRKIN, MARIE, *Way of Valour: A Biography of Golda Meyerson*, New York: Putnam, 1955.

VAN HORN, CARL, *Soldiering For Peace*, New York: David McKay, 1967.
VANCE, VICK AND LAUER, PIERRE, *Husayn of Jordan: My War With Israel*, New York: William Morrow and Company, 1969.

Secondary Sources

BOOKS

ABBOUSHI, W.F., *Political Systems of the Middle East in the Twentieth Century*, New York: Dodd-Mead, 1970.
ABDUL MUN'IM, MOHAMMAD FAYSAL, *Nahnu Wa Israel* (We and Israel), Dar Al-Sha'ab, Cairo, 1968.
ABIDI, AQIL HAYDAR HASAN, *Jordan: A Political Study*, New York: Asia Publishing House, 1965.
ALI, MOHAMMAD ALI, *Israel Qa'dah Udwaniyyiah* (Israel: A Base for Aggression), Al-Dar Al-Qawmiyyiah, Cairo, 1964.

ALI, ALI MOHAMMAD, *Nahrul Urdun Wa Al-Mu'amarah Al-Suhyouniyyiah* (The Jordan River and the Zionist Conspiracy), Cairo: National Publishing House, n.d.

ANTONIUS, GEORGE, *The Arab Awakening*, 3rd ed., New York: Capricorn Books, 1965.

AL-ARABI, MOHAMMAD, *Kayfa Sana'a Al-Ingiliz Al-Urdun* (How the British Created Jordan), Cairo: n.p., 1960.

ARIF AL-ARIF, *Al-Nakbah* (The Disaster), Beirut: n.p., n.d.

ARSALAN, SHAKEEB, *Al-Wahdah* (Unity), Damascus: Arab Union, 1937.

AVNERY, URI, *Israel Without Zionists: A Plea For Peace in the Middle East,* New York: Macmillan, 1968.

BAHA'UDDIN, AHMAD, *Iktirah Dawlat Filistin* (A Proposal For a Palestine State), Beirut: Al-Sharikah Al-Haditahah Lil-Tiba'ah, 1968.

BENERJI, J. K., *The Middle East in World Politics,* Calcutta: World Press, 1960.

BARRACLOUGH, G., *Survey of International Affairs: 1956-58*, London: Oxford University Press, 1962.

BARRAWI, RASHEED, *Mashru' Syriyyiah Al-Kubra* (The Great Syria Plan), Cairo: Makatabat Al-Nahadah, 1947.

BEN GURION, DAVID, *Rebirth and Destiny of Israel*, New York: Philosophical Library, 1954.

BERGER, EARL, *The Covenant and the Sword*, Toronto: University of Toronto Press, 1965.

BILBY, KENNETH, *New Star in the East*, New York: Garden City, Doubleday, 1950.

BIRDWOOD, CHRISTOPHER, *Nuri As-Sa'd*, London: Cassel, 1959.

BROCKELMAN, CARL, *History of the Islamic People*, New York: Capricorn Books, 1960.

BULLARD, READER, *Britain and the Middle East,* London: Hutchinson, University Library, 1952.

BURDETT, WINSTON, *Encounter in the Middle East,* New York: Atheneum, 1969.

CAMPBELL, JOHN, *Defense of the Middle East,* Revised ed., New York: Praeger, 1960.

CHACE, JAMES, (ed.), *Conflict in the Middle East,* New York: H. W. Wilson Company, 1969.

CHILDERS, ERSKINE, B., "Palestine: The Broken Triangle," *Modernization of the Arab World*, Edited by J. H. Thompson and R. D. Reischauer, Princeton: Nostrand, 1966.

CHRISTMAN, HENRY, *The State Papers of Levi Eshkol*, New York: Funk & Wagnals, 1969.

CRABB, CEICIL, *American Foreign Policy in the Nuclear Age,* 2nd ed., New York: Harper, 1965.

DANN, URIEL, *Iraq Under Qassim,* New York, Praeger, 1969.

DARWAZAH, MOHAMMAD IZZAT, *Hawla Al-Harakah Al-Arabiyyiah* (Concerning the Arab Movement), 6 Vols., Damascus, 1950.

——, *Mashakil Al-Aalam Al-Arabi* (Problems of the Arab World), Damascus: Dar Al-Nahdah, 1953.

DAYAN, MOSHE, *Diary of the Sinai Campaign*, New York: Harper and Row, 1965.
DEARDEN, ANN, *Jordan*, London: Robert Hale, 1958.
DECONDE, ALEXANDER, *A History of American Foreign Policy*, New York: Scribner, 1963.
DIB, G. M., *The Arab Bloc in the United Nations*, Amsterdam: Djambatan, 1956.
DRAPER, THEODORE, *Israel and World Politics*, New York: The Viking Press, 1968.

EDEN, ANTHONY, *The Suez Canal Crisis of 1956*, Boston: Beacon Press, 1968.
ELLIS, HARRY, *Challenge in the Middle East: Communist Influence and American Foreign Policy*, New York: Ronald Press, 1960.
EMERSON, RUPERT, *From Empire to Nation*, Boston: Beacon Press, 1959.
ERSKINE, STEWART, *King Faisal of Iraq*, London: Hutchinson, 1933.
EYTAN, WALTER, *The First Ten Years: A Diplomatic History of Israel*, New York: Simon and Schuster, 1958.

FARAJ, MOHAMMAD, *Al-Ummah Al-Arabiyyiah Ala Al-Tariq Ila Wahdat Al-Hadaf* (The Arab National on the Road to Unity of Purpose), Cairo: Dar Al-Fikr Al-Arabi, 1964.
FINER, HERMAN, *Dulles Over Suez*, Chicago: Quadrangle Books, 1964.
FISHER, CAROL, *The Middle East Crisis*, Washington: The Middle East Institute, 1959.
——AND KRINSKY, FRED, *Middle East in Crisis: A Historical and Documentary Review*, New York: Syracuse University Press, 1959.
FISHER, SIDNEY, *The Middle East: A History*, New York: Knoph, 1969.
FITZSIMMONS, M. A., *Empire By Treaty*, Notre Dame: Notre Dame University Press, 1964.
FLIESS, PETER, *International Relations in a Bipolar World*, New York: Random House, 1968.
FRYE, RICHARD, (ed.), *The Near East and the Great Powers*, Cambridge: Harvard University Press, 1955.

GABBAY, RONY E., *A Political Study of the Arab-Jewish Conflict: The Arab Refugee Problem*, Paris: Libraire Minard, 1959.
GALLMAN, WELDEMAR, *Iraq Under General Nuri*, Baltimore: John Hopkins University Press, 1964.
GERVASI, FRANK, *The Case for Israel*, New York: The Viking Press, 1967.
GHANIM, MOHAMMAD HAFEZ, *Al-Alaqat Al-Dawliyyiah Al-Arabiyyiah* (Arab International Relations), Nahdat Misr, Cairo, 1965.
GHAZAL, BURHAN, *Al-Ahdaf Al-Qawmiyyiah Wa Al-Dawliyyiah Li Jami'at Al-Duwal Al-Arabiyyiah* (National and International Objectives of the League of Arab State), Damascus: Hashimiyyiah Press, 1953.
GHOBASHY, OMAR Z., *The Development of the Jordan River*, New York: Arab Information Center, 1961.
GLUBB, JOHN B., *Britain and the Arabs*, London: Hodder and Stoughton, 1959.
——, *A Soldier With the Arabs*, New York: Harper Brother, 1957.
——, *The Story of the Arab Legion*, London: Hodder and Stoughton, 1948.

HAFEZ, MAHMOUD, *Istiragiat Al-Gharb Fi Al-Watan Al-Arabi* (Western Strategy in the Arab World), Cairo: Al-Mutba'ah Al-Faniyyiah Al-Hadithah, 1967.

HAKIM, SAMI, *Mithaq Jami'at Al-Duwal Al-Arabiyyiah Wa Al-Wahdah Al-Arabiyyiah* (The Charter of the Arab League and Arab Unity), Cairo: Anglo-Egyptian Press, 1966.

HAMMOND, PAUL, *The Cold War Years: American Foreign Policy Since 1945,* New York: Harcourt, 1969.

HAYKAL, MOHAMMAD HASANAYN, *Khabaya Al-Suez* (Secrets of Suez), Cairo: Dar Al-Asr Al-Hadith, 1967.

——, *Nahnu Wa Amrika* (We and America), Dar Al-Asr Al-Hadith, Cairo, 1967.

HEBREW UNIVERSITY, *Israel and the United Nations,* New York: Manhattan Publishing Company, 1956.

HERTZBERG, ARTHUR, (ed.), *The Zionist Idea,* New York: Doubleday, 1959.

HODES, AUBREY, *Dialogue With Ishmael: Israel's Future in the Middle East,* New York: Funk & Wagnals, 1968.

HOURANI, ALBERT, *Syria and Lebanon,* New York: Oxford University Press, 1946.

HOWARD, MICHEAL AND HUNTER, ROBERT, *Israel and the Arabs: The Crisis of 1967,* Adelphi Papers, No. 41, London: The Institute of Strategic Studies, October, 1967.

HUREWITZ, J. C., *Middle East Politics: The Military Dimension,* New York: Praeger, 1969.

——, *Middle Eastern Dilemma,* New York: Harper Brothers, 1953.

AL-HUSARI, SATI, *Al-Urubah Awwalan* (Arabism First), Beirut: Dar Al Ilm Lilmalayeen, 1955.

IONIDES, MICHAEL, *Divide and Lose: The Arab Revolt, 1955-58,* London: Geoffrey Bles, 1960.

IRELAND, PHILIP, *Iraq: A Study in Political Development,* New York: The Macmillan Company, 1938.

——, *The Near East,* Chicago: University of Chicago Press, 1942.

IZZIDDIN, NAGLA, *The Arab World,* Chicago: Henry Regnery, 1953.

JARVIS, CLAUDE SCUDAMORE, *Arab Command: The Biography of F. W. Peak Pasha,* London: Hutchinson, 1943.

KAMIL, MISHIL, *Al-Mu'amarah al-Amrikiyah fial-Urdun* (The American Conspiracy in Jordan), Cairo: Dar al-Fikr, 1957.

KERR, MALCOLM, *The Arab Cold War,* New York: Oxford University Press, 1967.

——, *The Middle East Conflict,* New York: Foreign Policy Association, 1969.

KHADDOURI, MAJID, "Fertile Crescent Unity," *The Near East and the Great Powers,* Edited by R. N. Frye, Cambridge, Mass.: Harvard University Press, 1955.

——, *Independent Iraq,* London: Oxford University Press, 1960.

KHADDURI, MAJIDA, *The Arab-Israeli Impasse,* Washington, D. C.: Robert Luce Inc., 1968.

KHATTAB, MAHMOUD, *Al-Wahdah al-Askariyyiah al-Arabiyyiah* (Arab Military Unity), Cairo: Modern Technical Press, 1969.

KHOURI, BISHARA, *Haqa'iq Lubnaniyyiah* (Facts About Lebanon), Beirut: Awraq Lubnaniyyiah, 1960.

KHOURI, FRED J., *The Arab-Israeli Dilemma*, Syracuse, N. Y.: Syracuse University Press, 1968.

KILANI, HAYTHAM, *Al-Mawqi'al-Istiratigi al-Arabi* (The Strategic Position of the Arab World), Damascus: Wizarat al-Thakafah wal Irshad, 1966.

KIMCHE, DAVID AND BAWLY, DAN, *The Sand Storm: The Arab-Israeli War of 1967*, New York: Stein and Day, 1968.

KIMCHE, JON AND DAVID, *Both Sides of the Hill: Britain and Palestine War*, London: Secker & Warburg, 1960.

——, *A Clash of Destinies*, New York: Praeger, 1960.

KIRK, GEORGE, *Contemporary Arab Politics*, New York: Praeger, 1961.

——, *The Middle East, 1845-1950*, London: Oxford University Press, 1954.

——, *The Middle East in the War, 1939-1946*, London: Oxford University Press, 1952.

LACQUEUR, WALTER Z., *Communism and Nationalism in the Middle East*, New York: Praeger, 1956.

LATHAM, EDWARD, *Crisis in the Middle East*, New York: Wilson, 1952.

LAUTERPACHT, ELIHU, *Jerusalem and the Holy Places*, London: October, 1968.

LENCZOWSKI, GEORGE, *The Middle East in World Affairs*, Ithaca, N.Y.: Cornell University Press, 1956.

——, *Oil and State in the Middle East*, Ithaca, N.Y.: Cornell University Press, 1960.

——, (ed.), *United States Interest in the Middle East*, Washington, D. C.: American Enterprise Institute, 1968.

LEWIS, BERNARD, *The Middle East and the West*, Bloomington: Indiana University Press, 1964.

LILIENTHAL, ALFRED, *Other Side of the Coin*, New York: Devin-Adair, 1965.

LONGRIGG, STEPHEN, *The Middle East*, Chicago: Aldine, 1963.

AL-MADI, MUNIB AND MUSA, SULEIMAN, *Tariekh al-Urdun Fi al-Qarn al-Ishrin* (History of Jordan in the Twentieth Century), Amman: n.p., 1959.

MERLIN, SAMUEL, *The Search For Peace in the Middle East*, New York: Thomas Yoseloff, 1968.

MONROE, ELIZABETH, *Britain's Moments in the Middle East, 1914-56*, Baltimore: John Hopkins University Press, 1963.

MORRIS, JAMES, *The Hashemite Kings*, New York: Pantheon, 1959.

MUSTAFA, HASAN, *Al-Musa'adat Al-Askariyyiah Li Israel* (American Military Assistance to Israel), Beirut: Dar Al-Talai', 1965.

MUSTAPHA, HASAN, *Al-Ta'awun Al-Askari Al-Arabi* (Arab Military Cooperation), Beirut: Dar Al-Talai, 1965.

AL-NASHASHIBI, NAIR EDDIN, *Matha Jara Fi Al-Sharq Al-Awsat* (What Happened in the Middle East), Beirut: Al-Maktab Al-Tigari, 1961.

O'BALLANCE, EDGER, *The Arab-Israeli War, 1948*, New York: Praeger, 1957.

PEAK, F. G., *A History of Jordan and Its Tribes*, Miami, 1958.

PERETZ, DON, *The Middle East Today*, New York: Holt, 1964.

PFAFF, RICHARD, *Jerusalem: Keystone of an Arab-Israeli Settlement,* Washington: American Enterprise Institute, 1969.

PHILLIPS, P. G., *The Hashemite Kingdom of Jordan,* Chicago: University of Chicago Press, 1954.

PRITTIE, TERRENCE, *Eshkol: The Man and The Nation,* New York: Pitman Publishing Corporation, 1969.

——, *Israel: Miracle in the Desert,* Revised ed., Baltimore: Penguine Books, 1968.

PAUX, GABRIEL, *Deux Anne'es Au Levant Souvenirs De Syrie et du Liban, 1939-40,* Paris, 1942.

RATIB, AISHA, *Al- Alaqat Al-Dawliyyah Al-Arabiyyiah* (Arab International Relations), Cairo: Dar Al-Nahdah Al-Arabiyyiah, 1968.

RIF'AT, MOHAMMAD, *Al-Tawjih Al-Siyasi Lilfikrah Al-Arabiyyiah Al-Hadithah* (Political Direction of the Modern Arab Thought), Cairo: Dar Al-Ma'arif, 1964.

RIZK, EDWARD, *The River Jordan,* New York: Arab Information Center, 1962.

RODINSON, MAXIME, *Israel and the Arabs,* New York: Pantheon, 1968.

RONDOTT, PIERRE, *The Changing Pattern of the Middle East,* New York: Praeger, 1959.

SAFRAN, NADAV, *The United States and Israel,* Cambridge: Harvard University Press, 1963.

SAKRAN, FRANK, *Whose Jerusalem?* Washington: American Council on the Middle East, 1968.

SAYIGH, ANIS, *Al-Hashimiyyoun Wa Qadiyyiat Filistin* (The Hashemites and the Palestine Question), Beirut: Al-Maktabah Al-Asriyyiah, 1966.

——, *Al-Hashimiyyoun Wa Al-Thawrah Al-Arabiyyiah Al-Kubra* (The Hashemites and the Great Arab Revolt), Beirut: Modern Press, 1966.

——, *Min Faysal Al-Awwal Ila Abdel-Nasser* (From Faysal I to Abdel-Nasser), Beirut: Al-Mutba'ah Al-Asriyyiah, 1965.

SAYEGH, FAYEZ, *The Dynamics of Neutralism in the Arab World,* San Fransisco: Chandler, 1964.

——, *Arab Unity,* New York: Devine-Adaire, 1958.

SEALE, PATRICK. *The Struggle For Syria: A Study of Post-War Arab Politics 1945-58,* New York: Oxford, 1965.

SEATON, WILLIAMS, M. N., *Britain and the Arab States: A Survey of Anglo-Arab Relations 1920-48,* London: Luzac, 1948.

SHARABI, HASHIM, *Government and Politics of the Middle East in the Twentieth Century,* Princeton: Van Nostrand, 1962.

——, *Palestine and Israel,* New York: Pegasus, 1968.

SHARAYHAH, WADI, *Al-Tanmiyiah Al-Iqtisadiyyiah Fi Al-Urdun,* Cairo: Mutba'at Al-Nahdah Al-Jadidah, 1968.

SHMAYS, ABDUL-MUN'M, *Siyasat Adam Al-Inhiyaz* (Policy of Non-Alignment), Cairo: Al-Dar Al-Qawmiyyiah, 1964.

SHWADRAN, BENJAMIN, *Jordan: A State of Tension,* New York: Council For Middle Eastern Affairs Press, 1959.

SPARROW, GERALD, *Hussein of Jordan,* London: George Harrap Company Ltd., 1960.

STEIN, LEONARD, *The Balfour Declaration,* New York: Simon and Schuster, 1961.

STEVENS, GEORGIANA, *Jordan River Partition,* Stanford: Stanford University Press, 1965.

——, *The United States and the Middle East,* Englewood Cliffs: Prentice Hall, 1965.

STEVENS, RICHARD, *American Zionism and U.S. Foreign Policy, 1942-47,* New York: Pageant Press, 1962.

STOCK, ERNEST, *Israel on the Road to Sinai: 1949-1956,* Ithaca: Cornell University Press, 1967.

STOESSINGER, JOHN, G., *The United Nations and the Super-Powers,* 2nd ed., New York: Random House, 1970.

SULTAN, HAMID, *Al-Mushkilat Al-Qanuniyyiah Al-Mutafarri'ah An Qadiyyiat Filistin* (The Legal Problems Resulting from the Palestine Question), Cairo: Mutba'at Al-Nahdah Al-Jadid, 1967.

SYKES, CHRISTOPHER, *Crossroad to Israel,* London: Collins, 1965.

SYRKIN, MARIE, *Golda Meir: Woman with A Cause,* New York: Putnam, 1963.

AL-TANDAWI, SAMIR, *Ila Ayna Yattagihu Al-Urdun* (Which Direction Will Jordan Take), Cairo: n.p., 1958.

TAYI, AHMAD, *Safahat Matwiyyiah An Filistin* (Folded Pages on Palestine), Cairo: Al-Sha'ab Publishing House, n.d.

THAYER, CHARLES, *Diplomat,* New York: Harper, 1959.

THOMPSON, J. H. and REISCHAUER, R. D., *Modernization of the Arab World,* New York: Nostrand, 1966.

TORREY, GORDON, *Syrian Politics and the Military, 1945-58,* Columbus: Ohio State Press, 1964.

TUBJI, AHMAD KAMEL, *Al-Quwwat Al-Musallah Al-Arabiyyiah Wa Al-Salam Fi Al-Yaman* (Arab Armed Forces and the Peace in Yemen), Cairo: Al-Dar Al-Qawmiyyiah Lil-Tiba'ah Wal-Nashr, 1966.

TUQAN, BAHA-UDDIN, *A Short History of Jordan,* London: Luzac, 1945.

VATIKIOTIS, P. J., *The Egyptian Army in Politics,* Bloomington: Indiana University Press, 1961.

——, *Politics and the Military in Jordan: A Study of the Arab Legion, 1921-57,* New York: Praeger, 1967.

WARD, BARBARA, *The Rich Nations and the Poor Nations,* New York: Norton, 1962.

WEAVER, DENNIS, *Arabian Destiny,* Fair Lawn: Essential Books, 1958.

WHEELOCK, KEITH, *Nasser's New Egypt,* New York: Praeger, 1960.

WOOD, DAVID, *The Middle East and the Arab World: The Military Context,* London: Adelphi Papers, The Institute of Strategic Studies, 1965.

WOODHOUSE, C. M., *British Foreign Policy Since the Second World War,* London: Hutchinson, 1961.

WYNN, WILTON, *Nasser of Egypt: The Search for Dignity,* Cambridge: Arlington Books, 1959.

YAHYA, JALAL, *Al-Aalam Al-Arabi Al-Hadith Munthu Al-Harb Al-Aalamiyyiah*

Al-Thaniyiah (The Arab World Since World War II), Cairo: Dar Al-Ma'arif, 1967.

YOUNG, PETER, *The Israeli Campaign, 1967*, London: Kimber, 1967.

ZEIN, ZEIN, *The Struggle for Arab Independence*, Beirut: Khayyat, 1960.
ZIADAH, NICOLA, *Syria and Lebanon*, New York: Praeger, 1957.

NEWSPAPERS

Al-Ahram, Cairo, 1952, 1956, 1957, 1966, 1967.

BOCHKARYOV, Y., "The Jordan Events," *The New Times,* Moscow, May 9, 1957.

DAYAN, MOSHE, "A Soldier Reflects on Peace Hopes," *Jerusalem Post*, December 30, 1968.
Al-Difa'a, Amman, 1950, 1955, 1956, and 1957.

Filistin, Jerusalem, 1959, 1955, 1956, 1957 and 1959.
Al-Hayat, Beirut, April 21, 1957.
——, February 18, 1958.
——, April 1 and 2, 1960.
HEYKAL, MOHAMMAD, "Asl Al-Hikayah", *Al- Ahram*, January 6, 1967.
——, "Myths about Israel's Water Project," *Al-Ahram*, January 24, 1964.
——, "Tareeq Al-Malik," *Al-Ahram*, February 13, 1967.
Jerusalem Post, 1962, 1965, 1966, 1967 and 1968.
La Monde, 1954, 1966 and 1969.
Les Cahiers, Vols. V and VII.
London Times, 1946-1967.
Manchester Guardian, April 9, 1969.
——, May 8, 1969.
New York Herald Tribune, March 8, 1960.
New York Times, 1943-1969.
Oriento Moderno, 1936, 1939, 1947.

PERIODICALS

ABU-LUGHOD, IBRAHIM, "Israel's Arab Policy," *The Arab World*, XIV, Special Issue, No. 10-11.
ALAMI, MUSA, "The Lesson of Palestine," *Middle East Journal*, III, October, 1949.
ALAN, RAY, "Jordan: Rise and Fall of the Squirarchy," *Commentary*, XIII, March 1957.
"Anatomy of a Crisis," *New Outlook*, March, 1966.
AYAGU, ODEYO, "Africa's Dilemma in the Arab-Israeli Conflict," *Pan-African Journal*, I, No. 219, 1968.

CAMPBELL, JOHN C., "From Doctrine to Policy in the Middle East," *Foreign Affairs*, XXXV, No. 3, April 1957.

CHEJNE, ANWAR, "Egyptian Attitude towards Pan-Arabism," *Middle East Journal*, XI, Summer, 1957.

"Communism and Us," *The Scribe*, Cairo, II (May-June, 1961).

"Crossroads in the Arab League," *World Today*, IV.

DEES, JOSEPH, "Jordan's East Ghor Canal Project," *Middle East Journal*, XIII, No. 4, Autumn, 1959.

ELLIS, HARRY, "The Arab-Israeli Conflict Today," *The United States and the Middle East*, Englewood Cliffs, N. J.: Prentice Hall, 1964.

Economist, July 21, 1950; February 20, 1960; December 14, 1963; March 2, 1968; May 4, 1968; December 14, 1968.

FRERE, J. G., "Arab Chessboard," *Spectator*, June 7, 1946.

GHALI, BOUTRUS, "The Arab League, 1945-55," *International Conciliation*, May 1954.

HORTON, ALLEN, "The Arab-Israeli Conflict of June, 1967," *American University's Field Staff*, XIII, No. 2.

HOWARD, HARRY, "Middle Eastern Regional Organization: Problems and Prospects," *Proceedings of the Academy of Political Science*, XXIV, January 1952.

"Israel's Economy Slows Down," *New Outlook*, June 1966.

IVANOV, K., "Israel, Zionism and International Imperialism," *International Affairs*, Moscow, No. 6, June 1968.

Journal D'Egypte, Cairo, April 27, 1949; June 19, 1949.

KEDDOURI, ELLI, "Pan-Arabism and British Policy," *Political Quarterly*, XXVIII, April-June, 1957.

KHADDOURI, MAJID, "The Arab League as a Regional Arrangement," *American Journal of International Law*, Vol. 40, October 1946.

———, "Toward an Arab Union: The League of Arab States," *American Political Science Review*, Vol. 40, February 1946.

KIRK, GEORGE, "Cross Currents Within the Arab League," *World Today*, January 1948.

———, "The Syrian Crisis of 1957—Facts and Fiction," *International Affairs*, Vol. 36, January 1960.

KOCK, HOWARD, "June 1967: The Question of Aggression," *The Arab World*, June 1969.

K. S., "The Lebanese Crisis in Perspective," *World Today*, No. 14, 1958.

LAWRENCE, JOSEPH, "The Levant Chooses Socialism," *Middle Eastern Affairs*, IX, May 1968.

LENCZOWSKI, GEORGE, "Arab Bloc Realignments," *Current History*, December 1967.

LITTLE, TOM, "The Arab League: Area Assessment," *Middle East Journal,* X, No. 2, April 1956.

"Jordan and its Legion," *The Economist,* Vol. 59, No. 1, July 15, 1950.

LONGRIGG, S. H., "New Groupings Among the Arab States," *International Affairs,* Vol. 34, July 1958.

Middle Eastern Affairs, Vol. XIV, April 1962; February 1952; Vol. 12, May 1961; Vol. 9, June-July 1958; October 1958.

Middle East Journal, Fall, 1953.

Middle East Opinion, January 20, 1947; December 2, 1946.

"Middle East Stalemate," *Newsweek Magazine,* November 20, 1967.

MONKS, NOEL, "Trouble Builds up in the Middle East," *Daily Mail,* December 7, 1955.

DE MURVILLE MAURICE COUVE, *Vital Speeches,* Vol. 33, No. 19, July 15, 1967; Speech Before the United Nations General Assembly, June 22, 1967.

"Nasser and Arab Unity," *Editorial Research,* 1958.

New Outlook, Vol. 7, No.6; Vol. 9, No.4, September, 1968.

"Pan-Arab Challenge to Ankara," *The Economist,* Vol. 56, February 1, 1958.

PEAK, F. G., "Transjordan," *Journal of the Royal Central Asian Society,* XI, 1942, pp. 300ff.

PEARLMAN, M., "Fusion and Confusion: Arab Mergers and Realignment," *Middle East Affairs,* IX, April 1958.

——, "The Turkish-Arab Diplomatic Tangle," *Middle Eastern Affairs,* Vol. VII, January 1955.

PERLMUTTER, AMOS, "The Israeli Army in Politics," *World Politics,* XX, No. 4, July 1968.

"Political Trends in the Fertile Crescent," *World Today,* Vol. 12, June 1956.

RALEIGH, J. S., "The Middle East in 1956: A Political Survey," *Middle Eastern Affairs,* IX, March 1958.

——, "Ten Years of the Arab League," *Middle Eastern Affairs,* Vol. VI, March 1955.

ROSENNE, SHABATI, "Directions for a Middle East Settlement," *Law and Contemporary Problems,* Duke University Law Review, Winter, 1968.

SAMS, JAMES, F., "U. S. Policy in the Middle East Crisis," *Middle East Forum,* XLIII, No. 2, 3, 1967.

SHARABI, HASHIM, "Prelude to War: The Crisis of May-June, 1967," *The Arab World,* XIV, No. 10-11.

STEVENS, GEORGIANA, "Jordan River Valley," *International Conciliation,* No. 506 (Prepared for the Carnegie Endowment for Peace, 1956).

TOYNBEE, ARNOLD, "The British Mandate for Palestine," *Survey of International Affairs,* 1930.

"Transjordan and Iraq: Scheme for Union," *The Times Weekly,* 1946.

TUTSCH, HANS, "A Report from Jordan," *Swiss Review of World Affairs*, Vol. X, No. 11, February 1961.

World Today, Vol. IV, No. 1, January 1948.
WRIGHT, EDMUND, "Abdullah's Jordan: 1947-51," *Middle East Journal*, Vol. V, Autumn, 1951.

YOST, CHARLES, "The Arab-Israeli War: How it Began," *Foreign Affairs*, January 1968.

REPORTS

HARKABI, Y., "Fedayeen Action and Arab Strategy," *Adelphi Papers*, No. 53, December 1968, London: The Institute of Strategic Studies.

SABIN, ALBERT B., *et al.*, *The Arabs Need and Want Peace But—*, Mission of American Professors for Peace in the Middle East, June 24 to July 5, 1968, New York: no publisher.
Security and the Middle East, A report submitted to the President of the United States, April 1954.
AL-SHA'AB, MUHAKAMAT, *Mahadir Jalsat Al- Mahkamat Al-Askariyyiah Al-Ulya Al-Khassah* (Ministry of Defense; Proceedings of the Special Military Court, 1958).

INDEX

INDEX

ABDULLAH, viii, ix, 4, 5n, 6, 7, 8, 9, 10,
11, 12n, 14, 15, 16, 17, 18, 19, 20,
21, 22, 23, 29, 30, 31, 32, 33, 34, 43,
44, 45, 49, 50, 51, 99, 117, 137,
144, 145, 146, 147, 148, 149, 150,
151, 152, 153, 155, 156, 157,
159, 160, 161, 162, 163, 164, 165n,
166n, 186, 187n, 188n, 189, 190,
191, 192, 193, 194, 195, 196, 198,
199, 200, 219, 223, 224, 225, 242
260n, 265, 266, 268, 300, 301, 302,
303, 304, 305, 306, 307, 308
Abdul-Ilah (Regent of Iraq) 162
Abu Nuwar, General Ali, 278n, 289n,
297
Abul-Huda, Tawfiq (Prime Minister
of Jordan), 20, 23n, 26n, 32, 46,
47, 48n, 49n, 50, 126, 149, 150, 165,
166, 167, 170, 200, 202, 239, 241,
248, 258n
Acheson, Dean, 227
Afghanistan, 39n; relations with U.S.
S.R., 231n
Aflaq, Michael, 172
Ahdut Haavoda Party, 88
Al-Asali, Sabri (Prime Minister of
Syria), 238
Al-Azhari, Ismail (President of Sudan).
118
Al-Azm, Khalid, 274
Al-Bitar, Salah Al-Din, 172n.
Al-Dawalibi, Ma'rouf (Foreign Minis-
ter of Syria), 238
Allenby, General, 3n
Alexandria Protocol, 187
Al-Fatah, 109n; see also P.L.O.
Algeria, 118
Al-Ghazzi, Sa'ed (Prime Minister of
Syria), 205
Al-Hayari, General ali, 282n, 289n
Al-Hazb Al-Watani Al-Ishtaraki (The
National Socialist Party), 170

Al-Husayni, Ameen, 35, 190
Al-Khatib, Anwar, 166n
Al-Kilani, Rashid, Ali, 225n
All-Palestine Government (Hukumat'
Umum Filastin), 189, 190, 191,
192
All-Palestine Government of Gaza,
33, 35
Allon, Yigali, 37, 112
Al-Majali, Hazzaa' (Prime Minister of
Jordan), 32n, 45n, 48n, 51n, 164n,
165n, 213, 242n, 248n, 249, 250,
251, 252, 278n, 281n
Al-Misri, Hikmat, 166n, 280
Almond, Gabriel 7, 8, 9
Al-Mufti, Sa'ed (Prime Minister of
Jordan), 242, 248
Al-Mulqi, Fawzi (Prime Minister of
Jordan) 200
Al-Nabulsi, Sulayman (Prime Minister
of Jordan), 165n, 204n, 208, 209,
210, 211, 277, 278, 279n, 281n, 297
298, 307
Al-Nahhas, Mustafa (Prime Minister
of Egypt), 146, 186, 188, 193
Al-Qudsi, Nazim (Prime Minister of
Syria), 159, 164
Al-Quwwatli, Shukri (President of
Syria), 152n, 155, 156, 171, 203,
205
Al-Rifa'i, Abdul-Mun'em (Prime
Minister of Jordan), 133, 135n,
165n, 207, 209n, 252, 279n, 286n,
291n.
Al-Rifa'i Samir, 156n, 251, 262n
Al-Rimawi, Abdullah, 166n, 280-1
Al-Sa'ed, Nuri, 145, 162, 165n, 167,
168, 169, 188 229n, 233, 235 236n
240, 241n, 246, 248n
Al-Sallal, Abdullah, 214
Al-Shieshakli, Colonel Adib, 158
Al-Shurayqi, Mohammad, 150n

Al-Sulh, Riyad (Prime Minister of Lebanon), 164, 192
Altrincham Lord, 188n
Al-Za'im, Colonel Husni, 156
Amer, General Abdul Hakim, 72, 73n, 169n, 218, 247
Anglo-American Investigating Commission, Report of the, 15
Anglo-Egyptian Agreement (1954), 235n
Anglo-French Agreement (15 September 1919), 3
Anglo-Jordan Treaty (1948), 20, 149n, 202, 204, 210, 211, 226-7, 241, 243, 245, 249, 263, 269, 294n
Anglo-Jordanian treaties, v-vi
Anglo-Trans Jordanian Treaty(1923). 124
Aqaba, 45, 240; Gulf of, 44, 53, 125, 126, 226n, 268; port of, 307
Aqsa Mosque, 6
Arab Collective Defence Pact, 203
Arab Collective Security Part, 167, 206 233, 237
Arab Common Market 198
Arab Covenant (1955), 201, 202
Arab Federation, 174-80, 183, 184
Arab-Israeli War of 1948, 164
Arab-Israeli War of 1967, 52-6; Zionists' responsibility for, 86ff; reasons for Israel' victory 86n, 91-2; Consequences of 95-6, 110; Jordan and 96, 97-8, 99-100
Arab League, 146, 149, 152, 162, 163, 167, 186ff, 227; and Baghdad Pact, 236, 239-40; and Iraq, 201; and Jordan, 19-20, 187n, 188, 189, 190, 191, 193, 194, 198, 199, 200, 305; and Palestine 16, 19, 26, 189, 190 193, 194, 195; and Syria, 187; and Western Powers, 188n, 201
Arab League Defence Council, 74.
Arab Legion, 25, 26n, 124, 125n, 243, 256, 260n, 261
"Arab Prussia," 144
Arab Solidarity Pact, 169, 204, 210-11, 214, 270

Arab States, Causes of disunity, 30; on negotiations with Israel, 44-5, 103, 118,-19, 131, 138; and recognition of Israel, 110n
Argentina, 39n
Aridah, Anton (Maronite Patriarch), 154
Armistice Agreement of 1949. See RHODES AGREENENT
Ashton, Brigadier, 158n
Asqalan, port of 50
Aswan Dam, 236n, 274
At-Tall, Wasfi (Prime Minister of Jordan), 76
Attasi (President of Syria), 96
Austin, Warren, 26n, 128n
Avnery, Uri, 23, 131
Azzam, Abdul-Rahman, 191

BA'ATH PARTY, 87, 172, 173, 174n, 214, 248
Baghdad Pact ,vi, 144, 171, 173, 174, 178n, 181, 201, 209n, 212, 213n, 226, 227, 231, 232, 233, 234, 235, 236, 237, 238, 239, 240, 241, 242, 243n, 244-50, 252-4, 265, 266, 272, 273, 277, 280, 291, 307.
Balfour Declaration, 7, 8, 11
Bandung Conference, 248
Barbados, 39n
Bashyan, Burhan Eddin (Foreign Minister of Iraq), 211
Bayar, Jalal (President of Turkey), 242, 247
Beigin, Menachem, 107n
Beisan Valley, 112n
Ben Gurion, David (Prime Minister of Israel), 27, 28, 31n, 35n, 36, 37, 51 69, 70, 89, 105n, 107, 108n, 123n, 137n, 175n, 270, 279n, 282n, 284, 296n, 300
Bethlehem 12n, 31n
Bermuda Conference (1957), 253n, 282n
Bernadotte, Count Folke, 33, 128, 130n
Bernadotte Plan, 70

Bevin, Ernest, 20, 31n, 45, 187n, 227
Bevin Plan, 16, 17n
Bludan Conference, 16
Bogota, 124
Bolivia, 39n
Bourgiba, Habib (President of Tunisia), 113, 130
Bourke, Legge, 255n
Brazil, 39n
Brewster, Senator, 25n
Britain, Middle Eastern policy of, 3, 4, 13-14, 144, 181n, 182, 183, 188, 227-30, 232-3, 234n, 235, 241-2, 252, 271; Palestine policy of, 7n, 8, 9, 11, 12, 16-17, 19, 25; relations with Jordan, 4-6, 44, 45, 46n, 51, 146, 160, 161, 162, 163, 166, 167, 170, 171, 180n, 181n, 182, 183, 184, 187n, 196n, 198, 200, 201, 202, 205, 206, 207, 209n, 210, 211, 223-6, 241, 242-5, 248n, 252, 258, 259, 261, 262, 263-5, 266, 267, 269, Great Syria Plan and 144-5, 156n; Israel and, 126, 196n, 225, 226, 254, 259, relations with Iraq, 161, 177n, 184n, 201, 226, 232, 233, 235; Baghdad Pact and 227, 232-3, 241, 252, 253-5, 265; relations with Egypt, 204, 226, 255, 256n; relations with Syria, 172
British Royal Commission (1937), 11,12
Bruck, H. W., x
Buenos Aires Declaration (1936), 124
Bunche, Ralph, 44, 50, 51
Burundi, 39n
Buraimi Oasis, 254n
Byrnes, James (U.S. Secretary of State) 268n

CAIRO SUMMIT CONFERENCE (1964), 67, 72
Cambodia, 39n
Campbell, John C., 130, 287
Carmel, Moshe, 88
Casey, Richard, 145
Ceylon, 39n

Chaim, President of Israel, 108n
Chamoun, Camile (President of Labanon), 205, 206, 215
Chile, 39n
Churchill, 5n, 123
C.I.A., 55, 92
Coghill, Patrick, 261
Coleman, James, vii, ix
Collective security Pact, 197-8
Colombia, 39n
Communism in West Asia, 173, 174, 212n, 217, 229, 230n, 257, 269, 272, 273, 274, 290; and Jordan, 277-8, 279, 283, 284-5, 289, 291, 292
Congo (Brazzaville), 39n
Costa Rica, 39n
Crusades, 43
Cyprus, 39n

DALADIER, 147n
Damascus, 143, 144
Darwazi, Zuhayr, 166n
Dayan, Moshe, 57, 60n, 89, 95n, 111, 113, 114, 115n, 123n, 128n
De Gaulle, Charles, 136
Dead Sea, 112
Deir Yassin Massacre 23n
Dirkson, Senator 95n
Dominican Republic, 39n, 217
Druz, 197n
Dulles, John Foster, 103n, 229, 230, 231, 232n, 253, 255, 269, 271, 272, 275, 276, 281, 282, 283

EAST BANK, 97, 98, 99, 100.
East Ghor Canal Project, 270n
East Negeb, 44
Eastern Palestine, 164, 192, 305, 307
Eban, Abba (Foreign Minister of Israel) 39, 53, 57, 58, 88n, 92, 98n, 101, 102, 103, 104, 105, 110, 114, 134, 135, 296n
Ecuador, 39n
Eden, Anthony, 144, 188, 232n, 233,

234n, 238n, 240n, 241, 253, 254, 264

Egypt, Arab League and 186, 187, 188-9, Arab Palestine and, 121n, Baghdad Pact and 235-6, 237, 239, 246 247, 254; Britain and 204, 240n; Closure of the Straits by, 52, 54, 55; Fertile Crescent Plan and, 145, 146; relations with Iraq, 213; attacked by Israel in 1948, 28; Causes of defeat in 1948, 28-9; negotiations with Israel in 1949, 44; Armistice Agreement of 1949, 51; on direct negotiations with Israel, 135; relations with Jordan 75ff, 96, 188n, 189, 193, 197n, 199, 202n, 204, 213, 218, 247, 255, 278n, 202n, 204, 213, 218, 247, 255, 278n, 289; relations with Syria 143, 171-2, 173, 203, 213; and UNEF, 90, 91; and Turkey, 240n, and U.S.S.R. 95, 214n; and Yemen, 214
Egyptian-Israeli Armistice Commission, 90
Eisenhower, 120, 179, 253n, 269n, 270n 276, 283, 291, 293
Eisenhower Doctrine, vi, 144, 173, 181, 211, 212, 216, 267, 270, 271, 272, 273, 276, 277, 279-88, 290, 291, 295n, 297, 298, 307
El-Salvador, 39n
El-Azm Khalid (Foreign Minister of Syria), 154
El-Khouri, Faris, 148
Elat, 79; port of, 52, 259n; straits of, 90
Eretz Israel (Greater Israel), 93
Eshkol, Levi (Prime Minister of Israel), 53, 56n, 67, 94, 95, 96, 104, 110, 112, 114, 127, 128, 259n,
Essamu, 62, 63, 72, 74, 87
Eytan, Walter, 33n, 37n, 47, 48, 49, 50n, 107n

Faranjiyiah, Hameed (Foreign Minister of Lebanon), 151

Farouk, King of Egypt, 30, 152n
Far'oun Henry (Foreign Minister of Lebanon), 154
Faysal, King of Iraq, 3n, 4, 10n, 17, 144, 163n, 164, 165n, 171, 175n, 177, 179, 184n, 185, 205, 206
Faysal Ibn Saud, King of Saudi Arabia, 122n, 191, 216, 217, 218n, 269n
Fedayeen, 64ff, 129. See also P.L.O.
Fertile Cresecent Scheme, 145-6, 148, 158, 161, 172, 173, 185, 186, 236
Flanders, Ralph E., 287
Forestal (Sixth Fleet carrier), 284
Foreign policy, factors in understanding, x-xi
Formosa, 291n
Forrestal, James (U. S. Secretary of State), 128n
France, relations with Syria, 4-5, 6, 144 147n, 156-7, 277; and Great Syria Plan 145; and Egypt, 204, 271; and Israel, 97, 126; and Jordan, 160; and Arab-Israeli War of 1967, 97

Gabbay, Rony E., 26-7
Gaitskell, Hugh, 180n, 255n, 258n
Gaza, 97n, 111, 189, 192.
Geneva Protocol (1949), 112
George, VI, King, 15
Glubb, General John Bagot, 5n, 20n, 23n, 24n, 25n, 26n, 31n, 32, 45n, 48, 49n, 51, 75n, 89, 203, 205, 227, 241, 243n, 246, 247n, 248n, 249, 256, 257, 258, 259, 260, 261, 262, 263, 265n, 267, 304
Golan Heights, 96
Goldberg, Arthur, 40n, 126
Great Syria Plan, the 14-5, 33, 43, 144-5, 147-60, 164, 186, 187, 197n, 304, 305
"Greater Israel," 110, 111-2, 114, 116
Greater Jerusalem Master Plan, 38
Guatemla, 39n
Guinea, 39n, 218n
Guyana, 39n

HAGERTY, JAMES, 283
Hammarsk joid, Dag, 125
Hashem, Ibrahim (Prime Minister of
   Jordan), 251,
Hashemites, 4, 5, 144, 161; importance
   of Syria to 143 *See also* IRAQ,
   JORDAN
Hashim, Ibrahim, 281
Hayari, General Ali, 169n
Haykal, Mohammad, 54, 88n
Hegel, 137
Helms, Richard (Director of C.I.A.).
   92
Herut Party, 3, 107n
Hijaz, 147, 188n
Hilmi, Ahmad, 32, 190, 193
Hinnawi, Colonel Sami, 158
Holy Places, 96
Hondures, 39n
Hoopes, Townsend, 295n
Hoover, Herbert (U.S. Under Secretary
   of State), 125
Huda, Prime Minister of Jordan, *See*
   ABUL-HUDA
Husayn I, 227
Husayn II, King of Jordan, 10n, 19n,
   21n, 54, 62, 63-4, 72, 75, 76-7, 86,
   87n, 88, 96, 98, 99, 110n, 115, 117,
   118, 119, 120, 121, 131, 132, 133,
   135, 165n, 168, 169, 170, 171, 173,
   175, 176, 177, 179, 180, 181, 182,
   183, 184, 185, 199, 200, 201, 202,
   203, 204, 205, 206, 207, 210, 211,
   212, 213n, 214, 215, 216, 217, 218,
   219, 220, 223n, 226n, 232, 235,
   236n, 240, 241, 242, 243n, 247n,
   248, 249, 250, 251, 256, 257, 258,
   259, 260, 261, 263, 264, 265, 266,
   267, 269, 277, 278, 279, 280n, 281,
   282, 283, 284, 285, 286, 287, 288,
   289, 290, 291, 292, 293, 294, 295,
   296, 297, 298, 299, 302, 303, 305,
   306, 307, 308.
Hutton, Brigadier, 261

IBN SAUD, 188n

Indonesia, 39n
Inonu, Ismat (Prime Minister of
   Turkey), 10n
Ionides, Michael, 63
Iran, 96, 218n, 231, 232
Iraq, 3, 74, 99, 145; armistice agree-
   ments and 29, 44, 45, 51; relations
   with Britain, 161, 184n, 201, 234,
   235; Baghdad Pact and 233-36,
   239-40, 241n, 246-7; relations with
   Jordan, 148, 161-71, 174-80, 183,
   184, 185, 194n; Arab League and,
   201, 233, 236; relations with Syria,
   156, 172, 179n; relations with
   Egypt, 184n, 213n, 233; western
   Powers and, 179-80; relations with
   the U.S., 184n, 235; relations with
   Turkey, 184n, 240n; relations with
   U.S.S.R. 201; Palestine Question
   and, 234-5
Islamic Conference, 217-18
Israel, economic factors in the foreign
   policy of 56ff, 97n., 116; sources
   of funds of 56n, military superiority of, 51, 92, 94, 108, 109, 116,
   129; influence of the army in, 26-7,
   50, 55-6, 113; theory of encirclement of, 88-9; aggressive policy
   and conquests of 27, 28, 45-8, 50,
   55-6, 61n, 72, 74, 86ff, 93, 95-6,
   107n, 111, 112, 114, 116, 117, 128,
   129, 203; Palestinian refugees and,
   116, 130n; policy regarding the
   status of Jerusalem, 36-8, 39, 40-
   41, 108n, 112, 115, 123, 124n, Jordan River Dispute and, 67ff, Western support to, 50n, 146n, 228-30;
   United Nations resolutions and
   the attitude of 25, 28, 38-9, 91-97,
   108, 117, 120, 127-9; policy regarding negotiations, 44-5, 57-8, 101ff,
   115, 120, 130, 135, 138, 139; question of recognition of, 103, 105n,
   116; question of the Straits and,
   53-4; Baghdad Pact and, 237n,
   245, 346, 254; relations with Jordan, 44ff, 68f, 99-100, 115, 117,

119, 259, 266, 269, 279n, 281n, 284, 295, 298; relations with France, 97; Syria and 76, 87-80; U.S. Policy towards, 36n, 38, 39-42, 95, 109n, 128n, 255; relations with Turkey, 234; relations with U.S.S.R., 97

"Israeli Maginot Line," 112n

JAMAICA, 39n
Jarring, Gunnar (U.N. Mediator), 49 134
Javits, Senator, 95
Jaysh Al-Anqath (Army of Liberation), 19
Jericho Conference (1948), 34, 164
Jerusalem, 24, 88, 108n, 112, 115, 196n; Status of, 12n, 26, 31, 33, 96, 120-3, 124n, 125n, 138, 295n, Arab stand on, 35, 138; Jordan's Policy regarding, 25, 31, 32, 33, 35, 43, 119, 121-3, 138; Israel's Policy regarding, 27, 31, 33, 36-9, 125n; UN on the status of, 33, 38-40; Saudi Arabia's stand on 122n; U.S. stand on, 35n, 36n, 38-40, 42; Vatican's stand on, 122n.
Jerusalem Conference (1921), 4, 223
Jewish Agency for Palestine, the 712, 16
Jewish Immigration, 7, 9
Jewish National Home, 3, 5, 6n, 8, 15-16. See also ZIONISTS
Johnson, Alexis (US Under Secretary of State), 68n
Johnson, L.B. (US President) 42, 53 289n, 295
Johnson, Eric, 270n
Johnson Plan, 71, 167n
Jordan, as a Mandate, 3, 123; role of Abdullah, 4, 5, 6, 17–18; independence of, 15–16; internal problems of, v; pivotal position of, 300: the Partition Plan and, 7–1–7; military strength compared with Israel, 51;

Arab-Israeli war of 1945 and, 23–5, 50, 164; Civil war in, 65n; role of the army in, 256-8, 260–262, 264, 265, 267, 302, 303, 304; Palestine problem and, 6, 7, 8, 14, 16, 29–30, 31, 155, 164, 189–96, 216, 301, 302; Palestinian Arabs and, 6, 48, 120–21, 164, 176, 185, 301–02, 303, 304, 305, 307; Rhodes agreement and, 50, 51, 117, 155; effect of the 1967 war on, 96, 97–9, 135n; policy regarding, Jerusalem, 32, 33–4, 35, 43, 115, 119, 121–3, 138, 215; relations with Israel, v; 45–8, 62, 74, 99–100, 115, 117, 194, 237, 259, 266, 269, 279n, 281n, 284, 295, 298, 300, 306–07; desire for peaceful settlement, 21–3, 29, 44ff, 49, 99–100, 117ff, 131–7; Abdullah's Great Syria Plan, 6, 8, 15, 33; proposal for union with Iraq, 161–71; 174, 585; Arab policy of, 200ff; Arab League and, 187n, 188–91, 193–5, 198, 199, 200, 305; relations with other Arab States, v; 52, 74–5, 99; Arab nationalists and, 6, 8–9, 73, 302, 303, 304, 306, 308; policy towards Palestine resistance movement, 63ff, 216; influence of Nasserism in, 207–8, 277, 297–8, relations with Butan, 51, 146, 160, 161–3, 166, 167, 170–71, 180n, 182–4, 187n, 196n, 198, 200–02, 205–07, 209n, 210–11, 223–6, 241–3, 248n, 252, 258, 259, 261–7, 269, 302, 306, 307; relations with China, 209n, 277; relations with East European states, 216; relations with Egypt, 75ff, 96, 160, 175, 184n, 185, 188n, 189, 193, 197n, 199, 202n, 204, 212, 214, 215–8, 240, 247, 255, 257, 258, 279n, 289, 303, 305, relations with France, 160, 225n; relations with Germany, 124; relations with India, 216; relations with Iraq, 65,

161–71, 174–80, 183–6, 194n, 219, 240–1, 248, 306, relations with Lebanon, 153; relations with Saudi, 216, 217; Christians in, 301; Communism and, 277–9, 283–3, 289, 291, 292, 307, Zionism and, 139, 201, 203; Baghdad Pact and, 239, 242, 244–50, 252, 255, 266, 307; Eisenhower Doctrine and, 270–84, 286–8, 290, 297, 298.

Jordan River Waters Dispute, 67ff, 87, 98, 216, 270n

"Jordan TVA Project," 270n

KARAMAH, 62

Keating Kenneth (US Senator), 68n

Kelman Herbert, vii, ix, xi

Kennedy, John F., 275, 276, 296n

Khalidi (Prime Minister of Jordan); 279n

Khartown Summit Conference, 96, 98n, 103, 118-9, 218-9.

Khrushchev, 183n, 215

Kibya, 62, 89n

Kirkbride Alec S., 3n, 5n, 24n, 44n, 250n

Knesset, 88n

Koprulu, Fuad (Foreign Minister of Turkey), 231n

Kuwait, 177, 219

LATRUM, 75

Lawrence, T. E., 23n

League of Nations, 123, 161

Lebanon, 3n, 98, 105n, 145, 147; relations with Jordan, 153-4, 160,'282; opposition to Great Syria Plan, 151-4, 160; relations with Syria, 153, 154, 196n, 197n, relations with the U.S., 181, 183, 272n, 285, 286n; Eisenhower Doctrine and, 285, 286n, 290

Lerche Jr., Charles, x, xi

LeVine, Robert, ix

Lime Declaration (1938), 124

Lodge, Henry C., 126

London Conference on Palestine (1939), 13

London, Kurt, vii

Lybia, 118n, 219, 285

MAJALI
    See AL-MAJALI

Malaysia, 39n

Mali, 39n, 218n

Mallory, 288

Mardam, Jameel, 150

Maronite Christians, 153, 154

Mayhew Christopher, 88n

"Mazoumah," 100

McDonald White Paper, Bn

McKitterick, T.E.M. 128n

McMillan, Harold, 180n., 181n, 182n, 183n, 253n

McNamara, Robert, 92, 294n

Meir, Golda, 68, 104, 109, 279n

Menderes, Adnan (Prime Minister of Turkey), 234, 236n, 240n

Middle East Defence Organization, 201, 228, 229, 272

Minor Harold B., 273

Mohammad Ali 177n

Monroe, Elizabeth, 288

Morrison Plan, 16, 17n

Mulqi (Prime Minister of Jordan), 170

Murville (Foreign Minister of France), 138

Muslim Brotherhood, 235n

Myers, F. (U.S. Senator), 268n

NABLUS, 281

Nabulsi
    See AL-NABULSI

Nahhas See Al-Nashhas, Mustafa

Nazd, 188

Nasser, Gamal Abdel, 67, 68, 74, 75, 86, 87, 88, 90, 91, 96, 98n, 105n, 110n, 115, 117, 118, 119, 143, 171,

172, 173, 177n, 182n, 185, 203, 204, 205, 207, 212, 213, 214, 215, 216, 217, 218, 220, 235, 236, 240, 246, 271, 272n, 273, 278n, 282n, 290, 291, 292, 298, 299, 303, 306
Nasserism, 174, 207, 277
National Council of Churches, 122n
N.A.T.O., 228
Negeb, 27, 28, 67, 69ff, 96, 226n, 259n
New Zealand, 87n
Nixon, Richard, 109n, 274, 296n, 297n
North Arabian Federation, 145, 154
Northern Tier Plan, 253
Nuri Al-Sa'ed
    See AL-SAED, NURI
Nutting Anthony, 243n
Nuwar
    See ABU-NUWAR, ALI

O.A.S. CHARTER OF THE, 124
Old Testament, 51
Ottoman Empire, 161

PAKISTAN, 39n, 218n, 231
Palestine, 3, 4, 8, 13, 99, 121n, 123, 132, 175; Partition Plan, 12, 19-22, 31, 50, 119, 122n, 128n, 152n; Palestinian war of 1948, 21, 25-9, 50, 189; Jordan's policy in, 6, 11-12, 117-8, 120-1, 155, 164, 185, 190-6; problem of refugees, 3, 7, 50, 52, 96, 97, 114, 116, 119, 136-8, 176, 189-90
    See also ISRAEL, JORDAN
Palestine Fedayean Movement, 308
    See also PALESTINE LIBERATION ORGANIZATION PALESTINE RESISTANCE MOVEMENT
Palestine Liberation Organization (P. L.O.), 60, 64, 96, 109n, 118, 216, 256, 303
    See also PALESTINE RESISTANCE MOVEMENT
Palestine Resistance Movement, 59ff, 94, 100, 135, 207

    See also PALESTINE LIBERATION ORGANIZATION
Pan-Arabism, 13-4, 143, 174, 230, 271, 303
Pax Judica 108, 116
Puasux, Gabriel (French High Commissioner in Syria), 147n
Peel Lord, 12
Pentagon, 92
Permanent Mandate Commission, 4n
Persian Gulf, 3
Philley, John, 188n
Poincare, 147n
Powell, G. B., viii
Prittie Terrence, 53n

QALQILIA, 75
Qassem (President of Iraq), 179n, 184, 215
Qibya, 200
Qibyah incident, 260n

RABAT ARAB SUMMIT, 93
Rabin Izhaq (Chief of Israeli General Staff), 77, 92, 94
Red Sea, free navigation in, 95
Refugee problem
    See PALESTINE
Resolution 242, of the U.N. Security Council,
    See also UNITED NATIONS
Reston James, 92
Rhodes Agreement, 44, 45ff, 50, 59, 73, 98, 117, 119, 137, 155
Richards, James P., 283
    Rifa'i, A.M.
    See AL-RIFAI
Riyad, Mahmoud (Egypt's Foreign Minister), 172
Robinson, Prof, Max, 27n, 62
Rogers (U.S. Secretary of State), 42n
Roosevelt (President), 15n
Rouleau, Eric, 88, 127
Rusk, Dean, 92, 129n

SAFWAT, ISMAIL, 19
Said, Abdul, A., x
Said, Abdul Hameed, 14
Salem, Major Salah, 236n
Salient of Latrun, 119
Salman, Mohammad Hasan, 165n
San Remo Agreement (1920), 3, 161
Sapin, Burton, x
Saud, King, 171, 177n, 205, 212n, 214
    237, 238n, 279, 280n, 285
Saudi Arabia, 74, 118n; Baghdad Pact
    and, 237-8, 254; relations with
    Egypt, 214, 217-8; Eisenhower
    Doctrine and 279, 285-6; Great
    Syria Plan and 145; Jerusalem
    and, 122n; relations with Jordan,
    166, 171, 188n, 214, 279-80, 281,
    286; relations with Syria, 143,
    147n; relations with Yemen, 214
S.E.A.T.O., 277
Senegal, 39n
Sharette, Moshe (Foreign Minister
    of Israel), 28, 68, 103, 110n,
Shawayhat, Dr., 166n
Shieshakli, 171
Shukayri, Ahmad (Prime Minister of
    Morocco,), 118
Shuneh, 49, 162
Sinai, 89, 90, 92, 96, 117
Sixth Fleet, 282, 284, 286, 297n, 298
Smith, Donald Eugene, viii
Snyder, Richard, x
Somalia, 39n
South Korea, 291n
Soviet Union
    See U.S.S.R.
Special Units 101, 89
Stimson Doctrine, 124
Straits, the, 95
Straits of Elat, 90. See also ELAT
Sudan, 175°n, 218n
Suez Canal, 3, 52, 95, 111, 271, 307
Suez War of 1956, 52, 98, 125, 204
    See also TRIPARTITE AGGRESSION
    OF 1956
Sukhan, Memduh, 166n
Switzerland, 108, 116

Sykes Picot Agreement (1916), 3
Syria, 87, 90, 98, 99, 118; Central Posi-
    tion of, 143-4, 173; Arab League
    and, 187; Baghdad Pact and, 238-
    9; relations with Britain, 4-5, 172;
    relations with Egypt 157-8, 171-3,
    203, 213, opposition to Great
    Syria Plan, 151-5, 159, 160; rela-
    tions with Iraq, 156, 157, 158, 172,
    213; relations with Jordan, 144-6,
    147ff, 203; relations with Israel,
    71, 76, 87-8; relations with
    France, 4, 144, 147n, 156-7; rela-
    tions with Lebanon, 153, 154,
    196n, 197n; relations with Saudi
    Arabia, 157-8; relations with the
    U.S., 156n; Eisenhower Doctrine
    and, 281n; relations with U.S.S.R.,
    144, 173, 274
Syrian Congress, 144
Syrian National Block, 156

TA'IF, 214
Talal, King of Jordan, 162, 163n, 165n,
    166, 167, 168, 170n, 197, 219, 302
Talman, Jacob, 137
Tanzania, 39n
Tel-Aviv, 24, 25n, 75, 119
Templer, Sir Gerald (Chief of Imperial
    Staff), 243, 247, 249, 252, 256n
Tiran, Straits of, 52, 55
Tobago, 39n
Toynbee, Arnold, 224
Transjordan, 3-5, 11-12, 17, 123, 124
    145, 147n,
    See also JORDAN
Treaty of Joint Defence and Economic
    Cooperation, 237
Trinidad, 39n
Tripartite Aggression on Egypt (1956)
    117, 126, 169, 203
    See also SUEZ WAR OF 1956
Tripartite Declaration (1950), 228, 229
Truman (President), 15, 45, 128n, 269
Truman Doctrine, 275
Tunisia, 118n, 218n

Turkey 96, 153n, 162, 184n, 213, 218n,
   231, 234, 236n

UNITED ARAB COMMAND, 52, 67, 72ff,
   89, 94, 206
United Arab Republic, 87, 94, 172, 173
   174, 175, 178, 183, 184, 185, 305,
   See also EGYPT,
United Nations Partition Plan, 194;
   resolutions on Jerusalem, 31n,
   38; resolutions on 1967 war, 97,
   119-20, 138; Israel's defiance of,
   28, 38-40, 90, 97, 108, 117, 127-29;
   Observers, 87; armistice machinery, 102n, see also ISRAEL,
   PALESTINE
United Nations Charter, 120
United Nations Emergency Force, 75,
   76, 90, 91,
U Thant, 38, 90, 91,
United States, Arab Policy of, 25, 26n
   61n, 118, 124-5, 128n, 132n,
   181-3, 227-32, 253-5, 269-72,
   275-7, 284, 291, 295, 297, 299;
   Arab nationalism and, 215-6, 273;
   policy regarding Jerusalem, 35n,
   42; relations with Egypt, 211,
   215, 271, 276; relations with
   Israel, 16, 36n, 38-40, 42, 95,
   109n, 117, 126, 131n 255, 268-70,
   281n, 293, 295, 296, 297n, 298,
   299; relations with Jordan, 15n,
   44, 45n, 51, 68n, 176n, 211, 212n,
   215, 268-70, 279-99; relations
   with Iraq, 184n, 235; Baghdad
   Pact and 253-5; Lebanon and
   181, 183, 272, n; Yemeni
   Republic and, 215, fear of Soviet
   infiltration, 128n, 129n
   See also EISENHOWER DOCTRINE
U.S.S.R., 38, 100, 128n; Middle East
   and, 55, 117, 183n, 227-31, 271-
   2, 274, 275; Baghdad Pact and,
   227-31, 232n; Eisenhower Doctrine and 275, 276n; relations
   with Egypt, 95, 271, 274;
   relations with Iraq, 201, 233; relations with Israel, 87, 97, 271-2;
   relations with Jordan, 277, 278,
   288, 289; relations Syria, 144, 173
   274; Kurds and, 201.
   See also COMMUNISM

VERBA, SIDNEY, viii
Vyshinski, Andre, 170n

WALKER, PATRICK, 229n
Weisman, Ezer (Major-General), 66n
Weisman, Haim (President of Israel),
   69
West Bank, 44, 95, 96, 97, 111, 112,
   115, 117, 119, 133, 168, 169, 180,
   195, 215, 270
White, Lincoln, 283
Williams, Harrison (Senator), 68n
World Bank, 236n
World War I, 161

YEMEN, 75, 118n, 188, 194n; relations
   with other Arab states, 214
Yemen war, 217, 299, 306
Yost Charles, 53n
Yugoslavia, 38-9

ZAKARIA, MOHIEDDIN (Vice-President
   of Egypt), 55
Zambia, 39n
Zarqa affair, 211n, 280n, 282, 289n
Zayd (Prince), 167
Zayn (Queen Mother), 171
Zayn (Syrian Premier), 66n
Zionists, expensionist policy of, 3, 26-7
   51, 58-62, British attitude towards,
   4, 8, policy towards Palestinian
   Arabs, 52n, 59ff; policy regarding
   Jerusalem, 31, 63; War of 1967
   and, 86ff, 95-6; Fertile Crescent
   Scheme and, 145; policy regard-
   ing peace treaties, 102ff; United

Nation and 90, 128.
See also ISRAEL PALESTINE
Zorlo, Fateen (Foreign Minister of Turkey), 242
Zuater, Akram, 166n